C000273623

Becoming an English Country Squire

Becoming an
English
Country Squire

With best wishes
d'Arcy Henry

W. d'Arcy Henry

Illustrations by Annie Tempest

to

R.D.H.P.

and

'Maureen'

in memoriam

ISBN 978-1-870948-99-9
Copyright © 2014 W. d'Arcy Henry
Illustrations © Annie Tempest at The O'Shea Gallery
First published 2014

No part of this work may be reproduced in any form and by any means without prior written permission of the author or publisher.

Published by
JJG Publishing
Sparrow Hall
Hindringham
Norfolk NR21 0DP

Designed by Graham Hiles
Printed by Gutenberg, Malta

Contents

Foreword

The Heartsease Hall Estate in north Norfolk is one of only about 300 English estates – down from perhaps 3,000 at the height of the British Empire a century or so ago – which still retains most of its original buildings, many of their original furnishings and the prime of its original land.

On 19 May 1994, a little over 350 years after an ancestor acquired it, Sir Roald, 13th Baronet Festing, quietly abandoned the campaign he'd been waging to keep possession of this exquisitely handsome, historic property, and agreed to sell it to my wife Nikki and me, a pair of upstart Americans.

Sir Roald, or 'Rolly' as he was known to family and close friends and as in due course it became our privilege to call him, had led an extraordinary life. He was born in 1916 to Elena, the beautiful, accomplished, younger daughter of an Austro-Hungarian aristocrat, in Yekaterinburg in west-central Russia's Ural Mountains where his father Sir Torvald, the 12th Baronet – an author, composer and diplomat, and sometime gold prospector – was acting British Consul. (It was in Yekaterinburg that, notwithstanding Sir Torvald's spirited intervention, Tsar Nicholas II and his family were murdered by the Bolsheviks in 1918.)

An eclectic and multinational education for the young Sir Roald was decreed. It began formally at London's elite Westminster 'public' – that's to say largely upper-class, private – school, continued at Cambridge University where he 'read' (majored in) history and economics, and then the august *Ecole des Science Politiques* in Paris, and concluded at the venerable *Ludwig-maximilians Universität* in Munich. In the course of this extended pupilage, Sir Roald revealed himself as a gifted scholar, linguist and athlete.

Sadly, England's World War II confrontation of the Axis Powers – Germany and Italy in particular – had first claim on just such young men. Almost immediately the conflict began, Sir Roald was recruited by the British Special Operations Executive, a Resistance co-ordination and support group generally known by its acronym 'SOE', and sent to North Africa to carry out data verification and analysis; shortly after it ended, he was posted to Bulgaria as a member of that country's 'Control Commission', the post-war interim government the victorious Allies imposed.

Employment in journalism followed. In 1947, the Reuters news agency hired Sir Roald as its correspondent in Belgrade, capital of what was then the communist People's Republic of Yugoslavia; five years later, he became East European correspondent of *The* (London) *Times*, reporting out of Vienna. Over the next decade, Sir Roald went on to serve *The Times* with distinction in almost all of Europe's major capitals, in Tokyo – then the Far East's communications hub – and, albeit only briefly, in Washington DC.

A major career change was, however, in prospect. For in 1961, Sir Roald's father unexpectedly inherited the Heartsease Hall Estate from a first cousin. Managing such a large property on his own soon proved too difficult for the by-then-elderly Sir Torvald, and he needed his son back home to help him.

Accordingly, Sir Roald quit *The Times* and in 1963 became a consultant in information research to the British Foreign Office. This appointment, which allowed him to divide his time between Heartsease Hall and Whitehall, in London, continued until his father's death in 1976 when Sir Roald succeeded to the Baronetcy and the estate; from then until his own death in 1999, discharging the many and varied responsibilities of these hereditary offices and exercising some of their meagre rights was the focus of Sir Roald's life.

As Sir Roald fully appreciated, hanging onto the Heartsease Hall Estate – the ancestral, Festing 'Seat' – was always going to be a battle; by the time Yr Correspondent and his wife arrived on the scene that battle had, of course, effectively been lost. How so, you may ask?

Mental and/or physical exhaustion wasn't a major contributory factor; despite his advancing years, Sir Roald seemed remarkably immune to all of that. Nor, as is sometimes the case with men who enter upon privilege, were wine, women and/or song to blame – although Sir Roald clearly appreciated all three. Rather it was the heavy burden of inheritance taxes ('Death Duties', the British call them) and the resulting sharp reduction in funds available to keep up the estate – 'financial exhaustion', you might say – that did Sir Roald down....

Or as the vanquished himself summed up his position in a movingly understated, 'old-style' British, stiff-upper-lip, unblinking straight-to-camera interview with CNN shortly after Heartsease Hall had been put on the market: 'In certain circumstances... some things just aren't possible.' Even today, the thought of that noble *nunc demittis* almost brings tears to my eyes.

How we came to acquire the Heartsease Hall Estate forms part of the narrative which follows. Suffice it to say here that on 14 October 1994 – three days after completion (in the UK the definitive, final stage in the purchase of a property) was supposed to have taken place, and three *months* after contract exchange (the stage at which the buyer puts down a deposit and, in accepting it, the seller binds himself to consummate the trade) was supposed to have taken place, and with only a trifling sum of money (a part-payment for some Festing furnishings we were buying) having actually changed hands – Sir Roald and his wife Lady Maureen moved out of Heartsease Hall, and Nikki and I and our sons Piglet and Bapu moved in. Not until a week later did the property officially become ours.

A number of friends and acquaintances have exclaimed of our Heartsease Hall purchase: 'Oh, you're so fortunate! You've realized your dream!'

Well indeed: we're very, very fortunate. But owning an English-Heritage-Listed Grade I Hall with period outbuildings, rooms full of exquisite antiques, hundreds of acres of woodlands, lakes and rich farmland – in short, a splendid place physically to live – isn't really our dream any more than having perma-toned-and-tanned catwalk bodies garnished with lustrous blond hair and luminous teeth is really our dream. Our dream is to spend as long as practicable enjoying the estate, and then to pass on quickly and painlessly without imposing too much on Piglet and Bapu or those of our friends who may remain.

For what seems so often overlooked – nowadays, perhaps, especially – is that no matter how great our empire, no matter how much we own outright or control, we're all – whatever our sex or sexuality, race, colour, nationality or creed – still just tenants of this fraught, fragile earth. And as such, St Matthew's timeless caution against laying up 'earthly treasures' is surely apt; where we should live – or strive to live – isn't in material things but in our minds.

In one sense, however, Heartsease Hall is the realization of a dream – or so it seems to Yr Correspondent. It's a dream of a story: self-generating, easy... combining history, biography and autobiography, and music, art and literature, and English country life... with a whiff of intrigue, a pinch of violence and the occasional flash of sex. I hope I've told the Heartsease Hall story well and that you'll read it and enjoy it.

Finally, for the record: all of what follows is essentially true; while most of the book's *dramatis personae* are very real to me, two characters – Alter-natis and Sir Jacob Festing – carry no corporeality or, less expansively put, they're imagined; the portrayals of some of the other characters have been altered to protect their privacy; as well, a few place names have been changed.

Chapter 1

Tally-Ho!

To begin not quite at the beginning:

Work – especially hard, physical work especially in the deep country – is a good antidote to almost anything, I've found. So it's late afternoon on 19 May 1994, and I'm at Brambledown – the large-housed, 25-acre smallholding in the Cotswolds my maternal Aunt Gertie left me, where I live with Nikki (whom I generally call 'N'), my wife and helpmeet of 15-odd years, Piglet and Bapu, my two young sons, my flock of 60 or so sheep, and Piggy, our 400-pound, pet sow-pig – clearing the past year's accumulation of 'litter', aka 'trash' – some of it nature's detritus but most of it manifestly man-made – from deep within our front hedge. The hot sun's beating down; my back, shoulders and arms are starting to ache from the unaccustomed labour; periodically, divers biting and/or stinging insects make their fleeting presence felt.

Behind me and uphill to my left, the display gardens – 'May gardens' Aunt Gertie (bless her dear, departed soul!) lovingly called them because typically they were then at their extravagantly gladding best – are approaching perfection. Cascading terraces of flowerbeds array bellis, campanula, cerastium, myosotis, primula and stock; stilling them top and bottom like weirs (low dams), herbaceous borders offer ranked stands of bleeding heart, euphorbia, geranium, lupin, phlox and trollius. In the middle distance, 'The Meadow' with its self-sown carpet of buttercups, daisies and violets invites discreetly; beyond, a scattering of bluebells, ceanothus, choisya, lilacs and rhododendrons beckon from the wood's edge. A strong-armed outfielder's stone's throw back and to my right, clematis and wisteria...

· ·

All those bloomin' names, d'Arcy! And that retail from a man who can hardly bring himself to address the instructions on a 'How to Grow Your Own' seed packet....

You're right, Alter-natis: deep down I'm not a 'green-thumb' gardener like Aunt Gertie's good old Hughes was. He'd a genuine love of plants, years and years of hands-in-the-soil, horticultural experi-

1

ence and, above all, great patience.

A very appropriate apologia, if I may say; I couldn't have composed a better one myself!

But down deep in my soul, I do sometimes sense the stirrings of a good, old-fashioned, English country squire; if I had more land – an 'estate', even... maybe – he might work his way out. I'm pretty sure I could acquire the necessary skills....

. . . .

... clematis and wisteria escalade the front wall of our house and overhang its porch.

Immediately in front of me and therefore almost literally 'in my face', however, is the Fosse Way – a major thoroughfare dating from pre-Roman times which runs like a ruled line roughly northeast-southwest from Lincoln in Lincolnshire, past my domiciliary door, and on to Exeter in Devon – with its infuriating whisssh, whisssh, honk, *screech*, whisssh, *honnnk* noises, and NO_x and SO_x (the general oxides of nitrogen and sulfur) smells – as well, of course, as stealthy, odorless CO^2 (carbon dioxide) – of commercial and private road traffic. *Urbe*'s ugly, olid mug obtruding where most assuredly it's not supposed to be, I growl: here, *in rus.**

And arrantly audible from away down in our Tranquil-Village-That-Once-Was, the first few bars of Rossini's *William Tell* overture theme loop again and again through an electric 'calliope' (a steam-whistle organ) before ascending like some ill-conceived descant to the grinding vehicular *ostinato* up here; it's 'Mr Sweetie Treatie' in his truck hawking ice cream made from seaweed and soybean curd along the precious, 'olde worlde' High Street with its ubiquitous tack of tea shops and touristy-trinketry, and around the relentlessly-depersonal-izing, modern 'council estate', as the British call public housing.

Heavens! I lament to myself. This caricature – this *travesty* – of real country life is how we must live now? No! NO! Please God or Whomever, let it happen, I plead. Just let it happen. Let our offer to buy the Heartsease Hall Estate succeed!

At which point N shuffles over, head down, shoulders hunched like those of some miserable crone, trailing a wire lawn rake behind her as might a haphazard child a Tonka Toy on a string. No 'good, old, green-thumb Hughes' (re)incarnate there either, I observe wryly. But might she be an English country Squiress-in-Waiting? After all, she's

---

* The happier and more familiar form of this Latinism, *rus in urbe*, extols pastoral features such as gardens and parks in municipal settings.

shown herself to be pretty good at a pretty wide range of things.

N takes a few, seemingly desultory strokes at a scattering of dis-carded paper tissues, candy-bar wrappers and empty soda cans, and then a few twigs and dead leaves, before pausing – as is almost in-variably her wont – for protracted reflection. (My 'helpmeet' indeed!) I flick the sweat from my forehead before giving her – as is almost invariably *my* wont – my get-on-with-it glare. 'Well, Dar (short for d'Arcy)' N says casually – better, in retrospect, 'coyly' – 'for drinks this evening, shall we have some bubbly?'

Poor, innocent little Uxor ('*Uxor*', the Latin word for 'wife', is one of my pet names for N), I sigh, not attuning to her signal. I know it's a strain, this Heartsease Hall business: all the waiting and the uncer-tainty…. It's tough. Then my own pent-up frustrations start to ex-press. But when the going gets tough the tough get going, I self-avow. They don't take refuge in comforting little indulgencies or palliative little treats; they hang in there, tight, tight, tight.

And as for the vendor of the estate, Sir Roald Festing, I rail, and that oleaginous real estate agent of his…. Well (deleted) them; if they don't like our (deleted) money they know what they can do with it! My expression escalates toward explosion. 'Bubbly?' I roar. 'What's the matter? Has the old Stanford *summa*, the old B-Schooler, the con-sultant *emerita* of the (consulting) Firm, the old White House Presi-dential aide, gone soft… not got the *cojones* to hack it in the fast lane anymore?'

'No…. No, it's not that at all,' N giggles, suddenly straight-up-front bursting with sweetness and light. 'The real estate agent's just telephoned….' She eases agreeably on her rake and begins humming a tuneless little tune; I go immediately to full-emergency, fight-or-flight red alert. 'And *he* said….' She pauses to pick at a fleck of dirt or some such on the sleeve of her blouse…. 'He said Sir Roald's accepted our offer.' Another dramatic pause…. 'So, Big Boy, we've done it: we've acquired the Heartsease Hall Estate!'

Dumbstruck, for a moment – a long moment – I just stand looking at N, my mouth gaping and closing like that of some out-of-water fish drowning in fresh air. Then the questions I've so often asked myself – surely, there's no need to articulate them again – arise spontaneously in my mind: What have I let myself in for? And whatever it may be, am I up to it? The answers, I re-recapitulate – still without speaking – will be revealed only in the fullness of many, many years… the full-ness of my life, perhaps; there's no point in assaying resolutions right now, right here.

'Good Lord,' I mumble, 'what an astonishing deliverance; I simply can't think of anything else to say.' N lets drop her rake, reaches out, takes my near hand in hers and gives it a reassuring squeeze. 'My little proto-Squire,' she murmurs endearingly. And so we float off toward the kitchen and its fridge for a bottle, or perhaps two, of bubbly.

· · · · · · · · · · · · · · · · · · · ·

Now we go back and pick up at the beginning, d'Arcy?
Now we go back to the beginning.

· · · · · · · · · · · · · · · · · · · ·

Chapter 2

Find & View

According to the mighty *OED**, a 'squire' is 'a gentleman in England, esp. the main landowner in a rural community'. An old friend whose step-father actually lived that life offered a somewhat less spacious take: 'he's a guy with a great, thick mess (potage, or stew) of responsibilities over which a thin puff-pastry of rights has been dressed. And *le droit de seigneur* (the right to dally with a local maiden before her wedding night),' he concluded drily, 'isn't one of them.'

Whatever: in spite of nearly three decades spent living in the UK – a good part of that time in what some reckon to be 'country' – and admiring many aspects of 'the English way of life', becoming a squire was never an explicit ambition of mine. It just sort of happened.

What I did very much desire was lots of land somewhere 'far from the madding crowd's ignoble strife', as the 18th-century English poet Thomas Grey put it in his *Elegy Written in a Country Churchyard*, with fields and woodlands and waterways I could look after – that's to say farm and maintain and, perhaps, even improve. (Or better, the wisdom of age suggests, *oversee* the looking after, etc, of by younger, better-endowed, more-energetic others.)

Provided the land came with a good house – something, say, like Brambledown, with 3–4 principal bedrooms – the extensive realty I had in mind could have been almost anywhere so long as three conditions obtained: it was within the jurisdiction of a free-enterprise democracy; its ambient culture was deep and engaging; and from it access to deep and engaging cultures elsewhere in the world was relatively easy. Moldering away in some old outback simply wasn't my line.

Nor had N ambitions of becoming a 'squiress', although she too was long-resident in England and liked English country life. Her es-

---

* *The Oxford English Dictionary* whose first edition, begun in 1879, took 49 years (until 1928) to compile and whose second took 61 years (until 1989) to update. A third, online edition is in preparation.

sential requirements were also three-fold: to remove from the dark, dank Cotswolds; *not* to remove from there to Scotland – a possibility I'd often considered – which she knew to be darker and danker still (and, seemingly, bent on some form of secession from the UK); and, finally, as Tammy Wynette sang and Hillary Clinton somehow managed, to 'stand by (her) man'.

So when on 26 March 1994 – windy, rainy, cold: a typical 'spring' day in the UK – a brochure came in the mail advertising the Heartsease Hall Estate – hundreds of conjunct acres of farmland, woodland and lakes and 'the Hall', a magnificent, 18th-century mansion complete with contemporaneous domestic outbuildings, farm buildings and cottages – in rural north Norfolk, N and I were mentally primed and ready.... Or so we thought.

The front cover of the brochure pictured the Hall atop a hill overlooking a lake on which swam a pair of swans, and a tree-studded pasture where sheep and cattle grazed. Talk about 'situation, situation, situation'! But there was more... much more: the brochure described the Hall as Georgian-Gothic Revival in style with 'battlements' – side walls topped by stylized embrasures originally for shooting attackers through – and ditto military 'turrets' with finials, and said it was realised in 1787 to a plan by William Wilkins, Senior, whose Junior had among many celebrated commissions designed the National Gallery in London.

Indeed, the brochure noted, it was partly on account of its association with Wilkins that the Hall was referenced in the architectural historian Nicholas Pevsner's prodigious 1962 compendium *The Buildings of England*, and Burke's and Savills 1981 county-by-county, pictorial *Guide to Country Houses*, as well as 'Listed Grade I' by English Heritage – the curator-institution of the Realm's historic-buildings collection – because of its 'exceptional importance to the nation'. The estate's gardens and parkland, the brochure continued, were also originally designed by 'a name': Nathaniel Richmond, a working associate of the landscape greats Humphry Repton and Lancelot 'Capability' Brown.

And finally: the brochure told that the estate had been owned by the Festing family continuously since the 1640s (back then, New York City was known as Nieuw Amsterdam!) – something over *350 years ago* – and that it was one of only 300 or so properties in the entire of England which still retained most of its original buildings, many of their original furnishings and the prime of its original land.

Heartsease Hall. Drawn by P.J. Neale. Engraved by J.C. Varrall.

The place-name 'Heartsease', the brochure added for good, antiquarian measure, was a great deal older still, having been recorded in *The Domesday Book* – the UK's first-ever, national land registry – commissioned by William the Conqueror and completed in 1086, that's to say something over 900 years ago. What a huge historical compass!

In sum, the Heartsease Hall Estate was very substantially larger and higher-profile, in multiple senses of both adjectives, than anything N or I'd ever contemplated even towards the closing, 'what-if' stages of our regular, end-of-workday drinks hours. And predictably, its guide price was steep. But as Horace, the Roman poet and satirist, enjoined: '*Nil desperandum!*' – Never give up! And, we post-scripted: certainly don't do so before you've even started. For a possible, potential… presumptive, even, maybe… English Country Squire and *ipso facto* his Squiress, might not some way of acquiring the Heartsease Hall Estate be found?

On the day I received the Heartsease Hall Estate brochure, my putative Squiress was in Rome on assignment for Frederick Henry Associates (the international management consulting company she and I'd set up many years earlier; 'FHA' we called it) and therefore, in those pre-cell-phone days, unavailable for immediate comment. So I put the brochure on her desk, paper-clipping to it a note exhorting: 'This one we've got to see!'

. . . .

*What was it... what is it... d'Arcy, about this land-owning which
so allures? Is it because you equate owning land with being more
secure?*

Certainly, Alter-natis; just about everything I do – including things
which in the shorter-term may make me less secure – ultimately reflects my search for security.

*So what we now need to establish is: what kind of security you're
searching for. Are you searching primarily for material security?
Food and shelter for you and your family when the great revolution
– the final, definitive conflict between the world's haves and have-
nots – or some similar, awful cataclysm comes?*

*According to the multi-billionaire Warren Buffet, farmland's a
great investment – especially in times of economic uncertainty, like
now....*

As you know, I was brought up in the country, and I view the
productive capability of the land – 'The Good Earth', Wang Lung,
the hero of Pearl Buck's Pulitzer Prize-winning novel of the same
name, called it – as a kind of life insurance policy-*cum*-pension plan.
But when the world revolution comes, if it comes – and I fervently
hope it doesn't come – that fall-back may not stand; in revolutionary
times, landowners are usually among the first to take the heat.

*Or are you searching for spiritual security and, as a first step,
some kind of sanctuary like a high mountain or a deep abyss – even,
improbably, what Noel Coward in Private Lives called (north) Norfolk's 'very flat' plain – to which you can withdraw and reflect?*

A qualified 'yes' again; spiritual security is important to me. But
I don't know why this particular property – this Heartsease Hall –
so appealed. All I can say is I've always been happier outside in the
fresh air than inside, and I've always been happier outside in the
country, rusticating, than outside in the city.

It may be I'm an evolutionary tortoise who's unable to keep pace
with the present, rapid rate of change. I'm certainly not as clued-
up... as hip... as those urban hares who move with – *create*, they'd
probably argue – 'The Times'.

*A hunter-gatherer in 20th-century clothes. Hmmmm. Do you
think your condition's the result more of nurture or nature, or some
sort of epigenetic recessive of both? You remind me that you were
brought up in the country. But perhaps as well your DNA coding
is that of a countryman. Or maybe your brain just didn't develop
properly in utero... or you were weaned too soon.*

I don't really know and I don't really care. All I want to do is get
on with....

*OK; I'll let you get back to your ruminations. But just a few final
questions: why are you putting all of this heavy, introspection stuff
in what's supposed to be a nice, light read about buying and coming*

to live in a – or should I write 'an' – historic English country estate?

Because you have to nowadays if you intend to be taken seriously as a writer. Unless you weep and wail and throw yourself about a bit, confess your angst, bemoan your condition and the condition of the society in which you live – *la condition humaine*, even – people will conclude you're just a literary lightweight... a scribbler of footnotes rather than an emblazer of headlines.

Are you really going to include some sex as well, as you promised in the Foreword?

Certainly – and violence too when I feel it's appropriate to the storyline. I won't include sex or violence just for its own sake.

What kind of sex?

Well... between consenting, adult, heterosexual cattle and sheep and pigs for instance, and chickens, maybe, and peafowl... and cats and dogs and horses, if and when we get some....

Nobody today wants to read about those sorts of things! Aren't you going to write about boys and girls, girls and girls... boys and boys...

Alter-natis, I appreciate that in one guise or another sex is a driver – *the* driver, perhaps – of nearly all great literature...

... the three tendencies sequentially or, err, coming together as it were?

... but the boys-and-boys thing just isn't my scene. And as regards the other possibilities you reference, there's not a lot that hasn't already been said.

· · · · · · · · · · · · · · · · · · · ·

Pending N's return from the Eternal City, I carried out further researches. These revealed that 'Heartsease' is a Middle English folkname for the wild pansy (*Viola tricolor*, a love-token or valentine also called 'Kiss-me-quick') and that 'TRE' – *Tempore Regis Edwardi*, when King Edward the Confessor (whose successor Harold was defeated by William the Conqueror at Hastings in 1066) ruled England – the Heartsease Hall Estate's lands belonged to the great Benedictine Abbey at Cowhulme in what's today known as the Norfolk Broads. It had then one 'sokeman', or freeman tenant/manager, and was worth – 'including all the churches' – some five shillings and four pence*!

Throughout the nine-plus centuries since 1066 the property appeared to have had only five owners: the Abbey, that's to say the (then-Catholic) Church, which for a while continued to hold the ti-

---

* The UK abandoned shillings and pence in favour of decimal coinage in 1971; at that time the pound equalled roughly $2.40. A pound comprised twenty shillings, and a shilling comprised twelve pence.

tle; Henry VIII, that's to say the State, who appropriated it under the Dissolution of the Monasteries (Suppression) Act of 1536; the Boleyn-Cleres who, it's thought, acquired it direct from Henry VIII; the Hobarts who acquired it from the Boleyn-Cleres; the Festings who acquired it from the Hobarts... and now, maybe, the upstart-American Henrys. What a stupendous pedigree!

Without after all waiting for N to return, I contacted the real estate agent and booked a viewing for 30 March at 1400 hours. Then I telephoned Nell, an old friend who lived in Saffron Walden (a town in Essex which was pretty much *en route*), to ask if she'd care to join us. She said she'd love to, and it was agreed we'd collect her on viewing day about noon.

· · · · · · · · · · · · · · · · · · · ·

In the immortal words of the great Chinese philosopher Lao Tzu: 'The journey of a thousand *li* starts from where one stands.' One *li* equals roughly 590 yards or about a third of a mile, we're told, so Lao Tzu was talking about a pretty good hike, Alter-natis.

Yes. And if at the time of booking that 30 March viewing you'd had the slightest inkling of where your Heartsease Hall 'hike' would ultimately take you....

· · · · · · · · · · · · · · · · · · · ·

In the meantime, Yr Correspondent's excitement grew apace; indeed, I could hardly sleep or eat. I read and re-read the Heartsease Hall Estate brochure last thing at night and again first thing in the morning, then at intervals throughout the day... unfolding and refolding its accompanying estate plan (map), so often it began to fray at the hinges. The fields, woodlands and lakes just on their own seemed to me too good to be true; a tent in the middle of them would have been more than enough. But to have as well the chance of a genuine, old-English 'Hall' renowned for its historical and architectural importance....

And all of this just over two hours by fast train from London! N, sensing salvation from Brambledown and Scotland, soon became almost as feverish as I was.

Successful 'viewing' – of real estate, for example, or pictures and statues and other *object d'art*... or a possible lifestyle or life-partner even – is a mixture of art and craft. The art part consists in developing a mental image or vision of what it is you think you want – what you think is 'right' for you – and then establishing how much you can afford to pay for it without winding up broke. ('Everything,' as the

10

Roman satirist Juvenal remarked, 'has its price.') This theoretical im-aging-and-costing viewing – this 'imagining', as it very often proves to be – can be done pretty much anytime, anywhere; if only on account of its physical facility, therefore, the art part of viewing is manifestly the easier element to achieve.

By contrast, the craft part of viewing is real-time and hands-on, that's to say it's something you have to go and do. It consists in look-ing closely at the that-which-is-out-there – the that-which-could-be-or-is-actually-on-offer – and sizing it up (sometimes literally, for ex-ample with a tape measure) and then analyzing it, pondering it... reflecting on it... to determine the extent to which it in fact represents your 'right' affordable thing – or, perhaps, by how much your nomi-nal budget cap for its acquisition may have to be exceeded. Even with the help of great search engines like Google algorithmically rummag-ing the internet, this 'craft' viewing can be just plain hard slog. So it proved initially with the Heartsease Hall Estate.

In those days before GPS went commercial, the first challenge was simply getting there. Norfolk – the UK's eastern-most 'lump' or, as its detractors say, 'rump'; it is, in fact, a 'Royal' County because Her Majesty the Queen has a residence there (Sandringham House) – turned out to be quite a long way from Gloucestershire. And although in the early stages of our drive the traffic wasn't too bad, the rain was heavy and continuous.

So it wasn't until after 1500 – that's to say an hour or so after the viewing was due to begin – that we exited the provincial capital, Norwich, and entered what was, clearly, the last stage of our journey. In all directions – often, as far as the eye could see – stretched gently-rolling fields and woodlands; nestled within them were picturesque lit-tle villages, their immaculate 'greens' edged with fire-engine-red mail boxes and telephone boxes and, inevitably adjacent, the pub, around which vicars and bobbies on bicycles doubtless patrolled... pictur-esque cottages, enclosed within wooden-paling fences, onto whose thatched and/or tiled roofs pink and yellow-flowering roses abun-dantly flowed.... And inter-linking this quintessential, British pastoral were picturesque little narrow, winding, secondary and tertiary roads, in places all-but overgrown with hedgerows and low-limbed trees – routings no behind-schedule crow would ever even consider – along which convoys of tractors and other big, slow-moving farm vehicles toiled....

So it wasn't until after 1600 hours – fatigued by the long, hard

journey and chastened by our failure to appreciate the distances involved, but agog almost to the point of catalepsis for our first glimpse
of our might-be, new-life abode – that we finally arrived at the entrance to the Heartsease Hall Estate. We turned through its tall, stone
gateposts and, leaving to our left its little gatehouse, started up its
long, winding, tree-lined driveway, crossed a narrow causeway dividing what we'd thought was just one single lake into two: an upper and
a lower one....

On first impression, the property didn't altogether impress; indeed,
it looked awful. For a start, the drive was full of potholes. And either
side of the drive – running to within 8–10 yards of the west elevation
of the Hall itself, in fact – wasn't the verdant sward we'd envisioned
but muddy, brown fields recently sown with spring corn (wheat, bar-
ley or oats, in English usage; American 'corn' is referred to in the
UK as 'maize'). And outlying wasn't the whispering greenwood we'd
envisioned but the cranked, bare branches of still-wintering trees. In
between, the lakes – fringed with a tangle of last year's bent and broken reeds – lay sullen and still; overhead, the dark-grey storm clouds
continued to spit rain.

The estate agent and behind him Sir Roald Festing, the owner of
the estate, and his wife, Lady Maureen, and behind them the estate
agent's tall, slim, wondrously-comely, young-woman assistant, all did
their best to compensate. Standing in the turning circle outside the
Hall's front porch – that's to say in the drizzle – they welcomed us
warmly and congratulated us on the achievement of what they characterized as our 'trans-Norfolk expedition'. Indeed, they acted as if
being two or so hours late for a viewing was pretty much the way
things were done in this part of the world.

If film crews had been around those 13.7 billion years ago when,
we're told, the Universe was created, the stupendous spectacle of 'Big
Bang' – or whatever happened – and, perhaps, the voice-over expli-
cations of its Pyrotechnician – assuming there was one – could have
been recorded for posterity; in short, we'd now know a great deal
more about what actually came to pass then. Ditto, in a micro-cosmic
way, the 'creation' of what would become N's and my 'universe': our
first viewing of the Heartsease Hall Estate. Alas no cameras, etc, were
on location there either, so no detailed record exists of exactly who
said what and when. General impressions degraded (or, just possibly, enhanced... occasionally) by the passage of time and selected and

shaped by Yr Correspondent and his wife – 'history' become 'this story', so to speak – must therefore suffice.

We began with the Hall or, more properly, 'the present Hall' – the William Wilkins' Hall – with which an ancestor of his had replaced an earlier, medieval one, Sir Roald said. Its extent was even larger than we'd expected. And with its vertical dimension and thus its volume exaggerated by the battlements and turret-finials – as well as three huge chimney stacks – it presented as something between a mini-cathedral and a mini-castle. Wow, I remember thinking: d'Arcy Henry and his little Uxor living... in a cathedral-castle?

Core construction of the Hall was of brick, Sir Roald told us, and in some places its walls were coming on for five feet thick. But what immediately caught my eye was the flint (a type of quartz) 'outer skin' or facing over the brick, which had been 'knapped' (shaped by hand-chipping) into squares and rectangles averaging perhaps three inches by four and then 'coursed' (laid horizontally). A quick estimation suggested there must be thousands upon thousands of these knapped and coursed flints; wet and glistening in the rain, they seemed to my then-heightened sensibilities like the scales of some giant dragon-fish.

Dressing this flintwork – as the fascia of the foundation, as plinth and cornice moldings at the bottoms and tops of the walls, as 'quoins' (from *coin*, the French word for 'corner') where the side and end-walls joined, and as copings on the battlements – was cut-limestone 'ashlaring', smooth-faced and straight-edged, quarried from the Isle of Portland in the English Channel. Portland-stone architraves, jambs and sills surrounded the Hall's windows and doors; Portland-stone string coursing (horizontal wall molding) indicated its ceilings and floors.

And then there were those turret-finials. Eleven or twelve feet high and also of Portland stone from which jutted carved, foliated *fleur-de-lys**, they stood skyward like a battery of SAMs (surface-to-air missiles) awaiting launch. The sense of ageless monumentality, solidity and mass... and yet of ephemeral lightness and grace... was simply staggering.

Inside, the Hall was 'Georgian-Gothic', literally. The entrance front and the rooms running along it had windows with sharply-pointed 'ogee' (recurvate) arches and neo-gothic interior decoration; the

---

* French for 'flower of the lily', a motif which forms part of the Bourbon royal coat-of-arms; in English architect-speak, they're referred to as 'crockets' or 'crochets' from the French for 'little hooks'.

rooms co-lateral with the garden front had windows with semi-circular arches and neo-classical interior decoration; the principal interior door, leading from the entrance hall to the main reception rooms, that's to say from the entrance front to the garden front, had Gothic panelling on one side and Georgian panelling on the other....

· · · · · · · · · · · · · · · · · · · ·

Why on earth would anyone want to build, let alone live in, an architecturally at-odds house like that?

Squire and Mrs Festing of yore just couldn't agree, I speculated at the time, he wanting to re-create the medieval Hall in which he'd been brought up, but she preferring the more contemporary and commodious Georgian mode. So they discussed the matter – perhaps heatedly and at length – then they stood back and had a chuckle or two over it, maybe... and, finally, they compromised. 'Compromise is almost always best,' I insisted....

Such a romantic tale: a shared aesthetic, a shared life... a shared house and home.... Two soulmates metaphorically playing the architectural duet they composed.

A decade or so later I learned about Squire and Mrs Ward, whose descendants became the Viscounts Bangor. In the mid-18th century, they jointly designed and had built for them a home on a property in Northern Ireland; Castle Ward, they called it and – like the present Heartsease Hall – it was Georgian-Gothic in style. Shortly after their great monument to connubial compromise was completed, Squire Ward and his wife separated.

Sometimes the music just stops, I suppose.

· · · · · · · · · · · · · · · · · · · ·

The estate agent emphasized that although the accommodation appeared large, it was in fact quite manageable. We could see his point: the Hall didn't have all that many rooms – there were only five principal bedrooms, for example (double or so that total, however, if you included the secondary bedrooms in its attics and conjoined, nursery annex) – and they were very simply and efficiently laid out. But by N's and my standards the rooms were huge! The drawing (living) room and the dining room each measured roughly eight yards by twelve, and four of the bedrooms were some six and a half yards on a side, or over 40 yards square. Whew, we exhaled! Are we really even considering this? Nell, an incorrigibly go-for-it former professional tennis player, punched the air with her fist and smiled encouragement; N and I tried to work out what just re-carpeting would cost.

Then, led by Sir Roald, we toured some of the outbuildings. Immediately adjacent were: a storeroom which had recently been converted into a single-bedroom accommodation called Dovecote Cottage; an old laundry, still with its washtubs and drying frames *in situ*; an old brewery with its ditto fermentation vats and barrel racks; and the used-to-be staff toilets which, because the estate was regularly 'open' (to sightseers), were now the public ones. Farther away – reached from the Hall's back door via a longish, brick archway referred to as The Tunnel – were a stable yard with its stable block and two carriage houses/garages (and, incongruously, a decrepit, 1960s-era mobile home), and an orangery – a good-sized, greenhouse-like building in which citrus and other fruits were formerly grown. All of these structures (except, obviously, the hideous mobile home!) were English-Heritage listed, Sir Roald informed us, and some, like the Hall, were listed Grade I.

I remember thinking: surely a nearly-complete suite of 18th-century outbuildings, all of them original and essentially unaltered, must be practically unique. I also remember thinking: Good Lord – what *would* it cost to restore and maintain them!

A drive around the farther reaches of the estate in Sir Roald's station wagon came next. We took in St Lawrence's Church – a simple, stone-built edifice adorned only by a 1000-year-old round tower, or 'keep', within which the local populace sheltered from Viking raiders, Sir Roald said, and where generations of his forebears now rested – a high-walled, 'kitchen' garden, perhaps 2–3 acres in extent, which used to supply vegetables and soft fruits to the Festing household, and a couple of 'derelict features' our guide deemed to be of possible interest: the trunk of a sail-less, tail-less windmill which once pumped water to the Hall, and a collapsed boat-house on the lower lake, its dock now silted up and overgrown with weeds.

Our viewing concluded in a pasture south of the lower lake – once the site of a summer-house and so called Pavilion Paddock, Sir Roald told us – near the spot where the cover picture for the real estate agency's brochure had been taken... at which point, *mirabile visu*, the storm clouds suddenly lifted. And lo! Swans lazed, sheep and cattle grazed... the sun shone down from an azure sky. The Hall – our Hall and my Esquiredom, perhaps – and a lifetime of away-from-it-all, deep-country living beckoned. Sir Roald mumbled something about Pavilion Paddock being in fine weather a wonderful place for a picnic. Nell inspired softly; N and I hardly breathed at all.

. . . .

'... and in that house they shall dwell, where there shall be no Cloud *nor Sun, no darkness nor dazzling, but one equal light, no noise nor silence, but one equal music, no fears nor hopes, but one equal possession, no foes nor friends, but one equal communion and Identity, no ends nor beginnings, but one equal eternity....'*

That's from one of the 16th/17th-century English poet John Donne's *Sermons*, Alter-natis, where he's reflecting on 'our last awakening into the house... of Heaven'. Obviously, Donne couldn't foresee all the time and effort N and I would have to put in fully to restore the Heartsease Hall Estate but, overall, you could say he prescribed our mind-set pretty well.

. . . .

On the Saffron Walden leg of our return journey Nell, N and I discussed what to do. For Nell, the Heartsease Hall Estate was a gift shot at championship point which, in her mind, she'd already put safely away: 'Your piano could go in the drawing room... in the far, right-hand corner, and that antique, *bateau-lit* sofa you bought in France would be just perfect in the entrance hall.' She'd even made a start on reconfiguring the display gardens. 'I'd be inclined to take out that little flowerbed on the south lawn below the kitchen window – there's no real point to it – and grass it down... maybe put some small statues there – a bronze goose or two, say. And I'd *certainly* alter the herbaceous border where it runs east of the orangery: curve its end around so when you come along the path you'll see, against a backdrop of shrubs and trees, ranks of biggish, boldly-coloured flowers.' As we dropped her home she added: 'Chrysanthemums, dahlias and peonies might go well.'

But on the second leg of our return journey, from Saffron Walden to Brambledown, and then over a late supper and before going to bed – *after* going to bed, even – N's and my deliberations were more subdued. N's main concern was that such a large, management-intensive enterprise would take a lot of time away from our FHA consulting practice; as well, she thought the Hall was too big and formal and – a cry straight from the Uxorial heart, this one! – that it would prove very difficult to keep warm in the depths of a north-Norfolk winter. Finally, N confessed to reservations about the atmosphere of the place; she said she felt it had 'something of the geriatric about it... by which I mean it seems a bit grey'.

'But flint *is* grey, or silver-ocher-grey,' I protested, 'that's the colour God or Whomever made the stuff.'

'And I don't like the kitchen; its layout is all wrong, and it hasn't been redecorated for ages.'

'We can change the layout N,' I entreated. 'Install a stand-alone, central workstation with a burl maplewood top and a sink, and an overhead rack to hang your pots and pans from... put up glass-windowed cabinets – maybe that'll inspire you to keep your spices and stuff tidier. And when we've done all of that, we can redecorate the kitchen any way you like: give it new wallpaper, new curtains, new lighting... new flooring, even.'

At which point... prompted, perhaps, by a more measured consideration of what would be required properly to renovate just one room, the enormity of the challenge which the Heartsease Hall Estate as a whole represented mentally, physically and financially began to sink in; Yr Correspondent too began to have doubts, which grew and grew. 'I don't really think we should attempt it, N, it's just too big a job,' I concluded as I switched off the bedside light. N's closing-down words were: 'Well OK, Dar, but let's sleep on it.'

The next morning, after getting a note off to Sir Roald thanking him for showing us around, N and I resumed our previous evening's deliberations. I still had doubts about the amount of work the property would need and whether I'd have the time and energy – let alone could acquire the requisite knowledge and expertise – to take it on. 'The ravell'd sleave of (N's) care', as Shakespeare's *Macbeth* puts it, had been well and truly 'knit up' by her sleep, however, and fine, new velvet cuffs with silver-gilt buttons sewn on. The large size of the Hall had overnight become 'its openness... its feeling of space', and its 'geriatric' greyness had become 'the perfect foil for bright, new realizations of interior design'. (Oh, yes....) Then taking a piece of scrap paper, she tossed off a sketch of her dream kitchen-to-be.

As to how we should go about the manifold, other works the rest of the estate required, N continued: 'You just need a detailed, strategic plan – call it "The Masterplan for the Restoration of the Heartsease Hall Estate" – specifying the things that need doing and the time-frames for getting them done.' Her eyes narrowing, she added: 'Of course, you'll have actually to meet those deadlines, Dar; there mustn't be any slippage, as sometimes happens with your FHA reports.' (Again: my little helpmeet....) 'But don't worry,' she concluded, 'I'll be there beside you; together, we'll get the job done.' (Oh, yes.... YES!)

And so – why ever not? – on to the financials. After a brisk consideration and an even brisker calculation – literally on the back of an envelope – my resident MBA determined that if we talked Sir Roald down a bit but added back a reasonable amount for repairs, got a good price for Brambledown and realized a little capital, we *should* only have to go into the money market for about – Yr Correspondent took a deep breath – about [...].

'Only [...]?' I exclaimed, the skinflint skulking ever within me sidling to the fore. 'Good Lord, do you know what that sum represents? That's [...] percent of our total net worth, N. Even Henry Ford would've blanched at such prodigal use of other peoples' money.' (Well... maybe....)

'Perhaps,' N countered in her most school-marmish tones. 'But the (econometric) back-testing I've done indicates that even at the top of the interest-rate cycle, rolling-average cash flow from just the estate's farming operations would support a current ratio – that's current assets divided by current liabilities you'll remember, Dar; it's a measure of solvency – of 2.71828. In addition, there'd be income from the cottages and other rents.'

. . . .

Hummm: '2.71828', I pondered. I couldn't at that moment remember exactly what it was, but I knew there was something very special about that number... other than, as you'd proposed, it's being a 'back-of-an-envelope' calculation specified to five decimal places.

I said I was pretty sure it had to do with the number's perceived relevance – or more likely, I seemed to recall, its irrelevance – metaphysically... ontologically... to our understanding of The Nature of Being. And I promised that as soon as I remembered what it was I'd let you know.

. . . .

'Well, of course... self-evidently,' I demurred. 'But suppose we can't talk Sir Roald that little bit down, or the repairs turn out to be more expensive than we reckon. And suppose we don't get a good price for Brambledown – not everyone may want to live at "The Gateway to the Cotswolds", you know – suppose we only get a nearly-good price. And suppose....'

'"Suppose, sch-mose",' N interrupted. 'Look, Dar: how is it, do you think, that crops get planted and harvested, pastures get fertilized and mown, lakes and woodlands get maintained and rents get collected. By supposers? No. By men of action. Squires, if you will. And Squires don't suppose; they don't have time to. They *veni*. They *vidi*. They *vici*... like the Roman historian Suetonius tells us Julius Caesar did. So: do you or don't you want to become an English Country

Squire? Because if you do....'

• • • • • • • • • • • • • • • • • • • •

Not, it struck me at the time, an analysis founded entirely in the rigorous, fact-based, methodologies renowned of the Firm, d'Arcy.
It was *very* gung-ho, Alter-natis. And all that research showing the critical importance to entrepreneurial success of good contingency planning was completely ignored.

On the other hand, as Ralph Waldo Emerson pointed out in his 1841 Circles *essays: 'Nothing great was ever achieved without enthusiasm.'*

• • • • • • • • • • • • • • • • • • • •

I nodded slowly, deliberatively... comfortably-nearly-resignedly... and recalled my feelings those many years ago as I'd waited with Anthony and Robin, my two best-men – my two 'supporters' as some British would say – at the altar-end of the nave in the Mission Chapel in Carmel, California, for N, my sweet little to-be Uxor – then all a-twit-twitter – to take up her place at my side 'until death us do part'. In proposing to take on the realty equivalent of a second wife, was I in prospect of another fundamental life-change?

'Little Uxor' – the flesh-and-blood Uxor... Uxor Number One – closed it down. 'But I think we really should have one more look at the property, Dar, just to make sure.' A second viewing, on 11 April – the day before we were due to fly off for a ten-day, FHA-business-*cum*-family-holiday trip to the US or, as we fondly referred to it, 'The Motherland' – was duly booked.

• •

In prospect was a very, very major decision for you and yours. Why were you acting in such haste, d'Arcy?
Three reasons really: I was increasingly desperate to move out of the Cotswolds and into 'real country', which north Norfolk appeared to be; the Heartsease Hall Estate was as close to perfection as any property I'd seen in roughly a decade of on-and-off looking; and, finally, we had that trip to The Motherland up-coming. There's nothing like a pending departure to concentrate the mind, you know, Alter-natis.
There was a fourth reason, wasn't there?
I don't recall it.
What about: your 'tide'.
My what?
Your tide. As Shakespeare in his play Julius Caesar *gives Brutus to say: 'There is a tide in the affairs of men Which, taken at the flood, leads on to fortune; Omitted, all the voyage of their life Is bound in*

19

shallows and in miseries.'
So?
In the spring of 1994 your tide was no longer 'at the flood'; it was on the turn... maybe even starting to ebb.
It was not! I was then only just entering the later stages of my prime!
On the basis of life expectancy in Georgian times, at the age you were considering purchasing the Heartsease Hall Estate you'd almost certainly have been dead. Your decision was, therefore, largely a matter of then or never.

· ·

And so to the practical matter of who might lend us the staggering sum of money N's calculations suggested we'd need to buy and renovate the Heartsease Hall Estate.

N remembered an old workmate from the Firm, now a venture capitalist specializing in 'improbable financings', as he engagingly put it, and set off to track him down. I started at the more terrene end of the trade: the Agricultural Mortgage Corporation, a UK-government-backed, lending-support body similar in function to the US's Fannie Mae and Freddie Mac.

Then, initiating a process which offered much early evidence of the easy-credit mind-set which would eventually precipitate the Great Crash of 2007–08 (would that I had taken more notice of it!), I groped up the greasy money-pole to investment bankers. In less than an hour, cold telephone calls to lending officers at five high-end institutions... produced warm, in-principle offers of the funding we required from each one of them. And what if, I asked, our calculations prove over-optimistic and we need even more money? 'No problem' or words to that effect every prospective lender replied without hesitation; indeed, one advised he'd be prepared 'to double or even triple' his offer. I selected what I thought sounded like the most responsible of these arguably *ir*responsible munificents and arranged for N and me to meet with him and his team at their London offices on 7 April. Then I settled down to draft a presentation and prepare for its possibly-critical Q & A follow-on.

· ·

I rehearsed you rigorously for your ordeal, you'll recall, to wit: 'On average, how much income do you expect to realize from your farming "investment" Mr Henry?'
Two-and-a-half to three per cent.... Say: three per cent per year in real terms.

'*Is that before or after deduction of the interest and other charges that would become payable to us as your bankers?*'

That's before deduc.... No, I mean *after* de.... Oh, I don't know, Alter-natis. These are just some very rough estimates which my wife, who's a Harvard MBA....

'*Indeed. But in round numbers we could say, couldn't we, your average annual return would be less than – very substantially less than, really – the long-run return from Gilts, that's to say what in your home country are called Treasury Bills, or high-grade corporate bonds.*'

There should be some capital appreciation; capital appreciation should be factored in....

'*Of course, if the Heartsease Hall Estate is farmed well. But, Mr Henry – you correct me if I'm wrong, please; my memory's not so good as it once was – didn't you say a moment ago you were an international management consultant with very little experience of larger-scale, commercial farming?*'

Well then there's the Hall – the magnificent, English-Heritage-listed, Grade I Heartsease Hall. That'll....

'*Ah, yes: your proposed residence which, as I believe you stated, requires certain renovations. What is the income from the Hall, Mr Henry; how much does it actually earn? After all, if we're going to regard the Hall as an asset....*'

. . . .

One heart-stopping moment excepted, however, our presentation went very well.

It took place in the bank's boardroom, an elegantly-understated wealth-and-power facility, amid deep-pile carpets and the softest of soft furnishings in muted beiges, blues and greys, and clusters of walnut and mahogany antique furniture which glowed rather than shone. On the big, oval, conference table in the middle, a Victorian silver coffee service – polished to gleaming perfection – sat surrounded by lustrous Sèvres china cups and saucers, and serving plates offering shortbread biscuits (cookies) which looked as if they'd melt in your mouth. The walls presented what purported to be genuine Impressionists, including a Chagall, a Dufy, a Monet and a hugely-exuberant head by Picasso of a one-eyed man... or, possibly, a woman... or, possibly, a goat. Present were four suits – three indians, who asked the questions, and their silent, stony-faced chief – a pretty, young secretary, and N and me.

I tried to approach my part in the proceedings as just another 'show-and-tell' not so very different from the many I'd made over

21

the years. But no; as a management consultant, you just present your conclusions and hope they're what the client wants to hear....

. . . .

Are you going to print that: 'present conclusions... the client wants to hear'? Are you actually going to...?

It does happen, Alter-natis. FHA would never stoop to that sort of thing, of course; our integrity is our *sine quo non*. But, I'm told, it does happen. Some unscrupulous management consultants are a bit like some financial analysts, and rating and regulatory agents, and 'investment' bankers, and accountants and lawyers and politicians....

. . . .

Whether the client actually did what I recommended and implemented my conclusions was, strictly speaking, none of my business. This time, however, if the 'client' didn't implement my 'conclusions'....

So with sweating palms and a face almost certainly more than normally rubicund I stood up, introduced myself, essayed a bit of warm-up patter ('Thank you very much for the opportunity to present to you today; being here is a great honor. Incidentally, that Picasso head: it's a life-portrait of one of the bank's former Chairmen, is it? Ha, ha.... Ha.... Ha.... I'm just joking, of course.') then pitched our main themes: what splendid people N and I were ('real buttoned-down over-achievers just like all of you') and what a fine investment the Heartsease Hall Estate would make for all of us in partnership ('one of only 300 estates in the whole of England, etc, *and* a current ratio based just on farming income of...').

Then I handed over to N for a detailed run-down of our purported business model, including estimates of revenues, expenses (building in financing costs...) and operating income 3–5 years out, and low, high and 'most-likely' cash-flow projections. Finally, after an exhortation please to: 'Help us achieve this low-cost/high-benefit opportunity... this opportunity which is so manifestly win/win!' N sat down. The most important presentation she and I'd ever made, perhaps – one of our most heart-felt ones, certainly – was complete.

But would the bankers buy it? Chief Stoneface and his Indians sat forward, brows knitted, lips pursed, conversing low-voiced and earnest; then they sat back, elbows on chair arms, hands clasped, upward-pointing fingers steepled, gazing into the middle distance... considering... reflecting.... Then they sat forward again; serious looks, gravid with import, were exchanged. A pause... a collective inhala-

INVESTMENT BANKERS

tion of breath…. Like a shroud, a wary silence settled over the beige, the blue and the grey, the walnut and the mahogany, the silver and the Sèvres; even the Picasso seemed to detumesce a bit.

Eventually all eyes locked onto the Chief. He continued to scowl, and it began to seem as if my hopes of becoming an Esquire, N's prayers for delivery from Brambledown and Scotland, and Piglet and Bapu's filial entitlement to happy, happy… oh, so *happy* parents, were about to be dashed. Seemingly in confirmation of my fears, old Stoneface suddenly rose to his feet and, positively spewing uncontent, turned to the pretty, young secretary. 'What time's old What's-His-Name coming in?' he snarled. Ms Secretary mumbled a few deferential words. Chief Stoneface nodded peremptorily, turned towards me and thrust out his right hand. 'I'm sorry, Mr Henry,' he said curtly. 'I'm very sorry. I'd like to be able to….'

My guts and N's, I later learned, wrenched. In the course of our business careers and also our larger lives, we'd faced bitter disappointment many times and more or less learned to cope; other opportunities – often better ones – almost always turned up. Even so….

'… I'd like to be able to stay around and talk to you,' old Stoneface continued, 'get to know you and Mrs Henry better, and hear more about the Heartsease Hall Estate – which sounds like an absolutely fabulous property. But I've got a meeting in a few minutes with one of our wealth-management clients who, to put it bluntly, is just about the most big-headed, small-minded, obdurate, quarrelsome… in short, tedious old (deleted) I've ever run across; just *thinking* about having to spend time with him puts me in a sour mood. Anyway, I'll get a letter off to you later today or tomorrow confirming our terms. If and when your purchase of Heartsease Hall is agreed… sure: we'll be delighted to do the financing.'

Yr Correspondent nearly shook Old Stoneface's hand off; N, it appeared for a moment, was actually – right there in the boardroom in front of everyone – going to hug and/or kiss him. And from the who-ever or whatever-it-might-be Picasso head staring balefully down I'd almost swear there came forth a cyclopean wink.

And so the blessed couple – the upstart-American, putative English country Squire and his Squiress – tripped back down the M40 (a 'motorway', or interstate highway analog, running north-west out of London) to Brambledown... to find a letter from another of N's former colleagues at the Firm advising that the weather in north Norfolk was typically 'very bleak and blowy' and its people 'rather cold and stand-offish'. 'The "feel" of the place is a lot like the Highlands and Islands of Scotland,' he concluded, unhelpfully. An alternative gloss – and one to which Yr Correspondent obviously inclined – was that north Norfolk must indeed be splendidly under-populated and un-spoiled and, therefore, just what we wanted. But to forestall any possibility of N's back-sliding, I propped a copy of the Heartsease Hall Estate brochure – cover picture facing out – against the big, earthenware pasta jar in our kitchen.

Old Stoneface's confirmation of financing having been received, N and I went back to the spreadsheet (or rather, back to the back of another envelope), this time to calculate the best compromise between what we felt we could offer for the Heartsease Hall estate and what Sir Roald might be prepared to accept for it. After a little massaging, a set of relatively plausible numbers emerged.

• •

That's what's so quaint about financial numbers isn't it, d'Arcy: the extent to which they can be derived 'in a box' on the basis of internally-arising, endogenous variables. It's as if the outside world – wherein may periodically be perpetrated 'Acts of God', aka force majeure *events, and acts of people aka human-behaviour events – didn't actually exist.*

Yes, Alter-natis; take those numbers out of their box and let an exogenous variable or two loose on them – virtually or actually 'stress-test' them, in other words – and all too often their plausibility comes crashing down. Just look at the accounts of so many national governments , state/country and municipal governments... even worse, of so many financial-sector institutions: all those definitive statements and/or projections of capital adequacy, and income surplus over expenditure.

And the accounts of today's baby boomers like you and me? Of course, some of us may have been a tad improvident from time to time....

....

Then, as the designated Writer-in-Residence, I proceeded – alone and armed only with my modest wits – to the word processor in my study to draft the formal letter of offer into which our artfully crafted numbers would be incorporated. For if we were to get away to The Motherland as planned, this instrument would have to be ready for dispatch more or less immediately upon the conclusion of our scheduled second view.

All very well in theory but, in practice, a few problems arose. First, to whom should I address the letter: Sir Roald or the real estate agent? I conferred with N who, purring that I was '(her) big, hands-on... man', said she favoured the principal-to-principal approach. Thus emboldened – girt for the epistolary challenge – I typed: 'Dear...' and ground to a halt. How should Sir Roald be addressed in writing, formally, as opposed to in conversation?

I checked my Debrett's *Correct Form** and started again... this time getting as far as 'Dear Sir Roald' before stopping. Writing a letter to a friend, a colleague, a client... a small-letter 'p' peer... was one thing; writing to a distinguished 13th Baronet – a capital-letter 'p' Peer as in 'of the Realm' – was quite another. Last but certainly not least, then: what, exactly, should I say and how, exactly, should I say it?

....

The end-points of the range seemed clear enough, d'Arcy. You could either pitch the text up-market to Sir Roald's level and try to give it a little courtliness... a little man-of-the-world savoir faire – always assuming, of course, you could manage it....

....

I keyed in: 'My wife and I would like to inform you that after very careful consideration we have decided to offer the sum of [...] for the Heartsease Hall Estate – subject, of course, to satisfactory contract and survey of the property – the which tender, I trust, you may find acceptable. I look forward to hearing from you at an early convenience. In the meantime I am, Sir, your most humble servant....'

....

Or as I think *you* proposed, Alter-natis, I could 'just let it all hang

---

* A reference book which sets out the system of titles and styles of personal address used in the UK.

out' and position the text well down, from middle-market, Made-in-America – or China, as was then more likely – me.

· · · · · · · · · · · · · · · · · · · ·

So alternatively: 'Nikki and I think Heartsease Hall's the most fantastic property we've ever, *ever* seen; it's, well… it's *just awesome*: *all* our best-est dreams come true. (I could even become an English Country Squire, my wife says, if I wanted to!) Will you take […] for it? Please say "Yes". We promise to cherish the Heartsease Hall Estate until the end of time or longer if necessary, just as you and your family would've done. Fingers crossed, and toes… and wrists and ankles…. Love ya'll….'

A great many drafts later, our offer letter – The Offer Letter – post-dated 11 April 1994, emerged from my printer. The original, duly signed, was sealed in an envelope addressed to Sir Roald *and stamped*; a copy was readied for the estate agent.

For our second viewing of the Heartsease Hall Estate – this time with Piglet and Bapu in tow (the latter, rising three, was a bit young to take it all in but Piglet, who'd be ten that September, understood something very important was going on) and a car overflowing with luggage containing the perceived necessities for our US trip – we managed to our considerable relief to arrive on time; indeed, we were a half-hour or so early.

So we didn't go straight in but, instead, drove around the perimeter of the property. After a couple of circumnavigations we parked the car and, like guests newly-arrived at a party – sipping our drinks, small-talking, listening to the music… building the mood to dance – made our way to 'The Brochure Cover Picture Place' in Pavilion Paddock.

The fields with their seeds now germinated – 'chitted' as, we learned, Norfolk farmers say – and the woodlands now just coming into leaf (what a difference ten days or so this time of year makes!) were a panorama of deep umbers, pale greens and the bright whites of flowering cherries, damsons and sloes. All but salivating, we anticipated what a bountiful harvest – for eating fresh, for cold-storing in the deep freeze… for conserving as jams and jellies – these last should in the autumn provide. The lower lake, rippled by a gentle breeze, sparkled invitingly in the warm sun. A cool respite on a hot summer's day for sure, I thought and, maybe, the repository of tasty eels and fishes. The pen swan was nesting now, guarded by her cob, on a little island of rushes just off the lake's south bank. How many little ones would they have, N wondered? Four? Five? Six? What a joy it'd be, we exclaimed, to watch them hatch out and paddle around in line, learning the rules of cygnine survival, and then moult from downy, matt grey to fully-fledged, adult, brilliant white. We turned and ambled back towards the car and, as we did so, the sheep and cattle herded up into a sort of honour guard and escorted us, baa-ing and lowing; 'Yes. Yeeesss!' they seemed to say.

Then we proceeded up to the Hall – the cathedral-castle with its exquisite Georgian-half-round and Gothic-ogee arched windows, its broad-shouldered battlements and crocketed/crocheted turret-finials, its great chimneys standing proud against the sky and its squared, knapped flints... its dragon-fish scales (some 25,000–30,000 of them, I'd calculated, at 80–100 'knaps' or chips per flint requiring, say, five minutes all told perfectly to prepare and shape each one, thereby yielding perhaps one hundred flints per man-day, and so requiring the better part of an entire man-year simply to make) – shimmering, silver-ochre-grey in the sunlight....

At the front porch, we were again cordially greeted by Sir Roald and Lady Maureen and their real estate agent (but, alas, no comely assistant). They had, of course, every reason to be cordial: relatively fortunate we must be – otherwise, presumably, we shouldn't have looked at the Heartsease Hall Estate in the first place – and now we'd returned, as only a small fraction of prospects do, for a second view.

But perhaps we might be *super*-fortunate and so taken with the property that we'd write them out a cheque more or less on the spot. ('Oh: not ready to close just yet? Well then, how about ten per cent *more* than the guide price?') Their welcome didn't seem of the forced, gimme-yer-money sort, however, but genuine and sincere. And soon all three excused themselves – 'Just make yourselves at home,' Lady Maureen insisted – leaving us to peer and poke about on our own.

N and I admired once again the light-filled, beautifully-proportioned, beautifully-laid-out rooms and, this time, also their appointments: lovely antique furniture mostly 200–300 years old and in 'best-country-house' condition – long lived-with and appreciated as chattels rather than shiny and Madison Avenue/Bond Street recently-restored-like-new – including bookcases, desks, chairs and a seven-leaf mahogany dining room table at which, Sir Roald proudly told us, Horatio, Viscount Nelson, the all-conquering, 18th/19th-century Admiral-hero and Norfolk 'native son' (lately, of course, of 'The Column' in London's Trafalgar Square) who was well known to the then

Festings, almost certainly dined; fine, leather-bound books in their hundreds, here neatly shelved by subject and author and there – the cast-offs of a too-brief moment's read – distributed about like confetti; and on the walls – everywhere, room after room, hallway after hallway – splendid 16th, 17th and 18th-century portraits of Sir Roald's forebears. There was even a pinewood model about the size of two jumbo suitcases side-by-side – made, it was thought, by or for the architect William Wilkins – of the Hall itself. Except as members of tour groups or on weekend stays with one or two higher-born friends, neither N nor I had ever beheld anything like it!

We decided to split up. I went outside to inspect for signs of movement in the Hall's foundations, then upstairs to the attics to probe for insect damage or rot; N descended into the cellars to confirm her wines could be adequately accommodated (could they indeed; the cellars included seven cool, dry bays, each easily able to take 1,000 or so bottles!) before recessing to the orangery to preview table and seating arrangements for her summer *soirées*.

Gradually, the Hall began to seem not so overwhelming... so intimidating... and its clustered outbuildings and extending acres not so extravagant. Rather these confederate elements – better, these *constituent* elements – became basic inputs which together with labour and management, and vision – and good luck! – would allow us to regenerate the Heartsease Hall Estate and make it sing again. If N and I could just get it together and keep it together, we and our children and our children's children, perhaps, could see out our days in this glorious, Edenic biosphere, sheltering within the Hall's resolute walls and beneath its doughty roof, and winning our food and our drink – our clothing, even – and our fuel from the estate's plenipotent fields, woodlands and lakes. Never again, I thought to myself, would we have to venture out or go abroad...

. . . .

No more jaunts to Algiers, Amsterdam, Bangkok, Beijing, Beirut, Berlin, Bombay/Mumbai, Budapest, Cairo, Calcutta, Cape Town, Djakarta, Hong Kong, Istanbul, Jerusalem, Karachi, Lisbon, Los Angeles, Madrid, Moscow, Paris, Prague, Rio de Janeiro, Rome, Sao Paulo, San Francisco, Singapore, Shanghai, Taipei, Tokyo, Vienna... New York, even, I asked you?

No Alter-natis, I replied, no more crowded flights to cheerless accommodation in homogeneous, over-decorated and over-furnished, indifferently-staffed, multi-starred and star-studded international hotels; we'll stay at home.

No more outings to concerts or the opera or the ballet or the the-
atre... or gallery openings and exhibitions, or literature and poetry
readings or lectures?
No; no more wondering helplessly while art-and-intellectual *glit-*
terati re-define and re-package 'genius' for the modern mass-market.
We'll read books – and try to write them, maybe – and paint, practise the piano and the organ, and watch public-service TV.
No more sprees to clothing stores, and cookware and dinnerware
stores, and IT/electrical stores, and CD and DVD shops, and....
No; no more waiting around for self-absorbed salespeople to
fetch merchandise we've already considered and decided against.
We'll shop online.
So no real face time; no warm, salute-the-seeing, savour-the-
scenting, hark-the-hearing, treasure-the-touching.... I can't think of
a suitable alliterative for 'tasting'...
Thank goodness!
... face time with other people?
There'd still be Piglet's and Bapu's school events like sports days
and founders days, and N's and my various class and other reunions
in the US, I suppose. And trips to the barber and the dentist and, almost certainly, I was beginning to sense, the psychiatrist....
How about the deli, I persisted? Every once in a while to mark
that extra-special occasion – what some Brits would call a 'hatch-
ing' or a 'matching'... a birth or a marriage... even a 'despatching',
that's to say a funeral celebrating a life well-lived – couldn't you...
wouldn't you... make just a little trip to the deli?
I don't do delicatessen (from *delikat essen*, German for 'elegant
or dainty foods'), Alter-natis; I'm basically a meat 'n' potatoes kinda
guy. You know: I like slabs of real-American, flash-grilled beef,
lamb... buffalo – all of it marbled and well-hung, of course, perhaps
with a side-order of chanterelles or morels from the Dordogne, in
France – or, in very cold weather, a slow-roasted... *en casserole*,
even... shoulder, brisket or short-rib/belly joint.
All those yucky animal fats! How about seafood? Seafood is so
good for you....
You mean like Chesapeake Bay rockfish and shad... and crabs
and oysters ... and North Atlantic cod, herrings and pollack, and
lobsters and clams... and fresh-run, North Pacific red salmon....
And maybe just the occasional fowl: chicken, duck, goose, grouse,
guinea hen, partridge... a nice, really plump pheasant.... Ooooooh!
Aaahhhh!
That's all very wholesome... but pretty basic....
Well: we *could*, I suppose, start off with Belgian or French *fois*
gras with truffles, or seared queen scallops wrapped in Parma (Italy)
or Seranno (Spain) ham – or just good old, down-home Smithfield

(Virginia, USA) ham – served on a bed of fresh asparagus...
And to finish?
... Austrian s*achertorte* topped with real-vanilla ice cream and maraschino cherries – or, as the healthier option, tree-ripened Basrahi (Iraq) dates, Ismiri (Turkey) figs and mangoes from the Nile Delta, perhaps – followed by a good, French cheese like *Reblochon* or *Vacherin*, or *Torta Basilico* cheese from Italy... *marrons, fraises* and *mirabelles glacées*, and root ginger crystallized in South-African acacia honey... Arabica coffee from the Malabar coast with double cream and chunks of unrefined, 'candy' sugar... and a little dish of dark-chocolate *truffes* with marzipan centres.
And then, after the deli – if you could fit it in before rushing back to milk the cows and feed the chickens, or hoe a few more rows of organic corn (I mean 'maize') or spin another fantastical yarn – maybe you could just stop through your friendly, neighborhood package-goods store....
Mais bien sûr, mon ami: oui, oui, oui, oui, oui, oui, oui! Bollinger and Dom Perignon champagnes... Chateau Latour, Petrus Pomerol and Puligny Montrachet wines – and for the oenophile N, of course, some of those wonderful, estate-bottled California concoctions – signing out with Armagnac de Montal, Benedictine... Cockburn's Vintage Port... and a Cuban cigar, hand-rolled on the inner thigh of a beautiful woman....
Once these deep-seated food-and-drink, etc, fixations of yours had been recognised, d'Arcy...
I'm sorry, Alter-natis; I probably did get a bit carried away.
... and their implications fully appreciated: that down deep you were very, very unlikely ever to become either an ascetic or a fully-committed, UK-based locavore...
I never said I *had* to have these *délices*; all I said was it *might be nice*, occasionally, to....
... were you still convinced that the Heartsease Hall Estate's 'glorious, Edenic biosphere', as you've above characterised it, really was the living for you?
· ·

Never again would we have to venture out or go abroad...

· ·
... except to buy a hammer and nails to re-fasten the slipped roof slates; a trowel and lime mortar – a precursor of cement and, you'll remember d'Arcy, the required binder when repairing elderly listed buildings in the UK – to re-secure the loose stonework and brick-work; and brushes, paint and putty to refurbish the windows and doors....
· ·

As our reconnaissance – and Yr Correspondent's musings – drew to a close, Sir Roald, Lady Maureen and the real estate agent (now, happily, rejoined by his comely assistant!) suddenly reappeared as if conjured out of the soft, spring ether. Had N and I any questions? The fixtures and fittings, I asked, and all those lovely, original marble fireplace over-mantles and surrounds? Included in the price, the estate agent said definitively. And the 18th-century gilded mirrors and console tables in the drawing room, and the ormolu wall sconces in the dining room, and the oak book cabinets and shelving in the library and, throughout, the period door and window furniture...? The agent looked to Sir Roald, who inclined his head obligingly, and back at me. Of course; they're in as well, he confirmed. Any more questions? No not really, I replied, but then... perhaps it would be helpful to have some idea how much Heartsease Hall costs to run: heat, light, water, rates (property taxes)... that sort of thing. Certainly, Sir Roald replied crisply. I'll post (mail) copy accounts to you tomorrow.

With as much calm and composure as I could manage, I nodded – 'head-bowed' more like, my ever-supportive Uxor later proposed – and advised Sir Roald gravely that we'd 'be in touch'. Then N, the boys and I, shaking hands and well-wishing all around, took our leave.

Just inside what we'd learned was referred to as the Main Gate (to distinguish it from the several other designated entrances to the estate), in the parking area for what, it transpired, was called the Front Lodge (the estate had an East Lodge as well), I stopped the car and convened one last conference. Should we or shouldn't we...? N, her eyes wide and unnaturally bright, unseeing looked at me; she murmured something about the amplitude of the rooms and, with their huge windows through which the sunlight flooded, their 'California-Mediterranean' quality... and the temperate capaciousness of 'her' wine cellars. I, unhearing, over-spoke her esquirely-authoritatively about the fertility of 'my' land and the way it lapped gently around the woodlands and the lakes, and the simple, 'organic' architecture of the historic Hall – its 'outdoors-indoors' aesthetic so similar to the house I'd long ago sketched for a property I'd inherited on Campobello Island* but never built – with its facing of knapped-flint dragon-fish scales.

---

* Off the northeast coast of Maine, in the Bay of Fundy; holidaying at his family's summer home there in 1921, the future President Franklin Delano Roosevelt contracted polio.

In the end there really was nothing to discuss. We'd drunk deeply of a most-gloriously heady brew; in our hyper-activated brains the music was pounding away, and we were lusting to engage, to party, to dance. I floored the accelerator and we roared off... only to brake hard at the first mailbox and drop in the offer letter addressed to Sir Roald. Then we drove up to London, stuck the copy offer letter under the estate agent's door and wafted down the M4 motorway to Heathrow.

. . . .

'*Alea iacta est!*' as Julius Caesar is said to have said upon crossing the Rubicon (river) from Cisalpine Gaul – of which he was Governor – into Italy, in defiance of Pompey's government in Rome. Protracted civil war from which Caesar eventually emerged victorious ensued.

In your description now of your then 'moment of great decision', you should write 'Alia iacta "erat"!' d'Arcy – that's to say 'The die was cast!' using the past tense, not 'The die is cast!' using the present tense.

As you will. But be aware, Alter-natis, according to Plutarch – one of Caesar's early biographers – the big man actually spoke the words not in Latin but in Greek.

. . . .

Chapter 3

Burning Scent

S hortly after we touched down in San Francisco, I telephoned Sir
Roald's real estate agent for news of our offer. The young man
coughed politely – I could almost see his patronizing wink to
his comely assistant and hear her barely-suppressed snicker in reply
– then advised me earnestly that, from the news standpoint, it really
was 'pretty early days'. What was the level of interest in the property,
I asked. Had many come to view? Again came the polite cough and,
probably, a reprise of the wink-snicker routine, followed by the intelligence that a dozen or so parties had been through so far and another
8–10 were scheduled. 'Quite an encouraging response for a property
of this size,' the estate agent opined, concluding: 'I'd be surprised if
Heartsease Hall didn't sell for a good deal more than its guide price.'
I summoned up something utterly disingenuous about how pleased I
was for Sir Roald, and said I'd contact him again in a few days…

… the first two of which we spent visiting with N's old friends
Cab and her husband Gary at their vast, new, lakefront 'Cottage'
in Tahoe. N and I were disposed in 'The Orchid Suite', known to
the staff as 'Guest Bedroom No. 9'; Piglet and Bapu bunked in 'The
Dorm' which, depending on the arrangements, could probably sleep
thirty or so. While the boys played and N napped, I sat by the pool
sipping an iced *piña colada* and studying the Heartsease Hall Estate
brochure and its plan, and also a large-scale, UK-government-issue
Ordnance Survey map of the north Norfolk area I'd brought along.

Around me all was as straight from the pages of a Sotheby's *International Realty* brochure: state-of-the-art modern, luxurious,
squeaky-clean. Great location, great house, great host and hostess….

· · · · · · · · · · · · · · · · · · · ·

*Ah, 'The Motherland': America. 'Oh beautiful, for spacious skies,
For amber waves of grain, For purple mountain majesties Above the
fruited plain!'*
I'll bet you can't tell me who wrote that.
Katharine Lee Bates, just over a century ago.
Good Lord, Alter-natis! How did you…?

I just… knew it. Anyway, there you were beneath a cloudless, blue, Rocky-Mountain sky with panoramic views over clear, sparkling waters almost as far as the eye could see. And no need to garden or farm or otherwise take any real care of it except, of course, in a longer-term, environmental sense. Let God, or Whomever, do the care-taking.

Ye-aaah! Right on, Brother!

So why did you offer for an expensive, time-consuming, megaresponsibility like the Heartsease Hall Estate?

Because I never learned to fly-fish? Or play golf? I dunno; 'because it was there', and it was beautiful, and N and I desired it.

And in dank, drear 'Old Blighty', as homesick British troops serving overseas used to call the UK, when you could have…?

We planned to keep our condo in Baltimore, Maryland, and our Campobello Island property.

That's not answering the question. Why did you commit so deeply to life as an expatriate in England?

Habit and a bit of preference, I guess.

'Habit?'

By early-1994 I'd been living outside the United States – mostly in England – for quite a while, you remember.

Yes. And when you first arrived in these Sceptered Isles you were so cute: trying to be 'more British than the British'.

It doesn't work, of course; I don't think you ever entirely shed what's formally known as your Domicile of Origin, or your Domicile of Birth. The British certainly don't; they take the full measure of their irascible British-ness with them to the grave!

Then, after awhile, you just sort of defaulted into being an Anglo-American·in England….

Yep. I got an interesting job writing about the Middle East; I got an interesting wife – a high-powered, career type, but a really first-class cook – and with her, I co-founded an interesting, political and macro-economic risk-management consultancy, started a family… and settled down into it. A momentum – an Anglo-tensive momentum drawing me ever more deeply into the UK and then, maybe, a mid-life inertia minding me to stay there; I don't really know – just sort of built up.

And 'preference'?

Pull factor was that Britain, with its great, globe-girdling, historical associations and frowzy little insular peculiarities, was a hugely interesting country in which to live. It's a commonplace, of course, that the most interesting people and the most interesting societies – those with the deepest, most questing inner lives – are often those who've enjoyed money and power and then lost it… like so many British and 'Great Britain', formerly 'of Empire', have.

Then there was the European Community thing. Britain's in some ways very much an integral part of mainstream Europe – its people are linked genetically to the Vikings (Scandinavia), the Romans, the Anglo-Saxons (North and West Germany), the Normans (France)... in East Anglia, especially, the Flemish (the Netherlands) – indeed, until some 9,000 years ago Britain was geo-physically conjoined with Europe; the Thames was just a large, estuarine tributary of the Rhine. Yet in other ways Britain's very much removed from the Continent....

And then there was, and is, the Anglo-American 'special relationship' thing, however that relationship may day-to-day be defined.

Was there a push factor too? Were you running away from something?

Personally, you mean? I might have been early on in my UK sojourn; I don't think I was by the time we were offering for Heartsease Hall. But, increasingly, I did sense about the US – 'the world's only superpower' – a jingoism... an imperialism, almost... with which I wasn't then and am not now entirely in accord. That crusading, 'by-divine-right' mind-set is, of course, captured in Bates's *America the Beautiful* very well.

If you could have whatever geo-political affiliation you wanted stamped on the cover of your passport – United States of America, United Kingdom, European Community, 'Planet Earth'... whatever – what would that affiliation be?

'Sustainable Free-enterprise Democracy'. National entities aren't so important as they used to be; we live in an irretrievably globalized world now.

But democracies tend to break down, lose their drive and their impulsion and, most importantly, their moral discipline. Liberalism takes hold....

'Thus conscience doth make cowards of us all...'

Ah, yes: the closing lines of Hamlet's tortured 'To be, or not to be' soliloquy.

'... And thus the native hue of resolution Is sicklied o'er with the pale cast of thought, And enterprises of great pith and moment With this regard their currents turn awry, And lose the name of action.' Amen!

Free enterprise, moreover, is regularly at the mercy of what the British economist John Maynard Keynes famously called 'animal spirits' whose excesses – often obscene excesses – despoil our environment, damage our bodies, deconstruct our minds and discomfit our very souls.

Indeed, as many in The Motherland and elsewhere have recently re-discovered; that's why I prefixed the adjective 'sustainable' to my fantasy-passport affiliation. But in many parts of the world – *most* parts, probably – what's needed right now is a good deal more equality of opportunity and political freedom.

Goodness gracious; you'll be dressing in fustian and hugging trees soon! One last question, however: in just two paragraphs of this short insertion, you've used the word 'interesting' six times. Is that bad self-editing, or what?

So far as I'm aware, I've only this one life to lead. And to build on the apprehensive words of the French philosopher Jean Baudrillard: 'The worst realization would be that it and me be boring.' The best realization would be that it and me be interesting.

Interesting....

. . . .

I roused from my musings, trudged into the 'Deal Room', as Cab called the glass-walled, command-and-control centre just off the front hallway of the Cottage from which Gary when 'off duty' directed his world-wide empire, and again telephoned the estate agent. He was out of the office – probably showing Heartsease Hall to some rich Dane, or German, or Gulf Arab, or Hong Konger, or Indian or Singapori, I supposed (in the mid-1990s, the Reader will recall, there weren't so many rich Chinese and Russians running around) – so I got his comely assistant on the line. Hearing her warm, attentive voice with its crisp English enunciation, imagining her long, lean, bikini-clad, California-surfer-girl body lying fragrant and golden brown in the sun... almost made me forget the purpose of my call. But oh, yes: was there any news on Heartsease Hall? Well, she advised, a couple of parties did appear to be quite interested; otherwise there was still nothing really to tell. I hung up and trudged back to my deck chair at poolside, my *piña colata*, my Heartsease Hall Estate brochure and plan, and my Ordnance Survey map.

Another 72 hours and I was on the telephone once again, this time from our Baltimore condo to which, N and the boys having flown to Sacramento to visit N's parents before returning to the UK, I'd retreated alone. The estate agent was, as ever, very polite, very correct, very professional... and very unforthcoming. It was still 'early days', he said – several parties, he told me, were intending to view or re-view – and the 'last shot' in the advertising campaign – a full page in *The Field* , a glossy, monthly magazine for real, deep-dyed country-lovers – wasn't due to be 'fired' until next week.

. . . .

The British are still a very martial people, Alter-natis... some of them, at least.

Not to mention boorish, rancorous, obstinate, devious, perfidious, self-impressed, vindictive, bigoted, xenophobic....
Refined, equable, obliging, straightforward, loyal, self-deprecating, magnanimous, fair-minded, welcoming....
• • • • • • • • • • • • • • • • • • • •

The ad would likely generate 'a number of offers', the agent believed. He concluded by asking me didn't I think Heartsease Hall would be 'a lovely place to live for at least the guide price'. I replied I thought it would be a lovely place to live for much, much more than the guide price, but that we'd 'have to see'.

I retired to the condo's patio full of gloomy thoughts. There could be... probably now were... dozens of people – more, maybe – tramping around the Heartsease Hall Estate, planning how *they* would crop its fields or stroll its woodlands or boat its lakes, choosing wallpapers and curtains and carpets to refurbish the Hall – *wondering at... presuming perhaps to stroke, even, its lovely, knapped-flint dragon-fish scales* – and submitting their own, higher offers.

The evening of 24 April, I boarded the red-eye from Baltimore-Washington International and flew back to Heathrow, then took the express bus down the M4 to Cirencester, in Gloucestershire, where N collected me for the short drive to Brambledown. *En route*, I read my horoscope and learned my 'instincts' must now be telling me I was in 'a uniquely opportune position'. Clearly, I concluded, this astrologer-person had precious little experience of long-haul, overnight flights and jet-lag. Other than that I was suffering from some sort of extraordinary cerebral dysfunction and whole-body muscle cramp, my instincts were telling me nothing!

But after a good, long, aerobic run and a nice, light, vinous supper followed by a couple of melatonin tablets and a sound, ten-hour zizzz in my own bed, I felt almost back to normal again; the extraordinary cerebral dysfunction, etc, was gone... leaving just the *ordinary* cerebral dysfunction... and a nagging sense of inconclusion and unfulfilment. Was there no relief from this purgatory of prospective esquiredom? (Tums? Advil? Super-strength Tylenol, perhaps, as advertised endlessly on American TV?) Well, yes there was... of course there was: somehow, I told myself, I had to regain The Initiative.

In an attempt to do, so I drafted a groveling letter to Sir Roald asking for his 'view' of our offer, that's to say whether he was inclined to accept it; to the letter I proposed to append, for his convenience of reply, my every possible contact detail: home address, office address, telephone, fax, email and ditto, I fairly-seriously considered, those of all my of-age next-of-kin (wife, mother and father-in-law... two or three first cousins). I concluded my draft by referencing 'an FHA client' with whom I might have to meet early the next week in Cambridge – a complete fabrication, Yr (Abject) Correspondent must now confess; apart from a few wretched university academics, I didn't know anyone in Cambridge – and asking if 'after my meeting, perhaps, if it wouldn't be too inconvenient, might I stop by at the Hall for a chat?'

. . . .

Shame on you, d'Arcy Henry, for even thinking such a ruse.
What? Who? Me?
And as for trying to perpetrate it on some poor, unsuspecting, British 13th Baronet....
But I never....
Even if in the extenuating circumstances which then obtained it could have been argued such a disgraceful, under-handed tactic was justified....
It could have been! And it wou....
It seems to me your 'stopping by' sentence has an awful lot of commas, conditionals and double negatives in it. Such a construction suggests supplication and/or weakness. I thought you always advised negotiating from strength.
Well, I couldn't require the man to treat with me, could I!
Indeed: 'treat'. So use of the word 'chat' when your real aim was to discuss business....
Awwww....
Finally, the drive 'from Cambridge to Heartsease Hall': that would have been a round trip of only a few hours. But, of course, you'd actually have been round-tripping not from Cambridge but from Brambledown – an excursion which would have chewed up the better part of an entire day.
Was there any indication whatsoever that your proposed subterfuge would've been time and cost efficient?
It would've made clear the intensity of my interest in and the sincerity of my commitment to the estate which, if Sir Roald attached importance to such things – as I sensed he did – might just have resonated.
It would also have made clear the near-desperation of your interest, etc, and in so doing put quite a lot of power in Sir Roald's hands.
Hmmmm.
. . . .

After conferring with N, however, I decided not to send the letter. Instead I mail-shot Sir Roald's 'messenger', writing to his estate agent that it was now over two weeks since we'd submitted our offer and, 'for a variety of reasons...

. . . .

First among them being fear of mental breakdown, I suggested.
   'Twas brillig, and the slithy toves Did gyre and gimble in the wabe; All mimsy were the borogoves, and the mome raths out-grabe,' as Lewis Carroll depicted in his *Through the Looking-Glass* of 1872.
   'Beware the Jabberwock, my son! The jaws that bite, the claws that catch! Beware the Jubjub bird, and shun The frumious Bander-snatch!'
. . . .

'... for a variety of reasons', the time was fast approaching when 'my wife and I would like to have the position with respect to our 11 April 1994 offer definitively clarified'. I suggested a meeting at the estate agent's premises in London the afternoon of 5 May, immediately fol-lowing my return from a long-scheduled, FHA research trip to the Middle East assuming, *insha'Allah*, my nerves held out that long.
   As to N's nerves, the day before I flew out – 28 April – was her '39th' birthday, an apparition of *tempus stabat* (as opposed to the more universally recognized *tempus fugit*) which we'd dutifully cel-ebrated each 28 April for the past eleven or twelve years. As usual I took her out for a 'quiet' supper in a local Cotswolds pub: its rows of garish slot machines chugging and dinging; its ubiquitous televi-sions blaring out that evening's football (soccer) Match of the Day; its massed, alcohol-over-testosterone-fuelled patrons booing and cheer-ing... and just plain screaming for the sheer, empathetic hell of it, apparently. Part way through, I gave N a big kiss and a little bottle of scent then, shouting over the din, I asked her if our bid for Heartsease Hall failed would she reconsider her proscription on living in Scot-land. N burst out crying.
   The next morning, while waiting in the departure lounge at Heath-row for my flight to be called, I thumbed idly through the current issue of *Big Farm Weekly*, a magazine aimed at larger-scale farmers and agricultural contractors; in it was an advertisement – placed by a major competitor of Sir Roald's real estate agency – for a big, indus-trial farm in Suffolk. The property wasn't a patch on the Heartsease Hall Estate, of course; to begin with, it was mostly Grade III, mid-

dling-quality land, unrelieved by either lakes or woodlands, and utterly without contour, that's to say as flat as the Great Salt Lake. And to finish: probably needless to mention, it had no Georgian-Gothic cathedral-castle robed in splendrous knapped-flint dragon-fish scales.

But in order to compare its particulars and guide price with those of the Heartsease Hall Estate, and on the off chance it might otherwise come in handy, I telephoned the competitor-agency and asked them to air-courier a copy of the Suffolk-farm brochure to me at my hotel in Cairo.

According to the astrologer for *The Egyptian Times**, my horoscope for the first week of May 1994...

· · · · · · · · · · · · · · · · · · ·

You and your horoscope, d'Arcy!
The need to believe – in a messiah, a prophet... an astrologer, even – is very deep isn't it.
It seems to be! But belief in these intermediaries... these agents... is just a proxy, of course.
A proxy? For what?
For the need to believe in something more fundamental: the existence of a paramount order or system within which everything – from specific atomic and sub-atomic quanta through to and including cosmic general relativities – inter-relates.
The thinking-person's Holy Grail: a grand, unified 'Theory of Everything', aka 'The Standard Model'....
And from this need to believe in a paramount order springs the ultimate question: if such an order exists, how did it arise?
Well go on, tell me: how *did* it arise?
I don't know.
Well, then... how did *the need to believe in it* arise?
Again, I don't know....
Alter-natis, you're not usually this unforthcoming....
But I don't think it arose out of any particular confessional imperative; I don't think there's some spirit – some 'force' – out there telling us we must believe in a particular way 'because it is meet, right and our bounden duty so to do'.
So how...?
Nevertheless, in an evolutionary sense – a Darwinist survival-of-the-fittest sense, perhaps – believing in an intelligible order seems to be very important. Indeed, some neuro-biologists think such a predisposition is hard-wired into that part of our brain called the

---

* Then Egypt's leading English-language newspaper; now replaced by the *Daily News Egypt* and bundled with the *International Herald Tribune*.

mid-frontal gyrus.

Why do...?

They call it the 'mid-frontal gyrus' because of its location, d'Arcy – in the middle of the brain's frontal cortex – and because of what it looks like from the outside: a 'gyrus', the Latin derivative of the Greek word 'guros', is simply a convolution or folding.

That's a very learned reply, Alter-natis, but it doesn't in fact address the question I had in mind asking... so you lose five points. What *I* want to know is: why do some neuro-biologists think believing in an intelligible order may be hard-wired into us?

Because our material existence as individuals, communities and societies substantially depends in the shorter term on our ability to perceive and understand order. The more we know about what makes us tick, and what makes tick the environment in which we live...

... our health, our wealth... Wall Street and the other financial markets, especially, and the implications of their wicked ways for our hopes of a comfortable retirement...

...the more likely we are, we think, to have the food, clothing and shelter we need. Put the other way round: if we didn't believe ourselves and our environment to be essentially ordered and intelligible – if, indeed, we believed these realms were essentially random and unintelligible; just one big brood or 'eyrar', as they used to be known, of Nassim Nicholas Taleb's construct Black Swans, say – there'd be very little point in our getting out of bed in the morning.

So why *do* we...?

But having gotten out of bed, we open the curtains... and what do we see?

We see another day's hard, hard living to be done and a hard, hard world to do it in!

We see earth and sky...

Not if our lower-floor bedroom looks out into the courtyard of a high-rise apartment block in some megalopolis like New York!

... and the flora and fauna in between and, beyond, a few, far-distant elements of that tiny speck of the Orion Spur – itself but an appendage of the humungous Milky Way Galaxy, with its 100 billion or so stars, many of them encircled by their own complement of planets – which is our Solar System and, beyond that, what we in our colossal ignorance quaintly refer to as 'Deep Space'.

Are these infinite or all-but infinite external 'orders' and our own internal mental and physical ones – the macro and the micro – linked in some way... within some 'everything' order perhaps? And if they are linked and if we better understood their linkage, would we lead materially more-comfortable and spiritually more-fulfilled lives?

As I just wrote: the thinking-person's Holy Grail – a grand, unified Theory of Everything....

However, the great conundrum seems to be that the more we learn, the less we know. Some peoples' reaction to this awful realization is so debilitating they fall into what Socrates called a state of 'aporia' – the Greek word for 'being at a loss about what to do or say'.

You don't appear to be much at risk on that account....

Trying to understand 'order' – really, fundamentally, understand it – is like looking for the pot of gold at the end of the rainbow: we search and search and search only to discover we haven't found it yet....

Even Albert Einstein, we're told, ultimately abandoned his search for a Theory of Everything. So too, it sometimes appears, has our contemporary Stephen Hawking.

Well! If they and all those other Great Searchers out there today can't find.... And if *they* can't, doesn't that imply some or all of what we think we know could simply be dead wrong?

Yes as, among many others, the renowned German physicist Werner Heisenberg suggested. The problem may be just a question of dimensional specification, of course; what present technology delimits as 'an order', future technology may unbound.

And/or a question of time-frame. An order may exist here-and-now today, but yesterday it didn't and it might not tomorrow....

And/or a question of perspective. Viewed one way, something may have the properties of an order but, viewed another way, those properties may disappear.

And/or a question of identity. The presumed order may exist within, or around the outside of, or alongside concentric-isms, or parallelisms – other universes entirely – which subsume, or suprasume or, even, consume it.

Heavens!

And/or a question of perception. That which we recognize as 'an order' could really be just a randomness or a chaos in drag.

Oh no!

And/or finally, it may be a question of brainpower. Given the limits of our individual, intra-cranial CPUs (central processing units), we might have to couple up, or down – with some fragrant woman-scientist, say – into iPPP mode – that's 'inter-personal parallel processing' mode... which, let me tell you, could be really, really hot! – to pull the gigs (gigabytes) we'll need to work all of this out.

What a stupefying prospect! How could anyone possibly know what to believe?

Exactly. So the important thing – the only *important thing, maybe – is to believe that we don't know it all and that someone else...*

some thing *else, even – God or an Almighty Whomever… a Supreme Ordering Immanence of some sort – might.*
And 'keep on searchin', of course.
You got it, Ole Buddy: jes' 'keep on searchin'. Recent research on human wellness suggests that, over time, nature favours the freely faithful, you know.
· · · · · · · · · · · · · · · · · · · ·

… my horoscope for the first week of May advised that in respect of 'certain outstanding matters' the positions of others 'will soon be revealed'. But it bid me to 'say what needs to be said… and it will then become clear why saying it was worth the effort'. My 5 May meeting with the estate agent, it seemed, could prove to be a momentous one.

Well good; let's get on with it, I told myself from the depths of my deep-cushioned armchair in the lounge of the Intercontinental Hotel in Abu Dhabi to where I'd flown from Cairo. It was early evening, and I was trying to write up my notes on the day's round of consultations and interviews. But my mind kept wandering….

I put down my notebook, took up my glass of *lassi** and sat back to watch the girls go by (in the most astonishing range of dress styles: everything from medium-mini skirts to floor-length *fustaan*, or gowns) and then the boys (a tall, young *bedou* in a flowing, white *dishdasha* robe and *keffiyeh* head scarf, with a hooded peregrine falcon – its jess dangling unsecured – perched on his gauntleted forearm, in particular caught my eye).

I put down my glass, sat up, and resumed my notebook: 'At the moment, there's very little of strategic regional consequence going on here,' I drafted, 'just a bunch of slightly bemused Gulf Arabs trying to adjust to the rapid rise in their living standards and a veritable tsunami of what they call *bidaa, i.e.* cultural imports – many of them exports from The Motherland – which aren't always entirely in keeping with their home-grown, traditionalist Islam.'

My thoughts turned from emerging Arabia, and political and macro-economic risk, to the eye-popping, state-of-the-art public utilities, and transportation and IT infrastructures all around me… to the distant swathes of still-unspoiled desert dotted with oases between which tenting nomads and traders with their camel-trains regularly trekked… and, finally, to the local peoples and the opportunities so many of them took so easily for long conversations – or just to reflect

---

* A sort of 'smoothie', often fruit-flavoured, made from sweetened yoghurt or buttermilk.

on the turning world – over salt-roasted pistachios and *demitasses* of sugary coffee or tea. The old, British-Colonial-era Trucial States with the new, 20th/21st-century UAE (the United Arab Emirates, constituted in 1971–72) plunked down on top: a vibrant, affirmative mix of the traditional and the *avant-guard* modern – just as the Heartsease Hall Estate would be when N and I'd finished properly doing it up.

On my return from the Middle East, and still in my travel clothes, I went straight from Heathrow to the real estate agent's office where I tried to establish the position in respect of our offer. 'How're we doing?' I began jovially. But they – the lead estate agent and another young man; no comely assistant was in attendance this time – were very skilled at parrying my thrusts. ('I know Sir Roald's received your offer, but I'm not sure we've had his guidance about replying to it yet. I'll just jot myself a memo [cue: faux-fervent scribbling] and see if, perhaps, my PA's had any "new news" [cue: anguished-attentive 'We're-here-for-you!' look]'.) So, on the pretext of wanting to refer to some papers buried deep in my brim-full briefcase, I took out the competitor-agency's brochure of the industrial farm in Suffolk and, for a weighted moment, laid it conspicuously on the conference table.

The two young men parried that one pretty well too. But then, *mirabile scriptu*, the discussion did in fact progress to the offer N and I'd made, how it'd been received and, predictably, whether we might be able to 'sweeten' it a bit. I took this as indication we were at least still in the running, so I replied we probably could improve our offer 'a bit'. I added, however – with what I hoped would pass for near-terminal impatience – that if we *did* improve it, we'd be looking for 'more or less instant gratification'. The two agents nodded gravely and scribbled some further notes. Finally the lead agent, in an intonation which in retrospect seemed over-heavy with innuendo, said: 'Well, why don't you improve your offer a bit.'

Two days later, N and I lodged with Sir Roald and copied to his estate agent a set of even more jaw-dropping numbers, along with our formal notice that 'however enjoyable (*sic!*) our exchanges to date have been, my wife and I would like to have this matter concluded, one way or the other, no later than the close of business on Friday, 20 May'. We then settled in for a fortnight or so's figurative abatement of breath.

· · · · · · · · · · · · · · · · · · · ·

As the revolutionary Thomas Paine – who, incidentally Alter-natis, was born in Thetford, in Norfolk – wrote in *The American Crisis* during that terrible winter of 1776 when the tide of our Revolution was turned: 'These are the times that try men's souls.' And, I'd have to say, that time in early-mid May 1994 certainly tried this man's soul.

For someone who was neither pubescent nor pregnant, nor going through andropause (male menopause) *you did seem pretty labile.*

Sometimes I felt N and I couldn't possibly win through; other times, I felt our success was almost predestined...

'... predestined'? You mean all you had to do was exist at the right moment, in the right place and, if He, She or Whomever willed it, the Heartsease Hall Estate would fall into your lap? What drivel! Humanism and The Enlightenment – d'Alembert, Diderot, Helvé-tius, Montesquieu, Rousseau, Voltaire... the above-referenced Tom Paine – they did away with all that predestination stuff, didn't they? They said men and women were inherently self-determining and free to do what they wanted... in other words: more or less fully empow-ered to try their luck.

That's just what we'd been doing, Alter-natis.

And in the end you acquired the Heartsease Hall Estate. But now, looking back, how do you think that acquisition came about?

It came about first of all because I – or, rather, N and I – defined our objective and then designed and implemented a strategy for achieving it. In life as in, say, baseball: if you don't swing you won't get a hit, right?

What if, to continue your sporting metaphor, no game had been in progress – better, no one had been pitching – when like Mudville's 'Mighty Casey' in Ernest Thayer's poem of that name you strode so purposefully to the plate?

Well, yes: serendipity... luck... does play an important part.

And what if you didn't have a bat because there wasn't one handy or you hadn't the means – the financial means, more precisely – of acquiring one?

Everyone's got a bat, haven't they? Something they can swing....

In deference to the sensibilities of Lady Readers you might con-sider re-phrasing that....

And if they haven't got a bat, they can make one out of an old broom-handle or some such. That's what democracy and equality of opportunity, liberty and justice for all... The Motherland and apple pie... is all about.

So could anyone have acquired Heartsease Hall? A Chinese peas-ant, for example, or an 'untouchable' Hindu – now, you'll know, re-ferred to officially as 'dalits' ('those who are oppressed')? Or a black person or a Hispanic from an inner-city ghetto?

Certainly, if they were able and worked hard and had that little bit of luck.

From what you know of China, India and inner city ghettos, etc: what probability would you assign to someone from that sort of background – from that sort of 'ballpark', you might write – acquiring the Heartsease Hall Estate?

Oooh... about the same as catching a falling star, I guess.

• • • • • • • • • • • • • • • • • • • •

Another Sunday – 8 May – and another race to the hebdomadal horoscope... this time to discover: 'Brilliant aspects early *next* week mean extraordinary opportunities. But, with the way things are going early *this* week, you'd be forgiven for wondering just how it will all work out'. I paused my reading: Please Mr Astrologer, I implored, I'm a hard-driving, Alpha-type male – at least, I like to think I am! Surely I can do something to break this impasse and progress my wife's and my interests? I resumed my reading: 'Just relax,' the astrologer counselled comfortingly; 'sit back and let things develop.'

And incredibly (or should I write 'inevitably') so, substantially, 'things' did. When, mid-week, I again telephoned the real estate agent he did indeed open, again, with the old, 'early-days' gambit. But then after a little wheedling...

• • • • • • • • • • • • • • • • • • • •

Mr Real Estate Agent... *Dear* Mr Real Estate Agent... Good, Kind Sir: it's now been more than a month since we submitted our first offer. And only a few days ago, you'll recall, we sweetened it a bit, as you suggested. I apologize for just *copying* our letters to you – not sending you originals – but could you... *would* you... tell me, please: are the 'late days' or the 'middle days', even, in prospect yet? Will they be coming soon?

• • • • • • • • • • • • • • • • • • • •

... after a little wheedling, the agent vouchsafed that our improved offer was being 'very seriously considered'.

• • • • • • • • • • • • • • • • • • • •

Ever the optimist, you at first thought the man was, in a roundabout way, communicating glad tidings. Something like: 'Just stick with it. Those other people who've looked at Heartsease Hall... they're just noise. Because Heartsease Hall's not a property for them – it's a property for you! So stick with it. You'll get it in the end.'

But I warned: 'Look out; that guy's trying to jerk you around....'

• • • • • • • • • • • • • • • • • • • •

I rushed off towards the kitchen to up-date N. But *en route* it occurred to me that, of course, any offer which wasn't rejected out of hand was *ipso facto* 'being considered', wasn't it? And given the amount of money involved, that consideration would almost certainly have to be – for anyone other than a Warren Buffet or a Bill Gates – 'serious' or 'very serious', wouldn't it? I slowed to a walk....

So what the sly-dog estate agent was really saying, I concluded, was that several offers were on the table. And while ours was indeed being 'very seriously considered', so were all the rest. In due course, a bidding war would break out. The price of the Heartsease Hall Estate would go up and up and up... at which point, having gone as high as – higher than, more like – we should really go, the estate agent would call for 'sealed bids'* and that would be that. Just outside the kitchen door, I came to a full stop and bellowed: 'It's simply not fair!' N, slaving away over our Aga stove – a wooden spoon in one hand and, to the other, Vol. I of Steven Parissien's definitive *The Styles of the Georgian Era* (a three-volume 'introduction' to 18th-century interior design) – looked up, startled. 'We were there first!' I cried.

For the week beginning Sunday 15 May, my horoscope – the last one, I promised myself, I'd ever bother to read – advised I'd now no choice but to 'be strong'. That directive seemed pretty *ex post facto* to me; so far as attempting to buy the Heartsease Hall Estate was concerned, I'd already been strong again and again and nothing had come of it. By way of further instruction, the soothsayer maintained enigmatically: 'Letting others continue to operate uncontrolled is not possible... you have much more important things to do with your time.' Well, I remember thinking, I *was* a little behind in my report on commercial prospects in the Arab Gulf.... I booted up my laptop and started in. Astrology, I snorted: what (deleted)! What hooey!

Work – especially hard, physical work especially in the deep country – is a good antidote to....

· ·

19 May 1994: isn't this where we came in?
Good Lord! Of course it is, Alter-natis; of course it is. My apologies; I must have been having a Senior Moment.
Or too much bubbly.
· ·

---

* A forcing device sometimes used by sellers or their agents in respect of very sought-after properties to extract absolutely the best price from competing buyers.

Chapter 4

Full Cry

The next day I was up bright and early (well, perhaps just 'early'....) with the birds, in spite of a poorly head. An English country squire – The Squire Apparent of the Heartsease Hall Estate – couldn't, after all, afford to lie long abed. He'd got neighboring landowners, local government officials, MPs and MEPs (members of the European parliament), ambassadors and other international statespersons and, of course, the factor (estate land-steward) and his staff – especially the rat catcher and the mole catcher – to meet. And he'd got work... important work, essential to the future of the estate... to attend to.

Well yes said N who, quite possibly, was also nursing a poorly head. But today, she pointed out, all we had to do was bring Toby, old Hughes's son, who'd been our gardener/handyman for many years and lived in our cottage, and Lauren, our South African *au pair*, into the picture – which we could just as well do later as sooner – and get Euan, our long-time lawyer, and The Suits at the bank moving. These last-referenced probably wouldn't even be at their desks until at least ten, she reminded me. So why didn't I just lie back down and shut up?

About noon, a letter arrived by courier from the real estate agent confirming Sir Roald had, indeed, accepted our offer, and asking if his firm might 'be of assistance' in respect of Brambledown, that's to say help us sell it. (Indeed, the agent said he'd already asked his Cotswolds colleague to make contact with us.) Contract exchange, the stage at which the purchaser puts down a deposit and, in accepting it, the vendor is bound to consummate the trade, was to be accomplished within 2–3 weeks – 'mid-June at the very latest', the agent declared certainly – with completion (the definitive, final stage in the purchase of a UK property) to take place 'the 1st or 15th of September'.

· · · · · · · · · · · · · · · · · · ·

Only 18 or so hours earlier, N and I'd been worrying if we'd succeed in buying the Heartsease Hall Estate; now we could begin worrying if we'd succeed in selling Brambledown.

Thus does the world turn, or as W. H. Auden put it in Birthday

Poem: *'In headaches and in worry Vaguely life leaks away.'*
What we faced seemed, at the time, more like a dam-burst than a
leak, Alter-natis.
 So what? You like worrying – and you're very good at it. Worry-
ing, you seem to believe, implies your petty strivings have purpose
and, ipso facto, *your mean existence has meaning. There must be*
a Latinism for it: something like 'Dum duro derigo' *translated as*
'While I struggle I matter'. That's a play on 'Dum spiro spero', *or*
'While I breathe I hope', d'Arcy.
 Anyway: the Indian guru Mehir Baba's take on life is much, much
easier: 'Don't worry; be happy!' is his advice.
• • • • • • • • • • • • • • • • • • •

How much actual selling-time did that final deadline give us? Select-
ing and instructing an agent; the agent booking advertising space and
preparing a brochure.... Two weeks – three, more likely – before the
house was fully established on the market; by then, we were nearly to
mid-June. Mid-July, mid-August, mid-September.... In all, we calculated, we'd a maximum of three months of English summertime – a
succession of national diversions which includes: 'The (see-and-be-
seen) Season' of Ascot (horse racing), Wimbledon (tennis, of course),
Henley (rowing), the Ashes (cricket), Goodwood (horse racing) and
Cowes (sailing); the 'Glorious Twelfth' (of August, the opening day of
the grouse hunting season); and, at last for the exhausted Everyman,
the tools-down, feet-up 'holiday' period itself (often referred to as the
'Silly Season'*), playing every evening (and now, some mornings and
afternoons) throughout the last two months of which is the world's
longest-running, most-eclectic, and best-attended and tuned-in-to
music festival, the Promenade Concerts (known colloquially as 'the
Proms') – in which to sell Brambledown and turn around the cleared
funds our proposed purchase would require. Even if we found a cash
buyer willing and able to move quickly, that was a very, very tight
time frame.
 While I got off a letter to the Heartsease Hall agent asking that
completion on the estate be put back a month, to mid-October, N
urgently consulted with former colleagues at the Firm about possible alternative estate agents and arranged interviews at Brambledown
with several of them.
 And when your agent-prospects arrive, I asked N, how're we going to decide which one to instruct? In a matter of minutes my little

---

* So called because, in the absence of hard news, UK media often resort to covering almost anything.

Uxor contrived the 'PREAQ' or, decrypted, the 'Prospective Real Estate Agent Questionnaire'. It consisted of four factual interrogatives – 'What is the state of the market for properties like Brambledown? How would you propose to market Brambledown? How long would you require to get the property onto the market? What should the guide price for Brambledown be?' – and a fifth, essentially-judgmental one designed to explore the interviewee's integrity and level of commitment: 'What do you, personally, really think of Brambledown?'

Each answer was to be scored one (lowest) to five (highest) on the basis of two criteria: its seeming plausibility and the extent to which N and I were actually persuaded by it.

This cunning device arrived on my desk just in the nick of time. For on 21 May, the Heartsease Hall selling agent's Cotswolds colleague telephoned to ask if he could come and see us. His name, as I thought I heard it, was a conjunction of syllables, hyphens and apostrophes – something like 'Atta-boy O'Barts' – which could have come straight from the anonymous, Old English epic poem *Beowulf*. And it was told to me in the upper-class, Edwardian-era articulation which the British call (and spell) 'plummy': leisured in pace, luscious and full in tone, suggestive of an origination which is ripe and oh-so-desirable… but, all too often, turns out to be a sort of botoxed prune. (I wouldn't have been surprised to learn old Atta-boy was speaking from the depths of a hot bubble-bath, a gin-and-tonic in one hand, a sponge [natural, of course] in the other, the telephone being held by his manservant.) Without so much as a participle of the PREAQ having been put, my plausibility/persuasion indicators began to flash a 'one' or, maybe at best, a 'two'.

After a lovingly-detailed re-cap of partridge and pheasant shootings, salmon fishings, deer stalkings and point-to-point horse-race meetings he'd recently participated in or attended – as well as 'teas in Tetbury' (a town in Gloucestershire), which I took as indicating social contacts with the Royal Family, some of whom have homes in and around there – it was agreed old Atta-boy would come and have a look at N and me – and even perhaps, if we behaved ourselves and asked him politely, at Brambledown – on 24 May.

As well as initiating the process of selling Brambledown, N and I also needed urgently to confirm the fabric of Heartsease Hall was as sound as we in our tail-wagging, prospective-purchaser enthusiasm wanted it to be; in other words, we needed to have it professionally inspected.

I got the names of several FRICSs, as Fellow(s) of the Royal Institution of Chartered Surveyors are sometimes called, and contacted
them about carrying out a survey... not an all-inclusive survey, I cautioned, just a good look at the Hall's major structural elements. 'After
all, the building's more than 200 years old,' I explained; 'it's bound to
have a few problems.' But no; each FRICS insisted he had to 'survey'
everything, from who built the Hall and how it was constructed – all
of which, of course, was referenced in Pevsner, Burke's and Savills, the
selling agent's brochure and, I assumed, the English Heritage Listing
– practically down to the last knap of the last flint.

And the cost of such a comprehensive survey, I enquired warily?
'Oh, round about [...] plus, you'll accept, our out-of-pocket expenses,' came the general reply, in each case as if the job had already
been commissioned. 'Good Lord!' I shrilled at one FRICS who so
presumed, 'I could take my whole family on a nice, long vacation for
that.' Then, deeper-voiced, essaying esquire mode, I added: 'or "establish", that's to say prepare the land and drill (seed), 65–70 acres
of corn'. Why's surveying so expensive, I asked? 'Liability,' the FRICS
confided in covered tones. 'If we didn't check everything out and,
subsequently, the Hall fell down Mister... ah, Mister... Mr Handy;
that's right, isn't it? If we didn't check everything out and the Hall fell
down, Mr Handy, you could sue us for negligence.'

· ·

*Litigiousness, the bastard get of greed: another of The Motherland's
iconic socio-cultural exports to an increasingly codified world,
d'Arcy.*
I'd have a much stronger case against old FRICS if he *did* 'check
everything out' and the Hall fell down, wouldn't I, Alter-natis?

· ·

Moreover, the soonest any of these FRICSs could fit us in was mid-
June – *after* contracts were due to be exchanged on Heartsease Hall
and, therefore, longer than we could wait. In desperation I called David B, a FRICS acquaintance of N's who, she'd reminded me, was
in the process of restoring a Grade I Cistercian abbey in Northumberland he'd bought some years earlier. Might he know of someone
who'd be willing and able to carry out a good, 'quick and dirty' survey for us fairly soon? Or better, I proposed, he could be persuaded
to do one himself? 'What a splendid invitation!' David enthused. 'Of
course; I'd be delighted to! I can come on Tuesday, May 31st, if that
date's convenient for you.'

And just for the record David, I asked cautiously, what would be the... err... the tariff... the bill? 'Oh, it wouldn't be very much,' David replied. 'I'd have *pro forma* to put the survey through my company but, all in, say [...]'. The equivalent of a weekend with just N in a reasonable roadside motel, I noted happily, or establishing maybe 6.5–7 acres of corn.

Belatedly, I wrote to Sir Roald – another of those difficult letters, which took much longer than it should have to compose – thanking him for agreeing to sell Heartsease Hall to us and pledging our best efforts to look after the property. My missive concluded: 'If, going forward, the Henrys can bring to the estate a fraction of the distinction the Festings have, we'll be very pleased.' Then I took time out from becoming an English country squire to reflect on the prospect of departing Brambledown.

Simply as a physical operation, it didn't seem saying farewell to our old abode was going to be as difficult as I'd feared. By then, N had to hand a long list of well-recommended real estate agents and, after several years of weakness, the housing market in the Cotswolds was said to be firming up. All we needed to do, it appeared, was get Brambledown in front of some prospective purchasers, sit back... and wait for the offers to come rolling in. For some probably best-left-unexcavated reason, the 1950s television entertainer Lawrence Welk's catchphrase 'Wunnerful, wunnerful!' wriggled up from the deeper sediments of my mind.

· · · · · · · · · · · · · · · · · · · ·

But emotionally? How difficult did you think saying goodbye to Brambledown would be emotionally? After all, your experience of the property – as a regular guest of your late Aunt and then as its owner-occupier – went back nearly a quarter of a century....

I didn't really have any expectations of house-leave-taking emotional difficulty, Alter-natis.

It was a very fine... a very handsome and well-built dwelling. And from it, the views up-hill of the terraced gardens, etc, and the lawns, and down-hill across the Windrush Valley, were very beautiful.

Yes, and it was lovely of Aunt Gertie to bequeath the property to me. But perched on that north-east-facing slope, even on sunny, summer days the building – with its low ceilings and small windows – could seem almost as dank and dark as the proverbial bat's cave. N and I put a good heap of living into it and started our family there, of course. But we could never summon the commitment fully to redecorate Brambledown – an indication, probably, that it always remained for us a house rather than a home.

And the Cotswold Hills: 'lovely, dark and deep' as you, borrow-ing from Robert Frost's poem Stopping by Woods on a Snowy Even-ing, *used to call them. Surely....*

Until a half-century or so ago, the Cotswolds – with its mounts and vales, its enfolded fields, its narrow, leafy lanes and the quaint hamlets they interlinked – must indeed have been an enchanting venue: so elemental and basic... so unspoiled. The remains of several Iron Age settlements have been found there, you know.

Straw Dogs – *Gordon Williams' 1969 novel which Sam Peck-inpah made into a film – was set in Cotswolds-like country. Its title speaks to an existence which the philosopher Lao Tsu characterized as elemental and basic almost to the point of inhumanity....*

But in the late-1960s/early-1970s, the Cotswolds began to be 'dis-covered'. Day-trippers from Birmingham, Manchester and the rest of the teeming British Midlands, second-homing weekenders from London, tourists from Europe and Japan... and The Motherland, of course – 'grockles', the locals called them – began to arrive in their thousands, their tens of thousands... their hundreds of thousands....

For many local merchants, this 'invasion' was a boon. But in the elapse of only a decade or so, a long-established, land-based socio-economy driven by the real needs of real people was almost totally subsumed by flash-and-trash consumerism.

'I have promises to keep and miles to go before I sleep,' you said, again citing Robert Frost's Stopping by Woods. *And so you opted out. Did you think that by removing to north Norfolk – 'The Chel-sea (as in London) of East Anglia' some people now call it – you could escape all of that pullulating superficiality?*

No. But with a larger property in a more peripheral part of Eng-land, I thought perhaps I could hold it at bay for a while longer.

· · · · · · · · · · · · · · · · · · · ·

'Wonnerful, wonnerful!' was to remain my happy exclamatory in re-spect of buying the Heartsease Hall Estate. In respect of selling Bram-bledown, however, over the next twelve months those words gradu-ally acquired undertones of irony bordering on despair.

As if the Heartsease Hall Estate in and of itself weren't a sufficient acquisition, on 23 May we learned from the selling agent that the ancient title 'Patron of the Benefice' could attach to the property*.

---

* The title used almost invariably to pass with ownership of the land. But as an increasing number of England's greater estates began to be bought by persons who weren't members of the Established, Anglican Church, in 1986 the Church's General Synod tightened the rules and made conferral of the Patronage more at its discretion.

Would I be interested in the job? Yr Correspondent put the obvious question and was informed that the office dated from 1534 – when Henry VIII had become Head of The Church in England – and reserved to the State – represented at the local level by lay Patrons – certain now-largely-ceremonial rights such as rubber-stamping the selection of the local vicar.

The duties of the Patron wouldn't, I was told – 'shouldn't, anyway' – take up much time. I'd have to attend the occasional service of worship at which I might be called on to solo a response or two, and the occasional Diocesan Council meeting but, in general, my role would be 'essentially supernumerary'. A 'lounge (business) suit' only was required; there'd be no need, the agent assured me matter-of-factly, to acquire any 'gorgeous robes'.

. . . .

I remember reflecting: W. d'Arcy Henry, the upstart American – an ecumenical agnostic, if anything – installed as a lay 'Patron' in the Anglican Church...

Yessss....

... and, thereby, displacing from that quintessentially English-Establishment role, the venerable Festings – more specifically, the venerable 13th Baronet, Sir Roald Festing....

Indeed. To paraphrase Stephen Gosson in his 1579 Ephemerides of Phialo: *'little good results from (swapping)... a silke purse (for) a Sowes ear'.*

. . . .

N, however, my diligent *carpe-diem*-ist, took the view that as it was on offer, reasonably priced (it would come with the estate) and likely to provide interest, I should go for it. But Yr (Shy, retiring) Correspondent, recalling the decisive words of General William Tecumseh Sherman on the US presidential candidacy proposed for him in 1884, determined otherwise. 'I will not accept if nominated and will not serve if elected,' I declared.

On 24 May, Prospective Real Estate Agent Number One – old Atta-boy and his wife, who was also a real estate agent, we learned, and with the same firm – arrived to appraise N and me and, *en passant,* Brambledown... and to be PREAQ-ed. The wife was all right – quite a little honey, in fact: lovely, animated face, nice tight, athletic body... good, all-over oestral glow – but the Cotswolds wasn't officially her patch, we were told firmly, so she was really just along for the ride.

Atta-boy was something else, however, with a face and form – and

name, now that I'd access to his business card – which could indeed
have come straight from the pages of some Old English epic and, so
far as could be immediately determined, a customer-service mentality
to match. When I asked him if he'd be interested in taking on Brambledown, he said he wasn't sure it was '(his) kind of property' or that
he'd have enough time. I looked at N and formed the thumb and index finger of my right hand into a circle. 'That's a "zero",' I mouthed,
'on Question Five.'

Eventually, however, we got down to business... and the thorny
question of 'guide pricing': the price at which Brambledown should
be offered on the market. Had old Atta-boy some numbers he could
lay out for us, N asked? My thoughts wandered to my UK graduate
business-school students and the guest-lectures I had then occasionally to suffer upon them:

. . . .

Ladies and Gentlemen... Class... good morning, and welcome. Just
to make sure everyone's where they want to be... or, at least, where
they've signed up to be: this is the 'How It's Done 101' module
of your International Management degree course. My name is W.
d'Arcy Henry. You may call me Professor Henry... or just d'Arcy, if

you prefer – as, I expect in this egregiously egalitarian age, most of you *will* prefer.

Yes, yes: come in... come right in; find yourself seats... quickly... quickly. I'm so glad you two were able to make it. Just try to remember that, as is clearly stated in the University Curriculum, this seminar starts at nine o'clock sharp.

For a variety of reasons, most of which are entirely personal, I'd like today to plunge right in at the deep end and discuss 'guide pricing' which, as I'm sure you're aware, is a very important aspect – *the most important aspect*, perhaps – of marketing, and marketing, it's said, is 'The Mother of Money' – '*Umm Fulous*' in Arabic, I believe. This marketing/money-mothering relationship is, presumably, a subject in which you've all got some interest.

But first, I'd like to offer a little basic-economics 'refresher'. Market-making, of course, requires at least two parties: a willing seller and a ditto buyer. Let's take the seller first. His or her main concern is what? Young man in the middle of the third row... tall, well-built... wearing an Athletics Department tee shirt which, I take it, means you either are or want to be seen as some kind of jock. 'Big Swinger' – 'BS' for short – could be a good class nickname for you. Perhaps, BS, you'd tell us what the seller's main concern is?

No? Well, that's a tricky one... a tricky one... I'm sure. How about the neatly-dressed... 'primly-dressed', we might say – Indeed... ha, ha... we *have*, in fact, *just this minute already said!* – young lady to my left and a couple of rows behind BS: wire-rimmed spectacles, hair gathered in a bun... nice, plain, shift-style dress... toying with the pendant – from up here, it looks to me like a cross, made of olive wood from the Holy Land, perhaps – on her necklace. 'Ms Gospel', we'll call you. Would you....

Yes, you're absolutely correct: get a good price. The seller's main concern is to get a good price for whatever he or she's selling.

Here, I'd like to fast-forward... not spend time discussing what a 'good' price is – since 'good' is a highly-subjective notion... unless you're a practising evangelical – and go instead to the question of pricing strategy. What are the seller's three basic options? Intense, focused-looking young man toward the back over by the door: red 'power' tie, blue shirt, gray pin-striped suit... jabbing away at his calculator; could be an aspiring commodities trader... or some kind of banker. Either way, 'Gravy Train' or 'GT' might be an appropriate handle. Yes, my friend, you: what are the seller's three basic pricing options?

That's right; that's the first one: ask a high price and be prepared, if necessary, to come down a bit. What's the second option? You got it... it's just the opposite: ask a low price but, if the opportunity presents itself, push for a bit more. Now: what's the third and final option?

You don't know? I'm surprised! Well, the third option is to price at and stick to a price you believe to be fair... or *just slightly above* fair, perhaps... the 'don't want no more; won't take no less' price beloved of older-time farmers. How's that? Yes, GT: I appreciate you've not met many farmers, but it's OK; nobody of your generation has. Farmers, like blue-collar workers generally – the 'unsung heroes' of the modern, IT-driven economy, I'd call them – are pretty thin on the office-blocked, carpeted and desked-over ground nowadays.

What did you say, Ms Gospel? I didn't hear your comment. Oh. Yes; I entirely agree, Ma'am. The older-time farmer's option is a very, very dull option, indeed – not at all the sort of stratagem a really cutting-edge international manager would consider. If only as an expression of the noble humility of the agrarian mindset, however, I believe the 'don't want', etc, formulation has very considerable merit.

Now let's explore the buyer's concerns. He or she, too, wants to get a 'good' price, of course. So what are his or her basic options? Anyone care to.... Yes... near the back, over by the window: dark, shoulder-length hair, wrap-around sunglasses, camouflage jacket, an ear-clip made of some kind of white metal – silver or stainless steel, I assume.... 'Che' we'll call you, after the late Latin American revolutionary Ernesto 'Che' Guevara of whom one or two of you may have heard. So, Che.... Yes, that's right; the buyer's options are the reciprocal of the seller's. Bid a low price and be prepared, if you have to, to advaaaance higher; bid a high price but, maybe, find some excuse to withdraaaaw lower....

It seems to me you're pretty well onto this one, so I won't bother to run it all the way through....

I will just remind you, though, that these two principals – the seller and the buyer – by means of their asking and bidding, establish what may be called the 'price-discovery model'; assuming good input data, that model should yield the amount for which the item on offer – in my case, my house – could fairly be sold. In theory, the model's pretty straightforward. In practice, owing to contingent and/ or cascading variables, it can get very complicated. For example: what happens to the model if, in addition to sellers and buyers, we add other principals, like selling and/or buying agents? *Real estate* selling and/or buying agents, say?

Yes. Young lady... Ms Gospel, again. How can an agent be a principal, you ask? What a good question! And the answer is... relatively easily. After all, the person wanting to assist with the sale or purchase of something – a property, for example – has, *ipso facto*, his or her own agenda: to win the agency contract, to achieve the sale or purchase, to make the best possible commission on that sale or purchase... and brings to that agenda – or *should* bring to that agenda – quite a substantial weight of ability, expertise, commitment and, most important, market access. Agenda plus ability, etc, is, I'd argue, more than sufficient to establish someone as a principal – or, at least, a secondary principal....

But I appreciate where you're coming from... and could be going to. In an attempt to get there before you do, let me quickly agree: 'secondary principal' *is* something of a contradiction in terms. Yes, it is. But to return to my question: how does the addition of selling and/or buying agents, that's to say secondary principals, affect the pricing model?

Young lady on my right, second row... long, blond hair in a po-nytail, enormous gold earrings *and* gold bracelets, red fingernails... just now putting her hand over her mouth, covering what – Good-ness, gracious me; would you believe it! – appears to be a yawn. Your eyes, your nose... your lips – Particularly your lips! – remind me a bit of Sophia Loren.... You remember: the 1960s actress who married the film director Carlo Ponti not once but twice.... No? Well, the 1960s was quite a long time ago. Anyway: we'll call you 'Ms Goldstar'.

So, Ms Goldstar: can you answer my question? No... you don't think you can. OK, I'll tell you: adding secondary principals – who in turn, of course, may have *their own* secondary principals: peo-ple who, from the principal principal's standpoint, are effectively tertiary principals – can turn the basic price-discovery model into almost rocket-science stuff. But to return to my – I mean, *our* – main interest, guide pricing.... To establish a guide price which takes full account of all of the various variables, you really have only two op-tions: either speed-dial Karl Case or Robert Schiller – the economists who, you'll recall, in the late 1980s developed a method of forecast-ing house-price trends – or just fly it.

· · · · · · · · · · · · · · · · · · · ·

In the event, old Atta-boy didn't speed-dial Mr Case or Mr Schiller. When taxed with that most vexed question – the guide price at which Brambledown should be offered – he replied immediately and with Delphic certainty: 'The guide price should be [...].'

N suggested the possibility of a lower guide price – in effect, a variation of the 'pile 'em high and sell 'em cheap' approach, thereby 'commoditizing' Brambledown – in the hope of encouraging more prospects to view. 'Establish some interest; get two... maybe three or four parties bidding against each other; then raise the price a bit... and then raise it a bit more....'

'Raising the price like that smacks of "gazumping" (putting up the price, especially of a house, after its purchase has been agreed),' Atta-boy averred categorically. 'It wouldn't be ethical. I'd certainly never consent to do business that way,' he concluded sniffily.

'But raising the price *before* you've agreed to sell... that's not gazumping; that's just a means of getting top dollar,' N protested. 'Some friends of ours in London raised the asking price on their house a couple of times; they got an additional three or four per cent. Everyone – excepting, obviously, the under-bidders – seemed reasonably content.'

'Ah well that's London, isn't it. A jungle – an *absolute* jungle – like Paris or Rome or Tokyo... or New York. Quite different rules apply here in the gentle English countryside.'

N tried again. 'We've been told,' she ventured, 'a commercial market could exist for this type of property: someone looking to convert Brambledown into a small, "boutique", country-house hotel, perhaps. They might be persuaded to pay over the odds, mightn't they?'

'Unlikely,' old Atta-boy intoned in his plummy voice. 'There's not much Category A1 or A2 tourism, that's to say higher-end trade, around here; mostly, it's Category B and C – middle-middle and lower-middle tier stuff.'

'But,' I protested, 'there's a very good, small, country-house hotel just a couple of miles down the Fosse Way, with a Michelin-rated restaurant; it's so fully booked you can hardly ever get a table and, if you do, the cost is coming on for £60–75 (in mid-1994, $90–110) per person, excluding drink.'

'You're referring to the Rockin' Horse Hotel, of course; it's clearly the exception that proves the rule. And I expect one Rockin' Horse's more than sufficient "mount" – Ha, ha... ha.... Get it? (I didn't... but I nodded anyway.) – to satisfy any likely future demand.'

N and I exchanged glances the gist of which was that she, like me, was having trouble taking old Atta-boy seriously.

· · · · · · · · · · · · · · · · · · · ·

And moreover....
  'Moreover', Alter-natis?
  Moreover, there's nothing so demeaning for a principal principal – especially an upstart-American, English-Country-Squire-Apparent principal principal and occasional graduate business-school guest lecturer – as having some secondary principal play him for a fool.

· · · · · · · · · · · · · · · · · · · ·

Given old Atta-boy's flagrantly laid-back manner and the fact that he was also unnecessarily tall, thin and good-looking – not to mention ostensibly well-bred – I had no difficulty concluding he wasn't for us. ('But perhaps your charming little wife-honey might care to...?')

Later that day, I received a letter from Sir Roald saying how 'relieved and delighted' he and Lady Maureen were to have found in us purchasers who 'so appreciate the beauty of Heartsease Hall, and the history and traditions attaching to it'. The letter concluded by wishing N and me, and Piglet and Bapu, 'long lives and great happiness there'. Imagine, I magnified, after 350 years: such a generous, graceful valediction.

A couple of days later, prospective real estate agent No. 2 presented himself for PREAQ-ing. Not too tall, thin or good-looking – and manifestly not too well-bred – with a nice, simple surname derived from some distant forebear's occupation, and saying over and over again what a lovely property he thought Brambledown was and how much he'd like to take it on....

. . . .

That put up a 'five' for Five before the integrity, etc, question had even been asked!

. . . .

In short, the man was a refreshing change. N and I quizzed him on the state of the market for Brambledown; how he would go about marketing the property; how long he would need to get it onto the market – receiving in reply to all three questions answers which seemed eminently plausible and persuasive – and, finally, what he thought Brambledown might fetch. Hummmm. After what appeared to be very careful consideration, PEA 2 dropped a number fully 15 per cent higher than Atta-boy's purported 'guidance'. N raised her eyebrows; I pursed my lips....

'It's easier to climb down than climb up,' PEA 2 advised cheerily, hunching slightly forward onto the balls of his feet and rubbing his hands briskly together.

'But perhaps more dangerous?' I proposed, on the basis of a long-ago holiday spent ski-touring/mountaineering near Innsbruck, in Austria's *Stubaier* Alps, during which I'd fallen heavily a couple of times while descending. 'If you have to climb down and consider an offer below the guide and, for whatever reason, Brambledown still doesn't sell, surely the property could appear "damaged"... compromised in some way... as with, for example, a picture whose reserve at auction was set too high. You'd then have either to consider an even lower price, or "buy in" the property – "warehouse" it, so to speak – until a new cohort of potential buyers ignorant of or prepared to ignore the "failed sale" came forward....'

'Possibly... but, in today's buoyant market, not very likely,' PEA 2 replied equably, straightening back up to his full height and folding his arms comfortably atop his ample stomach. 'There're lots of buyers around.'

· · · · · · · · · · · · · · · · · · · ·

Enthusiasm... confidence... determination – the holy trinity of effective sales-craft – and the prospect of this estimable package driving a significantly better deal for us: what more could we have wanted, Alter-natis!

Indeed. And, ultimately, whether you got a higher price or a lower one for Brambledown wasn't the issue; with completion on Heartsease Hall still scheduled for mid-September, the issue was whether, by then, you'd get any acceptable price at all.

· · · · · · · · · · · · · · · · · · · ·

I told PEA 2 that N and I'd like a little time to think the matter over, but the likelihood was that we'd instruct him....

While we were seeing off our probable secondary principal, the mail arrived; in it was a letter from the selling agent agreeing 'the middle of October' for completion on Heartsease Hall. N and I fairly jumped for joy! For Brambledown, we now had four weeks' more selling time!

Tuesday 31 May was sunny and warm... a picture-postcard late-spring/early-summer English day; I spent it traipsing around the Hall as 'surveyor's mate' to David B. My mentor being a confirmed 'bottom-up' man – 'A house is only as good as what it's built on, you know,' he opined – we started with the foundation. After a considered sight along its length and width, David pronounced this sub-structure to be in excellent order. 'It's amazing how solidly these big, 18th-century houses were made!' he enthused.

'Lots of mortar in the footings,' I nodded agreeably.

'They didn't use mortar in the footings when this house was built,' David replied. 'They used only sand and a bit of "shingle", that's to say coarse gravel. Such a mixture packs down like concrete.'

Oh. I tried again to evidence my 'knowledge': 'What about those fascia stones with the cracks in them? They should probably be re-placed, shouldn't they....'

'They're "blown",' David advised, 'that's to say burst open from the inside by pressure from the rusting iron "cramps" – "pins" in layman's terms; iron expands as it oxidizes, you know – let into the stones to secure them in place. It's the same with the cracks in the quoins and the jambs. Unsightly they may be but, structurally, they're nothing really to worry about.'

'And the patches where the flintwork's bulging out? They look pretty ominous,' I proposed in one last, vain attempt to acquire some cred as a site-works squire.

'Most likely just loss of bond between the flints which, as you know, are only an outer skin or veneer, and the real, load-bearing exterior wall which is made of brick and three... maybe three-and-a-half feet thick. "Delamination" we call it. Take the bulging flints off, clean down the brickwork and set some stainless steel ties into it, mortar up, course the flints back on again.... It comes out as good as new... in fact, probably better than new,' David affirmed.

'And the inward-leaning merlons – isn't that what those up-stand-ing sections of the parapet wall are called?' I asked (From my pre-vious evening's dip into *The Penguin Dictionary of Architecture*, I knew I'd got at least the word right!), 'particularly the two or three just over the southwest bedroom.... Each one must weigh half a ton or more. Surely....'

'Rotted wall plates, I'd expect. That's not unusual in a building of this age.'

'Wall plates?'

'Thick baulks (roughly squared timber beams) run along the top of the brickwork to distribute the downward thrust of the roof trusses.'

'Roof trusses?'

'The principal rafters and their associated king and queen posts, collar beams, tie-beams and struts – that's to say their vertical, hori-zontal and diagonal support members. Together with the ridge pole, common rafters, purlins and roof boards – onto which, ultimately, the slates are fixed – they hold the roof up.'

'If the wall plates aren't replaced, will the merlons topple over?'

Hoots of laughter from David. 'Yes! And if the merlons topple over, the trusses will almost certainly collapse and, like Jericho's walls, your roof will come a-tumblin' down. But dealt with in time – as I'm sure in this case it can be – it's not a difficult problem to remedy... just an

expensive one.' (More hoots of laughter from David.) He continued:
'Until you can get the wall plates replaced and the merlons rebuilt, I
suggest you designate the room just below a guest bedroom. Anyone
staying longer than three days – you know the old joke: about fish
and guests... starting to stink – just tell them about the rotted wall
plates, etc.' (David practically incontinent with laughter.) 'Now,' he
concluded, 'shall we do the attics?'

From my previous, cursory viewing of this tenebrous realm I remembered only some disused rooms – originally servants' bedrooms,
apparently – and, separating them, a great central void transected by
wooden beams receding into the darkness. Now, armed with David's
powerful headlamps and encyclopedic knowledge, all was revealed.
The wooden beams – the largest of which measured perhaps 12 x
15 inches in section and 22–23 feet in length – were, in fact, the tie-
beams of the roof trusses; they cross-cut the deeper attic space into
seven equal segments. Lengthways down the midline of the attic – the
midline of the Hall – ran the great 'spine wall': the main interior wall,
made of brick and, in places, 4–5 feet thick, into which the tie-beams
were keyed; from its top, the Hall's three great chimney stacks rose
like the boles of giant trees. Above was a canopy of rafters and roof
boards underhung with dusty spiders' webs; below was what seemed
like acres of glass-fibre insulation traversed here and there by narrow,
wooden planks – walk boards laid, presumably, across the ceiling
joists of the rooms immediately below.

'Where do we begin, and how?' I asked, resuming my attempts to
sound in-control and esquire-like. 'Shusssh!' hissed David. 'Quiet! We
begin right here... by listening.'

'Listening?' I whispered, incredulous. 'What for?'

'For woodworms and/or wood beetles. If they're active and having
a nice meal you can usually hear them munching away.'

I closed my eyes and held my breath, listening intently....

'And then we smell,' David said ambiguously but authoritatively,
lamped head up, nose out, testing the musty air like some bi-pedal
hound-dog. 'Wet-rot and dry-rot fungi have a very distinctive aroma
similar, some say, to that of truffles.'

I assayed a sniff or two... tried, with only partial success, to stifle
a sneeze....

'No. No woodworm or beetle or rot here,' David announced tri-
umphantly. 'We'll just have a bit more of a look around to be absolutely sure,' he continued, scuttling off across one of the walk boards

and beckoning me to follow. 'Mind how you go,' he cautioned, merrily. 'These planks are a bit teetery; if you lose your balance, there's only a thin layer of lath and plaster between you and....'

After a few more circumspections and some final probings of the darkness with his torch, David declared himself satisfied with the attics. It was time, he announced, to move on to the last major task: close external examination of the roof.

I didn't really want to ask such a dumb question... but how on earth would we get there, I wondered? A ladder from the outside? No: the vertical distance from the ground to the top of the parapet wall was forty feet or so. Given the need to stand the ladder off from the wall at the bottom and allow some extra height at the top to get safely up and over.... Mentally, I ran Pythagoras' trusty '3, 4, 5' right-triangle formula...

. . . .

Imagine: actually making use of something you learned all those years ago back in high school in Baltimore.

Now let's see: what was the name of that particular branch of mathematics? Geometry? Trigonometry? Tensor calculus?

. . . .

... right-triangle formula. Good Lord! That suggested we needed a ladder with a working length of well over fifty feet. Did they make domestic-use ladders that long? And if they did, was there one available here, on site? And if there wasn't, what was David going to do: call in the Fire Department? Whistle up a chopper?

'That's where the hatchways giving access to the roof slopes should be,' David said off-handedly, pointing toward the Hall's west gable-end wall. Hatchways.... Ah ha! We shone our headlamps, peered intently through the gloom... and sure enough, set across the entrances to what could have been low, walk-in dormer windows, one to our left and one to our right – facing roughly south and north – were two little square doors.

'Why the *west* gable end? Why there?' I asked.

'Since most of the UK's weather comes out of the west, putting the hatches in the lee of the west wall gives them the most protection,' my mentor replied.

David decided to inspect the south roof-slope first. Just getting to its access-hatchway proved a major undertaking; to do so, we had to tram our way along the ceiling joists leading either side to it (there weren't even walk boards there!) all the while crouching lower and lower, ape-like, as clearance under the rafters reduced. Then we had to get the hatchway door open – something which clearly hadn't been accomplished for a very, very long while. Bent nearly double, like underground miners of old hand-working a low seam, we prized and huffed, pulled and puffed... and, when the door did finally yield – suddenly and completely – all but derailed off the joists and down....

Our sedulously sought final destination still hadn't been achieved, however. Instead what confronted us, at the end of a passage perhaps two yards in length, was another little square door. David called this one the 'lucarne' door – 'a Provençal word, as in Peter Mayle's *A Year in...*' he added; 'I don't know why they're called that' – and confidently predicted it would give onto the parapet gutter at the bottom of the roof slope. We crawled forward on all fours, picking our way around a selection of battered kitchen pots and pans – testaments to leaks long lost in time, I devoutly hoped, and therefore now redundant – prized and pulled at the lucarne door... and eventually emerged just where David had predicted.

If, as Robert Louis Stevenson observed in his *Virginibus Puerisque* 'El Dorado' of 1881, 'to travel hopefully is a better thing than to arrive'...

· · · · · · · · · · · · · · · · · · · ·

It certainly may be in the case of life's journey, d'Arcy, because in that context 'to arrive' could mean.... Well; you know what it could mean. But in the case of this extended structural-survey section, 'arriving' has a lot to recommend it.

· · · · · · · · · · · · · · · · · · · ·

... than to arrive', before us was strong corroboration: the south roof slope was just a very large area of silver-grey-green slates – 'Westmoreland slates'* according to David, and 'still the best you can buy' – graduating in size from perhaps 2 x 3 feet at the bottom of the incline, where we were standing, to 8 x 12 inches at the roof's ridge. Here and there, a slate had cracked or slipped. Around the perimeter of the slates were lead crests, soakers and guttering, parts of which were starting to corrode. All of it was important to survey, of course and, as required, eventually to repair. But compared with our perilous trek upwards and outwards, this 'summit' was pretty mundane, ordinary stuff.

So while David inspected his way around – tapping here with his

---

* Coming from an area in northwest England which is now part of Cumbria.

hammer, probing there with his screwdriver... using a makeshift incli-
nometer, or plumb-bob (a bolt-nut suspended from a length of string),
to estimate how far the inward-leaning merlons over the southwest
bedroom were from their guest-discomfiting tipping point – and jotted his notes, Yr Correspondent did what any successful summiteer
would do: he took in the view.

To the far southeast, the gold-flecked, blue-grey-ochre of the North
Sea glistered; due south, in the mid-ground, a great arc of fields and
woodlands lay, their springing foliage shimmering in the warm sunshine and riffling in the gentle breeze; to the southwest, a narrow
pavé ribbon that was the driveway ran through more fields, over the
causeway... then beneath verging trees down to the front lodge and
the main gate. Immediately below reposed lawns and gardens, and
what remained of Nathaniel Richmond's 'regulated wild'*: a mini-
parkland of tree-studded pastures with the reed-fringed upper and
lower lakes curling through. The southern hemisphere of the Heartsease Hall Estate – 'our' Southern Hemisphere – in panorama... in
overview, I gasped; it was simply breathtaking.

· ·

*'In Xanadu did Kubla Khan, a stately pleasure-dome decree: Where
Alph, the sacred river, ran through pastures measureless to man
Down to a sunlit sea....'*
It's been suggested Samuel Taylor Coleridge's 1816 raptures owed
to an analgesic drug or 'anodyne' as they were then called, Alter-
natis. Stone-cold sober, that's to say 'clean', should one – could
one – really propose even to tenant such surpassing beauty as I then
beheld?
*'I'd restore that dome in air, That sunny dome.... But all should
cry, Beware! Beware! For he on honey-dew hath fed, And drunk the
milk of Paradise.'*
· ·

David pronounced his verdict: that the roof – indeed, the whole of
the Hall – was 'very sound... remarkably sound, really, for a building
of its age'. He concluded: 'It's as sound as your American dollar, you
might say.'

· ·

Was that just a figure of speech, I wondered? Or did David know

---

* A term thought to have been coined by the English poet James Thompson in
1730 to describe the natural-looking landscape at Stowe, in Buckinghamshire –
which, as Thompson well knew, had been carefully crafted by man.

something about The Motherland's macro-economy that we didn't, Alter-natis?

Looking back from our vantage point today, I think it was just a figure of speech.

· · · · · · · · · · · · · · · · · · · ·

After David had gone, I telephoned PEA 2 formally instructing him to sell Brambledown on our behalf. Then, unable to summon the (? decency) to speak to him in person, I wrote PEA No. 1 'regretfully' declining his services. Now, as earlier proposed, there really was nothing to do but sit back and wait for the offers on Brambledown to come rolling in....

A few days later, I was discussing some minor business with Euan on the telephone. Toward the end of our conversation, he drew my attention to the *caveat* in the Heartsease Hall sale brochure that 'fixtures and fittings not forming part of the English Heritage Listing* may be excluded from the sale'. It was probably nothing to worry about, he assured me, especially since our purchase of the major fixtures, etc, had already been verbally agreed. But perhaps we should just have 'a quick squint' at the Listing? If, as was sometimes the case, its inventory was 'light', that's to say not much was listed, and there was some last-minute disagreement – over contract details, say – we could wind up buying a Georgian-Gothic shell, he warned.

I telephoned the selling agent and asked him to send us a copy of the English Heritage Listing asap.

Shortly afterward, the EA – formerly known as 'PEA 2' – arrived to reveal to N and me what he called his 'Way Forward'... which is to say the three of us held a planning session. He told us his agency had already completed the necessary pre-marketing paperwork on Brambledown and 'registered' it, and that advertising space in *The Times* and *Country Life* was in the process of being booked. The next day, he said, preparation of the brochure would begin, with its body-copy expected to be in proof by early the following week... but his preferred photographer was at present on holiday, so no shoot was possible until 15 or 16 June... so the finished brochure probably wouldn't be available until Monday of the week after that, etc, etc... 'assuming all goes well'. The EA paused, as if to say: 'So that's my job done'...

... and then looked hard at N and me. 'You may be thinking you can now just sit back and wait for the offers on Brambledown to

---

* Typically, a summary description of a building and its important attachments.

come rolling in,' he began.

. . . .

Those were the very same words you'd been using, d'Arcy. Had the fellow pirated from your typescript? Or have you engaged in a little 'mis-remembering' for literary effect....

. . . .

'But,' he continued – I swallowed hard – 'as vendors, you too have responsibilities. Your main one is to keep the property looking spick and span but, at the same time, buyer-friendly,' he intoned. N, whose responsibility this responsibility would almost certainly largely be, asked how such a fine balance might be achieved. 'First do a really good tidy-up,' the EA replied definitively, 'and then go back and create a few reassuring messes.'

N nodded slowly. 'O... K....'

Next, the EA advised, we must strive to 'enhance, emphasize and project' Brambledown's country-house character. My resident MBA – as ever, conscientious to a fault – was again quick to the interrogative. 'Give it a bit of "hearty-arty",' our EA enjoined. 'You know: display some walking-in-the-rain gear, like waxed-cotton Barbour jackets and Hunter rubber boots, and also a pair of binoculars and a guide to the identification of birds or butterflies, and some old Christie's and/or Sotheby's sales catalogues... that sort of thing.'

N affirmed that yes, she could also manage that.

Finally, the EA said, we'd got to 'bring the outdoors in'. This time anticipating N, he continued: 'Always have some fresh flowers in the front hall, the drawing room, the dining room... possibly the master bedroom.... And in the kitchen, on the drain board next to the sink, say, put a 'trug' – that's a long, shallow basket, traditionally made of wood – heaped with fresh vegetables, preferably with the dew still on....' The EA paused for breath... 'or you could just sprinkle them with tap water.' Another pause.... 'Oh yes: and distribute a few vanilla pods inconspicuously around – on the window sills behind the curtains... south-facing windows, preferably... and next to the kettle on the warming plate of your Aga stove.'

'Vanilla pods?' N queried incredulously.

'When heated, they give off a fragrance which some prospective buyers find seductive.'

Our EA summed up: 'Brambledown and its associated outbuildings – the gardeners cottage, the garages, the stables... the greenhouse – must look as if featuring in *Town & Country*.... That *is* the name of your American *Country Life* equivalent, isn't it? And the flower beds, lawns, paths and hedges – indeed, the entire of the grounds – must look as if ready for exhibit at the Chelsea Flower Show.'

I made a mental note to contact as soon as possible the home and office-cleaning firm we sometimes used for FHA, and to ask Toby if there were any gardening requisites he needed.

• • • • • • • • • • • • • • • • • • •

Was he finished, Alter-natis, I asked you? At last, was that all?

Tha's it, Man, I replied. Dey's no more comin'; de Dude's all done. But....

• • • • • • • • • • • • • • • • • • •

Literally as he was walking out of our front door, however, the EA tendered one longer-focus and more-vexing 'responsibility'. 'When, in mid-October, your purchase of the Heartsease Hall Estate is complete,' he began innocently, 'are you planning to go and live there?' N and I looked at each other.... I guess so, I replied; we've been so busy, we haven't given that matter much thought. Why do you ask? 'Well,' the EA continued, 'it's very, very unlikely, of course – a remote improbability, you might say – but if Brambledown was then still unsold (gasps of disbelief from Yr Correspondent and his Uxor!) you shouldn't count on taking much furniture from here with you when you remove.'

After a pause to let the full import of his words sink in, the EA summed up: 'Unfurnished houses are notoriously difficult to sell; it's absolutely essential, therefore, that Brambledown – its kitchen, especially – continue to look like your home.'

That evening, as N and I were reflecting on the EA's various prescriptions, the telephone rang; violating my all-but-inviolable rule, I answered it. 'Hello d'Arcy,' a male voice began brightly, 'it's [...]'. The name didn't register but, in the interests of diplomacy, I replied in a similarly well-burnished vein... and bided my time. Sure enough, more or less immediately came forth my first clue: 'My child (? boy ? girl) is in your son's class at Leverets (the local primary school).' He'd heard, the caller continued, 'via the grapevine', we were putting 'Bumble-roun' (*sic*) on the market. Could he come over and discuss the matter with me? Perhaps there was something he could do to help. Ah so, I said to myself, our caller's a late entrant in the EA stakes.

I told the man we'd already instructed a real estate agent but by all means to stop by if he was so inclined – perhaps, in view of the tight time-frame, some sort of joint agency would be in everyone's best interest – and proposed 1100 the next day; in the interim, I thought, perhaps N or I'd be able to work out who he was. But even as the specifics of our conference were being agreed, there began to build in my mind's eye the image of a large, square-built, ruddy man, egregiously hail-fellow and well-met and, typically, turned out as Beau Brummell* might have got himself up for *Horse and Hound.* Oh no; it was [...]! Please no; not him!

The next day, [...] indeed – morphologicals essentially as described above and clad in a pea-green Harris Tweed jacket, a blue shirt with red stripes, a yellow-ground tie patterned with big, brown, polka dots, lilac-pink corduroy trousers, sky-blue ankle socks above thick-soled, 'champagne' (coloured) leather *Veldtschoen* (sturdy, outdoor shoes)...

· · · · · · · · · · · · · · · · · · · ·

I expect the Reader's got the picture....

· · · · · · · · · · · · · · · · · · · ·

... *Veldtschoen* – arrived at the appointed hour.

He was just as N and I'd remembered: nice enough in a cudding-bovine sort of way but without any appreciable cognitive faculty. And as for taking on 'Bumble-roun', it now transpired old [...] was only into 'big agricultural properties, really: industrial farms, estates... you know, that sort of thing', and was under the impression that Brambledown had much more land... 'a minimum of 70–100 acres, say'. If so, he could certainly have found a buyer for us 'right off... just like that'. But with only some 25 acres, the property wasn't really '(his) line of country'. 'Sorry, Old Boy, but that's how it is. It's a tough world out there, and I've got to call things as I see 'em,' he concluded.

And so Yr Correspondent was spared the onus of having to do likewise.

Later that day, the English Heritage Listing for Heartsease Hall arrived in the mail. It was a model of professional, macro-architectural summary: 'House.... Brick faced with knapped coursed flint with ashlar dressings. Slate roof. 2 (*sic*) stories and attics. North front bay†
2:3:2, the centre projecting, sides 3 bays....' I remember thinking: yes, that sort of describes the exterior of our new-home-to-be... I guess. What about its fixtures and fittings, then? Under 'Interior', the Listing

---

* The byname of George Bryan Brummell, an English, Regency-era 'fashionista' and friend of King George IV.

† As used here, the vertical division of a structure by some repeated feature, in this case, windows.

itemized a couple of exemplar windows, a couple of ditto doors, some plaster cornice and wall mouldings, the main staircase(!)... but nothing else. Absolutely... nothing... else. Talk about 'inventory-lite'....

Frantically, N and I searched our hard-copy and mental files. At our second viewing, surely honorable selling agent – after referencing various important period items: the fireplace surrounds, the mirrors and console tables nail and/or screw-affixed to the walls in the drawing room and the dining room, the manifold, ditto, wall sconces, the book casing in the library... the door and window furniture throughout – had said: 'yes, all of these... all of these beautiful and historic appointments... are yours with the Hall,' or words to that very close effect. I heard that. You heard that, didn't you N?

So what to do? Just relax and let this sleeping dog lie? 'Where's my horoscope!' I shouted. Ummmm ; it says developments this week require 'an active rather than a passive response'. I therefore had another, more-explicit conversation with the selling agent: 'Look here, My Friend, what about these fixtures and fittings, eh?' The agent, sounding as if he was caught on the hop – up to something with his comely 'assistant', perhaps – said he wasn't quite sure what had been agreed, and that he'd have to talk to Sir Roald. I re-stated N's and my view that the above-referenced items did indeed form part of the sale – indeed were, in our view, a very important part of the sale – and hung up.

N and I then turned our attentions to the critical question of who would have what operating responsibilities at Heartsease Hall. Most of the genuinely important line and management positions were, by acclamation, assigned to their Brambledown incumbents. In respect of the Top Job, however, Yr Correspondent's natural reticence – and the view in certain quarters that he was too old and inexperienced – proved problematical. Again as conjured up for my business school students:

· · · · · · · · · · · · · · · · · · ·

So, Class: 'Running the Enterprise'. What are the two essential categories of input – *material* input – which every well-run enterprise must have? 'Ideas' you say, BS. Yes, ideas are very important... but they're not exactly what we'd call a 'material' input, are they. How about 'a strategy... a game plan', you say. 'Yes,' again Big Fellow but, also again, a game plan's not exactly a material....

Don't know? Well, I'll give you a big hint: one of the inputs is capital... as in 'capital for investment'; that's the input we're into our Suits for. So what's the other one? Che, over by the window, trying not to get noticed.... You know the answer; I'm sure you do. Come on: Karl Marx... Friedrich Engels... *Das Kapital*.... The enterprise needs capital and.... Yes! Labour: human resources... staff... *bo-dies*, with arms and legs and brains – well... hopefully – who can actually *do* things.

What, Che? Would I take care of these 'inputs' and look after them well? Of course I would! Even Khufu, we're told – 'Cheops', as the Greeks called him – the builder of the Great Pyramid in Egypt, understood a workforce has to be properly fed and housed; over time, exploited labour simply won't be optimally productive.

Anyway. Labour... human resources... implies a staffing chart, doesn't it. Let's put one together for our case study: running the Heartsease Hall Estate. We'll deal first with the 'core' functions – the functions necessary to keep our enterprise ticking over – and move on to the more important 'development' functions – those, such as improving farm output, which will actually drive our enterprise forward – later, if we've got time.

What core staff are we going to need? First and foremost we'll need someone to look after Bapu, and Piglet when he's home from boarding school, and generally run our household. That slot, fortunately, is already well filled by the lovely Lauren who's about as energetic, resourceful and committed, not to mention easy on the eye, as any man – err... 'male parent'; better make that 'male parent' – could hope for.

Next, *extra mures* – that's Latin for 'beyond the walls', in this case those figuratively enclosing the Hall, our to-be Corporate HQ – we'll need at least one full-time gardener-handyperson... possibly more during the summer if we decide to keep the estate open to the public. Toby would certainly fill the position very well, but will he want to relocate from the Cotswolds to north Norfolk? It'd be the right thing for him to do, I think; he and his family could live in Keeper's Cottage, which should suit them very well. But not everyone's so mobile – so prepared to pack up and move on to new possibilities – as Mrs Henry and I are.

What about the farming operations, you ask? Good question, GT; a banker's always got to nosey about his client's revenue stream. As I was just about to say, there's already in place a team of highly-skilled farming tenants and contractors carrying out the day-to-day fieldwork; I may adjust their contracts slightly but, *pro tem*, my instinct is to go with them. The grassland farming – the sheep, pigs and, maybe, the cattle and horses – I'll see to myself.

Then we'll need someone to look after our finances, that's to say a Chief Financial Officer or CFO. My wife – who's a Harvard MBA... formerly of the Firm – is a natural for that role; given the chance, she can look *after* money – see it into some smooth-talking wine merchant's pocket or away to 'money heaven' – almost as fast as she can earn it. No, Ms Gospel, I don't really mean that; Mrs Henry's very good at managing money....

That leaves only one more core position – but the one with the most profound, longer-term implications for our corporate business development, however – to fill, right? And which one's that? Young man in the fifth row.... Yes...? No...? Someone else.... Ms Goldstar? Yes! YEE-SSS! You got it! The Big *Numero Uno*. The Chief Executive Officer or CEO. The super-man with the knowledge and the experience, the political and the technical skills, the charisma and the determination and the vision... really to progress the Heartsease Hall enterprise. To grow it on from that vulnerable, little-bitty acorn-sapling into that defiant, over-arching, monarch oak.... To rebuild its infrastructure and its outreach, its top line and its bottom line.... To make its 'two plus two' equal five or six... or even seve....

Yes: Che again. What? Gosh! You're right: we *are* starting to run out of time; there're only a few minutes of today's session remaining. So quickly, Class: who's the CEO of the Heartsease Hall Estate going to be? Anyone in-house – 'Home-grown' might be more apt in this agri-business context.... Ha, ha... ha! – with the ability to do the job? A farming smallholder-*cum*-management consultant and graduate business-school guest lecturer like me, perhaps? Ms Goldstar, what do you think?

I'm not properly qualified, you say. Oh, OK.... That's pretty much my wife's view. Well, what about with the ability to *grow into* the job? I've left it a bit late, you think. No, no, young lady; I'm not disappointed. Well, not *really* disappointed. But I do take exception to your inference that I'm somehow past it. I've still got all my own teeth, you know, except for the ones that got knocked out in my ice-hockey days....

What are we going to do, then? Last word to Ms Gospel.... Good idea! Why don't we reserve our position in respect of the Heartsease Hall Estate CEO slot – think again, perhaps, about whether anyone in-house might be up to the job – and make that part of our assignment for next time.

· · · · · · · · · · · · · · · · · · · ·

On 7 June, a comb-bound copy of David B's 'quick-and-dirty' structural survey arrived. Only five pages in length (plus a short appendix of 'Useful Addresses for Owners of Listed Buildings'), it confirmed our longed-for conclusion that the Hall was, indeed, 'very sound' and its principal outbuildings likewise. I copied the report to the selling agent noting, probably superfluously: 'My wife and I are therefore delighted to proceed, as planned, with our purchase of the Heartsease

Hall Estate.'

....

'Certainly *superfluously'*, *d'Arcy, not just 'probably' so, because as
the English lexicographer and critic Samuel Johnson wrote in his
1749* The Vanity of Human Wishes: *'(The) superfluous'* – *by which
he mainly intended the spoken word, but also the written word* –
'lags the vet'ran on the stage'.
    What on earth is that supposed to mean, Alter-natis?
    It means an experienced actor's message – *and, by extension, an
experienced communicator's message* – *is almost invariably proclaimed in his deportment... his posture, gestures and mime... well
before he verbalizes it. His words are, therefore, superfluous. Many
politicians and the like devote much time and effort to 'wronging'
their private deportment, etc, so as to get it 'right' from a public relations standpoint, you know.*
    'Body language' has been spoken for quite a while, then....
    Since The Origin of Species, *Charles Darwin would probably
have argued. Only the conversants and the tongues they use have
changed.*

....

I also raised again the fixtures-and-fittings ownership question.

The second week of June brought rain and more rain. Inside, Brambledown and the cottage were more or less ready for the EA's photographer but, outside, the lawns and gardens, etc, were a sodden
mess. Fortunately, N and I nervously reassured ourselves the early-
afternoon of Sunday 12 June, we still had 3–4 days until the shoot....
    Almost immediately therewith, the relentless rains ceased. The
'glass' (barometer) rose; the sky cleared; the sun came out.... With
those extra days now back in hand, everything, we rejoiced, was –
after all – really going to be all right. I yawned contentedly, relaxed
back into my big, easy chair in the study and resumed my... reading
of the weekend newspapers. About mid-afternoon, however, I was
awakened by a telephone call from the photographer – now returned
from his holiday – who said a gap had opened up in his schedule and
that he proposed be with us the next day, Monday 13 June, at 0900
sharp. 'I hope my earlier arrival won't inconvenience you; it'd mean
your brochure will be ready sooner, of course,' he crooned. I ground
my teeth...
    ... and summoned N, Toby and Lauren from their respective Sab-
bath rests. Telling them we'd a maximum of roughly 72 hours (18

hours x four people) of near summer-solstice working time to get everything ready, I assigned them their tasks: N and Lauren were to weed and dead-head the hanging flower baskets and the urns, and the display-flower beds; Toby was to edge the lawns and rake the paths, then put the cut-flower beds (producing flowers for indoor exhibition), the vegetable garden and the greenhouse, and the garages and the stables in order – N and Lauren coming to his assistance as soon as they were free.... Yr Correspondent, meanwhile, would tidy up around the front entrance, the driveway and the house forecourt before giving all the lawns a quick, last-minute cut....

'Any questions? No? Good! Off you go! Our next *rendezvous* will be at 2200 hours in the kitchen to review progress.'

The next morning the photographer arrived bang on time which, perhaps needless to record, was just as Yr Correspondent was about half-way through mowing the last – but from the standpoint of pictorial presentation, likely the 'first', or most prominent – lawn.

. . . .

I told you you should've given that lawn higher priority.

And you were right, Alter-natis. In the event, I left it until nearly nightfall, by which time – with the grass dewy-slick and only the lights on the mower to guide me – it was too late. After cutting a few swathes, I had to give up.

All those daisy and dandelion flowers, and plantains with their seed-heads sticking proudly up through the grass. I said you'd better hope your prospective purchasers include a naturalist or two.

. . . .

Predictably, the photographer said he'd like to do the outside shots first while the light was right and everything looked, as he put it, 'dawn-of-the-new-day fresh'. But, he continued, it would take him 'a few minutes' to get set up. I detailed N to slow him down with a cup of coffee and some chat, then raced back to the partly-cut lawn, tried to fire up the (deleted) mower... but couldn't get it to start. (Deleted!)

Otherwise, everything went more or less according to plan... which was just as well. For while I was showing the photographer possible camera positions for the gardens, he remarked, in what seemed to me a rather practised 'off hand' way: 'A good brochure... its photographs, especially – I don't want to sound too self-impressed, of course – can often make or break the sale of a property, you know. And it's a funny thing about photographs: they always seem almost to highlight – to exaggerate, you might even say – any problems in the way a house and/or its gardens are prepared and presented. You know, like if the dining room tabletop's got a patch of dust on it, or the edging around a lawn isn't perfectly curvilinear or straight....' (Ummm, so you say.... Psssst! N... or Lauren...? Quick! Take one final look in the dining room, will you? Make sure the.... Toby? Just have a last sight along the lawn edges, please. Check that they're....)

The morning of 20 June – or, otherwise put, some 4–5 days after calendar 'mid-June' – I readied the deposit monies owing for our Heartsease Hall Estate purchase and telephoned Euan to establish when, exactly, these funds would be required. Euan replied that as no instructions had been received from Sir Roald's solicitors, he hadn't a clue. I remember at first thinking: Well, N and I certainly don't mind keeping the cash in our account for a while longer.... And then reminding myself: but isn't contract exchange the point at which the vendor binds himself legally to consummate the trade? Up until that moment....

The possibility that 'other possibilities' had arisen for Sir Roald – a better offer for Heartsease Hall which his trustees simply wouldn't let him refuse, perhaps – couldn't be ruled out, so I asked Euan immediately to contact his opposite number and report back.

Throughout the ensuing long... long... afternoon, N and I amused ourselves with an advance copy of the completed Brambledown brochure which had arrived by courier about lunchtime. It was a fine, thoroughly-professional piece of work: beautifully written, photographed and laid out; only the daisy and dandelion flowers, and the plantain seed-heads – clearly visible in the front-cover picture of the house and its most-prominent lawn – stood (!) between it and perfection.

Finally, as the business day was drawing to its close – and our reserves of patience were nearing exhaustion – a fax came in from Euan. It read in part: 'I've just spoken to Sir Roald's solicitors. They appear to attach very little urgency to contract exchange, although they did tell me they "hope" to have the necessary papers ready in a week or so. As to "other possibilities", they confirmed that "none have arisen... or are likely to".' N and I heaved the proverbial sigh of relief... and cracked a chilled bottle of bubbly.

· · · · · · · · · · · · · · · · · · · ·

This is England, d'Arcy, part-bred of Germany, the heartland of Protestant 'Vorsprung durch Technik', or 'pre-eminence through technology'. Respect for the law, fair-play, and discipline – self-disci-

pline – are regarded as paramount virtues... most of the time....

I know that.

It's not Rome-ish France, with its preening 'BCBG' – that's 'Bon chic, bon genre': people who're stylish and well-connected socially – or Italy with its posturing 'bella figura', which is the Etrurian equivalent of BCBG. Here in England, nearly everyone does what they say they'll do when they say they'll do it... most of the time....

Of course, Alter-natis.

That's why, in common with a lot of other northern European nationals, so many Brits find membership of the European Community, with its unelected and largely-unaccountable 'government' in Brussels, and its metastasizing codes of rules and regulations – which southern-European nationals simply ignore... or routinely break – so exasperating.

Even so, it was very reassuring to have confirmation that in this slick, in-your-face, greedy world there were still people – like Sir Roald – whose word was their bond and who expected your word to be your bond.

That's how 'gentlemen' are supposed to behave.

I know that's how gentlemen are *supposed* to behave. But if they all in fact did, a substantial proportion of the world's legal profession would have to take early retirement.

· · · · · · · · · · · · · · · · · · · ·

The next day I telephoned Sir Roald, essentially just to stay in touch. We small-talked then, as we were concluding, he said there were a number of estate-related matters he'd like to discuss with me in person and asked when I might be available to come down. I replied I was pretty well booked for the next few days but that if the matters were urgent, I'd make time. 'No, no; there's nothing urgent,' Sir Roald replied. 'In due course, however, we should discuss what's best to do with the family portraits, and the furniture and the books here in the Hall, and the sitting tenants in the cottages... and, probably, the donkeys.'

'The *what*, Sir Roald?'

'The donkeys. My wife has two donkeys which, you'll understand, we may not be able to accommodate about our new premises. How *very* forgetful of me; I was absolutely sure I'd mentioned them to you....'

On 23 June, we got a letter from Euan saying Heartsease Hall's fixtures and fittings were 'ours without question', and that contract exchange was now firmly scheduled for 8 July – 'only three weeks later than originally planned' – with completion ditto for 11 October, 'probably'. Notwithstanding these 'mere pieces of paper', Euan's advisory concluded: 'the process of your purchasing the Heartsease Hall Estate should now be regarded as fully established'.

N and I heaved another sigh of relief, cracked another bottle of bubbly... and focused even more determinedly on getting Brambledown sold.

Chapter 5

Hilltoppers & Babblers

We welcomed our first Brambledown prospects – a man and a woman, both probably mid-late 30s; a husband and wife, I assumed – just after 1100 hours on 24 June. As they drove up the driveway I noted glumly their elderly, economy-model car, its bodywork grimy and covered in dents; if they couldn't afford better transport, I muttered to N, how could they possibly stretch to Brambledown. After they'd parked and were getting out, N remarked that rather than appearing up-beat and enthusiastic – eager to contemplate the opportunities of a new home – the two had about them a sort of hangdog, fugitive air.

Determined, however, that these 'books' shouldn't be judged by the battered, paperback 'cover' in which they'd arrived, or their curiously uninspired 'title pages', N and I marched out of the house and onto the forecourt to greet them. Or rather....

Following our Way Forward meeting with the EA, N and I'd had a number of discussions about who'd have what role in showing the house. N's view was that she should take the public lead. 'It's not that you're not basically a nice person, or kind and caring, Dar,' she'd argued repeatedly. 'It's that sometimes, when you're under pressure, you can come across as a bit too "Alpha" and over-bearing.' That, she firmly believed, wouldn't be helpful. 'People who're considering buying something they think is important – a house... a car... even a new coat or a pair of shoes – need plenty of intellectual and emotional space,' she'd insisted. An hour or so before that first viewing, she'd put her foot down: 'You take yourself off somewhere for 15–20 minutes... to Top Field, say, and "make hay" – you don't actually *have* to go there and do *that*, of course; we're just talking scenarios – then you come back here in good time to deal with any man-of-the-house matters. But remember: when you arrive back, be gentle... be nice!'

And so N marched out all by herself to greet the prospects; Yr Correspondent sloped up the front stairs and prepared covertly to monitor as best he could from the first floor ('second floor' in American usage) the events as they unfolded below.

It being a fine day, N opted to do the outside, 'Cottage and Gardens View' first. As the trio perambulated, I followed their progress through a succession of hallway, bedroom and bathroom windows. The woman seemed to be asking a lot of questions which N, judging from her relaxed posture and fluent hand jive, appeared to answer easily... perhaps even, I mused, honestly! In short, the pitch to the distaff-side prospect – statistically, according to the EA, the likely final decision-maker – appeared to be going well. The man, however, kept scurrying on ahead of N and the woman, then back again to them, then ahead again like a dog wanting to be taken faster on its walk; from time to time, he looked anxiously at his watch. That perhaps wasn't such a good sign, methought.

In due course, N commenced the indoors, 'Grand Rooms and Domestic Offices View'. I sweated out my appointed time – and a bit more for good measure – 'making hay' in the upstairs wings, then I crept down the back stairs and, brushing imaginary bits of chaff from my clothes, made my 'happenstance' entrance onto the selling stage. 'Oh, hello; I'm d'Arcy Henry, Nikki's husband. Ha, ha,' I chirruped genially. 'Nikki has, I'm sure, given you the big picture with full commentary, but if you've any little techno-infrastructural questions: you know, like the location of the rising main and its stopcock – Ha, ha: that's the principal water supply pipe and its shut-off valve! – or the thermal-output rating of the central heating system or where the septic tank is.... Ha, ha.... Ha....'

There followed a protracted silence during which the prospects performed a gaze-aversion-*cum*-foot-shuffle *pas-de-deux* which seemed almost choreographed. The prelude to a purchase proposal, perhaps? More likely a pantomime of prevarication, I concluded. Then the prospect-male said well, yes, he did have a question. I nodded at him, I'm-your-go-to-man encouragingly. His watch appeared to have stopped, he said, so would I please tell him what time it was? I told him it was a little before noon.

The man started. 'Oh, it's that late is it?' he exclaimed, turning to the woman. 'Darling, we've really got to be going.' He turned back to N and me. 'Thank you *so* much for showing us around, Mrs Henry... Mr Henry. Brambledown really is a most interesting... a *most* interesting... a *most beautiful* property. We'll let you know our decision with regard to it one way or the other just as soon as possible.'

Well, N confided as we waved them off, Brambledown isn't really right for them. Oh, I said, marvelling once again at my little Uxor's ability to ferret out crucial intelligence, why not? They're married, N replied, but not to each other. 'So what they really want isn't a family house but a cozy little hide-away for – well... you know what for – weekends.'

'What on earth prompted them to view Brambledown, then?' I asked.

'They liked the name, and they didn't think the property was going to be so big.'

On 26 June I drove to north Norfolk, dropped N and the boys off at Sea Palling (a beach about ten miles northeast of Heartsease Hall), then backtracked inland for my 'in due course' meeting with Sir Roald. As I turned through the estate's main gate, I slowed the car and took a deep breath. 'So, we've done it,' I exhaled. 'This entrance, this front lodge, this driveway...' then, as the wider realization began to sink in, 'this Hall, this estate, this little corner of England and the world... is where N and I – the Squiress and her Squire – may live out our mortal days.' A great surge of wonder and joy at all the new life-possibilities now opening up – and a tiny twinge of regret at all the old life-possibilities now closing down – ran through me.

· · · · · · · · · · · · · · · · · · ·

Curious, isn't it, the serendipity thing.

How do you mean, Alter-natis?

Who would ever have thought that the boy from Baltimore, Maryland and the girl from Oakland, California would wind up meeting in the UK, marrying, settling down... and buying one of England's finest, historic, country estates. Did you plan it that way?

Of course not, Dimwit; it wouldn't have been 'serendipity' if I had.

Did you ever 'in your wildest dreams' imagine it that way?

No....

So why, Dimwit, do you try so hard to shape... to 'order'... your life? Eating, sleeping and awaking at specified times; striving to achieve first this goal and then that one; relaxing only when your schedule allows...? Why don't you just 'go with the flow'?

Ivan Pavlov's 'conditioned reflex', I suppose. Striving is what I'm programmed to do; it's part of my genetic coding, and how I was nurtured and raised.

· · · · · · · · · · · · · · · · · · ·

Sir Roald greeted me in the turning circle outside the front porch, just as he had on that 'historic' afternoon two-and-a-half months earlier.

We shook hands then, for the most intense, flicker of a moment, we just looked at each other. No words were exchanged – but to me, at least, it seemed an understanding... a trust... passed. Then Sir Roald turned and led me briskly up the porch steps and into the entrance hall.

It was the first time I'd had the opportunity – better: *taken* the opportunity – to regard my counter-party closely. Notwithstanding his 77 or so years, Sir Roald seemed still a very good physical specimen: of average height and build – perhaps 5'9"–5'10" and 140–150 lbs – lean but well-made, with the natural athlete's balanced, graceful carriage and sure gait. His face was more squared-off than rounded in outline, and craggy, weathered, outdoorsman-handsome... with a full forehead beneath shocks of silver-grey hair, prominent cheekbones, an aquiline nose and a strong, clean jaw well set into a sinewy neck. It was Sir Roald's eyes, however, in that Middle English characterization of eyes as 'wyndowes of the mynde'...

· · · · · · · · · · · · · · · · · · ·

'Occulus index animi est,' or: 'The eye is the index of the soul.' It's a Latin proverb, d'Arcy.

· · · · · · · · · · · · · · · · · · ·

... 'wyndowes of the mynde' which particularly caught my attention. They seemed at once both to draw me in and engage me and yet, from a distance, to analyse and assess me as a high-court judge might some callow probationer or a great eagle some snack-time prey.

At an opportune moment, I screwed up my courage and – somewhat more diplomatically than the words immediately following suggest – asked Sir Roald what he'd done with his life. He replied that after 'coming down' (graduating) from Cambridge University where he'd 'read' (majored in) history and economics and 'gotten a Blue' (lettered) in track, and 'fooling around' for a few years at the *Ecole des Science Politiques* in Paris and the *Ludwig-maximilians Universität* in Munich, and 'harassing "Jerry" (the Germans)' as part of 'a UK-led, European Resistance co-ordination and support group'*, and serving on The Allied Control Commission (post-War government *pro tem*) in Bulgaria, he'd been taken on by Reuters, the international news agency, as its bureau chief in Belgrade, the capital of what was

---

* That 'group', I later discovered, was the super-secret 'Special Operations Executive' or 'SOE' which at the end of the war was absorbed into what is now the UK's Military Intelligence Section Six (MI6).

then the dictator Josip Broz Tito's People's Republic of Yugoslavia.

('Does that mean you speak Serbo-Croat,' I asked? 'I've always been fairly good at languages,' Sir Roald replied modestly which, I eventually learned, meant he was *fluent* in Serbo-Croat – not to mention Russian and most of the major East-European tongues and, of course, all the major West-European ones… and had, as well, 'a little Japanese'.)

From Reuters, Sir Roald continued, he'd been head-hunted to *The* (London) *Times*, serving as their correspondent in various European capitals and then the Far East. (He'd also, he revealed, briefly reported from The Motherland, working out of Washington, DC.) While he was bureau chief in Tokyo, however, his elderly father, Sir Torvald – the 12th Baronet Festing – unexpectedly inherited Heartsease Hall from a first cousin, and it soon became clear the old man needed help running the estate. Accordingly, Sir Roald quit his post at *The Times* and, in 1963, signed on as a part-time 'information research consultant' with the Foreign Office, dividing his workweek between Heartsease Hall and Whitehall, in London. This arrangement continued until 1976, Sir Roald concluded, when he himself succeeded to the baronetcy and the estate and, in his words, 'like some geriatric Beelzebub – as I'm sure you know, Mr Henry, that "honorific" comes from the Hebrew "*ba'al zebub*", meaning "lord of the flies" – began seriously to involve myself in the affairs of the Heartsease Hall community.'

'Goodness, Sir Roald,' I stammered, 'yours was a career most people would die for.'

'I've been very, very fortunate, Mr Henry,' Sir Roald said simply.

Partly in consequence of the above, lengthy preliminaries, but primarily because the pressures of the past few months on Sir Roald and, to a lesser extent, on me were now largely relieved, the proposed *raisons d'être* of our meeting – the Heartsease Hall pictures, the furniture, the books… the sitting tenants… the donkeys, even; 'the collateral of some three-and-a-half-centuries' guard being changed', as my host put it – were raised only briefly and then allowed to drop; for the most part, Sir Roald and I just chatted and began to get to know each other.

On 2 July, the two Misses Brown – sisters, pushing the limits of that 'certain age' – arrived to view Brambledown… sort of. Brown 'A', attired in a neat, floral-print dress, was tall and spare, with greying,

carefully-permed hair and a complexion from which any hint of vital-
ity had been ruthlessly face-powdered out. 'Magisterial' of deportment and speech, she seemed a near-perfect reincarnation of the ach-
ingly-archly prime Miss Jean Brodie exulted by Dame Maggie Smith
in Ronald Neame's bittersweet 1969 film. Brown 'B' was her almost
total *alter ego*: short and stout, with bobbed hair, a button nose and
eyes like currants in a bun. Clad in a blue smock-blouse of what appeared to be curtain or upholstery material below which were baggy,
mid-grey (? canvas) trousers, she scampered around and around as
might a spaniel in a cornfield, all the while talking nineteen to the
dozen.

N being in Stockholm for the day, it fell to Yr (Deconstructed Al-
pha-male) Correspondent to front the viewing. 'What would you ladies like to see first: the gardens? The cottage and the outbuildings?
The main house?' I asked.

'We'd like to see the stables, Mr Henry,' Brown A, her hands
clasped in front of her, advised sternly.

'Oh, yes, please. The stables, that's what we'd really like to see,'
echoed Brown B from the far side of one of the big planted-up urns in
Brambledown's forecourt whose flora she'd been closely inspecting,

'because, Mr Henry, we....'

'We breed llamas, Mr Henry,' Brown A announced. 'As you may know they're *camelids*; that's to say: members of the camel family.'

· · · · · · · · · · · · · · · · · · · ·

I *did*, actually, know that, Alter-natis.

And, commendably, you just stood there... albeit offering the two ladies that trademark rictus-smile of yours. I doubted you'd have been capable of such restraint even a few months earlier, and I wondered what might have triggered the sudden irruption of your self-control.

Their proper, Latin name is '*Lama (sic:* only one 'l'*) glama*'; isn't that sweet?

Your wife's constant example and her occasional, sharp reminder-precept, viz, 'be gentle... be nice', certainly had something to do with it. But acquisition of the Heartsease Hall Estate was the likely, critical agency, I eventually concluded, because with it came the pos-sibility of your being – for the first time in your adult life, perhaps – really, truly, 'at home'.

· · · · · · · · · · · · · · · · · · · ·

'Yes, we have 17 llamas: one *macho* – "Themistocles" we call him, after that greatest of Athenian statesmen , or "Themi" for short – six breeding *hembras* and, at the moment, seven darling little *crias* most of whom, sadly, we'll have to sell,' Brown B detailed from the south end of the herbaceous border running along the front of the house.

Machos, hembras and *crias*, that's to say males, females and ba-bies? Whatever; I ran the numbers, as years of management consult-ing had drilled into me – one, plus six, plus seven... that's 14 llamas, not 17, isn't it, Ma'am? – and displaced my mind elsewhere, as years of management consulting had also drilled into me. Only 14 llamas there may be Big Boy but, until you see clearly how this one's going to play out, you stay low. Brown A, however, was made of sterner stuff.

'No, Binkie, that's not correct,' she advised firmly. 'We have seven *hembras* – We've had seven for ages and ages! – but only six little *crias* now; Mrs Thistlethwaite purchased one, remember? And on Thursday while you were at the WI*, she came by with her trailer and collected it.'

Two-thirds of the line items having been revised, I waited to hear if either of the Misses Brown would take the opportunity to adjust the sum total. It was a wait in vain, however; in spite of every enumera-

---

* The Women's Institute, a British and Commonwealth society concerned with family and community issues.

tion to the contrary, the incorrect '17' entry was allowed to stand. Good Lord, I thought: suppose inspection of the stables reveals accommodation adequate for, say, a dozen or so llamas but too small for 16–18. Should I advert to a possible, lower (? herd? flock) total and one just about right for the space available? What would N do I finally, in desperation, asked myself? She'd smile amiably and keep shtoom, I concluded.

So biting my tongue... off to the stables with the two ladies I went (or, rather, off I went with Brown A; Brown B, that's to say Binkie Brown, was already half-way along the path, scenting round its every twist and turn) and in the event – as I've found is so often the case – the anticipated problem wasn't the one that arose. The size of the accommodation was deemed more than adequate....

'We could even increase our herd, Binkie,' said Brown A, her hands still clasped in what was clearly a signature pose. 'Yes, Sis (Ah so: it's Binkie and Sis, I registered); we could have 20–25... 30 llamas, even, in here!' said Binkie Brown, from the far corner of one of the stalls. 'Divide these big boxes (stalls) into halves – quarters, maybe, and....'

Rather, it was our location on the exposed flank of a high-Cotswolds hill which proved problematic.

'But we couldn't keep llamas here, Binkie,' said Sis, her right forearm now wrapped around her waist, her left hand supporting her chin. 'No, Sis,' said Binkie, from deep within the corn store. 'These stables are all very well and good but outside, in the pastures, there's no proper shelter from the wind.' Popping up her head like a meerkat on sentry-go, she looked earnestly at me: 'Llamas don't like wind, Mr Henry; they know it can give them chilblains*. If only your property was lower down – right in the valley, say....'

Sis Brown saw the matter differently... but only slightly so. 'The real problem isn't *wind* Binkie,' she pronounced, 'it's *wet*. In winter it's going to be very, very wet up here! All those storms driving in from the southwest and emptying their rain over these pastures....' Eyes narrowing, she scanned out the open door of the stables, across the lawns and up the terrace gardens to Top Field where grazed contentedly – as they did even in the dead of winter – our flock of sheep. 'No, llamas just wouldn't like it here, so they just wouldn't thrive – or, as we here in England say, they just wouldn't "do". Binkie's right, Mr Henry, if only your property was lower down....'

---

* Clinically, 'pernio': in humans, an inflammation of the extremities caused by prolonged exposure to moisture and cold.

Wait a minute, I thought: in the wild, don't llamas, with their deep-pile... insulating, in other words, and lanolin-coated... damp-proofing, in other words, fleeces – very much like those our sheep have, only finer-fibered – live high up in the Andes, where it can be windy and wet... not to mention bitterly, bitterly cold? Sensing I'd little to lose, I proposed these recullections from some long-ago issue of the *National Geographic* to the two gentle ladies.

'Llamas do indeed live in the Andes, Mr Henry,' Sis Brown replied, her hands once again clasped in front of her. 'And the weather can be very hard there. But, mostly, they inhabit the mountains' central plateaux and landward, eastern slopes where it's relatively sheltered and dry. Up here where you are, on this high hill, even though you're east-facing, it's like the seaward, western slopes of the Andes: cold and windy and *wet*.' Nodding her head emphatically, she recapitulated her main theme: 'Llamas don't like wet; under wet conditions, they just won't do.' Then, as an afterthought, she added: 'In that regard, they're a lot like many of us, Mr Henry.'

· · · · · · · · · · · · · · · · · · · ·

I was going to say that. And more: I was going to observe that the old 'Glama-lama' – or whatever you tell me they're properly called – and a certain female Homo sapiens *of whom you're most fond have almost identical distastes in weather.*

· · · · · · · · · · · · · · · · · · · ·

Binkie Brown hammered the final nail home: 'Yes, Mr Henry,' she said, shaking her head slowly, 'llamas are really no different from you or me. If they had their druthers (choice), what they'd really like is to be snuggled up in front of a big fire all cozy and warm with a nice, milky, sugary mug of tea!'

With a trill of giggles from Binkie and, from Sis, a polite but definitive 'thank you and good day', the viewing ended. Without troubling to inspect the rest of the property – the other outbuildings, the farther gardens, the gardener's cottage... or, indeed, Brambledown house – the two Misses Brown took their leave.

· · · · · · · · · · · · · · · · · · · ·

Reams and reams have, of course, been written about the British and their obsession with animals and, especially, with pets. The way they just sort of collect them...

... and, having collected them, the way they treat them: like members of their family.

It's well known that having animals around lowers stress levels, thereby promoting good bodily health and a more general sense of wellness, particularly in those who live alone.

The psycho-theraputics of transgenic bonding, aka 'ENSS' or Everybody Needs Somebody Syndrome.

But, surely, the depth and intensity of British transgenic bonding with animals – not to mention the extravagance of their anthropomorphizing – is extreme?

That's partly a function of the Brits' relative wealth; in less-fortunate socio-economies, you'll understand, the tendency is not so much to pet animals as to pot them...

Yeesss.

... and, I think, partly a function of the Brits' vaunted emotional self-containment, that's to say their 'reserve'. As you're acutely aware, relating to people can be very difficult: first, you have to get to know them, and find things to talk about and do with them... then you have to maintain a meaningful level of on-going contact.

It all requires a lot of time and energy. With animals, you just have to provide for their bodily needs and give them a cuddle from time to time. And if you choose to talk to them...

... they don't, as the notion's usually applied, talk back.

• • • • • • • • • • • • • • • • • • •

On 8 July, I telephoned Euan for a progress report on our Heartsease Hall purchase. 'I take it things are moving smoothly along toward contract exchange?' I asked, breezily. 'No "things" aren't,' Euan replied but, he added quickly, everything was 'under control'.

• • • • • • • • • • • • • • • • • • •

That construction's often a sanitised synonym for 'SNAFU', or Situation Normal: All (Deleted) Up', I reminded you.

• • • • • • • • • • • • • • • • • • •

Early one afternoon a few days later, a lean, mean, corporate-high-flyer type came to view Brambledown arriving, to N's and my huge delight, in a top-of-the-line BMW fairly bristling with telecommunications aerials. His wife had been through the day before, when I'd been in Brussels, and 'absolutely loved' the place, N told me, so it could be the husband was calling through just to sign off. I uncrossed my fingers long enough to shake hands and do the 'Welcome!' bit then, not wanting to risk a clash of testosterone, I turned Top Gun over to N and made myself scarce.

Eavesdropping discreetly while he and N do the Grand Rooms, etc, View, I hear N referencing enthusiastically all the features his wife had liked (and ignoring, presumably, those she hadn't!) and pointing out Brambledown's convenience for business travel: 'There're two or three small, local airports for your executive jet, and Heathrow's only an hour or so away....' (Oh? We've never been able to drive there that quickly....) The two of them then set off on the Cottage, etc, View, so I climb into my easy chair in the study for a read of the newspapers and, possibly, a little kip. And why not, I rationalize? Yesterday was long and hard.... Zzzzzzzz.... Suddenly: 'Knock, knock!' I snatch myself awake and resurrect a newspaper just as N and Top Gun come convivially through the study door.

'I've given Mr Johannson the full tour, Dar...'

'Hey, you guys, that's great!' I exclaim, leaping genially to my feet. 'By the way: I'm sorry *I* wasn't able to show you around, Mr Johannson, but I had to take an important conference call; one of our clients in New York....'

'... and he says he likes Brambledown very much. Particularly the gardens. He says they'll give his wife something to do while he's away on business – "Keep her out of trouble," so to speak!' Wink, wink... nudge, nudge... ha, ha... ha.... N rests her case and, together, the three of us enter upon the ritual, agenda-completed silence which segues into the ritual, pre-departure professions of goodwill, accommodation and accord and, from Top Gun, the revelation that he's got a meeting in central London in two-and-a-half hours. We quit the study and process amiably out to the forecourt; I attend closely for some hint of what may come.

'Well, Mr Henry, I've got to be in the Far East pretty much all of next week. But I'll ask my lawyers to get in touch. This is certainly just the sort of property my wife and I've been looking for. Just the sort! It's so peaceful... so quiet... so relaxing here.'

Top Gun slumps sidewise, head-propped-on-hand, over the roof of his car: the hyper-drive of the Fortune-500 senior executive on the verge of capitulating to the bone-weariness of the frequent long-haul flyer – the disposition N and I knew fairly well and had witnessed often – then wills himself into full take-charge, face the grumbling grunts, the maundering middle managers, the vaunting V-Ps, the Compensation and/or Audit Committees, the Board of Directors, the shareholders, the Securities and Exchange Commission... whatever... mode, thanks me, shakes my hand, opens the car door, gets in, turns on the ignition, powers the driver's-side window down.... 'As I was saying, Mr Henry, I'll ask my lawyers...' he repeats; my lower legs, my ankles, my feet... my toes... essay a little jig....

At that moment the most enormous percussions erupt overhead as a brace of Royal Air Force F-14 jet fighters out of their base at nearby Brize Norton scream past – as was their occasional wont – on a low-level training run. Top Gun winces mightily. 'I'll ask my lawyers,' he begins again, as the tumult diminuendos slightly then, 'missiles away', the F-14s go full-thrust into emergency climb. The heavens percuss and repercuss, again, and again... and again... as the terrible back-blast from their engines sunders the sky.

Top Gun arches an eyebrow. 'These overflights: are they a regular occurrence around here, Mr Henry?' he asks.

'Oh no, not at all. Not at all, Mr Johannson. They happen maybe once a... once a....'

'A week, Mr Henry?'

'Oh no, not as frequently as that, sir. No, no, not that frequently.'

'A fortnight, then? Once a fortnight? Once a month? Once every couple of months?'

'Well, perhaps something like that. Once every couple of months, maybe.'

As we all – N and I, and Top Gun, of course – know, all too well, survival in the upper canopies of the corporate jungle is, first of all, a matter of natural mental ability and physical stamina, next a matter of nurtural advantage and luck and, finally, a matter of who can out-bluff whom. Top Gun gives me one of those withering glares such as must have set many an under-performing subordinate quaking in his or her shoes; I look back as innocently as I can, trying to get some reassuring nonchalance into my demeanor....

Top Gun fastens his seatbelt, settles himself purposively in his... cockpit... slips the big Beamer into gear and starts off. At the top of the driveway he stops, looks briefly at the now-dissipating contrails of the F-14s and then at me, looks somewhat longer – wistfully, I think I sense – at the 'so peaceful... so quiet... so relaxing' Brambledown that might have been, and then accelerates away.

By mid-July, the 'spring' property-marketing window had effectively closed. And although we'd shown Brambledown nineteen times, not a single offer had we received. It came as no surprise, therefore, when on 18 July we got a fax from the EA advising us that house sales in the UK had 'slowed very markedly' in the three months to end-June. He summed up: 'I believe we may have some decisions to take. To that end, perhaps we should have a talk.'

Indeed. In the meantime, N and I pondered a preemptive meeting with The Suits to arrange a bridging loan and started to work out how, even with the energetic support of Lauren and Toby, we were going to cope with two pretty-major properties 175 or so cross-country miles apart – the better part of four hours' drive by car – an international management consultancy... and two young sons.

On 23 July I took a telephone call from Sir Roald – our first communication in about a month – reminding me of the issues he wanted to discuss – 'needed' to discuss, now, he said – and asking if I might find the time to come and see him. 'You must have some "matters arising" as well,' he added. Uncharacteristically, Sir Roald sounded somewhat weary and urgent.

Three days later, I again drove with the family to north Norfolk. In my briefcase was a two-page *aide mémoire* covering everything I could think of, from 'purchase monies: currency and method of payment' to 'milk and rubbish (garbage): delivery and collection days' – a total of nineteen separate headings.

(By now, I was getting the routing down a bit better... which is to say I only got lost twice: near Aynho, in Gloucestershire, and then just west of Buckingham [? Tingewick], where a new section of motorway was being built. But Bapu's stomach or, rather, 'vestibular system'* continued to be very unhappy about the dozen or so roundabouts punctuating a ten-mile stretch of the Milton Keynes northern by-pass [beltway] we had to run.)

I delivered N and the boys to our hotel, then continued on to Heartsease Hall. Sir Roald, looking as focused mentally as ever, but physically slightly pale and drooped, greeted me at the front porch, then ushered me into the library and towards two modest armchairs either side of the fireplace. I sat in one; he took the other; we exchanged pleasantries... and began the transition from small talk to business. I took up my carefully-prepared *aide mémoire*... but Sir Roald, it quickly became clear, would be in charge of the agenda. I put down my *aide mémoire*....

'Lady Maureen and I have, as you know, our premises in London,' Sir Roald began, 'and it's our intention in due course to purchase a small country house, perhaps in Aldeburgh or Southwold, on the Suf-

---

* The organs of the inner ear which detect motion and help maintain balance; over-stimulation of them, while travelling in an airplane, boat or car, for example, can cause nausea (!).

folk coast... someplace like that – not too far away but, on the other hand, not too near....

'Which raises the matter of what to do with the furniture and the books, and the Festing family portraits here in the Hall. There's far more of everything than we could ever find room for or, more's the point, ever need. We can, of course, sell some of the furniture and the books and put the rest – including the portraits – into storage. But there's always the possibility of damage; the portraits, you'll understand, are quite fragile. If there was any furniture which you and your wife would care to purchase... or any books, perhaps? And the family portraits: if you didn't mind, perhaps *pro tem* they might continue to reside here?'

. . . .

The portraits.... Good Lord: they'd struck me – positively hammered me, more like – from almost the first moment of our first view.

I do remember your mentioning....

I counted at least 18–20 of them, mostly dating from the 17th and 18th centuries – one or two probably late 16th-century – ranging in size from about 30 x 40 inches to perhaps 1.5 x 2 yards. Of these was a suite of ten, all of a piece and in matching, carved, gilt-wood frames. There was no need to know who painted them, except out of scholarly interest; even my eye could tell most of the portraits were very well-realized indeed.

My eye too could tell that, d'Arcy!

Among them was an exquisite pair of Restoration-era (c 1660s/ 1670s) portraits – the same composition, the same palette... probably by the same hand... the same size, framed up the same way – one, obviously after Van Dyck, of Charles I; the other, Sir Roald advised, of Isaac Festing, a Roundhead (a supporter of Parliament in the English Civil War), who was deputed by Cromwell to 'look... well and properly after' King Charles prior to his beheading in 1649 and from whom, Sir Roald told me, his ancestor had received – 'on the scaffold... as a token of that unfortunate Monarch's gratitude for his good care' – an emerald ring.

Curious, wasn't it: the Festings oppose Charles I... but then, about the time the Monarchy is restored and Charles II – the son of the executed king – accedes to the English throne, they commission these pictures to represent solidarity with him. Very curious!

There was even, Sir Roald pointed out, a portrait of Henry Festing, who was George III's Commissioner of Customs in Massachusetts at the time of the original 'Boston Tea Party'.

That dastard! He had to flee for his life back to England, didn't he? But to return to Sir Roald's proposal that the pictures continue to reside in Heartsease Hall and your risibly-unsuccessful attempt to conceal your delight in this possibility: you'd a number of fine, old, d'Arcy Henry and Harryman portraits, at Brambledown and in Baltimore....

Not in this lifetime was there any likelihood of N's and my having, even for a few months, such a quantity of portraits – let alone portraits of such quality and historical appropriateness – to hang on Heartsease Hall's walls. Would we *mind* if the Festing portraits stayed here *pro tem*? Would we mind if a selection from the British National Portrait Gallery in London or the American National Portrait Gallery in Washington were suddenly made available on what might turn out to be an indefinite loan?

Just the recollection of that moment causes you to hyperventilate.

And to be able to offer for some of the antique furniture and books as well!

But, again, you and your wife had many lovely things, some of which you'd inherited and some of which you bought yourselves.

Yes we did. But the scale of much of our furniture was wrong. It was fine for the smaller, more intimate dimensions of Cotswolds houses like Brambledown but not the grander proportions of Heartsease Hall. And, in any event, even if the scale of our furniture had been right, there wasn't anywhere near enough of it. Heartsease Hall was big!

And books?

We'd a goodly accumulation of books, sure – more, by many multiples, than we'd ever read. But my *credo* was and is – even in this age of electronic publishing... *especially*, perhaps, in this age of electronic publishing – never pass up the opportunity to acquire and display a few more. Books give a room... a house... a house-owner – maybe even an up-start American English country squire – an aura of genteel intellectuality.

I observed then and I observe again now: for someone who professes to be in search of spiritual security, you certainly spend a lot of time and energy pursuing material things.

· · · · · · · · · · · · · · · · · · · ·

Predictably, probably... I replied I'd be delighted to consider Sir Roald's proposal; Sir Roald said the furniture had been inventoried and that he'd send N and me a 'Consignment List' to peruse. Item One of his meeting agenda having been disposed of, we moved on to....

'Then there's Groome,' Sir Roald continued, 'our *factotum* (handyman) of many years; you met him briefly when you visited in June. Old Groom's been of great assistance to us. If you've no objection, could he remain here for awhile? In his mobile home?'

On first impression, Groome – tall and dark, and with a hint about him of The Highwayman, the eponymous hero of Alfred Noyes's dark ballad... albeit a somewhat dishevelled and slightly hippy highwayman – had struck me as savvy, willing and able; I'd very much taken to him. Moreover, his continued, sturdy presence would help secure the property while the Festings, N and I, and the estate were in transition, I reckoned.

But, I remember thinking, the mobile home? Oh, no! With its photo-degraded, Perspex windows, its bleached, algae-encrusted paintwork and corroded aluminum trim, its rusted iron frame buttressed with scrap-wood timbers, its moldering tires... its surround of litter – old car batteries, beer and wine bottles... a discarded TV or two – this dilapidated vehicle, etc, wasn't exactly what the English country squire apparent had in mind to accessorize his new premises. I sat myself boldly up, squared my shoulders, took a deep breath, smiled broadly... and said certainly Groome could remain 'for awhile'.

'Good. That brings us to Maggie and Jubie – Lady Maureen's two donkeys, that is. Several parties have expressed interest in having them; to date, however, that interest has proved more theoretical than real. We can, of course, make other arrangements. But if you felt, perhaps for your boys.... They'd come with bridles and saddles and all that... and a couple of useful carts; we sometimes use the donkeys and the carts to fetch in firewood....'

. . . .

So that's the rub, I thought: furniture, books, portraits *pro tem*, trusty old Groome... and then the thrust home – donkeys. Was the Old Boy trying to put one over on me? No, no, of course not, I rebuked myself. He's much too fine, too decent, too up-standing... too savvy... a man ever to seek to foist a pair of dolesome jill donkeys onto some poor, benighted American man and his Stanford *summa*, etc, American wife. And yet.... And yet....

The package Sir Roald was proposing would at one stroke have solved most of his remaining removals problems, d'Arcy.

Indeed, Alter-natis.

I reminded you of the words attributed to St Matthew: 'Why beholdest thou the mote that is in thy brother's eye, but considerest not the beam that is in thine own eye?' Just two donkeys – they couldn't eat that much, or need that much looking after, I noted – as quid pro quo *for the opportunity to offer for some lovely antique furniture and fine-bound books and to lock in, on whatever basis for however long, those splendid portraits on the walls....*

. . . .

'Certainly, Sir Roald,' I said, 'we'd *love* to have Lady Maureen's two donkeys. What did you say their names were?'

'Maggie's the older one; she was born in 1975, just before Margaret Thatcher became Leader of the Conservative Party. Jubie's her daughter; she arrived about the time of the Queen's 1978 Silver Jubilee. They're very good natured, generally, and they don't require much care: a quarterly hoof trim, and a good currycomb and brush from time to time....'

Done; and thank you, sir. 'By the way, Sir Roald, what's the average life expectancy of a donkey?'

'They can go on for as long as 50 years, I'm told, but 30–40 years is more the norm. Your Maggie and Jubie are really pretty much still in their prime.'

. . . .

Today, Class, I'd like you to cast your minds back to our last session – early June it was, I think – when we considered staffing and how important it is to make timely and appropriate provision for staffing needs. In our case study, the acquisition of the Heartsease Hall Estate, we identified people to manage some of the critical core functions of our enterprise, especially our corporate finances. We also talked about who might make a good estate CEO – although I seem to remember we didn't, in fact, crack that one.

Recently, a new staffing requirement has been identified; we need someone to look after a couple of donkeys. So the question I'd like now to explore with you is this: should we hire in a person specifically to do this job, that's to say a dedicated groom-*cum*-stable lad or ladette? Or should we leave it to Lauren or Toby? What do you think, Class? Keep the staffing chart short and simple, and stick with Lauren or Toby, even though they've no experience of donkeys? Or go into the labour market and find someone with precisely the right mix of aptitudes and skills?

Yes... Ms Goldstar, reclining in your seat looking so... well, err... so... so tasty, like a Fragonard odalisque – What? No, I'm not going to tell you what is a Fragonard odalisque*; after class, you go and look it up! – head tilted back and to one side, lips slightly parted, gazing into the middle distance... or are you in fact eying up Che? I get a sense there's someone or something – or maybe both – extracurricular on your mind. Shame on you! Aren't you interested in these finer points of support-staffing?

Un-hunh. You think we should hire a specialist donkey person.

---

* A slave girl or concubine, such as might have been painted by the 18th-century French rococo artist Jean-Honoré Fragonard.

Now why's that? Oh, I see: UK Animal Welfare, and Health and Safety at Work regulations make clear we could be in serious trouble if we had someone looking after the donkeys who wasn't properly qualified. If something went wrong – the person looking after the donkeys got kicked or bitten, say, or contracted 'strangles'; clinically, that's known as 'equine distemper', I believe – we might be liable for very considerable damages.

But wouldn't our general insurance cover that? No? So you say: working with animals is the subject of very specific exclusions in most policies written nowadays; *including* this sort of coverage could cost quite a lot of money. I hadn't realized that; thank you for telling me.

By the way, if you don't mind my asking: how is it you're so very well informed about this... how should I put it... this rather unlikely subject? Oh, I see. Your father used to be a donkey concessionaire selling rides on the beach at Scarborough – the seaside resort often billed as 'The Pleasure Capital of Northeast England', and home of the fabled-in-folk-song 'going-to' Fair, I believe – and, during your school summer holidays, you used to work as one of his donkey-girls, tacking the donkeys up and leading them with their paying-passenger riders along the Scarborough Bay foreshore... that sort of thing. Very interesting; yes....

So how does being a business-school student compare with life as a donkey girl? It's the what? Again, please? Oh, yes: the 'S' word, plural – *'merdes'* in French, I believe. Ummmm. Ms Goldstar: are you really sure you want to pursue a career in corporate management?

· · · · · · · · · · · · · · · · · · · ·

Early on the afternoon of 30 July, just as N and I were finishing a light, *alfresco* lunch on the patio, the EA telephoned to advise that 'a VVIP' from the United Arab Emirates – 'He's the Chief of one of the principal local tribes, I'm told; they're not going public with his name' – was coming to view Brambledown and could be arriving 'pretty soon'.

It seemed a very long shot. But if only on the grounds that the man's visit would let me return some of the hospitality I'd so often enjoyed during my travels in the Middle East, I said OK. Then I detailed Lauren to hit the high spots with the turkey-feather duster, freshen the flowers and the vanilla pods in the front hall and the drawing room... and drizzle the vegetables in the trug in the kitchen... and Toby to rake the paths. Finally – before myself racing upstairs to shave – I dispatched N to the Tranquil, etc, Village to buy a selection of whatever fresh fruits and fruit juices she might be able to find.

About twenty minutes later – seconds, literally, after N's return from the Village – a dark-blue Rover, then a Rolls Royce, a Bentley, another Roller, a stretched Mercedes limo and, finally, a second dark-blue Rover convoyed up the drive and into the forecourt before stopping, line-abreast, facing back out. From the first Rover, a fit-looking, immaculately-tailored young man with a bright red lapel pin and a 'hearing aid' in one ear ('Must be a *rubella* baby,' N, at my elbow, advised gravely) emerged, introduced himself and, opening a black box about the size of a small laptop, asked if he could 'just check a few details'. I said 'of course'. 'This *is* the for-sale property known as Brambledown, isn't it?' the man enquired, looking intently at his black box's screen.

'Yes,' I replied.

Hurriedly, the man keyed some data into the box, then re-engaged with me. 'And you *are* Mr Henry, are you?'

'Yes.'

'Would you let me have your mother's maiden name, and her date and place of birth, please.'

'"Harryman", born 31 October 1904 in Annapolis, Maryland, in The Great US of A,' I proclaimed in a strong, patriotic voice.

Black-Box Man nodded briskly and input more data into his little device. 'And this is your wife, Mrs Henry?' he asked, nodding at N.

'Yes.'

'Ma'am, would you let me have *your* mother's maiden name, and the date and place of her birth, please.'

Eyes round like saucers, mouth agape, clutching to her chest plastic shopping bags practically bursting with cartons of cranberry-coconut, orange and grapefruit juice, as well as quantities of dates, mangos, papayas, pomegranates... kumquats, even (who knows what exotic delights may be available in that olde-worlde, Cotswolds, down-town today!) my little Uxor – speaking... ve-ry... slow-ly... and... care-ful-ly – eventually managed: '"Keller", born 27 May, 1919 in Alameda, which is just outside of Oakland... in Califormia.'

'And also for your information,' I interjected with mock bravado, 'we don't smoke, drink only two or three units of alcohol per day – well... sometimes a few more – eat berries and nuts by the handful, take lots of exercise and bath or shower on Tuesdays, Thursdays and Saturdays – if there's enough hot water, that is; in the summer we like as much as possible to rely on our solar-thermal system. And we're regular readers of the *International Herald Tribune*, the *Financial*

Times and the *Economist*,' I concluded. 'But without first speaking to my lawyers, I'm not prepared to disclose....'

Black-Box Man rolled his eyes Heavenward, sighed heavily, cash-iered me with a thin, pseudo-indulgent smile... then adjusted his ear-piece and entered still more data into his device... from which shortly came forth a burst of high-frequency beeps.

'Good,' the young man said, all cordiality now. 'I just had to con-firm we're at the right place and talking to the right people.' He turned and nodded smartly in the direction of the two blue Rovers... from which quickly descended three more immaculately-tailored, fit-looking young men with bright red lapel pins and ear pieces ('Poor things!' N puzzled. 'Where they've come from there must have been some sort of *rubella* epidemic!'), who spaced themselves around the perimeter of the forecourt, facing outwards, before coming to stand with their legs apart and their hands clasped behind their backs 'at the watch'.

At another a nod from Black-Box Man, this time toward the lead Rolls Royce, its doors and those of the rest of the cars in the fleet tripped open and, as from a racecourse starting-gate, some 25–30 people – old men with walking sticks, young women with babies in their arms, middle-agers, teenagers and young children; the men dressed in *thobis* (loose-fitting robes) and *keffiyehs* (head-dresses) or beautifully-cut Saville Row suits, the women in *abayas* (ankle-length cloaks) and *hijabs* (head-scarves) or bright, boldly-coloured, Parisian *haute-couture* dresses and trouser-suits... the *et al* in polo shirts or tee shirts, chinos or blue jeans... or some manner of style or variation in between – tumbled out.

Among the last to emerge was an elderly man wearing a flowing, bright-white *keffiyeh* with a gold-threaded *agal* (brow band) and a matching *thobi* similarly gold-girdled. '*Ahlan wa sahlan*,' I intoned, smiling and bowing deeply. 'Welcome to Brambledown.'

'Mr Henry, this is His Excellency Sheikh [...],' our former inquisi-tor announced reverentially, carefully closing his little black box and tucking it under one arm.

'*Ahlan wa sahlan*,' I repeated. 'Welcome....'

'You sbeek Arabeek?' His Excellency, clearly delighted, exclaimed.

· · · · · · · · · · · · · · · · · · · ·

Uh-oh....

· · · · · · · · · · · · · · · · · · · ·

Desperately, I tried to cool him down. 'No, not really,' I protested.

'I only know a couple of....' But it was too late. Overjoyed at having found – in the middle of the high Cotswolds, no less – what he took to be an Anglo-Saxon Arabaphone, His Excellency rattled on. Every once in a while I managed to catch a word or two: 'Dirty city... fresh, green countryside... grow fig trees, date palms... breed racing horses... perhaps racing camels too....'

All this on just 25 acres, I mused? Well, I tried to persuade myself, our Shaikh's probably already bought a suitably-large estate (in the Tetbury area, perhaps!) and now he's after a house for his head trainer, stud manager or one of his junior sons. Meanwhile, the various members of His Excellency's tribe began to fan out across the lawns, exclaiming the height and girth of this tree, the habit and foliage of this shrub, the colour and fragrance of that flower... and making themselves comfortable in fold-up lawn chairs or on picnic blankets which from somewhere began suddenly to appear.

Abruptly, His Excellency shifted into business-to-be-done mode. 'And, bleeze,' he asked, turning to me, 'Where eeze the house?'

'This is it,' I replied, pointing to our abode. 'This is Brambledown; this is the house.'

'No, bleeze, I mean the beeg' – he gestured expansively with both arms – 'the Beeg Brambledown...the Beeg House?'

'This is it right here,' I repeated, brightly. 'Brambledown House: 3–4 principal bedrooms, 4–5 secondary bedrooms, three and a half bathrooms and a cloakroom, front hall, parlour, drawing room, morning room, study, dining room... the usual suite of domestic offices, including a large kitchen.... Just over there,' I turned away slightly and gestured back, over my shoulder, 'is the three-bedroom gardener's cottage....'

'No, bleeze,' His Excellency pronounced, this time – the unhappy truth dawning – half regretfully, half apologetically. 'Eeze house no enough beeg. My fam'bly: many wives, many sons, many daughters, many grandchildren... nieces and nebhews....' He swept his white-robed arm in an arc through the plane of the gardens... paused, as if trying to establish whether any of his entourage might have wandered off into the adjacent fields and gotten lost... then arced it back again. 'I must have beeg house – really *beeeeeg* house – weeth....'

'Many apartments. Many, separate apartments,' I concluded for him, resignedly.

His Excellency's eyes began to glow with patriarchal pride. 'Yeess,' he intoned. 'Weeth many abartments. You see... my fam'bly not al-

ways one beeg habby. So I must have *hareem* with sebarate abartments for women, and *majlis*... conference room with lobbies... for
men.'

· · · · · · · · · · · · · · · · · · · ·

That first couple who viewed: they thought Brambledown was too
big, Alter-natis. Then along comes His Excellency the Sheikh, who
thinks the property's too small....

*As older-fashioned, 'huntin' 'n' shootin' Brits might say: it's 'hors-
es for courses', d'Arcy.*

I've never been quite sure what that old saw means.

*Literally, it means which horse you choose depends on how and
where you want to go and over what kind of terrain you have to
travel. By extension, it can connote almost any selection process. As
I've just proposed, for example, it means: 'which house you choose
depends on how and where you want to live and the number of
people you need to accommodate'.*

Those choices sound easy enough to make....

*Metaphorically, of course, it's all about travelling 'the course' of
life – as an individual, a society, a community of societies... a sustainable, global anthroposphere – and, along the way, having to rec-
oncile the necessary co-contingent ends and means.*

Wow! Going from choosing horses for courses to reconciling the
co-contingent ends and means necessary for a sustainable anthroposphere.... That's tough, Alter-natis. That's *really* tough. Are enough
people out there prepared to attempt it? Are you and I prepared to
attempt it?

· · · · · · · · · · · · · · · · · · · ·

With the arrival of August's 'dog days'*, pretty much every constructive activity on which Yr Correspondent relied to keep himself
amused – selling Brambledown, buying the Heartsease Hall Estate...
completing, on time, his FHA reports – effectively ceased. It was very
frustrating. To maintain at least the illusion of constructive endeav-
our:

In respect of selling Brambledown, after much desultory discussion
N and I decided to do that which was in effect already done: withdraw the property from the market for what remained of the summer
and re-offer it in the autumn... at a lower price, of course.

In respect of buying Heartsease Hall....

The full implications of the UK's summer recess for progressing

---

* The hottest days of summer and so called by the ancient Greeks and Romans,
we're told, because Sirius – the 'Dog Star' – is then ascendant.

our purchase began to be revealed on 15 August when I telephoned Chief Suit, aka Old Stoneface, and put to him our probable need for a bridging loan. He said 'yes' immediately but then advised affably that it 'might be awhile' before he could get the supporting paperwork turned around. That wasn't the sort of expedition Yr (Executive-executive) Correspondent was looking for.

Chief Suit then asked what we intended to use as collateral for our previously-agreed mortgage facility: Heartsease Hall, the farmland, or the estate as a whole. Until that moment, no one had actually flagged this issue, and I'd therefore assumed it was a relatively unimportant one. Could it, in fact, be critical? Egad! I confessed to Chief Suit that I didn't have a formal, considered answer to his question but, off-the-cuff, I suggested perhaps a loan against the farmland would be best since our interest expenses should then be able to be offset against farm income. 'I'll talk to our advisers and get back to you as quickly as I can,' I assured him. 'That'll be just fine,' Chief Suit replied mellifluously before adding that, owing to staff vacations, his office was now more or less closed 'until after the Summer Bank Holiday' – that's to say roughly the next two weeks. There was therefore, he confided, 'no need to hurry'.

Well, I thought, at least I can wrap this business up *my* end and get it off *my* desk. So I telephoned our accountant to get his opinion on which was the best surety to pledge... only to be told by his secretary that he was on the beach in the south of France and, therefore, 'out of touch'. So I sought the counsel of Euan... whose para-legal vouchedsafe she was 'pretty sure' he was 'sailing with his family somewhere off the coast of Cornwall' but that, wherever he was, she'd been instructed to disturb him 'only in the case of life-or-death emergencies'. (Imagine: a time, not all that long ago, when higher-level service-sector professionals on holiday felt free to turn their cell phones off!)

In desperation and because, obviously, our mode of collateralization could have implications for structuring the contract or contracts of sale, I got off a letter to Sir Roald asking which of the three options under review best suited him. (I also apologized preemptively for whatever problems this late-arising issue might pose, pointing out – almost certainly unnecessarily – that N and I'd never bought a heartsease hall estate before and doing so was proving to be 'very much a voyage of discovery'.)

A few days later – Hooray! – Sir Roald wrote back to say that so far as he was concerned any of the proposed collateralizations was entirely acceptable, so N and I should do whatever best suited *our* purposes ... 'always assuming there are no objections from my trustees or my lawyers... none of whom, I regret to report, have I been able to contact'.

· · · · · · · · · · · · · · · · · · · ·

It was 'Summertime', d'Arcy, and as DuBose Heyward – a Carolina native (but later, a New York City resident) who probably never imagined cool, rainy, UK-like summers could ever, anywhere, obtain – put it in his 1935 hit-song, 'the livin' (was) easy'. No one was bothered about the sale of some musty old estate to you then.

N and I could, I suppose, have just capitulated and joined everyone else on holiday....

But I assured you your urgence would win in the end. Because behind it – informing and driving forward virtually all of the concerned parties – stalked that most plenipotent of motivators: what the great, Scottish economist Adam Smith called 'self-interest'.

And you wittered on and on about the need for me to be patient. Ambrose Bierce, I pointed out, in his *The Devil's Dictionary*, defined patience as 'a minor form of despair disguised as a virtue'.

In the meantime, I advised, you simply must sit back and relax – 'chill out' as your elder son used to say. Que sera, sera.

I felt an Oren Arnold moment coming on. In his Prayer of the Modern American, he wrote: 'Dear God, I ask that you give me patience... and that you give it (to) me right now!'

· · · · · · · · · · · · · · · · · · · ·

Even the asinine-accommodation issue proved impossible definitively to resolve.

On 2 August, I'd received a letter from Sir Roald dealing with several matters left open at our 26 July meeting (the status of the sitting tenants in Front Lodge and Bottom Cottage, and N's proposed purchase of some cases of wine stored in the Hall's cellars) at the end of which he advised me in his usual, graceful way that 'a complication' had arisen over the donkeys. With bated breath, I read on. A neighbour, it now seemed, wanted to have them and, for a variety of reasons, Sir Roald had decided – 'assuming (my) agreement' – to proceed with this alternative arrangement. He concluded: 'It may be this news will come more as a relief to you than a disappointment.' It does indeed, I chortled!

But in a lengthy postscript to his subsequent, advisers-uncontactable 'collateralization' letter, in which he dealt with more unresolved 26-July matters (some furniture in the Hall belonging to his sister Oriana, who lived with her husband and two daughters in Vienna, and a damaged Festing memorial plaque – formerly hung in the round-towered, St Lawrence's Church but now propped against a wall in the estate's stables – in which English Heritage was interested), Sir Roald revealed: 'It seems the donkeys may not after all be favoured with accommodation at our neighbour's.' If they aren't, he continued, 'may I assume you remain ready to take them on as previously agreed?'

. . . .

Well, of course, Sir Roald. Like you, I'm a man of my word....
    (Deleted!)

. . . .

In the midst of all this indeterminacy came a sad little moment: the departure from our household of the lovely Lauren. Some weeks previously, she'd given N her notice saying she wanted 'to travel and see the world' but, with so much going on, the import of her message didn't really sink in until just after lunch on 12 August when a girl-friend arrived with her car to pack Lauren up and take her away.

The official farewell was scheduled for 1600 hours in Bramble-down's forecourt. As that hour approached, I found myself wanting to be neither too near the designated point of Lauren's departure – 'hovering with tender intent', so to speak – nor too far away, that's to say out of her sight and, maybe, out of her mind as well. So I withdrew to one of the terrace gardens – a middle distance – where I plucked disconsolately at some weeds. At the appointed time, Lauren bounded out of our front door – she hardly ever walked anywhere I recalled, fondly – put her luggage in the girlfriend's car, bounded up the path and over to me, put her hands on my shoulders, looked deep into my eyes, gave me a lingering kiss on the lips... and then bounded off.

Now, I mourned, there'd be no more light-hearted squabbles over politics, religion and 'the meaning of life', no more deadly-serious attempts to grind me down during cross-country runs, or squash or tennis matches... no more flouncy, flirty eyes, no more wholesome, winsome smiles bridging cascading tresses of gold.... Lauren was one of my very favourite *au pairs*, for her strength and goodness of character, the enthusiasm and thoroughness with which she did her job, and the occasional *frisson* of.... Oh, I don't really know what of...

. . . .

Oh yes you do, d'Arcy!

. . . .

... she brought to our lives. It was indeed, I concluded, as the 16th /17th-century English writer Richard Barnfield lamented in his *The Shepherd's Complaint*: 'all is amiss (because) Love is dying, Faith's defying, Heart's denying.' Amen.

But as the ever-ready Barnfield soon enough rejoiced in a follow-on piece entitled *The Shepherd's Content*: 'Fortune is full of fresh variety.' And so it came to pass that towards the end of a fine, sunny afternoon (14 August to be precise, just two days after Lauren's departure) arrived our new *au pair*: Fiona – soon to be dubbed 'Big Fee' – a tall, curvy, former catwalk model and beach-volleyball semi-professional from New Zealand with the most lovely dark hair and mocha-cream skin, and a smooth, forward-going leg action which, were she a four-hoofed filly, would surely have attracted mega-bids at any bloodstock sale.

Wow! Did I long to do *hongi* (touch noses in greeting as Malayo-Polynesian peoples may do) with her. (If only she'd lean down, or I'd a box – some sort of mounting-block... perhaps – to stand on....) Indeed, I wondered why on earth N was prepared to have such a glorious package about the premises. Perhaps, in the job interview, the young woman had said she couldn't abide even the sight of short, fat, older men....

. . . .

Even privately to admit to such an aversion would be very unwise, I cautioned. In this era of mindless egalitarianism, for a woman to dismiss a man merely on the basis of his height, BMI (body mass index) and/or age is bound to be actionable in some court of law.

. . . .

A few days later, while N and I were enthusing – as we regularly did – about the lovely Festing-family heirlooms we'd soon be acquiring, and rejoicing in how greatly they'd enrich our Heartsease Hall living, N proposed that Sir Roald and Lady Maureen should have in return some keepsake, however modest, of the d'Arcy Henrys. I quickly agreed and determined that on my next trip to Baltimore I'd retrieve one of my father's family's old silver spoons. Dating from the time of America's Revolutionary War*, that's to say shortly before the present Heartsease Hall was built, and initialed 'J. d'A. H.' ('Joshua d'Arcy Henry'), it should be just the thing, I felt.

---

* The British, understandably shy of being styled for the historical record as tyrants wanting top(pl)ing, generally prefer to reference America's 'War of Independence'.

Chapter 6

Settling to the Line

Ispent the turn of August into September 1994 on FHA business in India. As I flew back to London from Bombay (now Mumbai) – where, let my suffering for the weal of Our Firm be acknowledged, the temperature in the International Departure Lounge hovered around 112° F; the air conditioning system, we were told, had broken down – I had, in addition to my consulting assignment, a lot on my mind.

First, of course, was selling Brambledown. The so-called 'autumn property marketing window' in the UK was then or would very soon be ajar and, in the hope of persuading a crush of prospects to barge through it, we'd scheduled further advertisements in *The Sunday Times* and *Country Life*. Then there were the two earlier-referenced issues associated with buying the Heartsease Hall Estate – the bridging loan we needed until the funds locked up in Brambledown could be released, and the purchase-contract restructuring we wanted to tax-optimize our mortgage – as well as a third and even more critical issue which, in Euan's memorable understatement, had 'somehow just popped up': confirmation that Sir Roald's legal title to the estate was 'clear', that's to say that he did, in fact, own the property.

• • • • • • • • • • • • • • • • • • • •

Surely, d'Arcy, after 350 years in the same family....

• • • • • • • • • • • • • • • • • • • •

And all of this, I groaned, against the background of the UK's Summer Bank Holiday: a three-day celebration analogous in some respects to Labor Day weekend in the US, which is usually held over the last Saturday, Sunday and Monday in August.

When I first arrived in England, I reflected, the designated Monday – literally, the Bank Holiday; the day when all banks were officially closed – was taken off, and that was that. Now, many people quit work the Thursday before the holiday weekend 'to avoid the Friday traffic', and don't return to their offices until the Wednesday (or Thursday) after it 'to avoid the Tuesday (or Wednesday) traffic' or, in extreme cases, until Monday of *the following week*. My schedule, I noted wistfully, didn't permit such an excess of leisure and, I added testily, neither should theirs.

· ·

More evidence of the UK's decline and, by implication, the decline of The Motherland and the West, the German philosopher Oswald Spengler would probably have observed. Anyway, you've always had trouble taking time off... kicking back and relaxing.

Not when I was younger, Alter-natis. At school and at college, I used to take weeks, months... entire years off.

You've changed then?

I'm getting older; I see that my time is limited.

That's a bit of a non-sequitur, isn't it? Surely you could argue in favour of kicking back and relaxing even more now, so as to better enjoy your 'limited time'.

I like working, generally; in particular, I like the focus and the definition it gives me. And I've got to leave my mark, that's to say accomplish something.

So you've finally succumbed to the Protestant work ethic: the need to justify your existence – in your case, your very privileged existence – by doing worthwhile things.

What's 'Protestant' got to do with it? Are you suggesting that non-Protestants, for example, Catholics – not to mention Jews, Muslims, Hindus... Buddhists and so on – don't do worthwhile things?

No; peoples of all faiths do worthwhile things, of course. But as the German sociologist Max Weber proposed about a hundred years ago, the roots of modern, free-enterprise capitalism lie in Protestant asceticism. The phrase 'Protestant work ethic' simply acknowledges that brief period in human history beginning, say, two hundred years ago, when Protestants and the socio-economic systems they created reigned supreme.

You refer to that supremacy in the past tense... as if it's over now. Has the period of Protestant asceticism and free-enterprise capitalism come to an end?

Protestant 'asceticism' certainly seems to have; in the UK and parts of northern Europe – southern Europe never really embraced Protestantism, let alone asceticism – and especially in The Motherland, the past half-century has seen the rise of a veritable pandemic of conspicuous consumption and other forms of self over-indulgence and, as you know, the accretion of colossal public and private-sector debt!

But 'free-enterprise capitalism'? I don't know. It has, self-evidently, a very considerable capacity for dysfunction and self-harm which it's the responsibility of all of us who rejoice in it to try to contain.

In China, India, Brazil and many other emerging markets, however, the evidence strongly suggests that capitalism – often top-down, 'dirigiste', state capitalism but, in many of its bottom-up specifics, egregiously free-enterprise – is growing and expanding... winning new converts every day.

By the way, Alter-natis: what do you mean by 'doing worthwhile things'?

Whatever you mean by 'accomplish something', d'Arcy.

'I met a traveller from an antique land Who said: Two vast and trunkless legs of stone Stand in the desert... Near them, on the sand, Half sunk, a shattered visage lies, whose frown, And wrinkled lip, and sneer of cold command....'

Alas poor Shelley. His dispirited English-romantic-era traveller famously concludes: 'And on the pedestal, these words appear: "My name is Ozymandias, king of kings: Look on my works, ye Mighty, and despair!" Nothing beside remains. Round the decay Of that colossal wreck, boundless and bare, The lone and level sands stretch far away.'

. . . .

It was therefore with a mixture of surprise and delight that I found on my return to Brambledown letters from: his excellency the Chief Suit confirming our bridging loan was OK, our accountant confirming collateralization of the farmland was OK and, finally, Euan confirming Sir Roald's title to the Heartsease Hall Estate was OK.

. . . .

Surely, after 350 years in the same family... that last hadn't much news value.

No. The news value was tucked away in a short advisory toward the end of our lawyer's letter: that, in reaching their conclusion, the UK Land Registry people were statutorily obliged to search back only twenty years. In theory – and as in practice we learned to our dismay more than a decade and a half later – if Sir Roald's title to the estate had been compromised in some way, say, twenty years plus one day ago....

. . . .

In short, the British nation's aestivation seemed finally to have concluded and the great gearwheels of its financial, accounting and legal machinery – perhaps even, I prayed, the little cogs of its Cotswolds estate-agency machinery – to have resumed their turning. Or alternatively put: Yr (Increasingly anxious) Correspondent's elevation to the status of English country squire suddenly began to loom much, much larger. In anticipation of this Great Leap Upward, I scheduled two meetings for the afternoon of Friday, 23 September: with a chartered surveyor to value the Heartsease Hall Estate, and with its then land agent (in the UK, the professional manager of an agricultural property) to review its farming, etc, operations. For the Saturday morning following, I arranged with Sir Roald and Lady Festing that the Henrys would all stop by the Hall and take one last, pre-purchase look, as a family, at what they were letting themselves in for.

In the interim, I received from Sir Roald the Consignment List of furniture available for our purchase. It set out nearly one hundred lots – all offered at prices which seemed fair almost to the point of self-abnegation – and included a number of the pieces N and I most coveted; among them was the magnificent, seven-leaf 'Lord Nelson' dining room table.

. . . .

An acquisition opportunity almost as exciting as that of the Heartsease Hall Estate itself, I remarked.

Yes, I reflected with quiet pride, now the Hall could be furnished substantially as it should be furnished, that's to say authentically, in late 18th- and early 19th-century style...

... which is to say in the style to which you were already largely accustomed.

I'd always liked Georgian arts and crafts both for themselves and as expressions of the enlightening, humanist mind-set from which they sprung. In particular, the unassuming elegance and, of course, the easy utility of Georgian furniture struck me as pleasing. My parents' house in Baltimore contained some very good American Georgian, or 'Colonial', pieces: a wardrobe, a couple of drop-leaf desks, a dining room table and a set of twelve chairs, all of mahogany.... Georgian is what I grew up with; I was literally at home with that style then and I still feel at home with it now.

Indeed....

On the other hand, I've always thought what fun it would be to live in a modernist house: one designed by Louis Henry Sullivan, the Boston-born architect who coined the famous phrase 'form ever follows function', say, or Frank Lloyd Wright, or Adolph Loos, or Walter Gropius, or Mies van der Rohe, or 'Le Corbusier' (as Charles-Edouard Jeanneret styled himself) or Philip Johnson... to name just a few. I like the clarity and rectitude of the architectonic statements modernist structures make externally, and the freedom implicit in their open-plan, 'minimalist' interiors. Decorated in neutral colours such as whites, off-whites and beiges, and boldly appointed with furniture precision-engineered from metal and glass, or clean-cut from wood and stone....

Paintings and sculptures – artworks of all periods and places: out-of-Africa pre-historic, Eastern-Mediterranean and Asian ancient, European Renaissance, Baroque, Romantic and Impressionist... everything, really, including North and South American and global Modern and Post-modern – show so well in simple, uncluttered, modernist settings....

Indeed....

But then I've also long admired fortified medieval manor houses. There're still a few of them remaining in the UK: Aydon Castle in Northumberland, Ightham Mote in Kent, Oakham Manor in Rutland, Ockwells Manor in Berkshire, Stokesay Castle in Shropshire.... 'Architects' as we know them weren't around when those rough and ready piles were raised, you know, Alter-natis; that role was accomplished by 'master builders'.

With their resolute exterior defences and thick inner walls, such structures always give me a feeling of sanctuary and security like somehow I'd managed to return to the womb. I've often imagined myself holding court in a 'Great Hall' – the business head office *cum* family living room, literally, which was the heart of the manor house – sitting in front of a roaring fire surrounded by blazing candelabra and sconces, with epic tapestries insulating the walls, and animal skins ditto the floors... and packs of rough-coated dogs, bevies of full-hipped wenches and pods of cherubic children loitering around.

Indeed, indeed! But what about a cave? A nice, snug cave... with a view... and a hearth, and a three-legged stool of some sort, and a simple, wooden table and a straw-mattressed pallet for a bed like some ascetics – the Saddhu Hindus in India, the Buddhist Shaolin in China... the Christian Copts in Egypt, for example* – often call home?

A cave? Why would I, a closet *bon vivant*, want to live in a cave?

For one who so ardently advocates greater spiritualism, your sense of 'self' still seems very deeply anchored in material things. If you stepped back from these temporal distractions and lived closer to nature, took more time out to offer thanks – it doesn't really matter to whom you offer those thanks; you can just 'thank goodness', as the American philosopher Daniel Dennett has suggested – simply for being alive....

You're right, Alter-natis; I should be more regularly thankful and, someday, I will be. But, right now, I've really got to....

· · · · · · · · · · · · · · · · · · · ·

Sir Roald's letter also enclosed a 'Loan List', as he called it, itemizing household furniture we were welcome to use until such time as he and

---

* Jews and Moslems, whose primarily desert living was fundamentally very hard, *ab initio* placed far less emphasis on self-denial and abstinence, we're told.

Lady Maureen bought another country house or we sold Bramble-down, 'whichever happens first'.

I decided to decline Sir Roald's offer of the loan items – it would be easier, it seemed to me, to scavenge *pro tem* the few things we might need from Brambledown – but I put a check next to two dozen or so lots on the Consignment List, conferred with N... and then checked two dozen or so more. All this finalizing of arrangements for disposing of chattels and furnishings, I mused, but still no contract exchange!

Sir Roald's letter concluded by saying how very much Lady Mau-reen was looking forward to seeing N, the boys and me when we came down at the weekend but that he, 'unhappily, (had) to be oth-erwise engaged'. Sir Roald gave no details of his otherwise 'engage-ment', but the infelicity he charged to it made me uneasy. Indeed, I feared the Old Boy might not be well.

And so it proved. When on 20 September I telephoned Heartsease Hall to confirm to him our likely time of arrival, Lady Maureen an-swered the phone. We exchanged pleasantries; I asked to speak to Sir Roald; Lady Maureen told me he'd just gone into hospital to have 'a growth of some sort' in his neck removed. 'It's been troubling him for the past several months or so,' she explained matter-of-factly, then quickly added: 'but he's expected to be out of action for only about a week'.

A 'growth' could, of course, be almost anything, I considered. But its removal from a fair-haired, fair-skinned, Nordic-phenotype of Sir Roald's age sounded ominous to me.

· · · · · · · · · · · · · · · · · · · ·

Imagine: all that... that, at best, health *uncertainty*... weighing on Sir Roald's mind throughout my extended negotiations with him, and he never referring to it.

The battle-hardened, WWII-era Brits – the 'get-on-with-it' types who, you'll remember, for years after the fighting itself ended had to endure strict food, fuel and clothing rationing – have upper lips as stiff as carbon steel! The post-war, 'entitlement' generation – or, at least, the vocal minority of it which attracts so much media atten-tion – is shamelessly softer and more effete.

In the wild, animals who're infirm whether through illness or in-jury are, almost inevitably, some hungry predator's next meal. The capacity to shrug off infirmity – dismiss it, even – can, therefore, be literally a matter of life or death, Alter-natis.

A certain calibre of human – the 'winners', it seems to me – some-how find the means of dismissing infirmity much as animals do,

d'Arcy.
. . . .

N, the boys and I spent the night of 22 September at our London flat, then drove to Heartsease Hall the next day. It was the first time we'd done the north-Norfolk-via-London routing – previously, we'd always driven straight from Brambledown – and in its opening, metropolitan stages at least, a hugely interesting journey it was: down King's Road to Sloane Square, turning south through Pimlico and *en route* getting a glimpse of Chelsea Hospital and its grounds, then east and north along the Thames, winding past the Tate Gallery until we reached Westminster Abbey and the Houses of Parliament, then an 'uphill' 270 degrees around Parliament Square – Buckingham Palace and St James's Park to the west and, to the north, Downing Street and the great government buildings of Whitehall (the Treasury, the Home Office, the Foreign Office, the Admiralty and the War Office) and also the Banqueting Hall, Horse Guards Parade and Trafalgar Square (with 'our own' Lord Nelson on his column, overlooking 'our own' William Wilkins', Junior's, National Gallery) – before returning, at Westminster Bridge, to the river with its *moto perpetuo* of commercial and pleasure craft, and going east along the Embankment below Charing Cross[*], the South Bank arts complex (now decorated with one of the world's largest Ferris wheels, the magnificent 'London Eye') to our right and Somerset House immediately to our left and, beyond it, Covent Garden, Bush House (on whose BBC World Service Yr Correspondent used occasionally to broadcast) and the Law Courts, then along Upper Thames Street – parallel to Fleet Street (out of certain of whose editorial offices Yr Correspondent used for some years to write) and Ludgate Hill – just south of the venerable legal societies of Gray's Inn, Lincoln's Inn and The Temple, and St Paul's Cathedral (now with its sight-line across the Millennium Bridge to the Tate Modern museum) passing below Pudding Lane, where the Great Fire of London started, and Mansion House, the Corn Exchange... the Bank of England, the Stock Exchange – the heart of the City's 'Square Mile', that's to say some of the most expensive commercial property on earth – under London Bridge (not 'falling down', but sturdily up-standing!) and along to Trinity Square, past the simple, stone memorial to merchant mariners MIA (missing in action) 'who

---

[*] Where, in 1290, King Edward I had erected a cross-memorial to his Chère Reine (Beloved Queen) Eleanor.

have no grave but the sea'... the Tower of London and Tower Bridge, then into Docklands (on part of which would later rise the Millennium Dome) with its view of the Canary Wharf business complex – intimations of new 'empire' arising from the detritus of the old – past London Airport and the awe-inspiring Thames Flood Barrier....

The historic and the contemporary, the staid and the swinging, the practical and the whimsical: a panorama of some of the world's greatest architecture in the heart of one of the world's greatest cities.

· · · · · · · · · · · · · · · · · · · ·

Why on earth have you included this extraordinary itineration?
Partly as a prose example of 'emotion recollected in tranquility' which, you'll remember, was William Wordsworth's 1802 take on the stuff of poetry. I find London's riverine cityscape absolutely enchanting but because of the heavy, fast-moving traffic, I can't sufficiently appreciate it while I'm driving through.

And partly because I thought Anglophile Readers – past and present visitors to London, especially – might enjoy this along-memory-lane interlude.
· · · · · · · · · · · · · · · · · · · ·

Shortly after 1500, we arrived at our hotel (in view of the foregoing, the Reader may be relieved that we arrived at all) and checked in; then, after dispatching N and the boys via our room to the hotel's swimming pool, I drove in fine, bright sunshine the short distance to Heartsease Hall in good time for the start of my 1600 meeting with the chartered surveyor...

... to find the chartered surveyor already well into his work – indeed, nearly finished his work. We shook hands – I winced as the big man's vice-like grip closed down, then I remembered being told he used to stroke the Cambridge University (rowing) crew – and set about confirming the apparent position. So, I asked, have you been around the fields and the woodlands? 'Yes,' the fellow replied, 'it's such a lovely day... there's no point wasting it, sitting in an office, is there?' And the farm buildings and the cottages? 'Un-huh; there's a pile of deskwork I could've done... should've done, probably. But with the season just on the turn like this, from glorious summer to glorious autumn....' So now you're surveying the Hall? 'Well, actually I've surveyed the Hall, mostly. It's beautiful! Absolutely beautiful! I might just have to go up onto the roof and check out one or two things – I'll bet there's a really fantastic view from up there; you can see right the way across to the North Sea, can't you? – but the numbers are pretty much done....'

Good Lord, I thought. This fellow's almost as taken with Hearts-ease Hall as N and I are; it's a wonder he didn't enter the competition to buy it. We then moved on to what I'll call 'A Lesson in How "The Game" Is Played'.

. . . .

Just remind me, d'Arcy: what are the rules of 'The Game'?

They're very simple: the chartered surveyor estimates – 'objective-ly', for The Suits – the market value of the Heartsease Hall Estate to confirm their loan is properly secured; I pay the chartered surveyor for his valuation. In sum, that's all there is to it.

Doesn't the fact you're paying the chartered surveyor create a potential conflict of interest for him? Suppose his valuation suggests you've agreed to cough up more for the property than it's actually worth? 'He who pays the piper calls the tune,' you know.

Perhaps. But the surveyor's publicly bound legally and profes-sionally – not to mention privately bound morally and ethically – to assign to the property the value he thinks is correct; if he didn't do so, the system simply wouldn't work. And, ultimately, of course, 'the market's always right...' or so we're told. In the meantime....

. . . .

Honourable chartered surveyor made a few final calculations and wrote down his valuation total – double-underlining it with a flourish – on his worksheet. Then, positively radiating conspiratorial glee, he turned to me and asked in a heavy stage whisper: 'So how much are you paying for it... the estate, that is?' With some misgivings – after

113

all, if his objectivity were to be strictly maintained, this was the one number he *shouldn't* know – I told him.

'Hmmmm,' he said pensively. 'Is that all?' I nodded. A look of dismay came over the big man's face. He returned to his valuation worksheet, penciled in an adjustment or two, and then made what was clearly the entry of some new numbers into his calculator.

'Let me just run through this again,' he said, drawing himself up to his full, 6'4"–6'5" height. 'You're buying the Hall and a very considerable range of outbuildings, five cottages and all of this farmland – of which I make it 700 acres at least is prime arable (very fertile) – together with a hundred or so acres of woodlands and lakes....' A long pause, then: 'Whew! You're paying about eight per cent – maybe as much as ten per cent – *less* than I think this property should be worth. That's not enough... not really enough... unless, of course, you're Sir Roald's preferred purchaser.' He paused again then, smiling resignedly, tipped me a big wink. 'You could, of course, raise your bid for the property; that would certainly be the decent... the *American* thing to do....' I scrunched myself down and in vain scanned the room for some 'rock' analogue I could hide under.... 'Otherwise, I'll just have to do the British thing and adjust my numbers.'

After some further massaging, a new valuation was printed out. 'There,' honorable chartered surveyor advised me genially, 'I took a bit off the value of the Hall – it probably *does* require more repairing than I'd allowed for – and on the grounds that the farming tenancy and contracting arrangements may prove more difficult than I'd thought to restructure, I've revised the estimated income, and thus the farmland values, down a bit. The new total's come out only 4–5 per cent above your offer.'

Chuckling grimly to himself, he continued: 'I've got a farm myself, you know, about the same size as the Heartsease Hall Estate; in fact, it's a little larger. And let me tell you: either you've got a real bargain here....'

· · · · · · · · · · · · · · · · · · · ·

My thoughts turned to poor Sir Roald lying in his hospital bed, Alter-natis.

If ever anyone deserved not to be on the wrong side of a bargain – even one in which the counter-party might be his 'preferred purchaser' – it was he.

· · · · · · · · · · · · · · · · · · · ·

'... or I'm not quite as fortunate as I'd thought I was,' the chartered surveyor concluded.

. . . .

EMT, that's to say *Efficient Market Theory. I've never felt I really understood its surmise, but doesn't it posit that the price at which something is bought or sold is,* ceteris paribus, *always the right price?*

Pretty much.

So how could you have gotten a 'bargain', d'Arcy?

Well for a start, efficient market theorists don't speak of 'bargains', Alter-natis. They speak of 'anomalies'.

What, in this context, are 'anomalies'?

They're things that are bought or sold at the wrong price.

Oh....

That's how the punters make their money. They buy or sell things which should be at the right price when, in fact, they're at the wrong price.

Why then, in efficient markets, do anomalies happen?

Because efficient markets aren't really all that efficient. In fact, over the short run – and, many economists would argue, even over the longer run – they're pretty *in*efficient.

Would you believe it: in*efficient, efficient markets! Surely one day pigs must fly.*

Behavioral economics and, more pointedly, the investment guru George Soros' notion of 'reflexivity', which proposes that certain asset prices are determined almost entirely by self-reinforcing, intra-market feedback systems rather than 'the iron laws' of traditional economics, address this issue....

. . . .

After a quick word with Lady Maureen – who assured me Sir Roald was 'just fine... absolutely fine' – I returned to the hotel for meeting number two, with the land agent, and 'Another Lesson in How...'.

. . . .

It must have been very chastening for you, an international man-agement consultant and business-school guest lecturer – as well, of course, as a seriously-knowledgeable American – to have to suffer so many lessons. And the rules of this second game?

The land agent's job is to maximize sustainable revenue from the Heartsease Hall Estate's farming, etc, operations and, in so doing, earn himself a fat little fee. As the estate's 'hot-shot, new-broom owner', my job is to rethink those farming, etc, operations with a view to finding as many improvement opportunities as possible, that's to say to sweep relatively clean.

Even if that means a reduced role and reduced fees for honorable land agent?

Even so, Alter-natis.

It was the conflict-of-interest thing again! You didn't then know very much about larger-scale arable farming, of course – and still don't. But if you struck lucky and by chance happened on an improvement opportunity, the land agent could feel tempted to argue against any changes you might propose....

Or fall on his sword.

. . . .

I greeted the land agent and his comely assistant (amazingly they were clones, almost, of the Heartsease Hall selling agent and his comely assistant...) in the hotel lobby, found an empty table with some chairs, sat down and ordered drinks. While the waitress was bringing them, I delivered my set piece. I had, I said, four broad concerns: to take a more active role in the management of the farming; to make the farming income-distribution system fairer such that I shared more of the risk and, hopefully, more of the reward; to fine-tune the farming and, thereby, improve farm productivity; and, lastly, to squeeze a bit more profit out of the farming.

Honourable land agent, his expression somehow managing to combine the absent-mindedness of the mad scientist with the total focus of the nursing vixen-fox surveying a full roost in the chicken coop, opined he had no quarrel with the theory of any of that... 'just, perhaps, the practice'. His comely assistant nodded supportively.

The first problem was legal, the land agent said. Several of the farming arrangements had been entered into only recently as part of a reorganization Sir Roald had carried out, he reminded me, and still had a number of years to run; the counterparties to these arrangements would be entirely within their rights not to entertain any changes – particularly changes adverse to their shorter-term interests – until the contracts came up for renewal. The second problem, he said, was 'atmospheric'. Farming folk in north Norfolk were pretty traditional in their thinking and suspicious of change, the land agent advised. A new landlord and – he switched into a sort-of ersatz cowboy drawl – 'one who's a 'Mmurrican as well', proposing too much change too quickly, might generate resentment. In the longer run, that would almost certainly prove counter-productive.

Finally, honourable land agent spoke to my intention to improve productivity and the possible implications of so doing for the bottom line. 'A few pennies' might indeed be trimmed from farming expenditures, he averred, and 'a few pennies' added to farming income.

'But, on the whole,' he assured me fluently, 'your good ship *HH* (Heartsease Hall) *Enterprise* is being sailed pretty tight.' With that, he drained his glass.

All, undoubtedly, very true, I replied diplomatically. So then: how best to address my concerns, I asked? Why... with another round of drinks, of course, 'this one on me'. With a merry wave of his hand, our waitress was summoned, our order placed and, shortly, fresh drinks arrived. We sipped and chatted, chatted and sipped....

Tired from the long drive and the strain of trying to deport myself as an English Country Squire Apparent, and nearly at the lucidity limit of my alcohol intake, my enthusiasm for business matters was fast fading, however. I made one last attempt to pin honourable land agent down and extract from the depths of his canny brain some inkling of how I...

• • • • • • • • • • • • • • • • • • •

Hadn't you better make that 'we', d'Arcy? How you and he, that's to say 'we....'

• • • • • • • • • • • • • • • • • • •

... how *I* might best proceed. I put the question one way; I put it another way... and then another. Honourable land agent and his comely assistant sat and sipped, he listening attentively, she taking notes.... After a while, I looked covertly at my watch; honourable land agent looked covertly at his; the comely assistant looked....

Suddenly, smiling broadly, honourable land agent sat forward in his chair and cleared his throat. 'Farming in north Norfolk is a very long-term commitment, Mr Henry,' he intoned sonorously, his eyes once again taking on that mad-scientist/nursing-vixen glint. 'The important thing is that you start as you intend to go on.' He paused for a moment, studying his now-empty glass. 'Yes, Mr Henry,' he repeated, rising grandly to his feet, 'that's the one most important thing: you must start as you intend to go on.'

I nodded and said I'd reflect on this sage advice – which, indeed, I did. What's more, over supper that evening in the hotel's grill room, I 'down-loaded' it to my resident MBA who (after suggesting 'up-loaded' might better characterise what I'd actually done) concurred that as 'a blueprint for action', it needed a lot more detail.

• • • • • • • • • • • • • • • • • • •

Welcome back, Class. I hope you've had a refreshing summer break because you'll need it. We've a lot of material to cover this term, and some of the concepts we'll be addressing are very challenging and complex – just, you'll find, as is life out there in the real world!

But let's kick off with an easy one. You'll recall our case study of the acquisition of the Heartsease Hall Estate; well, in that regard, the incoming CEO of the estate has just been strongly advised to 'start as (he) intend(s) to go on'. I'd like to begin this session....

Yes, Ms Goldstar: what incoming CEO, you ask? You're right; I should have kept you informed. During one of our earlier seminars – in June, I think it was – we drew up a staffing chart; at that time, we filled in most of the names, but the Class seemed to feel there was no suitable candidate for Estate CEO so we left that slot blank. (Our July session, you'll recall, was pretty much given over to asinine matters.)

Anyway, during the summer, a decision was taken to appoint.... Yes, Che, while you, perhaps, and probably many other northern hemisphere plutocrats were relaxing on holiday at the beach or in the mountains....

Ms Goldstar, again. Who took this decision, you ask? Errr... I mostly did, Ma'am, but.... Anyway, a decision was taken to appoint me as the estate's CEO. What? Shareholder approval? Not in the sense I think you mean and, strictly speaking, not required by our charter of incorporation. No, Ma'am. But I've reason to believe my wife Nikki now supports my appointment – she's a very important shareholder in Heartsease Hall – and The Suits, that's to say those who're financing us, they support it.

So to continue: 'start as you intend to go on'. What, exactly, do we mean by that exhortation? Yes BS, our jock. If you've arranged to meet some mates at the Boar's Head pub, you shouldn't stop off *en route* at the King's Arms pub. That's technically correct, of course, but it's not quite the answer I had in mind. GT? 'Build for the longer term... build for the future,' you say. Spoken like a really good, solid – and, I might add, increasingly hard to find – old-fashioned banker! You're on the right track... you're definitely on the right track.... Anyone else? Yes? No?

OK. I'd paraphrase my mentor's words as: 'Have a destination... know where, ultimately, you want to be.' Now is knowing where you ultimately want to be, in respect of restoring and further developing the Heartsease Hall Estate, say, difficult or easy? Yes, to my right: young lady, dark hair, yellow blouse.... We've lots of input from the ladies here today; what's the matter, guys? Going to let the gals.... Yes, it's difficult; it's pretty darn difficult. Why?

BS, again: because having stopped off at the King's Arms and sunk a few jars (drunk a few pints of beer), you could be so out of it you wouldn't be able to remember exactly.... Good Lord! Yes, Ms Gospel; why...? Indeed: you've got it. It's 'The Vision Thing'. To start as you intend to go on implies you've got a clear mental image, that's to say a well-informed understanding, of what your destination – in the case of our case study, the fully-restored and re-developed, 'ultimate' Heartsease Hall Estate – should be: in short, what it should constitute and how it should operate.

Now one final question: in general, do private-sector, corporate CEOs or, for that matter, heads of government and/or heads of state – public-sector, 'national CEOs' if you will – have a vision? Do they know where they want to be or are they just…? What do you think? Goodness; I've never seen to many hands go up – guys as well as gals! Yes, Che, again….

In a narrow sense you think yes, they do have a vision. They want to remain in power as long as possible, make themselves pots and pots of money and, maybe, even achieve a measure of 'fame'. But in a broader, moral and ethical sense…? You think no; a lot of corporate and national CEOs – the majority of them, perhaps – don't have a vision.

And what? I'm sorry, Ms Gospel, I couldn't hear you; would you repeat…. 'And their lack of a higher-order, longer-focus responsibility in large part explains why our developed-world, free-enterprise, democratic society is today in such a mess,' you say. Excellent; go to the head of the Class! Or better: next time, why don't you come up and stand here, where I am, and *take* the Class. After all, in just a few, short years that's what you'll effectively have to do!

• • • • • • • • • • • • • • • • • • • •

It's always astonishing, N and I later agreed, how much a couple of fold-away beds in a hotel room can complicate the logistics of family co-existence. Closed, as sofas, they frame an amplitude of space in which it's easy for everyone to unwind and relax. Open them up, however, and scatter about them a couple of boisterous boys with their clothes, computer games and other toys…

• • • • • • • • • • • • • • • • • • • •

You're right, Alter-natis: computer games – as distinct from computer simulations – aren't toys. No, no; they're much more… much more… well, 'something' than that. 'Life-like and challenging', that's it; computer games are much more life-like and challenging than toys, and even though their ambit is only virtual, they're really much more real.

And I accept that computer games – even the most fantastical ones – can help you develop useful life skills, to wit how to leap over erupting volcanoes or avoid decapitation by pseudo-Samurai swordsmen, for example, or muster into battle against hydra-headed invaders great swarms of autistic toads. What? No; of course I'm

being serious....
· · · · · · · · · · · · · · · · · · · ·

And so it was after what might, using litotes, be called an 'interesting' overnight at the hotel – which Piglet and Bapu greatly enjoyed, and N and I managed to survive – that we drove to Heartsease Hall for what was to be our final, pre-purchase look-around. Lady Maureen greeted us with the usual selection of issues: the donkeys, the gardens; the donkeys, the paddocks and the stables; the donkeys, their harnesses and carts; the donkeys in and of themselves.... But this time – perhaps because everyone's schedules and thus mind-sets had eased – a major breakthrough was achieved: we were taken out and, by name, actually introduced to the donkeys.

(I didn't know quite what to expect; given the representations to that date, I thought perhaps we might find the gentle jills wearing straw hats or some such, sitting on their haunches proffering their forehooves to be shaken. But no: before us were just two ordinary donkeys, standing with their heavy heads hanging over the paddock fence. Directly the introductions were completed, Lady Maureen asked if anyone would like to give the donkeys 'their little treat'. I volunteered; from a pocket in her cardigan, she produced a carrot and gave it to me. 'But you must feed them properly,' she enjoined sternly. My mind raced. Would that be with me on bended knee? Or worse, noot-to-noot [nose-to nose]? No: it just meant from the palm of my hand rather than with my fingers.)

In this my first, relatively-extended contact with Lady Maureen on her own, I tried to get a better fix on her and what made her tick. Physically, she was a powerfully-built, athletic-looking woman – an

inch or two taller than Sir Roald – strong-featured and handsome in her way. Mentally, she projected a similarly robust specification: that of a doer rather than a thinker – instinctive, energetic and resolute – who formed opinions quickly and offered them freely, often supporting them with emphatic gestures.

Within her private self, however, I sensed less assurance; it was as if Lady Maureen wasn't so much living her own, 'rightful' life as one patched together from the lives of people she'd read about or known. In part, this derivativeness reflected her role as wife to the charismatic Sir Roald – her Pole Star – to whom it was clear she was absolutely devoted and for whom in that time of his medical trial, she must have been verily a bastion of strength. But I felt as well there were a number of things – hard, perhaps even tragic things – Lady Maureen was running away from. And as with so many women of her generation who hadn't had a career (or in her case, sadly, children) – that's to say who hadn't had the chance of an 'own world', *sui generis*, in which to realize themselves – not many she was running towards.

Shortly, Lady Maureen departed saying she'd some shopping to do, leaving the Henry family for the first time all alone with their new home-to-be. The boys went off generally to 'explore' and so, in a more considered and specific way, did N and I. Initially, we just wandered around the exterior of the Hall noting with gradually-intensifying, eleventh-hour interest its blown foundation fascia, string coursing, architraves, jambs and quoins, its delaminated flints, its windows with their deteriorated frames and glazing bars; from ground level, we couldn't see the broken slates and perished lead crests, etc, on the roof....

Then, as our need-to-know gradually overcame our sense of trespass, we went inside for a penultimate review of the entrance hall, the library, the drawing room, the oval ante-room, the dining room, the gun room *cum* cloak room, the kitchen, the laundry, the boot room and the rest of the 'domestic offices' – many with their peeling wallpaper and flaking paint – the boiler (heating and hot water systems) room.... And this was just the ground floor, we reminded ourselves earnestly-off-handedly; above were 12–15 further rooms, all similarly well-lived-in and enjoyed or, otherwise told, all similarly 'tired'.

'Very sound... remarkably sound, really, for a building of its age' the Hall might be, I reflected, but many years of renovation and repair work nonetheless lay ahead. And beyond the Hall were the estate's outbuildings, its farm buildings and cottages, and its woodlands and waterways needing care and attention, and its hodgepodge of farming, residential-tenancy, and other contracting and contractual arrangements – nearly all of them delicate, local political, economic and social issues – needing reorganization.

· ·

What's it like, I asked you, the final moment... the 'Moment of Truth'... entering the astronauts' capsule, sitting down atop half a million gallons or so of high-explosive rocket fuel and being strapped in, hearing the hatch you've just come through – your could-be, last-chance emergency exit – close and triple-lock... before blasting off into the life-as-we-know-it nihility of space?

Ummm....

Or roping up to begin the final assault on the icy, wind-swept summit of Annapurna I or K2? Or setting sail, alone, to thread the stormy Strait of Magellan westward into the vastness of the Southern (Pacific) Ocean? Or armed only with a cape and a sword, confronting the better part of a ton of enraged and pain-crazed fighting bull? Or climbing into the saddle to ride one of the world's most-challenging steeplechases: the English Grand National or the Maryland Hunt Cup, for example?

Or, as a soldier, hurling yourself 'over the top' to advance into raking enemy fire... or padding softly out to defuse an unexploded bomb? Or covering a war, or some other hyper-hot spot, as a front-line photojournalist or reporter?

Yes, I persisted: the Moment of Truth before joining any capital challenge – one in which you put your life on the line.

I said I didn't know, Alter-natis, because I'd never joined any capital challenge. But I expected on the one hand there must be a certain *frisson* of apprehension and/or fear and, on the other, an eagerness – an impatience almost – to get on with it: to see if, after all those months and years of grueling mental and physical preparation, you could actually do what you'd set out to do.

By the way: why did you pose that 'what's-it-like' question then?

*I thought having to answer it would help you put your Heartsease Hall purchase into a proper – that's to say a properly-*modest* – perspective.*

· ·

N and I returned to the entrance hall and there, in spite of John D's, the chartered surveyor's, the land agent's, our friends' and families'... manifold reassurances – our own manifold reassurances, each to the other – and the reflections recorded herein immediately above, we had our own tiny, trifling, Moment of Truth:

'Dar,' N began, 'this isn't going be an exercise in exploring "the

122

good life" in semi-retirement or on holiday in a cottage in Provence or Tuscany, say.' She took a deep breath…. 'It'll be about hands-on managing, 24/7, a very large property – a residential and farming estate *producing* food, rather than gourmet-cooking and eating it – with a very high local, regional… to some extent national, even, profile; remember, Heartsease Hall's officially classified as being of 'exceptional historical and architectural importance to the British nation….' Taking my hands in hers and searching deep into my eyes, N concluded: 'Is this really how we want to spend the rest of our lives, Dar? I mean…the Heartsease Hall Estate's so big, and it needs so much doing to it.'

'Of course!' I replied, willing as much authority and decision into – and dubiety out of – my voice as I could. 'We've always known taking on Heartsease Hall would be much more than just buying a house….'

'I'll say,' N interrupted, 'it'll be like having another full-time job, another career….

. . . .

… another wife… another family, almost.

Yes. And now as you've proposed that link, Alter-natis, I have to write I've long thought male polygamists must have a screw or two loose…

… not to mention truly surpassing mental and physical energy.

. . . .

'Are we really up for this? Are we really, *really* up for this, Dar?'

I looked out of a window in the entrance hall and northwest to St Lawrence's Church, with its generations of Festings – d'Arcy Henrys in due course, maybe – recumbent in its ancient yard; I looked out of the oval ante-room window and southeast across the fields and woodlands… then I panned in to the far bank of the lower lake where disported Piglet and Bapu. No last-minute doubts or hesitations, it appeared, assailed them. From someone, somewhere – good, old Groome, perhaps, mining the tailings around his wretched mobile home – they'd acquired a pair of old fishing poles and, as N and I watched, were attempting their first casts.

'We'd better go make sure they don't fall in and drown,' I said, jokily; N nodded in agreement. Heads down, intent, pre-occupied… trying to get a few, last-minute pre-sights into and pre-confirmations of the only later life we'd ever live, probably, in the only world we'd ever live it in, probably, we found ourselves drawn as if by magnetic force to 'The Brochure-Picture Place' in Pavilion Paddock where the photograph on the front cover of the selling agent's promo had been taken... the place of our epiphany – of our 'miraculous conversion' – on 30 March.

We looked up and out at the herds of fattened cattle and sheep, the five nearly fledged cygnets, the harvest-ready corn shimmering in the breeze, the wild cherries, damsons and sloes, their branches heavy with ripe fruit... at the woodlands, their trees' leaves just starting to colour... at the clear, blue sky dotted with puffy, white clouds below which martins, swallows and swifts tracked to take their mid-day meals... at the Georgian Gothic cathedral-castle with its knapped-flint dragonfish scales – soon to be *our* Georgian Gothic cathedral-castle – standing so magnificently, so proudly... so 'well' as, we learned, the locals say simply... on its purported 'hill'. We swivelled our gaze to Piglet and Bapu with their fishing poles, now thrashing the water like demons. We looked again at each other....

. . . .

'If you can dream – and not make dreams your master; If you can think – and not make thoughts your aim....'

That's a pretty heavy assignment, Alter-natis... I mean, Mr Rudyard Kipling, sir.

'If you can fill the unforgiving minute With sixty seconds worth of distance run, Yours is the Earth and everything that's in it, And – which is more – you'll be a Man, my son!'

Gee! I get where you're coming from – at least I think I do: British, Edwardian-era, male-chauvinist-led, global imperialism. But I'm not sure I'm really....

Hmmmm. It may be Grantland Rice's softer, more liberal-democrat take, as in his Alumnus Football, *is more your style: 'When the One Great Scorer comes to mark against your name, He writes – not that you won or lost – but how you played the Game.'*

. . . .

'So: it needs a little doing up, does it?'

'More than "a little" doing up, Dar; it needs "quite a lot of doing up", really. And that'll tax our patience and our pocketbook for many, many years to come.' She paused, looked down, and prodded a tuft of grass with the toe of her shoe. Then she raised her eyes and peered intensely/calculatingly – and yet easily/comfortably – at me: 'But... so what,' she said.

'Yeah: so what!' I echoed. 'We've got to live somewhere, and it might as well be here.' Shouting to Piglet and Bapu to be careful, N and I turned and, arm-in-arm, walked back up the 'hill' towards 'home'.

On 26 September, Euan telephoned to advise that bar 'a few minor clarifications' we were finally ready for contract exchange. *Multo, multo bene! Multo magnifico!* I exalted.

· ·

Imagine! Only three-and-a-half or so months later than originally scheduled.
　　If, in The Motherland, such a laid-back approach to the paperwork had been taken, and at that late stage something had gone wrong, the writs would have fallen like rain.

· ·

Magnifico.... But wait! What was honourable solicitor in his gentle, unassuming way continuing on to say? That from the standpoint of efficiency – *cost*-efficiency, a concept he knows I'm big on – it'd in fact be better not to exchange right now but to do so at the same time as completion which, he told me, was now 'definitively' scheduled for Tuesday, 11 October, some two weeks hence? Well, OK....

　　Later that day, I wrote to Sir Roald relaying this new news and hazarding that the time when we could all 'crack a bottle of something nice' appeared at last to be in sight. In my letter were enclosed the marked-up furniture Consignment List and a check for [...] as a ten percent deposit on the items in which N and I were interested – the only monies of any sort in respect of our Heartsease Hall purchase we'd paid over to that date.

By the end of September, one-third – one-half, perhaps – of Brambledown's 'autumn marketing season' was completed, over with... done. And although our advertising campaign had generated about a dozen leads – each of which N, her secretary/PA or the estate agent had diligently followed up – we still had no real purchase-prospects.

　　But on 4 October, N's and my spirits were lifted by the arrival to view of a seemingly very promising, up-market, late-middle-aged, husband-and-wife team. From his uniform and 'swagger stick'*, and his side-armed 'chauffeur' – who, clearly, was also his bodyguard – I took it he must be a very senior military man... even before he told me so. She, I shortly learned to my cost, was a sometime concert pianist.

　　Once Brambledown's forecourt and side patio had been 'secured', Mr Military sets briskly off with the chauffeur/bodyguard to reconnoiter the gardens and fields; having nothing better to do, I offer to

---

* A short length of cane or wood, sometimes carried by army or other service officers on parade.

accompany him but am told my 'tagging along' would be 'wholly ancillary', which I took as a 'negative', so I stood down and, instead, offered myself to the ladies' brigade... who condescended to accept me.

Mrs Military, N and I go inside; we view the front hall and the dining room; we proceed to the drawing room.... Like a homing radar,
Mrs Military's attention locks onto our Bechstein grand piano and
the score of Frédéric Chopin's A-flat major *Polonaise*, Opus 53 – 'The
Heroic', as it's popularly known – open on its music stand. 'Which of
you plays?' the lady barks, looking first at N and then at me. Warily,
I raise my hand.... 'Well then,' she continues, in a voice which clearly
brooks no refusal, 'perhaps you'd care to attempt the piece for me?'
OK, I think; anything to progress a sale....

· ·

*When a certain ilk of Brit asks 'do you ride', what they sometimes
mean is have you recently won a major steeplechase like the Chel-
tenham Gold Cup or a flat race Classic like the Epsom Oaks/Derby
or the St Leger. This lady's ostensibly innocent 'do you play' question could be similarly over-loaded, I warned.*

I harked to you, Alter-natis. But other than feigning some sort of
indisposition – a bruised metacarpal, say – what could I have done?
· ·

I sit down and, after an extended pantomime of limbering up my
fingers, flail away at the first few bars of the piece in my usual ham-
handed way. 'No, *no*... NO!' cries Mrs Military, stamping her foot
impatiently. Lamenting that 'like so many men – my husband's a good
example – obsessed with the passing of their prime and their potency...'

· ·

And again, Alter-natis: what could I have said?
    *How about: '"prime"? Yes, Madam; undoubtedly. But "poten-
cy"? If you'll just hang on a minute – or maybe two – I should be
able to demonstrate that you're mistaken.'*
· ·

... their potency', I don't give the opening *Allegro* 'sufficient space',
she dismisses me from the bench, sits herself down at the keyboard
and delivers up a master (? mistress) class on the spot. 'This opening
section – pretty much the entire of the composition, in fact – must
be played *molto maestoso* (very majestically) with pronounced wrist
enunciation,' she directs. She pauses... then: 'You must remember, Mr
Henry, the *polonaise* is a dance for people of consequence: royalty,

landed aristocrats... big *burghers**.' Another pause... during which I ponder whether Mrs Military's glancing reference to Ronald Mc-Donald's super-marque was inadvertent or an attempt at humour and then, finally, the clincher: 'The *polonaise* isn't some hip-hop for sugarplum fairies!'

But to return to *our* main theme: the Militarys appeared to be *very interested* in Brambledown; indeed, they burbled on enthusiastically about which bits of their furniture would go where, and then how easily those dispositions could be altered 'for official receptions and our other important social events'. The viewing ended with Mr having 'reluctantly' to leave for a meeting, and Mrs asking if she could return the next day with her interior-design consultant 'to do some measuring up'. Surely, I reasoned, no one would invest this amount of time and energy if they didn't intend at least to put in a bid.

And indeed, about 48 hours later Mr Military telephoned to advise he'd be out of touch for a few days – 'I'm going on a mission; I can't tell you any more,' he snapped – but that I should expect 'a communication from (his) ADC (*aide-de-camp*/PA) soon'.

'Does that imply, sir, you're going to make us an offer?' I asked hopefully, looking hard at N who was standing nearby.

'Affirmative,' came the reply. 'That is my sure intention.'

I gave the thumbs-up to N – who did a little pirouette – said goodbye, and took myself away to the Bechstein and Chopin's A-flat major *Polonaise* to work on my wrist enunciation. At last, I rejoiced, we were going to receive an offer for Brambledown! Oh boy, oh boy!

N and I spent the afternoon and evening (morning and afternoon, US Eastern Standard Time) of 9 October watching the US dollar and the S&P 500 – the twin, 'Tier-1, core-capital' pillars on which we were relying absolutely to support our purchase of the Heartsease Hall Estate – decline sharply.

. . . .

What *is* it about October on Wall Street, other than the correlation with bear markets and, of course, the great crashes of 1907, 1929, 1987... and 2007–08?

It's the run up to Halloween, when hoydenish hobgoblins and other pranksters....

No: seriously, Alter-natis....

It's the fund managers 'dressing their windows', that's to say

---

* A Germano-Dutch word, now largely archaic, for merchants or tradespeople.

selling to lock in trading profits at the end their accounting year, and the arbitragers playing the 'shorts' off against the 'longs', one minute – or mille-second... as with 'flash-trading', aka 'HFT' ('high-frequency trading') – building positions up and the next taking them down again....

There must be more to it than that....

It's the financial markets – the writhing, venomous, snake-pit financial markets – fuelled by obfuscation, half-truth and lying, and driven by fear and greed, in which insiders ruthlessly exploit outsiders and nearly everyone games the system in the hope of making a quick buck. 'The casino culture', it's sometimes called.

That seems more definitive....

In sum, it's the veritable apotheosis of a free-enterprise, democratic system which has lost most of its raison d'être *and integrity.*

When you get the bit in your teeth, Alter-natis, you certainly....

After all, very few people today invest for the longer-term; in the main, they just trade, that's to say, speculate. Sure, some of the income generated by their various whiffles may, eventually, 'trickle down' to members of the population at large or, as J. K. Galbraith put it in his The Culture of Contentment: *'if one feeds the horse enough oats, some will pass through... for the sparrows.' That outcome (sic) is almost wholly incidental, however; mostly, traders trade only for their own direct and indirect gain.*

Ummmm.

At the end of the day, it's very difficult to see how all of this short-term cycling and re-cycling, at ever-increasing velocities and on ever-reducing margins, of largely-derivative 'assets' – especially when the inevitable marking-to-market of those 'assets' collaterally puts at risk the savings of innocent depositors, shareholders, bondholders and taxpayers – actually grows the nation's and the world's wealth.

That's why I believe such egregiously self-interested, society-at-large-be-damned trading should be heavily regulated or taxed nearly out of existence... or both!

I get it: autumn's financial downheavals are just more 'efficient market' nonsense....

· · · · · · · · · · · · · · · · · · · ·

Oh well, N and I consoled ourselves wearily, we could always try to persuade The Suits to underwrite the purchase of a bit more prime, north-Norfolk farmland....

Tuesday 11 October 1994, the Reader will recall, was to be 'Completion Day' – or, rather, 'Exchange and Completion Day' – on our purchase of the Heartsease Hall Estate. By that mid-afternoon, however, there was no indication either deadline was in fact going to be met.

I thought about contacting Euan – more out of curiosity than any sense of concern – but in deference to the old 'principal-to-principal' principle, I telephoned Sir Roald instead. Had he any idea what the hold-up was?

'No.... Well, the lawyers, I expect,' Sir Roald replied.

'Whose: ours or yours?' I asked.

'I don't know... both, probably.'

'Is it worth trying to put a bit of pressure on?'

'I doubt it; they'll just cover up.'

'Well, Nikki and I are quite content. But is this delay raising any problems for you?'

'None whatsoever.'

I started to move the conversation on to the conflict in Bosnia and the widening US-European rift over how to deal with it – a current international-affairs issue in which I was then personally and professionally interested – but Sir Roald interrupted me. 'By the way, Mr Henry, Lady Maureen and I are pretty much moved out of the Hall,' he began, 'and this weekend we're off for a short holiday in Leningrad, or St Petersburg... or whatever they're calling the place now. It's a trip we booked several months ago. We won't be coming back to Heartsease Hall again, to live.' He paused; I wondered idly what might be coming next. 'Once we're out, if you and your wife and your two boys would care to move in, you're most welcome to do so.'

It took a moment or two for the full import of Sir Roald's offer to register: that with no formal, written contract of any sort in place – nothing but our meeting notes, our exchanged correspondences, our verbal agreement that he would sell and N and I would buy, and a handshake or two – and excepting the small deposit we'd just put down on the consignment-list furniture, no transfer to him of any money, Sir Roald was proposing to turn over to us, more or less literally 'lock, stock and barrel', the Heartsease Hall Estate – his ancestral home of some 350 years – and just walk away.

. . . .

Did you think he really meant it?

Certainly. Sir Roald would never say something he didn't mean.

Did you think his lawyers and trustees would let him do it?

By then, my reading of Sir Roald was that on matters of principle he wouldn't let lawyers, trustees or anyone else stand in his way.

Wow! To exclaim again: a man whose word is his bond. It regularly seems to me there aren't so many of those around nowadays.

It's too bad there aren't more Sir Roalds, for example in business – especially in banking and finance – in the civil services... in government generally.... As you know, many sociologists believe the extent to which trust is formalized and institutionalized in a society's social, economic and political systems – its 'credit systems', broadly-defined – ultimately determines whether that society succeeds or fails.

If you've no faith in the integrity of a system, you won't make the effort to work within it or through it; co-operation, aka 'team effort' – that most basic building block of civilization – simply won't be achieved.

And even more fundamentally, Sir Roalds in families, for example as heads of households. It's vitally important that society in general – and its younger members in particular – have good role models... good exemplars... people they can look up to.

But having to treat with such a high-principled principal – a Sir Roald, for example – can put an awful lot of pressure on the counterparty. Were you sure you were up to it?

I had to be. Having campaigned for and then achieved 'The Office', I had to be up....

So you decided then and there to accept Sir Roald's offer.

Pretty much.

Remind me: what, exactly, did you say?

I was so stunned that, at first, I didn't say anything.

And then? Did you come up with something suitably grandiloquent? Something like: 'Your magnanimous offer is far beyond anything my wife or I could ever have conceived of, and our pleasure in accepting it is transcendent.'?

· · · · · · · · · · · · · · · · · · · ·

'I'll just check with Nikki, Sir Roald,' I replied. 'But I'm sure her answer will be: yes, we'd love to move in. Thank you very, very much.'

'Good; that's settled then. Groome'll be about, in his mobile home; I'll give the Hall's keys to him. Oh, by the way, Mr Henry,' he continued, 'the four kitchen chairs and the kitchen table: we told the removals people to leave them until last, so we'd have something to sit on and eat off and then, in the confusion, they were forgotten about. So they're still here. We can certainly arrange to have them taken away.... But perhaps they'd be of use to you?' I recalled the EA's injunction that we leave Brambledown – its kitchen, especially – looking like a home, and said 'yes' and 'thank you' once again.

The next day, I gave the d'Arcy Henry silver spoon a final polish and tucked it into its presentation box. That's the easy part done, I said to myself; now, I've got to fashion some words suitable to this extraordinary occasion and for someone who's not only learned and wise but also a man of letters. Please, God or Whomever, I implored, inflict not upon me, Yr (Humble-servant) Correspondent, an attack of Writer's Block. Please, let there be no Writer's Block now.

About an hour and a quarter later, my *parvum opus* (including salutation and complimentary close, it was only some 150 words long, implying a final-copy work-rate, give or take punctuation, of roughly two words a minute) was ready. For the record: I wrote that about the time the Festings were acquiring the Heartsease Hall Estate from the Hobarts in north Norfolk, some three thousand mostly transAtlantic miles away in the Crown Colony of Maryland, the d'Arcy Henrys were taking up a Grant of Land from Cecil Calvert, the second Lord Baltimore*. The enclosed d'Arcy Henry spoon, I continued, dated from roughly a century and a half later – just after the end of American's War of Independence, by when the d'Arcy Henrys had established themselves – and was made from melted-down British specie – then a standard of argentine purity and, by extension (for the purposes of my note, at least!), a proxy for the integrity of British mintage more generally – in recognition of which the spoon wasn't hallmarked, or stamped '925 sterling', but simply impressed 'coin'.

I concluded: 'We're all, one way or another, just tenants of this fraught, fragile earth. My wife and I hope that you who've tenanted Heartsease Hall so long and so well will be pleased with the estate's new tenants and come to visit them often.'

---

* To whom King Charles I had given the Colony in 1632.

Chapter 7

To Earth

O n Friday 14 October 1994, a day which will live in history – Henry family history, at least – N, Bapu, Big Fee and Yr Correspondent set off from Brambledown just after lunch to drive to Heartsease Hall for their first overnight – nay: their first weekend! – in their magnificent, new abode. (Piglet, sadly, wasn't able take an *exeat** and so couldn't be with us.)

N's and my anticipation of the life-change this journey implied was, to say the least, intense. It was as if we were retro-colonizers who, many years earlier – when we were in our mid-20s – having back-tracked the Spanish, the French, the British, the Dutch and all the rest across the Atlantic from the New World to the Old were, as well, now flipping Horace Greeley's oft-cited but apparently never as-such documented directive to 'go West'† and, instead, going East from the Cotswolds to north Norfolk in our metaphoric search for gold. An epic voyage into a great unknown was in prospect. We felt sure it would bring soaring new opportunities and manifold new rights and responsibilities, but also heavy new challenges....

• • • • • • • • • • • • • • • • • • • •

Oh, for Heaven's sake, d'Arcy! That first weekend, all you were re-ally doing was going on a sort of glorified camping trip!

• • • • • • • • • • • • • • • • • • • •

Our first challenge was to determine what the four of us would need simply to survive. Just inside the front door at Brambledown we laid out on the floor indoor and outdoor work and casual clothes and hiking boots, canned and fresh food and appropriate condiments, a quantity of drink, an assortment of cooking, serving and table uten-sils, washing-up liquid and paper kitchen roll, a basic tool kit and a ditto medicine-chest-*cum*-first-aid kit, some light bulbs and spare

---

* Literally, a 'Let him go out!', the Latin imperative used by some British board-ing schools to designate a home or other leave.

† Fred Shapiro, in his *The Yale Book of Quotations*, calls it 'one of the great examples... of misinformation about famous quotations'.

electric fuses (and, should the illumination problem prove more serious, two kerosene lamps), a step ladder, a broom, and a dustpan and brush, a couple of buckets, a wet-mop and some rags, pillows, sheets, pillowcases and duvets (and an alarm clock!), towels and toiletries, a hair dryer for the ladies, some reading material… and last but not least 'Crocodile', Bapu's favorite cuddle-toy.

Predictably, perhaps, the capacity of our 'estate car' (station wagon) proved too small to accommodate the above, and so our second challenge became to work out how we would transport it all. In the end, we hired a small truck… which provided far more space than we needed. To our essential survival gear we therefore added a quantity of 'luxuries' – a spare television and a ditto hi-fi and radio, a folding card table, three table lamps, two small bookshelves, a vacuum cleaner… bathroom scales – as well as a few summer-use items, to wit the barbecue, the badminton and croquet sets, some lawn chairs and a brand new, 52-inch, walk-behind rotary lawnmower all of which, we reasoned, might as well over-winter at Heartsease Hall as at Brambledown. Yr Correspondent was, of course, the designated 'packer' and given his matchless, manly skills… the hire-truck was soon – in that wonderfully evocative up-country phrase – 'as full as a tick'.

(It didn't remain so for long, however. Shortly after setting out, the truck's steering began to go slack. I pull over to the side of the road, stop, get out… sure enough: a tyre's going flat. And perhaps needless to record, the jack and the spare are stowed at the very front of the hire-truck's cargo bay. N, Big Fee and I unpack the truck and retrieve the jack, etc; the two women rejoin Bapu in the cab; I hunker down and set to work….

(After a while, Big Fee decides I need moral support. She exits the cab, ambles around to where I'm working, bends down, asks how I'm getting on, then stands up tall, hands on hips, her long legs – clad in skin-tight jeans – slightly apart, her spectacular [deleted] perfectly presented for the delectation of oncoming male drivers. Almost immediately, a car with three lads in screeches to a stop on the road shoulder in front of us then, wheels spinning urgently, backs up. The near-side front door bursts open and one of the young men jumps out; he asks Big Fee if he can help. I raise my head and am about to thank him, but decline his offer…. At which point he says: 'Oh, 'ello, mate. Is she with you?' I nod. 'Lucky man,' the lad enthuses, with just a hint of disapproval. Then he returns to the car and is overheard to say: 'Ahhh, never mind; she's with some old geezer. What a waste!'

The car roars off; I complete the tire-change; we pack everything up again....)

About three-and-a-half hours later, we're approaching the entrance to the Heartsease Hall Estate. I put the blinker on, turn through the main gate, go past the front lodge and start up the front drive, braking hard to avoid one crater in the road surface and swerving around another.... 'Home sweet home, Dar,' N croons, 'and well driven! Well done!' 'We've got to do something about these (deleted) pot-holes,' I grunt. 'Soon!' The reality of life as an English Country Squire, I ask myself grimly, has it just now begun?

· · · · · · · · · · · · · · · · · · · ·

Thus may the consequential, the momentous – 'the turning points of history' – fall prey to and be overwhelmed by the trivial. It's the old 'for-want-of-a-nail' thing, Alter-natis.

The 'old "for-want-of-a-nail" thing' proposes not that 'the turning points of history' – and by extension the turning, or 'tipping', points of all sorts of feedback or cybernetic systems – may fall prey, etc, to the trivial, but that they may actually be trivial.

Oh.

Thanks to environmentalists like James Lovelock and Peter Ward and, less-directly, the writer William Golding, we might now say: 'For want of a Kleenex, the sneeze of a rain-forest logger – or a trawlerman fishing the open sea – may give Gaia a deadly new 'flu...' or some such.

We might...?

In Greek mythology, d'Arcy, 'Gaia' or 'Gaea' or just plain, old 'Ge' – who became the goddess of Earth – was the first being to emerge from Chaos. She gave birth to Pontus (Sea) and Uranus (Heaven) and, by the latter – after a brace of immaculate conceptions incest, evidently, wasn't a problem – became the mother of the twelve original Titans.

Today's so-called 'Gaia', the name Golding gave to the hypothesis Lovelock developed, is essentially whole-earth science. It sees our anthroposphere – that part of the biosphere human beings impact... which is pretty much all of it – as a complex of inter-dependent systems which provide the physical and chemical environment for sustaining life.

Ward's so-called Medea hypothesis – named after the headstrong Greek goddess and wife of Jason the Argonaut who became a serial killer, first of her brother Absyrtus, then of the children she'd had by Jason and finally of the younger woman Jason eventually left her for – is that Gaia may not survive.

We *absolutely must* save Gaia, Alter-natis – even if we have to adopt more-frugal lifestyles and, figuratively, keep Kleenex ever handy!

· · · · · · · · · · · · · · · · · · · ·

And so we continue on over the causeway, past the front circle, and into the stableyard. 'I'll go roust out Old Groome,' I pronounce, authoritatively. 'Get the keys to the Hall so we can let ourselves in.' I stride briskly over to Groome's decrepit mobile home. I rap on the door and shout; I look 'high and low', as they say. No Groome. N, Bapu and Big Fee – already restive from the long drive – now declare their urgent need of 'the facilities'. I refer them to the outside, public toilets, then return my mind to the vexed question of how, in the absence of the key, the new squire and his entourage are going to get in. I stride briskly through the tunnel and along towards the back door of the Hall to research the options more closely. The Hall's back door's wide open.

After establishing our base camps – lower ones in the kitchen for cooking and eating, and in the library for reading, listening to music and watching TV; and upper ones in various Hall and annex bedrooms and bathrooms – Bapu and Big Fee depart to stretch their legs and check on the donkeys; N and I repair to the drawing room with a bottle of bubbly the Festings have left for us. Apart from the beautiful 18th-century console tables and over-mirrors which had come with the Hall, the only furnishings in the room are two early 19th-century, wooden-framed library chairs – their original (? brocade) coverings in tatters – which were part of the consignment we'd bought. As N and I flop exhilarated but exhausted into these last we wonder, idly, where we should set our glasses down; almost immediately I think I hear, from somewhere over by the fireplace, a voice saying in an English accent I'd never before encountered: 'On the floor, Silly! Set your glasses down on the floor!'

Anyway, I tell myself, what a petty concern. For, somehow, the lack of furnishings... the lack of clutter... give the ambience and the occasion an especial clarity of definition and depth of appeal. N and I look at each other, toast the Fredericks and the Harrymans and the d'Arcys and the Henrys – our familial 'ancestral voices' and, more to the point, their generous gifts, legacies and bequests – and, in turn, Sir Roald and Lady Festing... clink and substantially empty our glasses; then we stroll over to the drawing room's west window and gaze in delight at the rose-and-violet-slashed sunset sky silhouetting the trees beyond the upper lake. How many Festings had admired such a view from the Hall or its medieval predecessor, we ask ourselves? And how many Henrys will admire it from the Hall or a futuristic successor? Irrelevant questions... and, yet, not so irrelevant ones. Verily, we conclude: only time will tell.

I awoke early the next morning to a fine, autumnal prospect. The blood-orange sun, back-lighting the big woods to our southeast – Neate Wood, the plan said it was called – was just starting to burn off the mist which over-lay the lower lake like a quilt; beneath this coverlet, cozily out of sight, geese honked, ducks quacked, coots (? cooted). The view – almost exactly as I'd imagined it would be – was simply exquisite. And excepting the raucous waterfowl, and the melodious songbirds, it was so quiet...

· · · · · · · · · · · · · · · · · · · ·

'And, behold, the Lord passed by, and a great wind rent the mountains...; but the Lord was not in the wind: and after the wind (came) an earthquake; but the Lord was not in the earthquake: And after the earthquake a fire; but the Lord was not in the fire: and after the fire a still small voice....' That's from I Kings Chapter 9 of *The Bible*, Alter-natis.

'Quiet' is what it's all about, d'Arcy. *In the re-worked, re-applied words of the American foreign correspondent Amy Goodman, what you must do is:* 'Go to where the silence is and (hear) something'*.
· · · · · · · · · · · · · · · · · · · ·

... so quiet; the only sound was the whispering of a gentle breeze through the trees. I went down to the kitchen, made a couple of cups of coffee and took one up to N.

· · · · · · · · · · · · · · · · · · · ·

Yes, Alter-natis, it was *that* fine a morning!
· · · · · · · · · · · · · · · · · · · ·

After a hearty breakfast, we set about rearranging some of the furniture we'd acquired from the Festings – in particular the beds, bedside tables, bureaux and chests of drawers. Before these dormitory items could be assigned their 'permanent' places, however (places which over the years have, in fact, proved remarkably permanent), one most-crucial matter had to be decided: in which of the bedrooms would the new Squire and his Squiress sleep?

There were essentially three choices. The largest bedroom of all – the 'master bedroom', so-called because Sir Roald and Lady Festing had made it theirs – was in the middle of the front elevation of the

---

* Ms Goodman, recognizing the journalist's obligation to report what's not been reported, actually enjoined: 'Go... and say something'.

house directly over the entrance hall. It had its own, *en suite*, 'master' bathroom (formerly, its dressing room) and was the only bedroom in the Hall to be so complemented. And it had a lovely aspect – sweeping from the shrubbery with its great walled garden across to the woods-fringed upper lake, framing in between rolling fields and the 1000-year-old, round-towered St Lawrence's Church.

This aspect was to the north and west, however; N and I greatly preferred to look out to the south and east.

Either or both of the two eastern bedrooms along the back or 'garden' elevation of the Hall, at the head of the main staircase, offered such a view. Originally, these rooms comprised Lady Festing's bedroom and sitting room and, on this account, they had an interconnecting door. The sitting-room 'bedroom' was particularly grand, and its fireplace had a beautiful, brown-and-grey figured marble surround either side of which were three-quarter-height niches into which bookshelving had been built....

But did N and I really need two large rooms just for our own, later-life conjugality, we pondered? Even considering N's extensive, all-continents, all-seasons, work-and-play wardrobes, and my habit of accumulating bedside reading materials, that was an awful lot of space....

And, if we didn't need that much space, it seemed only right that we should 'connect' – that's to say 'share' – with someone. But who, we asked, would we share with? One of the boys? (Think of the noise and the smell and our lack of privacy, N said.) The occasional houseguest? (Think of our lack of privacy, and *their* lack of privacy, I said.) The Whomever, in the unlikely event He or She came to stay? (Did He need a bedroom; if He did, could this one actually accommodate Him, or would He transcend it; would such close proximity to Him keep us awake... or damage our mitochondrial DNA and, thereby, accelerate our ageing and/or increase our vulnerability to disease?)

In the end, we decided to allocate these two bedrooms to the boys against those late nights/early mornings when, in future years, they'd likely be rollicking noisily home.*

That left the western back/garden-elevation bedroom – the *original* master bedroom, used by the of-this-Hall first owner-occupier Fest-

---

* As well, N proposed, the inter-connecting door would allow the brothers to communicate more easily with each other and thus to bond more deeply. Within weeks of their officially moving in, however, 'the brothers' had closed and effectively sealed the door by putting pieces of furniture either side of it!

ing… or, less assuredly, the one directly under the rotted wall plate which John D had jokingly proposed should be the guest bedroom. It had a lovely outlook over the lower lake, as did its dressing room, and the above-referenced master bathroom was just across the Hall. Finally, there was its original, 18th-century, carved-wooden, floral-patterned, door, window and dado moulding, and its ditto fireplace surround, swaged across and down either side with tasseled 'drapery' and surmounted by a tablet with a beautifully-sculpted Venus head on. The package was simply irresistible – and N and I didn't long try to resist it. Into the original master bedroom our dormitory furniture was shortly moved.

About mid-day the mailman arrived with, amazingly, two letters addressed to me. Who could have sent them, I wondered? The first letter, in a fine if barely-legible hand, was from one 'Sir Antony Huffton, C.B.E. (Commander of the Order of the British Empire)' of Brunstead Hall – a near neighbor, he wrote, who lived just a couple of miles down the main road – welcoming us, saying he looked forward to making our acquaintance in person very soon and, in the meantime, hoping we'd find Heartsease Hall to our liking.

· · · · · · · · · · · · · · · · · · · ·

Good Lord; a formal letter of welcome! I'd assumed that order of civility had, like the passenger pigeon, passed long, long ago.

It all-but has. Today, people mostly just email and/or text, or 'blog' or 'tweet' or 'twitter' – and these last, as often as not, to co-horts or groups of presumed like-minds rather than to individuals. It's called online social networking. Hardly anyone troubles to craft personal communications 'for posterity' now.

It's all so shoot-from-the-hip spontaneous! And because these messagings usually aren't printed out – as input for a diary, say – but only 'saved' to… to wherever they save that sort of stuff to: over there, up there… in 'the cloud' in cyberspace where, we're told, it could get lost or destroyed – it's evanescent almost by definition.

Hard copy can get lost or destroyed too, d'Arcy; through inadvertence or by design, it happens all the time….

No new epistolary troves will be created for future generations – or, indeed, the correspondent himself in later life – to happen upon or search out, and rejoice in or recoil from; the evidence of 'little' history – the history of individuals' day-to-day lives, and their family and friendly relationships – will simply cease to be!

There's always 'life-logging': the process whereby people create detailed audio and/or visual archives of virtually everything they do. Just what public good would come of this almost-incalculably vast accumulation of data, or how and when even life-loggers would benefit from it – they could, after all, see out their days just logging themselves tending their ever-expanding archive of logs – is utterly beyond me, however.

To *me*, it all sounds like just so much solipsistic navel-gazing! And if it takes over, 'big' history – the story of mankind's ranging in search of its future – will cease to be too!

Don't worry, d'Arcy; George Orwell's 'Big Brother' – and now, possibly, 'Big Sister' – and his or her swarming acolytes will keep big history grinding along. Remember: most established governments and churches are prodigious recorders and collators of almost any data they can lay their hands on; legal, accounting, credit-rating, financial, insurance and medical entities are generally similarly inclined. Then there're the archives collected up and laid down by the institutions of higher learning and research – consultancies like FHA, even – and museums and galleries, and libraries and publishing houses... and the media.

Don't forget sales and marketing facilitators... and Google, Amazon and Facebook....

There's also so-called 'Big Data': information – initially a sort of by-catch, incidental to the 'little' data actually being trawled for – about our individual words and deeds which, aggregated up and extrapolated, becomes a prescription for our very lives....

Good Lord: Big Brother or Big Sister – now with Big Data – coming soon to a vantage point near you! Alter-natis, do you think this book should include an Afterword about the importance of writing letters, and/or keeping diaries, so younger Readers, if there are any, will know what we're (t)wittering on about?

. . . .

The second letter, running to pages and pages of large, exuberant and, in its way, equally challenging manuscript was from Lady Maureen advising us what needed doing to which of the plants in the gardens and the greenhouse and – Oh, yes! – to which of the donkeys and when.

A Saturday-night celebratory 'feast' having been decreed, the afternoon of our first full day at Heartsease Hall was largely given over to preparations for same. While N and Big Fee slaved away in the kitchen base camp, Bapu and Yr Correspondent set to work in and around the proposed venue: the dining room. We gave the great Lord Nelson table a good waxing – using a floor polisher fitted with fluffy, new, buffer heads and some furniture wax we'd found in a closet – and in due course achieved a mirror-like shine. Then we set out rectangles of corrugated-cardboard packing as place mats, lengths of kitchen roll folded as napkins, our back-up, 'everyday' cutlery – chrome-plated but worn, with the brass substrate showing through – and plastic wine balloons. Finally, we carried in the four, battered, kitchen chairs the Festings had left behind, put one at the head of the table and the other three down its inside, fireplace side....

At last, tired and bedraggled, and badly in need of a bath and a whisky, I stood back with Bapu to admire our handiwork....

'Brrring, brrring... brrring, brrring... brrrrriiing!' (Deleted), I curse; it's a doorbell. But which doorbell? Having never before had to answer one here in the Hall, I don't know whether to attend at the front door or the back one. And at this hour, with evening drawing in, who on earth could it be?

· · · · · · · · · · · · · · · · · · · ·

I said maybe it wasn't anyone. Maybe it was... ghosts!
   And *I* said: grow up, Alter-natis! Act your age!

· · · · · · · · · · · · · · · · · · · ·

Eventually, I dispatch Bapu to the front door – the better-lit, more-patent entrance – and go myself to the back one; there's no one's there. I retrace my steps towards the dining room and, just outside it, encounter Bapu in haste retracing his. 'Daddy, there're three or four men... very tall and thin... and all dressed in black clothes...!' he tells me breathlessly. I order my disheveled raiment, smooth my unkempt hair, square my esquire-apparently shoulders and march off to confront the intruders.

Three or four tall, thin men there were indeed and at least that number again standing behind them, all immaculately got up in black bow ties, dinner jackets, waistcoats, trousers and overcoats or cloaks. And stretching away into the gathering gloom was a line of big, expensive cars. 'I'm very sorry to trouble you, sir,' began the apparent spokesman of the group sheepishly, 'but we're trying to get to the North Norfolk Conservative Party Association dinner. It's being held this evening at Beeston Hall. Is this Beeston Hall?'

No, I told the man heavily, this is Heartsease Hall.

Collective mutterings of great consternation ensued. 'Could you direct us to Beeston Hall, then?' the spokesman asked.

Wearily, I replied I'd very much like to, but that I was new to north Norfolk and didn't know where Beeston Hall was. 'I've got a good map of the area, though – a large-scale Ordnance Survey map – if you'd care to come in and have a look at it,' I offered. In the men came, their eyes raking curiously over Bapu and me and the generalized, in-transition jumble of packing boxes and packing that overflowed the entrance hall like waste-paper for re-cycling from a supermarket collection bin. From the folding card table I'd set up as a desk in the library, I fetched the OS map.

'This's the Heartsease Hall that's recently been sold, isn't it?' a member of the group ventured. 'I remember articles in the papers about it, and some news items on TV....'

I nodded, doing my best to seem hospitable.

'You look as if you've just moved in,' observed another.

I cranked the *façade* of hospitality up another notch or two.

'Well then: welcome to north Norfolk!' the group spokesman proposed, heartily. 'Here, here,' chorused his fellows: 'Welcome to north Norfolk!' A pause... then, tentatively, from someone toward the rear of the group, came a declarative-interrogative: 'You sound Canadian... or, maybe, American perhaps?

· · · · · · · · · · · · · · · · · · · ·

The dear old British: they can be very PC (politically correct) when they want to, Alter-natis.

Yes; an American taken for a Canadian will often acquiesce. But a Canadian taken for an American...? No way!

Why is it, do you suppose, that in spite of everything they do throughout the world to 'let freedom ring', as the 19th-century US poet and clergyman Samuel Francis Smith put it, so many Americans seem to be so widely so unloved internationally?

Shouldn't you finish writing this book, d'Arcy, before starting...?

· · · · · · · · · · · · · · · · · · · ·

'You wouldn't by any chance be interested in joining the UK Conservative Party Association, would you?' the man continued. Another added teasingly: 'We have special, introductory rates for overseas members....'

And so it wasn't until about 1900 hours, dressed in the gladdest rags we had to hand – which, as the Reader has doubtless already surmised, weren't all that 'glad' – that we gathered for our Grand, Inaugural, Henrys-at-Heartsease-Hall Dinner. I assigned places – me at the head of the table, N to my right, then Bapu, then Big Fee – carved and served up, lamented Piglet's and sundry dear friends' absence from this momentous occasion, intoned a short but profoundly heartfelt grace... and then sat down. I looked to my left, out the window and south to the now moon-lit lower lake; I looked to my right, up above and beyond N and the others, at the north wall of the dining room with its great, marble chimneypiece and array of Festing portraits; I looked straight ahead, along the length of His Lordship the Admiral Horatio Nelson's venerable table – its brilliant top reflecting yet more Festings on the west wall – across the oval ante-room, through the drawing room door and out its west window toward the upper lake, the woodlands and the fields....

I remember N interrupting my reverie; 'Dar, would you pass the salt, please?' she said. Just as I was about to do so, I suddenly heard that strange English voice again:

. . . .

'Mr Henry?'

Who... who're you?

'I'm Jacob Festing. I expect Sir Roald's told you about me.'

He's told me about Isaac Festing who gave succour to King Charles I on the scaffold and Henry Festing who scourged our brave Boston Patriots. But I don't recall....

'It doesn't matter; you'll find plenty of references to me in the estate's records. That's my portrait hanging there, just to your right... over the fireplace. I'm the Festing who built this Hall.'

I looked with renewed reverence up at the portly gentleman represented three-quarter length in his burgundy frock coat and cream-colored, sateen waistcoat, smiling benevolently down. You built...?

'Yes. Unfortunately, shortly before the Hall was completed, I was thrown from my horse and killed. But... those things happen, don't they! Whatever: it's wonderful the clean, uncluttered geometry of Georgian architecture and interior design, don't you think? Because for all its overlay of "Gothic-ness" your Hall is essentially Georgian... by which I mean it derives from the works of the Jacobean designer Inigo Jones who, of course, was greatly influenced by the Italian Andrea Palladio. Do you like it?'

Oh: my wife and I love Georgian architecture, Sir... Jacob; it's such an unpretentious, easy-to-keep-clean style. And we love Gluck, Mozart... Jacques-Louis David, Jean Auguste Ingres, maybe... Jean Antoine Houdon....

'Strictly speaking, those artists weren't "Georgian", Mr Henry, because they were all born and primarily worked in Continental Europe. They were "neo-Classical".'

Well then: William Byrd – although he died in 1623, as a composer he was very *avant-guard* – and Handel, except he was German-born... Thomas Arne, perhaps, who composed *Rule Britannia!* and *God Save The King*, the tune of which the just-above-referenced Samuel Francis Smith appropriated for his/our patriotic song *My Country, 'tis of Thee*... and Sir Joshua Reynolds, George Stubbs,

Thomas Gainsborough, George Romney and Johann Zoffany...
except the last too was German-born.... Simple, pure and spiritual. Then, in the space of only a few industrializing, imperializing
decades, British architecture descends via the flamboyance of the
Regency period into the self-congratulatory excesses of Victorian
materialism.

'"Self-congratulatory excesses... of materialism...." Hummm.
That characterization could be applied to very substantial swathes
of contemporary architecture in what, I understand, you call "The
Motherland", it seems to me. But are you saying that if Heartsease
Hall had been designed by Augustus Pugin or Sir Charles Barry –
one of those high Gothic-Revival/Victorian architects, for example
of the Houses of Parliament – rather than William Wilkins, Senior,
you wouldn't have bought it?'

No, not at all, Sir. You are styled 'Sir', aren't you... sir? For this
site and its glorious outlook, and this expanse of water, woodlands
and fertile, gently-rolling fields, we'd have bought almost anything:
a concrete blockhouse... a tent, even. The Hall's Georgian architecture was just icing on the cake.

'"Beauty is Nature's brag," that's to say "self-glorification" or
"boast", as John Milton wrote in his *Comus*. Milton was one of us,
you know: a Roundhead and supporter of Oliver Cromwell – and
Parliament – during our Civil War. And he didn't become totally
blind until the winter of 1651–52 when he was 43 years of age, so
he'd had plenty of time to acquire a visual appreciation of nature.
Anyway: that'll be all for this evening; I just wanted to introduce
myself and say I hope you'll feel at home here. We'll talk again when
you've settled in. Goodbye.'

Goodb....

. . . .

... and then I remember N snapping her fingers. 'Dar, what's the matter with you?' she said. 'Get with it! Pass the salt, please.' Starting,
I jerked myself full-upright in my chair, groped out my hand toward
the plastic, off-the-supermarket-shelf shaker we'd brought along....

When finally we'd finished our celebratory supper, Big Fee took
Bapu upstairs to get him ready for bed; a little while later, N and I
followed on to tuck him in and kiss him good-night. It was a scene
neither of us will ever forget: in the cast of the hallway light through
the open door of the late Lady Festing's cavernous bedroom, with its
enormous windows, its huge fireplace and hearth, and its seeming
acres of floor, was this little Squirrel-Nutkin figure in his little duvet-
nest bed, cuddling his beloved Crocodile. How could our precious
Bapu possibly settle and get to sleep in there, we asked ourselves?

Surely he must be tossing and turning and fretting up – trembling, even, with anxiety and fear – in the terrible, strange gloom.

'Bapu, dearest,' N called softly from the doorway, 'are you OK, honey? Is everything all right?' There was no answer. The Paternal took his turn: 'Bapu? It's Daddy and Mummy; we're here if you need us, Big Fella, just downstairs. We'll leave your door open....' We cocked our heads and strained forward in the semi-darkness awaiting Bapu's reply. But all we heard was a soft, sibilant breathing and the 'who-woo... who-woo' of an owl in a nearby tree.

After N had gone to bed, I poured myself a nightcap and returned to my tattered library chair in the drawing room to reflect on the day's events and what a lovely evening... a love(uph!)...ly evening... a lovely, lovely (burruph!) *lovely* evening... we'd just had! The beef wellington was lovely, I noted with great deliberation... the *lyonnaise* potatoes, and the parsnips – adding that splash of Armagnac was a wonderful idea! – were lov(whp!) lovely... and ditto the field mushrooms and the *al 'dente* celeriac – I tried to remember just how much and why I so adored parsley-butter sauce! – the broccoli *hollandaise* was lovely, and to wash it all down there was that lovely... lovely... (burruph!) lovely magnum of Leoville-Las Cases.

• • • • • • • • • • • • • • • • • • • •

But could any meal have been a match for the occasion itshelf? I mean (burrup!): had you ever before eaten with your family in an esshenshially original, unaltered, Georgian dining room?

Within walls and among pixtures and furnishings... (uuuph!) which if they could but shpeak would recall first-hand to you events of two, three and more shenshuries ago... away back to the days of your 'great' repeated ten timesh grandparentsh?

Or to put a shomewhat einer fedge on it, d'Arcy – I'm shorry, My Man, that should read: 'finer edge' – had you ever before eaten with your family in your own esshenshially original, unaltered Georgian dining room? (burrp!)

If you don't mind my shaying, Alter-natish – Awww... what the (deteled): even if you do mind! – the exhperiench really does take your breath away! (burrrrruph!)

• • • • • • • • • • • • • • • • • • • •

Indeed. But as runs the old Gaelic proverb: 'All good comes to an end – except the goodness of God.' Even so, I wondered the next day, must all un-Godly good come to *such* an end? Big Fee, it transpired, was up much of the night being sick and that morning could barely drag herself out of bed; Bapu made it down to the kitchen and through a little breakfast – during which he told us of the conversation *he'd* had with Sir Jacob – but then was obliged to retire; even my gastricly industrial-grade Uxor said she felt a bit queasy.

Was it too much rich food, etc? I puzzled. I'm usually the one whose stomach flags that sort of problem, and I felt fine. It must be some sort of flu, I concluded. Whatever: after the high of the Grand Dinner the previous evening, our Heartsease Hall inaugural ended physically as well as spiritually low.

On Tuesday 18 October, I telephoned Sir Roald to say how very much we'd enjoyed our weekend 'in (his) ancestral home'. He was just off the plane from St Petersburg and sounded raring to go but faced, he told me, the prospect of 'another few days' in hospital. ('Nothing serious… just some tests,' he said.) We chatted on for a while, then began our close-down… at which point, as if suddenly recognizing some far-distant oversight, Sir Roald exclaimed: 'By the way, Mr Henry, what's happening in respect of contract exchange and completion? Have my lawyers sent the papers to you yet?'

No they haven't, sir, I replied. 'Well,' Sir Roald said pensively, 'it's time these formalities got sorted out. After all, we can't have you and your family "squatting" (living illegally) in the Hall indefinitely.' He chuckled before continuing: 'Not that it really matters, of course; as Thomas Draxe noted in his *Adages* of 1616: "possession is nine points of the law" and, *de facto*, last weekend you must certainly have established most of those nine points. (More chuckles.) Anyway: I'll get on the telephone, try to find out what the problem is and get back to you with an update as soon as I can.'

A few hours later that update came. All the paperwork had, in fact, been finalized Sir Roald told me and was 'as we (spoke)' being couriered to Euan for his review and N's and my subsequent signatures. That accomplished, the documents would make their way to him, he would sign, 'certain monies would change hands', Title to Heartsease Hall would be officially transferred… 'and that'll be that!' Sir Roald summarized, sounding almost relieved. 'They said they could have it done by the end of this week,' he added.

How wonderful… how marvellous, I exulted to myself: an American English country squire is just about to be legitimized! Hallelujah! With what hindsight suggests was certainly the wisdom of experience and may even have had undertones of mischievousness, Sir Roald concluded solemnly: 'Very soon, you'll be in full charge of the Heartsease Hall Estate, Mr Henry. Total responsibility for each and every aspect of the property's day-to-day and longer-term management will be yours and yours alone.'

And so the paperwork did indeed proceed. The morning of 20 October, N and I met with Euan to read through and sign the exchange and completion documents. (After all the intellectual and emotional issues had been resolved, and all the financial and legal ones, there wasn't really much to it: just some figurative scratchings of roller-ball pens on papers. Even so my hand was shaking.) The documents then went off to Sir Roald *et al* in London and at about 1700 hours the following day – Friday 21 October – while N and I were driving to Heartsease Hall in heavy, rush-hour traffic and relentless, torrential rain – this time with Piglet as well as Bapu and Big Fee aboard – N's cell phone rang. It was Euan reporting that title-transfer had been accomplished and that the Heartsease Hall Estate was, at last, officially ours. N and Euan maundered on awhile before signing off; Yr Correspondent – read: tired, bleary-eyed chauffeur – considered raising another 'Hallelujah!' or two but, in the event, couldn't summon the energy.

Our first awakening at Heartsease Hall as *de jure* owners was – like our first awakening there as *de facto* occupiers – fine and bright.

For most of that morning, N and I pretty much just kicked back and pondered our incredible good fortune. But in the afternoon, initiating what I hoped (? feared) would become a long lifetime's regular labour, I gave the front lawn its first Henry cut. In addition to the extent of the lawn – well over an acre, I guessed; the back lawn, I noted warily, was roughly twice that size – and the cardio-vascular benefits trekking the many miles back and forth across it would over time doubtless confer, what struck me was how very sweet... perfumed, almost... the new-mown north Norfolk grass smelled.

· · · · · · · · · · · · · · · · · · · ·

How many more of these fulsome eulogies are we likely to have to endure, I asked?

Probably not many, I replied, expecting our home-making honeymoon would end soon. But I also commented on how extraordinarily comfortable – intellectually, emotionally and physically – I felt at Heartsease Hall. It was almost as if....

'As if' what?

As if in some anachronic way I'd returned home, Alter-natis.

The contour of the land around the estate, its flora and fauna and, when the wind's out of the east, the perception in the air of proximity to open water, does call to mind your parts of The Motherland's east coast: the southern littorals of the Chesapeake Bay, for example, or seaboard New England and Campobello Island.

Indeed. I sometimes wonder, however, if my sense of home-coming could be rooted even deeper. The d'Arcy Henrys, you'll remember, were Huguenots – that's to say north-European Protestants – some of whom fled to East Anglia in the 16th century to escape persecution by Catholics in Belgium and France; my paternal ancestors could have been among them.

And on my mother's side, several ancestors – part of the 17th-century 'Great (Puritan) Migration' from the UK to New England – almost certainly came from around here.

• • • • • • • • • • • • • • • • • •

In the midst of my mowing and scenting (and genealogizing) came my first direct contact with another north Norfolk landowner: Joscelyn Steele, the squire of the Caiston Hall Estate – a property a couple of miles north-east of Heartsease Hall – who'd stopped by to collect an old, oak, trestle table he'd bought from Sir Roald. For some reason, the encounter made a lasting impression on me.

At first sight, Joseclyn appeared to be almost a caricature of the traditional, upper-class, English 'toff': tall and slim, and with an easy ambulance all-but oozing *noblesse-oblige*. (In public contexts he often styled himself 'Commander', I later learned, in testament to his distinguished naval career.) Closer scrutiny, however, suggested a far more complex persona. Indeed, to me Joscelyn's visage seemed that of the high-browed and heaven-ward tending scholar-ascetic (I certainly couldn't immediately discern in it much militaristic swagger.), and his aspect overall that of a pilgrim embarked on an extended journey of self-discovery in a strange and somewhat alien land.

• • • • • • • • • • • • • • • • • •

'Who would true valour see, Let him come hither (but pronounced 'heather'); *One here will constant be, Come wind, come weather. There's no discouragement Shall make him once relent His first avow'd intent To be a pilgrim.'*

That's an allegory of man's unremitting search for God, and Truth, from the 17th-century English writer and clergyman John Bunyan's *Shepherd Boy's Song*. I recognized that extract immediately, Alter-natis. What a strange passage to have come into your mind!

We're all pilgrims 'embarked on an extended journey', etc, d'Arcy – you... me... the Reader, even – although not all of us are aware of our condition. One reason why your meeting with Steele so affected

you, I suggested, was your instinctive appreciation that, psychologi-
cally, you and he had a lot in common.
· · · · · · · · · · · · · · · · · · · ·

On Sunday 23 October, the apprentice English Country Squire and
his family – psychologically and sartorially primed – attended their
first-ever service at the round-towered, St Lawrence's Church. Before
setting out, I lined everyone up for inspection. N, in country tweeds,
offered a sort of 'ho, hum... another meeting in the (White House)
Oval Office' demeanor; Piglet – as ever, intent in his search for new
learning to pack away – was resplendent in his boarding school's
'Number Ones' (emblazoned jacket and tie); Bapu, his back ramrod-
straight, was collected... focused... three going on thirty... prompting
Yr Correspondent to wonder who was inspecting whom; Big Fee was
beautifully coifed and made-up, and wearing a skirt of some gauzy
material which couldn't fail to make clear – to some bachelor, yeo-
man-farmer, perhaps – what a fine figure of a young woman she was.
I made a final check of my wristwatch – arriving punctually well as
properly turned out was, I felt, crucial to this most-important paro-
chial debut – then marshaled everyone into the car for the short drive
to the church....

Hmmm. That's *very* strange, I remarked, as we pulled into the
small field (one of the estate's) part of which served as the church's
parking lot: there aren't many cars here... in fact, there aren't any. Ah
well, I reassured myself, it's a country parish and on fine mornings
like this everyone probably walks... or rides their horses or drives
their carriages... to church. But no horses or carriages were to be
seen either. And the church was absolutely deserted; not a creature
was stirring, not even the vicar. What could be wrong? I thought I'd
checked the 'Announcements' of services and events in the parish
carefully enough.... But was this one of the 'close' Sundays when no
service was held? Or had we....

· · · · · · · · · · · · · · · · · · · ·
That's right! Use the first person plural; diffuse the blame....
· · · · · · · · · · · · · · · · · · · ·

Or had I misread something? Piglet's propositive cut through my consternation: 'Today's the day winter time (Greenwich Mean Time, or
GMT) begins, isn't it? I remember one of the masters at school re-
citing that mnemonic about clocks' hands "springing forward into
spring; falling backward into fall".' Indeed; the service wasn't for

another hour. So to the Hall we all returned for one of those little segments of down-time professional operations research people say over-achievers – *real* over-achievers – optimize use of. While I strolled the south lawn admiring the view and Big Fee and the boys kicked a soccer ball around, N brewed up a fresh pot of coffee.

Then back we went to the church for what proved to be a rather better-attended (e)stately entrance. I parked the car – backing it into the space so as to be ready for a quick get-away – then shepherded the family and Big Fee along, N in turn shepherding Big Fee and Piglet and Bapu along, Big Fee shepherding Piglet and Bapu (all this precedence and succession: was it pecking-order or stage-fright... or both, I wondered?) Piglet shepherding Bapu... and so indeed in the words of The Great Isaiah to the wayward people of Judah: 'a little child (an innocent) shall lead them', to the porch of the church where the vicar – a sea-faring type, judging from his weathered face and full beard – greeted us, then into the nave... the usher conducting us down the aisle past row after row of swiveling heads and scrutinizing eyes to, at long last, the front pew... the pew reserved by centuries of tradition for The Squire of the Heartsease Hall Estate. Pushing the family and Big Fee ahead of me, I scuttled in, sat down – then knelt down – and offered my small musings to the great Whomever above....

Thereafter, Yr Correspondent found little of much note. The service consisted of simple matins from the 'BCP' – the 1662 Anglican Book of Common Prayer which, I learned, was a matter of strong local preference – there were some vaguely familiar hymns (the elderly organ and the ditto organist wanted some rejuvenation, perhaps); the vicar delivered a succinct if somewhat inconclusive sermon and pronounced the Benediction and the Grace in a clear, strong voice.... Finally, came the Silent Prayer – which went on and on and on... and on... in the course of which on-going Yr Correspondent sensed a certain impatience building in the congregation as with a football or baseball team during the pre-game playing of *The Star Spangled Banner*, or a fox-hunt awaiting the off.

I smiled reassurance across at N and the boys; N and the boys scowled askance back at me. I averted my gaze up to the vaulted ceiling of the ancient church with its plaster ribbing – installed in the first years of the 19th century, I remembered Sir Roald telling me, and a copy of the ceiling in the Heartsease Hall entrance hall – then down to its 14th-and 16th-century stone-mullioned windows with their clear and stained-glass leaded lights, then around to the profusion of

Festing funerary monuments and 'hatchments'* crowding its walls... and, finally, to its furnishings: the pitch-pine pulpit, lectern and pews, hand-made and all-of-a-piece; the finely cast and wrought brass chandeliers and sconces, with their un-lit candles standing at the ready; the simple altar-table, with its embroidered linen cover-cloth.... The usher suddenly materialized at my elbow.

'They're waiting for you and your family to leave, Mr Henry,' he whispered deferentially. Slowly – too slowly, manifestly – I re-booted my brain. 'The congregation's waiting for you, Mr Henry, sir,' the usher repeated, more urgently now. 'They won't go out until you do.' Ohmygosh!

I nodded gravely – the way I thought Sir Roald might – arose and stepped with what I hoped would pass for 'seemly dignity' into the aisle, motioning my entourage to follow. After a reprise of the shepherding shuffle such that Bapu, 'the little child', once again led, we recessed down the aisle, exchanged some final compliments with the vicar and beat a retreat to our car. From the generality of the now-emancipated congregation came sighs of relief and, from at least some of their number, what sounded like giggles.

That afternoon we took our first family walk around the Heartsease Hall Estate.

. . . .

My, my (puff... puff). This estate's pretty large, isn't it, I observed.

Yes (puff... puff), Alter-natis, I concurred. It's nearly as big New York's Central Park or the Imperial Gardens of the Summer Palace just outside Beijing. Configured as a circle, its circumference would be well over four miles.

You must get some riding horses (puff... puff) soon, I advised!

. . . .

We hadn't gone very far, however, when I noticed a Land Rover – its headlights flashing and its horn toot-tooting – tearing along one of the estate's tracks and moving more or less in our direction. What an impertinence, I thought. Going that fast and creating all that commotion on our land; if I get even half a chance, I'll certainly give whomever's driving it a piece of my mind.... And hey, Big Boy: here's your half-a-chance! The Land Rover's coming, coming... coming right over... and

---

* Heraldic memorials, often painted diagonally across a square, black-framed wooden panel or canvas which, to enable normal, i.e. up-right viewing, is then hung 45° askew.

stopping just in front of us.

A great, burly bear of a man with a bull neck and arms which hung like brawny parentheses either side of an oak-trunk body swung down from the Land Rover's cab; what seemed an equally-imposing figure remained inside. Racked across the cab's rear window were a bolt-action rifle and two double-barreled shotguns. Ummmm....

'And 'oo might you be, then?' our Ursus (the Latin word for 'bear') began, assertively.

'I'm d'Arcy Henry,' I replied, squaring up to the challenge as best I could. 'Yeah?' the big man growled. 'Yeah!' I squeaked. From the figure in the cab – quite a pretty woman I now saw – came a heavy 'Pssssst!'. Ursus hulked over to the open window on her side of the Land Rover and through it a few whispered words were exchanged. Ursus, all smiles now, hulked back, started to proffer a paw about twice the length, breadth and thickness of mine and then, respectfully, withdrew it.

'Mista 'Enry, Sir. Welcome! I didn't know you was movin' in so soon. I'm Thomas Warrener, the gamekeeper 'ere. An' this's my wife Rosalie. Welcome to 'Eartsease 'All, Mista 'Enry. Welcome, Sir, to Th' 'All.'

The next day came a welcome of a different sort: our first Heartsease Hall wind-storm. The anemometer on the weather station I'd just installed quickly revved to 80 or so miles per hour – to be sure, a mere zephyr compared with Caribbean/American Gulf Coast or South Asian blows, but I couldn't remember being in gales like this ever before except perhaps on Campobello in (? 1958) when the hurricane passed through. (Of course, I realized suddenly, we're on top of a 'hill' here, that's to say a full 70–75 feet [sic!] above sea level, where the same sweeping panorama and 'big sky' we delight in so much in calm weather means, in stormy times, no shelter whatsoever.)

And the noise! Outside, the tempest literally howled around the merlons and turret-finials atop the parapet walls; inside, unlatched doors banged as gusts found their way through the elderly window-frames and eddied about the Hall itself. (The lower sash in the master bathroom window, lacking keeper rails, was particularly afflicted, flapping out on its cords like a spinnaker sail whose sheets had let go; our emergency attempts to 'cleat' it were only partly successful.) And from the front porch – exposed nearly broadside to the full force of the storm – a minimalist mini-symphony rose: the trailing ends of the wisteria vines over-growing it rapping and tapping... percussing... against the glass panes of its windows, and the copper weather-stripping around its inside door vibrating like a saxophone's reed and giving out a low, melancholic, moan-like sound.

The afternoon of 27 October, we made another Brambledown-Heartsease Hall trek, this time in our Land Rover with our horsebox in tow. In the back of the Land Rover, carefully bubble-wrapped and packed, was what I referred to as my 'mural comfort blanket': a selection of favourite oil paintings, most of which I proposed to hang in the Hall's drawing room. In the horsebox was a load even more esteemed in some ways: Applesauce and Mustard – the two pure-bred, wild-boar weaner pigs we'd acquired only a few weeks earlier via a wildlife centre in the Cotswolds – and the earlier-introduced Piggy, our 'Large White' (the common name/descriptive of a breed of commercial pig) 'house' sow – that's to say a sow who was part pet and part the generatrix of pork for our table – who was then heavily 'in pig' (pregnant).

The pigs' rations having been considerably reduced the day before, loading our little swine-herd wasn't a problem. I made up a batch of especially savory swill, served it into a trough placed deep within the body of the horsebox, and then stood back out of the way; like aspiring buyers to an Apple or Microsoft new-product-launch/sale, the pigs swarmed in. As soon as they were feeding, I closed and barred the inner gates of the horsebox, lifted the ramp, and slid its locking bolts home.

Unloading the pigs was a somewhat longer and more suspenseful story, however. To encourage the Reader's anticipation to build:

As the Reader may be aware, driving a loaded horsebox requires care if its occupants aren't to be badly inconvenienced... or worse. Acceleratings and brakings must be smooth and gradual; turnings and roundaboutings must be smooth and slow. And perhaps needless to mention, the foregoing, going constraints must be observed pretty much regardless of the antics, stratagems and ploys of competing road users.

As the Reader may also be aware (see Ch. 2), driving cross-country in the UK – as distinct from driving between major conurbations – almost invariably involves stretches of narrow, twisty-turny back roads. Moreover, as will be recalled (Ch. 5), about a third of the way along our Brambledown-Heartsease Hall route lies the Milton Keynes northern 'by-pass', or beltway-analog, with its many roundabouts (our son Bapu's stomach's nemesis) preceded, separated and succeed-ed by lengths of 'dual carriageway', that's to say interstate-highway type roads.

Back roads are regarded by some British drivers as opportunities to hone their rally-driving skills. They tail-gate aggressively then, at the earliest opportunity – even before that opportunity, occasionally – they attempt to overtake. Road systems such as Milton Keynes' northern by-pass are, in turn, regarded as opportunities to hone their Formula One racing skills. They speed along the 'interstate straights', down-shift and brake hard into the roundabouts – sometimes 'drift-ing' (skidding sideways) through them – then they accelerate out... and all of this even at the height of the rush hour, sometimes.

But – Sorry, folks! – not that late-afternoon of 27 October rush hour. From stressed-out, home-bound commuters stuck behind Yr Correspondent and his loaded horsebox, you could almost hear the shouting and cursing and gnashing of teeth.

Shortly after exiting Milton Keynes, I stopped at a gas station to refill the Land Rover's tank and buy some snacks for N *et al*; as well, I checked on the three passengers in the horsebox and gave them some water. Applesauce and Mustard were, manifestly, a bit wound up, but Piggy was as she ever was: serene, seraphic, sedate... perhaps, even, half asleep. We proceeded on to Heartsease Hall; I dropped N and Bapu off in the stableyard, then drove the Land Rover, etc, down the track to the walled garden – the pigs' designated new 'sty'. By then the light was starting to fade, and I recall thinking how nice it would be to get the pigs out and re-settled in before it went com-pletely. I backed the horsebox up to the entrance to the walled gar-den, set some 'hurdles' – sections of portable wooden (or, increasingly now, metal) fencing – from the horsebox to the entrance to define a runway, unbolted and lowered the ramp, opened the inner gates, and waited and waited... and waited... for the exodus to commence. After a minute or so of no action, I poked my head around the back of the horsebox and peered in.

At the very front of the vehicle's hold, barely visible in the gather-ing gloom, Applesauce and Mustard caromed around like bumper-cars run amok; they were certainly ready for out. But about half-way in and lying diagonally athwart the horsebox like some vast sack of grain – effectively blocking the young boars' exit – was our dear Pig-gy, grunting periodically. And in the straw on the floor of the horsebox looking like big, pink maggots lay… a quantity of piglets. 'Ar-rrugnnnph,' grunted Piggy, depositing yet another big, pink 'maggot' on the horsebox floor.

Remove this bunch to their new home now, under these conditions, I considered? Not a chance! After putting in fresh water and swill, I closed the gates of the horsebox, raised the ramp back up and bolted it shut… and trudged wearily down the track to the Hall.

· · · · · · · · · · · · · · · · · · · ·

All these anecdotes… these divertissements: *I thought this book was supposed to be about you and your wife buying a historic English country estate and you becoming an English country squire.*

It is. But that sort of narrative… that sort of 'plot': boy and girl meet property; boy and girl fall in love with property; boy and girl buy… is hardly the stuff of compelling literature, Alter-natis. For compelling literature, you need to treat consequential, enduring themes like life, struggle, death… transfiguration, even… maybe.

The English Romantic poet William Blake in his Auguries of In-nocence *sought 'a World in a Grain of Sand, and a Heaven in a Wild Flower'.*

Now you're getting there. I'm trying to see a World….

In a farrowing Large White sow-pig and her plague of piglets?

Many very fine authors have characterized pigs, viz: Roald Dahl in *Pig*, A. A. Milne in *Winnie the Pooh*, George Orwell in *Animal Farm*, Beatrix Potter in *The Tale of Pigling Bland* and *Pig Robinson*, Dick King-Smith in *The Sheep Pig*, E. B. White in *Charlotte's Web*, P.G. Wodehouse in… to name just a few.

'Pig-lit', you might say, with apologies to your nick-named elder son: like 'belles-lettres', a literary sub-genre but, obviously, lacking that mode's intellectual appeal. See also 'chick-lit' (French: 'chic-litte'), 'environmenta-lit', 'socio-cultura-lit', 'lifesty-lit', 'trave-lit'… perhaps even 'gustatoria-lit' (aka 'cookin' 'n' 'eatin' [l]it')….

That's enough, Alter-natis!

· · · · · · · · · · · · · · · · · · · ·

The next morning, counselled by N and Bapu from deep within their chosen redoubt – the cab of the Land Rover – I resumed my efforts to get Applesauce and Mustard, and Piggy *et al* out of the horsebox and into the walled garden. My intrepid advisers positively hemorrhaged advice:

'Do like you do with the sheep, Daddy, when you want to move a ewe and her lambs into the barn, say. Open the wooden gate into the walled garden, gather the piglets up and carry them in…. Piggy'll then just follow on through.'

That's a *really good* suggestion, Bapu; we might give it a try later. But remember: to get the piglets out means I've got to go in and confront a quarter-ton or so of lightening-quick, fiercely-protective porcine maternity within the close confines of the trailer's hold. One rip of Piggy's up-curving, razor-sharp tusks....

'Well, get her some of her favorite food, Dar. What's it she really likes? Porridge with milk and raisins and brown sugar? Put *it* in the walled garden.... When Piggy comes through to take the food, close the wooden gate behind her and lock her in. *Then* gather up the piglets....

That's first-class lateral thinking, N; you do Stanford and the B-School and the Firm... the White House, even... proud. But Piggy's probably not all that interested in food just now; in the wild, a post-partum sow generally lives off her reserves of fat until her piglets are able to travel and, therefore, may not go out to feed for several days.

And incidentally, the proposal both of you made that I 'gather up' Piggy's brood: good, healthy piglets typically activate like – and sound *somewhat* like – car alarms. So long as no one bumps them or tampers with them – tries to 'steal' them, say – they're nice and quiet. But disturb one... 'gather (one) up'... and the most ear-splitting screech is triggered. Before you could say 'I'm only trying to help!' Piggy would almost certainly be back on station – in the horsebox or in the walled garden, closed and locked wooden gate or no – looking to shred every animate intermeddler she found.

The best solution for Piggy, *et al*, I therefore decided, was for them to stay right where they were for awhile. The horsebox was dry and comfy and, as the nearest road was a mile or so away across heavy country – an all-but impossible trek for the stubby-legged, neo-nate piglets – I could leave its gates open and its ramp down; whenever Piggy decided her brood needed a walkabout, she could safely indulge them. So enjoining Piggy to 'Have a nice day!' N, Bapu and I departed.

(I did, however, eventually manage to extract Applesauce and Mustard through what's called the groom's door*. Indeed, when I opened it, the poor, terrified little beasties nearly knocked me over in their haste to exit.)

Later that morning, I received two letters of note. One was from Sir

---

* A small door in the front of most horseboxes by means of which having led the horse in, the groom makes his or her way out.

Roald saying how very much he and Lady Maureen were 'moved' by N's and my gift of the d'Arcy Henry spoon, and that they looked forward to taking up our invitation to visit 'very soon'.

The other was from the real estate agent who'd sold us Heartsease Hall. After congratulating N and me on our purchase – which he described as 'perhaps the most exquisite property (he), in (his) twenty-five years in the business, (had) ever handled' – and wishing us 'an eternity of happiness' there – a wonderful wrap-up touch, N and I thought – he disclosed that he'd been approached by a program maker for the BBC who wanted to do a television documentary about first-time owners of important English country estates. Might we be persuaded to participate, he asked?

· · · · · · · · · · · · · · · · · · · ·

Suddenly, after all those years of oblivion, the curse of fame was upon you.

'Station inflation', Alter-natis: the attribution of eminence to someone who's maybe slightly above-average good and/or just plain lucky.

And yet purchasing the Heartsease Hall Estate was or could be viewed as a distinction no more insubstantial... no more unworthy... than that which many political people, movie, theater and show-biz people, print, small-screen and radio people, athletes and 'personalities' of all sorts tout nowadays.

Those people hardly have fame... *real* fame. They have 'celebrity': a hollow simulacrum of fame – almost invariably media-driven – which the under-educated, under-employed, intellectually and emotionally un-fulfilled embrace like 'sex and drugs and rock 'n' roll', to borrow Ian Dury's phrase...

... and for the rest of us to embrace: wine and food. Don't forget compensatory indulging in wine and food, and shopping... and gambling... and on-line social networking, even!

... in an attempt to furnish the emptiness of their lives and give a semblance of substance to their self-esteem. 'A celebrity is a person who is known for his (or her) well-knownness,' as the historian Daniel Boorstin put it in his book *The Image*.

It's people like us who enable celebrities to achieve their well-knownness, you know....

People like you, perhaps, but not me!

We identify with them, lavish attention and tribute on them... try, even, to emulate them by buying into their so-called enviable lifestyles. In short, we build 'em up...

... like the false gods and goddesses they are...

... and then we knock 'em down. As any number of observers

have remarked, the lives of many celebrities ultimately become –
figuratively generally but, occasionally, literally – the modern-day
equivalent of one of mankind's oldest rituals: the blood sacrifice.
Hummmm....
And you and I are right there in the van, gawping at the gore.
So what, then, is 'fame', Alter-natis? Real, *bona fide* fame?
It's a sort of halo which in the fullness of time certain summa(e)
summora(e) *– the highest of the mortal high – may be given to wear.*
As a real-life goal to be sought, however, my estimation is that
fame's probably overrated; even in the very, very unlikely event you
achieve it, most of the benefit will accrue to your heirs.
· · · · · · · · · · · · · · · · · · ·

That evening, a Friday, N and I went out 'to take the air' as the British say (or used to say, before so many of them became so sedentary)
and count our blessings. We strolled the front lawn and admired the
view of St Lawrence's Church, then we walked around to the back
lawn and dittoed St Michael's Church. The ecclesiastical antipodes
of the Heartsease Hall Estate, I reflected, their axis running nearly
through the center of the Hall itself, 'as they are and ever (may) be'.
The landscape's doubtless somewhat altered over time, I supposed,
but otherwise...

· · · · · · · · · · · · · · · · · · ·

'Every valley shall be exalted and every mountain and hill shall be
made low: and the crooked shall be made straight and the rough
places plain,' in the words attributed to Isaiah by certain of the 47
or so scholars King James I of England deployed to re-translate the
Bible with which his name is associated, and which Handel set so
beautifully to music in his Messiah. Such a masterful description of
geologic change!
... and by extension, of mankind's societal and genomic change,
that's to say the global 'melting pot' in action.
· · · · · · · · · · · · · · · · · · ·

... but otherwise, all must be pretty much as it's been here through
peace and war, salubrity and pestilence... years fat and lean and
countless ordinary, everyday years.... The sense of tranquility – of
Earthly and Heavenly concord, almost – was so profound....
When, like a tonal thunderclap, from the carillon tower of St
Michael's Church a peal came ding-donging – 'tintinnabulating'*
– through the twilight still. What a glorious, exuberant, uplifting

---

* The onomatopoetic coined by Edgar Alan Poe in his poem *The Bells*, and well
known to many of Yr Correspondent's age and ilk.

noise it was! And it reminded me that before wire (? fixed) line and wireless – but after drums – bells were society's means of 'instant' communication, summoning local people and, perhaps, their farther neighbours, sounding the alarm and the all clear, proclaiming births, marriages and deaths and other sorts of installations and demissions, sending dispatches in code... or simply marking the passage of time. The Festings and the Hobarts before them – and before them, assuming this carillon existed then, the Boleyn-Cleres – would have heard these bells or their predecessors ringing out their message of man in the countryside, man in north Norfolk and The Motherland and the world... The Spirit in man.

(As we later learned, this particular clamour signified nothing either toward or untoward but rather owed to a group of campanologists having their weekly 'ring'.)

The following Sunday while out walking the donkeys, that's to say continuing...

• •

I can see the headstone now: 'In memoriam W. d'Arcy Henry, 1942-[...], first American Squire of the Heartsease Hall Estate. "He walked donkeys and bred swine".'
You mustn't refer to Piglet and Bapu like that, Alter-natis; you'll hurt their feelings! Just because they don't always keep their bedrooms neat and clean....

• •

... continuing our exploration of our new property, we had two further interesting 'encounters'. First, on our outbound journey, Piglet leading Maggie, and Big Fee leading Jubie with Bapu up: 'The estate plan says the ice house* ought to be over there, Dad,' Piglet shouts, pointing into the depths of Neate Wood; trailing Maggie, off he sets. That gets Big Fee's orienteering juices flowing. With Bapu hanging for dear life onto Jubie's mane, she and her charges plunge into the woods too. Moments later from Piglet comes the triumphant cry: 'It's here! The ice house is right here! Wow; it's big... and deep... and dark! Most of its roof's fallen in, though.' In a few moments, N and I too have discovered another of the Heartsease Hall Estate's enchanting (or given the resources likely required to restore it, I reflected, perhaps that should be '*dis*enchanting') ruins.

---

* Where, before the advent of modern refrigerators, blocks of ice cut from the lower lake in winter would have been stored for summertime, 'icebox' use.

Then as we meandered home, evening starting to fall, a creamy-brown owl – a barn owl... *Tyto alba*, to give it its Latin name; a 'protected' species in the UK and the first one I'd ever seen in the wild – was patrolling the edge of the Shrubbery (a misleadingly-named small woodland). With its great, slow wing-beats... leisurely wing-beats, almost... and its seemingly effortless alteration of altitude and attitude – now falling away to the left; now stroking up to the right – the apparently-lazing raptor seemed a metaphor of dalliance and blithe fancy-free. But all of a sudden, after an almost imperceptible stall: whuumpht! Down like a landing sky-diver flaring his canopy it collapsed onto some unsuspecting prey – a field mouse, I supposed. For a moment the owl lingered on the ground. Then, its deadly talons locked into the mouse's body, up it flew to the top of a nearby fence-post (a 'plucking post', I learned they may be called) where it dismembered the hapless rodent and, gobbet by bloody gobbet, swallowed it. A twisting, turning, upward stretch of the neck – to compose the gobbets in its proventriculus (crop-like, upper stomach), presumably – a preen of a disarrayed feather or two, a seemingly bemused, slo-mo peri-scope of the surrounding countryside... and *T. alba* was away again in search of its next course.

On 31 October, N and I drove to London for an evening out 'painting the town'. (In the event, our preferred local pizzeria... was full of overwound trick-or-treaters and their chaperones – recognition of Halloween as a commercial opportunity may have come late to UK merchants, we sighed, but when it came it came big-time – so instead we had a Chinese take-away in our flat.) With us we took some letters for Sir Roald and Lady Maureen which had been delivered in error to Heartsease Hall. Wanting some exercise after the long drive, I decided to jog the mile or so from our premises to the Festings' and forward the errant mail by hand. I arrived to find Lady Maureen just starting out on a walk with Phoebe, the English Cocker Spaniel puppy she'd recently acquired. I asked after Sir Roald's health; Lady Maureen said he was nearly fully recovered from his operation but that he'd found his hospitalization 'very tedious' and was 'in desperate need of someone interesting to talk to'. Wouldn't I please 'go in and entertain him'? Entertaining the 13th Baronet could, I knew, be a pretty tall order. But professing delight at being asked to try, in I went.

Although I'd spoken frequently to Sir Roald on the telephone, I hadn't seen him in the flesh since our meeting on 26 July and, as was immediately clear, during those intervening three or so months his illness had taken its toll. Sir Roald made no reference to his medical trials, of course; as usual, his mind was orbiting so high over matter as to transcend such mundanities altogether. And when I asked him how he was feeling, he replied with an impatient shrug: 'Very well indeed, thank you; absolutely fine.' But he looked thinner, greyer... older.... And running from behind his left ear down and along the hollow of his jaw he'd a fresh scar which, although apparently well healed, was surrounded by angry, reddened skin. I thought to myself: Oh dear, oh dear!

As usual, we began our 'chat' with a review of current international developments.* Then we moved on to European, American and British news and, finally, to north Norfolk and local, parish-pump 'news'... stopping just short of the one topic I felt must be pretty-well forward in Sir Roald's mind but which, I sensed, he thought it inappropriate that he himself should raise: how N, the boys and I were getting on in his ancestral home.

• • • • • • • • • • • • • • • • • • • •

The British, especially the more intelligent and/or better-travelled ones, tend on the whole to respect your privacy... your 'personal psychological space'; Americans are typically more intrusive... more 'in-your-face'. Why is that, Alter-natis?

Not so many more-intelligent, etc, Brits think they have so many answers, probably.

• • • • • • • • • • • • • • • • • • • •

So into a lull in the conversation I inserted: 'Living at Heartsease Hall is a great pleasure, Sir Roald; my wife and I and our two boys... all of us as a family... like it there very, very much.' As if a switch had been tripped, Sir Roald's weary, distressed eyes lit up. 'You do, Mr Henry?' he said. 'You really do?' In an uncharacteristic gesture of familiarity, he reached out and gently patted my knee. Then slowly, quietly, and with evident content he said simply: 'I can't tell you how glad that makes me feel.'

... on which note my audience with Sir Roald... my amiable audi-

---

* One topic was whether President Clinton's compulsive womanizing or President Yeltsin's heavy drinking posed the more-immediate threat to world peace. Sir Roald's judgment was that the Russian leader's dipsomania did but, he advised, no one really need worry on that account. 'Boris' Kremlin minders will keep him well away from "The Red (nuclear) Button"!' he chortled determinedly, through pain-clenched teeth.

ence, certainly, my intimate audience, perhaps – such as might obtain between a tutor and his pupil, or a God-parent and his God-child, or an uncle and his nephew... or even, if the Reader will excuse the presumption, a father and his proxy son and heir – drew to its close.

Chapter 8

Blind Country

With its expanse of scuffed floorboards and worn, grey-brown, broadloom carpet, its compass of sallow walls and faded-yellow, brocade curtains... its vasty, soot-scumbled, off-white ceiling – its spare emptiness, in short, which not even my 'mural comfort blanket' of paintings, most of which I'd hung there, was able really to relieve – Heartsease's drawing room seemed to N and me a bit like 'The Wilderness' or desert, famed of wise men's wanderings, and as such we regularly referred to it.

But within weeks of our coming to live in the Hall, Piglet and Bapu had transformed this 'barren sand' into a Lego and Brio-land oasis, plenteous with delight. Plastic-block gas stations, shopping malls and castles – as well as palm-shaded islands with pirates and their treasure – had sprung up and been encircled by wooden, model-railway tracks with stations and trains. Ah, the envisionary creativeness of young minds, N and I marvelled, seeing – and realising – in The Wilderness a potential our older minds had ignored.

On 2 November, I received in the mail from Sir Roald a thick, A4-size (slightly larger than American 8" x 10") envelope. In it was a detailed structural survey of the Hall which he'd commissioned in 1993, and an apologetic note saying he'd meant to give me the document months ago but had misplaced it during his house-move. Some 25 pages long, and complete with drawings and costings, and – best of all – conclusions essentially in accord with those David B had reached, Sir Roald's survey was just the sort of platform I needed to support 'The Masterplan for the Restoration of the Heartsease Hall Estate' N had proposed on 31 March, the day after we'd first viewed. I sat down at my 'desk', that's to say the opened-out folding card table, in the library – hereinafter, when appropriate, to be referred to as 'the estate office/library' – took out a fresh pad of paper and a clutch of newly-sharpened pencils:

. . . .

I'm very sorry, Class, to have had to re-schedule our last lecture. But my wife and I were then just moving into the Heartsease Hall Estate – about a week later, we actually bought *and paid for* it! – and I just couldn't find the time....

Anyway: today, I'd like to talk about forward planning and, perhaps, further develop a plan I've been working on – 'The Masterplan', I call it – for the restoration and renovation of the Heartsease Hall Estate. To help us, and to provide his own, very distinctive perspective, I've brought along Alter-natis – 'natis' is an archaic word for 'buttock', or 'butt', by the way – who's my.... Well, I'm sure you bright guys can work out who he is.

So, why are we waiting, 'Master'? Unveil the Masterplan!

'What's your mission statement going to be, Prof?'

You're quite right, Che, quite right... amazingly.... We must begin, of course, with that most-esteemed of business management tools: 'The Mission Statement'.

Now, BS.... I'm sorry to interrupt your daydreaming – better, perhaps, your time-out; were you on the football field scoring the winning touchdown, or somewhere well removed from gridiron activities 'scoring' more euphemistically? Tell us, please: just what is a 'mission statement'? Give us an example.

'To make big bucks.' OK, and.... How's that? You say you placed a couple of limit orders yesterday... and now you need to check if they've been executed.

Well you're right: 'to make big bucks' is a mission statement, in a sense... a declaration of what you want to accomplish... what you want to achieve... although I'm bound to point out that senior corporate executives are generally encouraged to define a 'mission' somewhat more broadly. Yes.... Oh: I see. You're asking if you may be excused for a few minutes... to telephone your stockbroker. OK, but make it quick. For the rest of us, struggling along here under the heavy burden of our own and now, collectively, a lot of other peoples' mortgages... which, we devoutly hope, in fact are 'Triple A'....

The mission statement I've arrived at with respect to Heartsease Hall, Class, is as follows: to achieve an input/output-optimized, authentically restored and renovated, residential farming estate.

Wow! All those great, big buzzwords!

'Sir, you've got to keep it simple. Why don't you – at least conceptually – take it one step at a time. First draw up a plan for, say, the critical, money element of the estate: the farming.'

The farming's pretty well under control, GT. We're already getting a reasonable income from the crops we produce – although I'm sure that income could be improved – and as regards income from livestock, there're only a couple of things I've got to do: decide which fields and parts of fields will revert to trees and grassland – that's to say which fields, etc, will be 're-emparked' – and put some fencing around them; and install cattle grids (barriers to transit by hoofed animals) at the top and bottom of the front drive so we can graze its verges.

'See, Professor Henry: planning's very straightforward. Title One: Farming. Schedule One: Arable. Item One – 'T1S1I1' we'll call it, for ease of reference – rationalization of contractual arrangements. Farming... Schedule Two: Livestock. Item One, or 'T1S2I1': determination of new grassland areas/re-emparkation, and erection of perimeter fencing. T1S2I2: installation of cattle grids. So, on to Title Two or 'T2': 'Residential'.

Yes, Ms Gospel. Well... O...K.... On to residential, I guess. The first thing we need is a comfortable home for my family and me. That means renovating parts of the Hall. So... Title Two: Residential. Schedule One: the Hall....

'That's it, Sir. You're getting the hang of it. Now: what's going to be the first actual line item? The outside of the Hall? The inside? The top... the sides... the bottom?'

The 'bottom'.... Yes... indeed: exquisite... *absolutely exquisite*, don't you agree, Alter-natis? *The way hers just sort of....* Errr, sorry; my mind wandered.... I mean: you can delete 'bottom', Ms Gospel; Heartsease Hall's foundations are absolutely solid as a rock. And, would you believe it, there's no mortar in the footings – the builders used only shingle and a bit of sand! Over time, such a mixture packs down like concrete, I'm told.

'Right, then, sir: on to the outside. Or the ins...?'

We'd better begin with the outside, GT.

'The top? The sides?'

Well, the roof's just old. It's not actually leaking....

Oh? So what, then, are those damp spots around the cornice moldings in your younger son's bedroom and on one wall of what, because of the color of its wallpaper, you call the Orange Bedroom?

Those? They're from leaks in the parapet guttering, Alter-natis, not actually in the roof itself.

A pretty fine distinction, if you ask me....

But the walls.... They've a couple of sections which need work, like on the northeast gable end... and the western end of the southeast elevation.

You mean right above the original master bedroom where you and, more importantly, your beloved wife now sleep each night.

Hmmmm; perhaps we should make the walls 'item one'. And we'll consider the windows – re-painting, re-puttying... re-glazing, where necessary – part of the walls. So, as you're logging it: T2S1I1: The Sides.

'That's the old, fighting spirit, sir. You're really into it now!'

Next: Residential; The Hall; Item Two, or T2S1I2: The Top.
Yes – and the 'parapet guttering', as you tell us it's called.
Then, Item Three; we start inside.
'Where "inside", Professor Henry?'
Well… the electrics are pretty good, Ms Gospel – in fact, the Hall's recently been almost completely rewired. And the heating and hot water system isn't too bad. It's not quite big enough, perhaps, for the job it's supposed to do – you could put in a more-powerful boiler and add a few radiators if you really wanted to – but the system itself is entirely adequate.
That's not what your wife says. She says winter's only just beginning and already she's feeling cold. Indeed, she's started comparing Heartsease Hall's interior micro-climate to Brambledown's… or that of a castle in Scotland….
'What about the bathrooms and the kitchen, d'Arcy?'
The bathrooms. Good Lord! All but one of them are positively antediluvian!
The bathrooms. Yes, Ms Goldstar…. The original bathrooms are, indeed, very, very interesting. In the late 18th century, when the Hall was built, indoor plumbing… plumbed-up indoor bathrooms, especially… were a luxury and only for the very rich, you'll understand. The fact that the Hall was actually designed with bathrooms, therefore, is striking in itself. The 'stacking' of the original bathrooms, one above the other in a three-floors-into-two, mezzanine arrangement – which offered great efficiencies from the standpoint of pipework – is particularly noteworthy. Of course, some of the sanitary ware has a few chips… and a few cracks….
Surely you can keep the stack of three bathrooms, that's to say the architectural phenomenon, but replace the sanitary ware, so as not to have to toilet every day in something George Washington – or rather, George III – might have used!
'It sounds to me, Professor Henry, like the bathrooms will have to be very substantially renewed.'
But Ms Gospel….
'Architectural authenticity… architectural integrity… must of course be respected. But these constraints mustn't be allowed to take precedence over the reasonable needs of day-to-day, contemporary living.'
All right, then: T2S1I3, the bathrooms; I4, the kitchen; I5, rebuilding the end of the annex which, Sir Roald – that's Sir Roald Festing, the previous owner of the Heartsease Hall Estate; I don't believe I've introduced him to you before – advised me, had 'got lost' many years ago… 'burned down', he thought. That would give us two more bedrooms and a further bathroom – which could form part of a 'granny flat', as you British call them, for my wife and/

165

or me to retire to someday – as well as a proper food larder and, of course, the family farmhouse kitchen-*cum*-snug we all want.... And that would be that.

Thank goodness! At last: the wretched Masterplan's complete. Now we can....

'Hang on a minute, sir! What about the rest of the buildings? The old laundry, the old brewery, the stables, the carriage house, the orangery, the boat house, the ice house.... What we might call the estate's original domestic 'plant'.

Aarrragh! I don't know about you, Class, but I'm finding all this planning stuff pretty heavy going... and I'll bet the Reader is too. Couldn't we take a little break?

'And most important of all, Prof, the cottages for your staff and the rented cottages, and the cottages you intend to rent...?'

Ummmm. I'd forgotten about the cottages, Che. We can't have our staff and our tenants living in premises which aren't up to scratch, can we? No sirree: that's not how a squire... a real, caring English country squire – or a real, caring country squire of any nationality, presumably – would behave....

'What's... what's that strange noise, Professor Henry? It sounds like the lowing of cattle wanting food and/or water, or the baying of angsty, kennelled hounds.... Sir? Can you hear it? It seems to be coming from deep in the basement somewhere... and trembling the floorboards beneath our feet.'

It's the sound of generation upon generation of cold, wet, ill-housed English country staff and tenantry, moaning and groaning and hooting derisively from their graves.

So, Ms Gospel. Title Two: Residential; Schedule One – that's to say 'T2S1' – to become 'the cottages', then. Make The Hall T2S2....

'What time-frame have you specified, d'Arcy?'

What what, Ms Goldstar?

'What "time-frame". That's: "How long is all this work going to take?"'

Two to three years, Ma'am...?

Is that a declarative or an interrogative?

Two to three years, Ma'am!

'And "benchmarks", sir. How're you going to ensure the work's carried out to an acceptably high standard?'

Err, by.... Ummm... we'll just do the best we can, GT.

Your debt-holders and shareholders – and, in particular, English Heritage – may not accept such a relaxed, go-with-the-flow approach....

'Finally, Professor Henry: operational constraints. Are you aware of any factors which might negatively impact the implementation of your so-called Masterplan?'

Lack of time, Ms Gospel. Lack of money. Lack of knowledge. Lack of experience....

'Oh, get real, Prof. It can't be that bad.'

... not to mention, Che, what seems to be a lack of understanding of or sympathy for my predicament.

Well, if it is that bad, you and your wife shouldn't have bought Heartsease Hall in the first place. So, come on: pull yourself together. Get a grip on....

Ouch!

No need to grip yourself so hard... or right down there!

'Sir, I think we should talk about these purported operational constraints of yours.'

OK, GT: time and money. I'm supposed to be employed, you know, helping run an international management consultancy and lecturing you lot occasionally. So there's only a certain amount of time I can devote to Heartsease Hall. And, as regards money... unless we want to go back again to The Suits – who, you may recall, we're already into for a mortgage and a bridging loan – we'll have to be careful how we spend.

'Given Heartsease Hall's "Listed Grade I" status.... Surely, Professor Henry, the government will help restore such a notable component of Britain's built heritage?'

They do offer some assistance, Ms Gospel. But Sir Roald didn't find the government very forthcoming.

'What about charitable bodies here and in the United States, sir? And the Anglo-American "Special Relationship" thing... and the Puritan "Great Migration" thing?'

There's lots of competition for that sort of money, young lady, but it's certainly worth a try. More to the point, it's certainly worth my wife's trying – she's FHA's engagement partner. But, in the meantime.... By the way, Ms Gospel, when you knit your brows together, as in concentration, did anyone ever tell you how very, very attractive...?

'Professor Henry: *please*! In the meantime, we'll have one titled, scheduled and itemized – "TSI'd" – Masterplan for the achievement of an input/output-optimized, authentically restored and renovated, residential farming estate. We told you it wouldn't be all that difficult.'

At last, it's done! What a relief!

Thank you very much, Class. I'll just tidy The Masterplan up and give it more detail....

· ·

Which I did. And having thus further diminished my fresh pad of paper, and worn down even more the points of my newly-sharpened pencils, I sat back to watch while the elemental forces of Mother Nature revised The Masterplan to *their* specification....

· ·

'As flies to wanton boys, we are to the gods; they kill us for their sport,' in the words Shakespeare gave to King Lear.

· ·

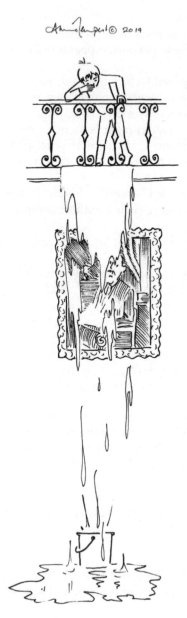

For on the evening of 3 November, another (see Ch. 7) almighty storm broke, this time with rain the like of which I'd only ever experienced in India's Western Ghats, where the monsoon can drop three or so feet of water in as many days. Down through the holes in the corroded parapet guttering and into Bapu's and the orange bedrooms the deluge drained and, apparently, up and under the slipped, etc, slates on the weather slope of the roof it drove because, within minutes, we'd a miniature Victoria Falls – in the rainy season, it becomes the world's largest cataract by water volume, we're told – pouring from the ceiling of the staircase hall to the ground floor some 30 feet below.

In his capacity as CEO of the Heartsease Hall Estate, Yr Correspondent immediately directed that appropriations formerly reserved for repairing the sides of the Hall – T2S2I1 of The Masterplan – be applied to repairing its top.

'Charity' – from the Latin word *'carus'* meaning 'precious' or 'dear' – is in theory an expression of love as, for example, St Paul's usage in his 'First Letter to the Corinthians' makes clear.* *Ipso facto*, charity must be freely-given, without any pre, per or post-conditions, that's to say without any binding ties or attached strings.

But in the real world, of course, there's 'no such thing as a free lunch'; *applied* charity presupposes some sort of implicit or explicit contract. Typically, the donor-party – be it a private individual or institution, or a government, that's to say the public sector acting as agent for the taxpayer – makes available what Winston Churchill might have called the increase of the 'blood, toil, tears and sweat' they've expended in the past; in return, the recipient-party pledges their future 'blood', etc, to using what they've been given responsibly and well… or, at least, that's what they *should* do.

N and I certainly weren't charity cases. But, we persuaded ourselves, in restoring the Heartsease Hall Estate – that's to say in restoring a small but important part of the UK's built heritage and, by extension, of The Motherland's… and the world's built heritage, why not? – we'd, in a way, be performing a small public service. Shouldn't we therefore be entitled to a little UK public money? So far so arguably good.

The problem, as we saw it, lay in the British government's 'mandatory public access' requirement. Rightly or wrongly – and probably rightly N and I had, in the end, to admit – this proviso establishes that in accepting public funding, obligations to the ultimate source of that funding – the UK taxpayer – are also accepted. More specifically: if we took public funds to restore the Hall, the Hall should be open to the public; if we took public funds to restore the estate's grounds, the grounds should be open to the public.

N and I looked forward to interested individuals and groups visiting Heartsease from time to time at our invitation – 'permissive public access', as it's often called – indeed, we felt braving such visits went with the turf of owning a historic property. But government-imposed, *mandatory* public access…? We were very much in two minds about that possibility.

. . . .

'Mind' number one: shaped by rugged-individualism as you and your wife knew it in The Motherland of your youth. 'Mind' number two: tempered by 'rugged individualism' – note my use of quotation marks – as, in mid- and later-life, you and your wife came to know

---

* 'Charity suffereth long, and is kind; charity… beareth all things, believeth all things, hopeth all things, endureth all things. Charity never faileth.'

it in the UK and Europe. The two modes are very, very different, you know.

I'd never seen our dilemma in quite that way, Alter-natis...

America's rugged individualism has always been largely synonymous with capitalism and free enterprise. Europe's once was... but for most of the past 100 years or so it's been increasingly subverted by what Herbert Hoover in 1928 described as 'paternalism and static socialism'. (A fulsome realization of this process is, of course, the European Community.) In consequence, rugged individualism in Europe – real rugged individualism, as incarnate in the 'old-line', WWII-era Brits you so revere – has been marginalized almost to the point of extinction.

... but my sad suspicion is that you're right...

That same process of marginalization is now well-established in The Motherland, of course. For although the default mode of many Americans remains rugged individualism – often rugged individualism run riot, some would argue – the cost of servicing the agendas of 'empowered' government agencies and their 'entitled' constituent interest groups and individuals implies America too must eventually go the way of paternalist/socialist Europe.

... and, maybe, right again. So what can my wife and I do?

Accept that rugged individualism – once the rule throughout most of the developed world – is now the exception. That's probably why 'My Way' – the song written by the French duo Claude Francois and Jacques Revaux which, translated, Paul Anka and then Frank Sinatra made famous – has such a powerful resonance.

Anything else?

And keep pushing for 'sustainable free-enterprise democracy'.

Anything else?

'Don't worry, be happy.' To advise again, you'll almost certainly live longer that way.

. . . .

Many people had warned us, however, that the restoration of older properties was a financial black hole. Whatever 'reasonable limits' we might try to impose on costs, they cautioned, once work was initiated, our expenditures would inexorably grow and grow; a succession of humiliating, cap-in-hand meetings with our suits – if not actual bankruptcy – could then ensue. In such an eventuality, N and I concluded, a bit of fall-back funding from the UK government – even funding with strings – might be no bad thing.

And as N knew from her time in Washington, sometimes the public-sector's strings weren't as firmly attached as they appeared... or, if they were, they weren't pulled (? jerked) very hard or very often.

In return for the UK government's assistance in restoring the Hall, say, we might be obliged to open it only for a few days each year, and then only to particular groups – persons interested in Georgian-Gothic architecture or 16th–18th-century British portraiture, say – and to those groups, even, substantially at our own convenience. In short, some reasonable compromise between generalized, large-scale public access and selective, small-scale public access might be able to be achieved.

The Frederick-Henry 'Campaign' to raise money for the restoration of the Heartsease Hall Estate was, therefore, duly inaugurated. N and I decided to beat first the bushes closest to home, that's to say the UK ones – the ones whose interest in a restored Heartsease Hall would, we assumed, be the most direct – and then to beat those farther afield, especially potential donors in The Motherland.

My little Uxor was rearing to go. Literally within hours of our decision to proceed with the campaign, she reported she'd identified and scheduled meetings with the three most-relevant British organizations: the Historic Houses Association (HHA), which offers advice to, and lobbies on behalf of, owners of historic houses; the Country Landowners Association (CLA), which dittoes for owners of large and/or historic estates; and English Heritage, the curator of the nation's historic buildings collection (first referenced in Ch. 2), which has a substantial budget and may actually provide hard cash. With a view to preparing for these meetings, N booked a lunch with Lord Gowrie, a friend of a friend of hers from the Firm who was then a government Minister involved with funding the arts.

The afternoon of Sunday, 6 November, found the Henry family at Caiston Hall, to where they'd been invited for 1600 hours by Joscelyn Steele and his wife Leonie to 'take tea'*. In the event, the 'tea' *qua* tea was just a sideshow.

Shortly before the appointed hour N, the boys and I packed into the car, set out and, after a couple of back-road miles, arrived at Caiston Hall's main entrance. I drove through and started up the drive, aiming for what I could glimpse in the distance was a house of very grand proportions. A half-mile later came a crossroads; I turned in

---

* Tea taken in the afternoon is largely a middle and upper-class conceit and may be followed within hours by supper or, more formally, dinner. In working-class British parlance 'tea', consumed in the evening, typically comprises the main meal of the day.

the direction I thought must be towards the grand house... and in due course wound up at the stables. Ah well: that's life in north Norfolk, I consoled myself. As I was reprogramming, a young man in an exquisitely shabby sports jacket and matching trousers emerged from the stables' tack room. I asked him for directions; he gave them to me and, after another half-mile drive....

Caiston Hall is an imposing, red-brick structure somewhat in the style of Thomas Jefferson's Monticello but larger, and without the roof-top cupola and surrounding balustraded porch. Spilling from its portico-ed, double front doors and down its graduated Portland stone entrance steps that afternoon were a quantity of dogs, some chickens... and a dozen or so people. From the top step, framed by the portico's Tuscan columns and architrave, Joscelyn and a woman I took to be Leonie waved encouragingly. At the bottom of the steps, smiling impishly, stood the shabby-jacketed, etc, young man. As soon as I stopped the car, he tripped around to its passenger-side, opened its front door and, introducing himself as 'the footman', offered to hand N out.

Our host and hostess descended to greet us, then led us back up and into the Hall's main reception area.... Wow; it was as if we'd entered a museum! On the walls, framed family portraits and historical documents all but overhung one another like roofing slates; on the floor, serried ranks of full-length statues and busts on plinths jostled amid display cases overflowing with engraved silver cups and salvers, war medals and other decorations... dress swords, epaulettes... as well as what were referred to simply as 'souvenirs': a dried blow-fish (inflated), an ivory-mounted fly whisk, a Chinese mandarin's pill-box cap, a carved wooden nutcracker seemingly of Central European origin, a set of Ottoman Empire coins....

At last we were ushered into a smallish room about the size of Heartsease Hall's library – lined and re-lined with books, magazines and journals – where a sofa and four or five armchairs were circled in front of a blazing fire. In one of the chairs, an elderly woman fairly dripping diamonds sat wrapped in a mink cloak; she gave her name as Pamela Steele (correctly The Dowager Lady Steele, we learned, Joscelyn's mother) and apologised for not rising. Joscelyn made the rest of the introductions. There were his daughters numbers one and two, and the latter's son (about Bapu's age) and a nephew surnamed Williamson and one further of Joscelyn's daughters – a mezzo-soprano with the Royal Opera House in Covent Garden – and her boyfriend, 'and my son Harcourt, our "footman" whom you've already met', and two of Harcourt's friends from Cambridge University and, entering lately *en pointe*, wearing a tutu… someone's girlfriend. (Keep calm, I kept telling myself, it's just an ordinary, extended, upper-class English family enjoying an ordinary Sunday afternoon at home; N later confided she felt as if she'd just arrived on another planet.)

With the alimentary tea (and the inevitable problems of taking it: balancing your cup, saucer, stirrer/spoon and biscuit in one hand; using the other as required to convey the refreshments to your mouth or fend off other, similarly-preoccupied tea-takers; generally maneuvering around without spilling or dropping anything… all the while trying to be a good guest….) came Question Time, conducted in that courteous but probing style for which a certain ilk of Briton are renowned. ('Is Heartsease Hall your "dream house", then?' 'In many senses, Leonie, many….' 'Mr Henry, why does America hold national elections every two years? Surely, that makes for very choppy governance.' 'It's a deep, US Constitutional thing, Harcourt, and….' 'Do you like chickens, d'Arcy?' 'Do you mean to eat, Lady Steele? Yes, I love….' 'We keep "Norfolk Greys" here; they're *very* civilized, you know, and they give us *such* good eggs.') After an hour or so of trying to keep the conversational ball in the air, Yr Correspondent began to feel as though his tether's end was nigh. As soon as 'tea' was concluded, he offered thank-yous and good-byes all around, withdrew his nuclear, middle-class American family back to their… spacecraft… and sped away home.

. . . .

England and the United States: two countries – better, perhaps, two cultures – 'separated by the same language', as George Bernard Shaw is said to have observed.

. . . .

The following Tuesday, 8 November, I got a letter from Sir Roald saying how much he'd enjoyed my 31 October visit with him in London and referring again to Heartsease Hall's archives most of which, it now seemed, he'd like to entrust to our care.

. . . .

More magnanimity! I hardly knew what to say.

I suggested you say you'd be honored to have the estate's archives – that they'd add a wonderful historical depth to your new living – and thank you very kindly, sir.

But we'd already accepted so much, Alter-natis! Was it right, I wondered, that we just continue to accumulate – to take ownership of, in a sense – what is, after all, properly the property of others?

This sort of cycling and recycling of stuff goes on all the time, d'Arcy. Isaac Watts, the great 17th/18th-century English hymnist, put it wonderfully in his re-make of Verse 5 from Psalm 90: 'Time, like an ever rolling stream, bears all its sons away...

'... They fly, forgotten, as a dream Dies at the opening day.' I think that's just the most beautiful, beautiful jeremiad; every time it comes into my mind, I almost cry.

And 'all time's sons' physical possessions' we might add – if it weren't such a mouthful! Time also bears them away. Then along come Christie's, Sotheby's, Bonhams, Hotel Drouot and sundry smaller auction houses – eBay, even – serving new 'sons' building new collections, and bear many of those chattels back again.

The relentless 'Hegelian dialectic' of thesis, anti-thesis and synthesis....

Errr... no, d'Arcy; not exactly. The so-called Hegelian dialectic is a sort of teleological Google: an algorithmic search-engine for Truth. Anyway, just think of yourself as a Festing 'anthologist', in the original Greek sense of that word: a 'flower-gatherer'. Given that you've acquired the Hall and its principal fixtures, fittings and furnishings, there's logic in your having the estate's archives as well.

But others may be more deserving ....

Good Grief: our very own Uriah Heap, touting humble pie*! As you know, the archives of the Festing family itself are secure in, among other places, the Norfolk Record Office and the Fitzwilliam Museum in Cambridge. What, therefore, are these land-and-buildings related papers to an elderly man with no direct heirs?

Things to cherish, certainly, and to reflect on as *mementi mori* (reminders of the inevitability of death), perhaps....

And then cheerfully to see through to the next generation. In the end, Heartsease Hall's archives – archives generally – are a by-product of life, not life itself.

. . . .

The next day, 9 November, began my formal introduction to real, hands-on estate management and farming – which is to say a whole, new learning-stage in my life began.

The morning's tutorial was taken by the land agent. Predictably, his exposition consisted mainly of observations on the delights of life in north Norfolk. But occasionally, as *intermezzi*, he did refer-

---

* 'Humble pie' is Charles Dickens' wordplay on an inexpensive meat dish made from 'umbles' – originally, apparently, 'numbles' – that's to say the heart, lungs, liver, etc, of a food animal.

ence a number of estate matters, most notably: its non-farming tenancies and rentals (those pertaining to the cottages, and way-leaves [rights-of-way] for the overhead electric-power and telephone lines, and 'certain underground cables belonging to the MOD' [Ministry of Defence]) which, being deemed 'pretty straightforward', it was agreed I should immediately take over the management of; and its 'more complicated' arable-farming ones (cropping plants as opposed to animals) which, until I was able to see more clearly what needed doing, honorable land agent 'humbly' recommended should be 'outplaced', that's to say managed by him.

At the time, I felt my hard-won skills as a management consultant – not to mention my privileged position as husband to a Harvard MBA and *emerita* of the Firm – were being undervalued. But, in hindsight, I'm bound to record the farming tenancies and rentals were a great deal more complicated than I'd thought: some of the arrangements had been entered into by Sir Roald as part of an agribusiness restructuring he'd carried out only a few years earlier, and thus were enshrined in detailed, written covenants; others appeared to date back almost to the time of the Norman Conquest and, so far as could latterly be determined, simply to have been agreed verbally (much as had been our purchase of Heartsease Hall, I noted with wry amusement!).

In all, a dozen or so different farming-tenancy and rental agreements and/or understandings were in force – or more accurately, it transpired, *presumed to be* in force. And in those few instances where similar agreements, etc, applied to land of comparable quality, the income accruing to the landowner varied very substantially – in the case of two almost-identical fields which actually adjoined each other, by almost 200 per cent. In due course, all of this contractual clutter would have to be tidied up, I told myself.

In the afternoon, Joscelyn's farm manager, Neville Sheen, took over as tutor. After detailing the agronomic characteristics of virtually every one of the estate's thirty or so fields and parts of fields (soil structures and ground-water levels, etc, across the property varied very considerably, Sheen told me), he ran me through the cropping rotations of the last three years, complete with inputs (seeds, fertilizers, herbicides, fungicides and insecticides) and outputs (harvested crops) by volume and value.... My brain fairly buzzed from having to accommodate so much new information; leaving the 'arable' to the professionals *pro tem* was undoubtedly the right decision, I concluded!

Finally, we moved onto more familiar territory: sheep and shepherding. In particular, we discussed various possibilities for over-wintering our 60-strong flock of SHB (Scotch Half-Bred) ewes: a very hardy breed known for their big, well-fleshed carcasses*. Most of the options seemed to involve not hay, which was their staple off-season diet at Brambledown, but 'fodder beet' and/or 'stubble turnips'.

As it was obvious any *Real* Farmer – any Real *Sheep* Farmer, at least – must *ipso facto* be fully conversant with these comestibles, I was loath to ask Sheen what, exactly, they were. Even so, two conclusions seemed perfectly clear: fodder beet and stubble turnips were a very palatable, nutritious and cost-efficient winter feed for sheep and, with winter just around the corner, we hadn't got any.

(After my meeting with Sheen, I did some research. Fodder beet, I learned, is a spring-sown root crop which, after being 'lifted' [dug up], may be fed throughout the winter to almost anything: cattle, sheep, pigs, horses... even, my reference book said, domestic and wild fowl. One acre yielded perhaps 14–18 tons. Stubble turnips, I learned, are sown in the autumn either just before – 'under-sown' – or just after a 'combinable crop'† is taken off, and then grazed beginning around Christmas or early in the New Year. Sheep can be 'creep-fed' their turnips bit-by-bit so as to control their intake, or allowed to feed *ad lib*.)

· · · · · · · · · · · · · · · · · · ·

As if your basic story-line – boy and girl meet property, boy and girl fall in love with, buy and prepare to renovate, etc, property – weren't a sufficiently challenging sell, now you're asking the Reader to take an interest in the minutiae of farming.

He or she should. Farming's end-product – food – is, after air and water, the ultimate personal, familial, tribal... regional, national, global... strategic resource – as a growing number of people even in the chronically over-fed developed world are now beginning to appreciate. Food's not a discretionary purchase, like a shiny new set of golf clubs or a fancy, latest-fashion frock; it's a commodity we literally can't live without.

· · · · · · · · · · · · · · · · · · ·

A meeting with the venerable builder who for the last 15–20 years

---

* In the UK, sheep are raised primarily for meat; their wool, used mostly for carpets, is essentially a by-product.

† A crop harvestable with a 'combine': the machine which today simultaneously performs, that's to say combines, the previously-separate functions of harvesting and threshing.

had been the estate's *de facto* fabric officer, that's to say nominally in charge of maintaining and repairing its buildings, concluded my home-instruction day. He told me what he'd been able to get done (mostly minor, often emergency, repairs); I told him what I'd like to do (renovating all of the cottages and much of the Hall); together, we concluded at least 4–5 years' of nearly-full-time work was probably in prospect for a firm of his modest size which, even if N and I could have afforded, he couldn't commit to. The Masterplan's proposed 2–3 year time frame would, I concluded sadly, have to be very considerably extended. (And, in the event, extended and extended again!)

The life of the upstart-American apprentice English country squire wasn't all tea-taking and talking, however; some jobs needing actual, hands-on doing in fact got done, *viz*:

1. I embarked on my first serious re-landscaping. Just off the southwest gable-end of the Hall was a small flower garden/sun lawn hedged on two sides by cypress trees (*Cupressus lelandii*, a fast-growing conifer often used as a wind-break) and remnants of the wrought-iron fencing and galvanized-steel rabbit-wire netting the cypresses had long ago replaced. The height of the trees was such that they largely obscured our view of the upper end of the lower lake; as well, I felt, they detracted from the setting of the Hall and would continue to do so even if pruned well down.

I therefore determined to take the hedge out. The cypresses and the iron fencing posed no problems: a good tug with a chain attached to the Land Rover and they were gone. Removing the wire netting – deliberately entrenched well into the ground to prevent rabbits digging under it and, over the years, invaded by the hedge's roots – was trickier, however; to get it out, you had first to find or make a free end of the netting and then, using the Land Rover, gently pull it back along its length – 'peeling' it out of the ground like the skin from a banana, so to speak – otherwise the strain on the individual wires became too great and the netting broke... in which case you had to dig down and find or make a new free end and start peeling back all over again.

With the hedge gone, the improvement to our prospect was very dramatic; indeed, you could then actually see the upper end of the lower lake instead of just, literally, 'overlooking' it. (Seemingly to protest the invasion of their privacy, some ducks and geese, and our lone, resident grey heron [*Ardea cinerea*] rose at intervals to fly around and reproach us.) The view of the Hall from the southwest also was greatly improved.

2. By way of encore, I began to tame the derelict, hedged holly (*Ilex aquifolium*) running north from the front elevation of the Hall. With its dense, smallish-leaved foliage, holly is fairly easy to keep trim and being, like box (*Buxus sempervirens*), relatively slow-growing, holds its cut shape well. For reasons I'll leave to the (psychoanalyst) Reader to elucidate, Yr Correspondent had always longed for his own well-kept holly hedge.

The holly hedge he'd acquired, however, had rotted stumps and bits of rusted fencing underpinning it, and ivy, brambles and scrub elder (*Sambucus*) growing through it. And, of course, there was the holly itself which, over time, had 'layered' – that's to say propagated new plants from offshoots of the parent one – so as to form an al-most impenetrable brake. Extracting the rubble and then reducing the holly so as to hedge it more precisely – all the while suffering pricks from the holly leaves' peripheral barbs – contributed much to my understanding of sadomasochism. (In my exclusively northern hemisphere experience, the only shrub more challenging to hedge is hawthorn (*Crataegus*), whose typically interlaced branches are armed with sharp spines an inch or so long.)

The results of Yr Correspondent's hard labours that 1994 autumn took many years fully to reveal themselves. But, if I may presume to write: Heartsease's holly hedge – *my* holly hedge – now looks very fine.

3. And then there was the 'adventure' in the course of which Yr Correspondent's knowledge of the estate and its ambient environ-ment – and of his own innermost, most-private self – was significantly deepened, *viz*: I, a relatively experienced, all-round outdoorsman, got disoriented and lost only 800–900 yards from my own front door. And painful though it is to record, being astray – one even that close to home – frightened me.

The incident occurred late one afternoon, as nightfall was well ad-vanced. I'd been 'farming paperwork' at my desk most of the day so, to dispel the stresses of sitting still, I went for a jog – down the track to the walled garden and out the 'back end' of the shrubbery, which all-but surrounds the walled garden, along a length of farm track and into a 50-60 acre field which had recently been harvested – intending to go as far as Long Wood, which lies just short of the northeast boundary of the estate. My mind in neutral, I was idling happily along....

When, part way across the big, recently-harvested – that's to say empty and largely featureless – field, a dense fog... a sort of grey 'white-out'... suddenly came down; so thick was it that I couldn't see where I was going, or where I'd come from or, unless I knelt down, even the ground immediately beneath my feet. A childhood memory of being lost one summer's evening in a fog-bound cranberry bog on Campobello Island powerfully revived and, in an instant, I was all-but shaking with fear.

And the longer I stood there in the cold, damp, sensory-suppressing miasma, the more fearful I became. What if, I wondered, the great, red-deer (*Cervus elaphus*) stag Warrener'd told me about, angered that I was on his turf and among his hinds, or the fierce, 'north-Norfolk puma', sightings of which had been reported in the *Eastern Daily Press* (the local newspaper, known as the *EDP*), hungry for some supper, suddenly emerged in front of me or, even more disconcertingly, behind me.... What could I do?

Or perhaps some modern-day highwaymen lurked who might attack and rob me (they wouldn't get anything, I consoled myself... briefly) or worse ('Your money or your life!'; that's what highwaymen said, wasn't it? And if I hadn't anything to hand over to them...). I pulled myself up to my full height and squared my shoulders; I bulled my neck; I took deep breaths and exhaled them slowly... and I told myself firmly that a reasonably fit and healthy man of my age and experience – an English country squire no less, even if only an apprentice one – on his own estate shouldn't be... *couldn't* be... so shamefully timorous.

But these self-admonitions were of no avail. Desperate to find a place of refuge, I turned around and started walking quickly – given the heavy fog, running wasn't an option – in the direction I assumed was towards the Hall. But before I'd taken more than a few steps, I bumped into the trunk of a great oak tree. (Ah: a landmark, I thought, initially with relief. For a 'mark' to be useful in relation to 'land' which you can't delineate or even see, however, the mark has to have a specific identity. As best I recalled, there were five or six great oak trees in that particular field. Which one was this one? Well, I reflected, at least it offered some shelter, and protection for my back.)

I leaned into the massive trunk and began, very tentatively, to pull myself together. I could stay right here for a while, I reasoned – all night, if necessary. I'd make a pallet and than a coverlet of the fallen leaves which lay thick on the ground, curl myself into a tight, fetal ball, snuggle down… and wait for N – or Big Fee, maybe! – or a search party with tracker-dogs to come and find me. And if no-one came, I'd just stay curled up under the tree until dawn when the rising sun would burn off the fog and I could see how to go.

But could I survive until dawn? In my thin, sweated-up, cotton jogging gear, I was already starting to shiver and the coldest part of the night – when the temperature could fall to freezing or below – was hours away still. My 'good life' had, thankfully, given me a thick layer of subcutaneous insulation. But, even so, what if hypothermia set in? That prospective overnight in the outdoors suddenly began to seem not quite so agreeable; indeed, I began solemnly to reflect on what I had done – and, more solemnly, *hadn't* done – with my all-too-brief life… and even generally to repent me of my manifold sins.

Just as my morale was nearing its nadir, however, a brisk wind began to blow and, as quickly as it had dropped, the dense fog lifted. 'Hallelujah! There's time for a little more doing… and, perhaps, even a little more sinning,' I shouted. 'May The Lord be praised!' The stresses of farming paperwork having by then been pretty much relieved, however… I gave the great oak a little pat of gratitude and, with relief lightening my steps, all but sprinted the 800–900 yards back to the warm hearth of home.

· · · · · · · · · · · · · · · · · · · ·

Alone and unarmed in open ground, not knowing what danger lurks or where refuge lies, man – 'The Ultimate Predator' – becomes just another prey species, Alter-natis. And his view of his world is fundamentally shaped by this dire recognition.

You'd had another little, trifling, 'Moment of Truth', d'Arcy, like you'd had back in September, just before you committed absolutely to purchasing the Heartsease Hall Estate. Only this time, your little wifey wasn't there to hold your hand….

But why was I so frightened, Alter-natis?

As the great 18th-century British lexicographer and critic Samuel Johnson was reportedly asked by his biographer, James Boswell: 'Is not the fear of death natural to man?'

What did Boswell say Johnson replied?

'So much so, Sir, that the whole of life is but keeping away the thoughts of it.'

It takes a particular sort to spend most days compiling a dictionary, I suppose….

Fear of failing socially in your adoptive, new community and/or of failing economically in the challenging job of estate restoration and management you'd taken on might also have underlain your distress. You're a Capricorn – and Capricorns can become obsessed with their projects and with being seen to make a success of them, you know. In some ways, this book could be an example of that....

Failing? We Henrys never give a moment's thought to failing.

Perhaps you should. Failing is to succeeding as Yin is to Yang, or as the songwriter Sammy Cahn put it in 1955 – before 'partnerships' became so popular – as love is to marriage: 'You can't have one without the other'.

But restoring and running the Heartsease Hall Estate and, especially, caring for its fields and lakes and woodlands so as to preserve them for future generations, does sometimes seem a pretty daunting task.

· · · · · · · · · · · · · · · · · · · ·

About this time a new and immensely satisfying chapter in N's and my relationship with Sir Roald and Lady Maureen was opened when they and their precious Phoebe ('she's out of one of Her Majesty the Queen's Sandringham bitches,' Sir Roald told me proudly) became our overnight guests in Dovecote Cottage.

· · · · · · · · · · · · · · · · · · · ·

Dovecote Cottage is only ten yards or so from the Hall's back door – indeed, it's effectively an extension of the Hall. Surely, even in the UK, property-vendors becoming their property-purchasers' house-guests is unusual, isn't it?

It seemed the right thing to do; Sir Roald and Lady Maureen both loved the country and, having moved out of the Hall, they'd nowhere to live except their London premises. So we invited them to stay in the Cottage, and they accepted.

· · · · · · · · · · · · · · · · · · · ·

In what over the next fifteen months or so was to become – for Yr Correspondent, at least – a hallowed, occasional ritual, shortly after 0830 the next morning, Sir Roald knocked gently on the library door and, at my invitation, came in.

I sat the Old Boy on the sofa – lately, of course, *his* sofa – took up my place behind my card-table desk and, after some preliminaries, we began to talk 'about this 'n' that', as Sir Roald came almost invariably to characterize the content of our conversations. Among that first morning's topics, I recall, was the level of confidence the KGB – the USSR-era State Security Committee (now re-named the FSB, or Federal Security Committee) – reposed in the East German secret police, the *Stasi* (the State Security Service, from *Sta[ats] si[cherheitsdienst]*), an office which at the height of the Cold War apparently employed some 500,000 agents to inform on perhaps six million people, Sir Roald told me – in other words, of the order of one-third of East Germany's total 18–19 million population was either spying or being spied on – and, in so doing, accumulated roughly 125 shelf-miles of hard-copy files. Did the KGB trust the *Stasi*, I asked? 'Not much, Mr Henry,' Sir Roald replied, his eyes glinting merrily. 'That's why the KGB station in Berlin was so over-large; instead of co-operating with the *Stasi* as part of a "national", *soviet* (government-council) intelligence team – which they might better have done – they were busy spying on them... and *vice versa*, of course.'

We also tackled the vexed question of what wine to drink with fresh, 'longshore' cod as they're called in north Norfolk: cod caught, often by hand-line, in coastal waters, as opposed to net-caught mesopelagic cod. 'I like a light red – a *Brouilly*, perhaps, or a *Chiroubles* if I'm in Scandinavian mode – otherwise, a nice *Pouilly Fumé*,' Sir Roald confided. In sharp contrast to his somewhat overcast mood in London on 31 October, throughout that morning's caucus the 13th Baronet seemed positively ebullient.

• • • • • • • • • • • • • • • • • • • •

After years of struggle and uncertainty, Sir Roald had given over the very considerable burden of owning and running the Heartsease Hall Estate.

And as a result of his operation, his health prognosis had, perhaps, improved....

One of the great Russian authors – Tolstoi, I think it was – built a lovely short story around this theme: an ageing, aristocratic landowner, exhausted mentally, physically and financially by years of managing his great estate, with its fine Hall, offers to trade places with one of his serfs, an ambitious Young Turk. His offer is readily accepted.

In some respects, that's like Sir Roald selling the Heartsease Hall Estate to N and me.

Fast forward a few years... and the landowner – now living in the serf's cosy, little cottage – is substantially restored in mind, body and bank balance, and hugely enjoying a whole new lease of life. Not so our Young Turk, however. He's over-worked, up tight and run down... on the verge of mental and physical collapse, almost. He begs the elderly landowner to let him have back his little cottage with its simple, secure way of life, but the landowner in effect replies: 'No way, Serge!'.

Alter-natis, did you ever fear I might go the way of the Young Turk?

Yes, d'Arcy; indeed, I'd have characterized the early stages of your struggle with Heartsease Hall much as Arthur Wellesley, later the 1st Duke of Wellington, did his 1815 battle with Napoleon at Waterloo: 'the nearest run thing in your life'. As you grew into the property, however, and it became for you not so much a badge of attainment as just a fine place in which to live, I concluded you'd be OK.

But I'd have to add, again borrowing from the Iron Duke: 'I don't think it would have been done if I' – by which I here intend me, your shy, retiring... Alter-natis – 'had not been there.'

. . . .

On the other hand, Lady Maureen – who I encountered later in the day – seemed a bit down. I attributed her depression to delayed-onset mourning for the loss of Heartsease Hall with its display gardens she'd nurtured so lovingly for so long, and separation from her beloved Maggie and Jubie, perhaps.

By way of contrast, hard on the heels of my amiable and informative exchanges with Sir Roald came a meeting with Mr and Mrs [...] – we'll call them Mr and Mrs 'X'; if they're still alive and able to take in what follows, they'll know who they are – who were the sitting tenants in Bottom Cottage, a 'two (bedrooms) up, two (living rooms) down' situated on low ground three-quarters of a mile or so along the estate's east track, just inside its east gate. Coincident with the institution of Yr Correspondent and his wife as owner-occupiers of the Hall, the Xs had stopped paying their weekly rent.

As this rent was relatively modest and, at the time of our meeting, both the husband and the wife were in full-time employment, *prima facie* there shouldn't have been any question of financial hardship or need – that's to say inability to pay. I therefore suspected what the British call a 'try-on' (deception).

The above notwithstanding, into the estate office/library the delinquent couple came. He was small-framed and of medium height, with lank, dark hair beneath which shifty eyes positively oozing truculence glared out; she was fair-haired and plump – pleasant-looking and seemingly agreeably disposed – but clearly not the lead horse in this rig. I waved the pair to the sofa, then retired to behind my desk; we all sat down....

'So,' I began jovially, 'what're we going to do... about this rent thing?'

'What "rent thing"?' Mr X asks, his eyes flicking like a snake's tongue from the floor in front of him to the window just beyond my right shoulder.

Hmmm, I thought. Trying to give the apprentice squire a rough ride, are you? I'll have to be more direct, I guess, and give you a figurative 'good whiff of grape-shot'* as the 19th-century Scottish essayist Thomas Carlyle put it and/or 'a prick of the old, cold steel' (a bayonet). 'You've not paid your rent for five weeks,' I say sternly.

'We don't owe no rent to you,' Mr X spits out. I do my best to fix him with my hard-man, I'll-have-your-guts-for-garters stare, but he keeps averting his gaze. 'No sir, we don't owe *you* no rent, Mister. Our agreement's with Sir Roald. It's his'n signature, not yer'n, what's on our rent contract.' ('Yer'n'? 'Urine'? For a brief moment, I wondered whether Mr X might have had the contract's paper tested forensically.)

I've got to consider this one carefully, I say to myself. Could there have been a back-office cock-up such that Sir Roald's lawyer's letter, advising Mr and Mrs X of their new landlords, etc, didn't get through? Or – they not being educated people – perhaps Mr and Mrs X just don't understand that ownership of Bottom Cottage, and hence entitlement to rent monies from it, has passed from Sir Roald to N and me. As gently as I can, I lead the pair through these great mysteries of a residential tenant's life.

'It i'n't a question of "lawyer's letters" or "ownership-passing", Mister.' (Old X seemed really to be getting up steam now; Mrs X – poor, pacific Mrs X! – was starting to look very uncomfortable indeed.) 'It's a question of *you*. We don't owe no rent *to you*.'

I thought: this fellow's been taking mendacity lessons from Pol Pot or Slobodan Milosovich or Saddam Hussein, and something tells me he's not yet played his last card. 'How, after what we've just been talking about – the new contract... the other papers which you say you've received – can this be?' I queried, trying to draw the man out and give him the benefit of every possible doubt.

'Cause you 'ad our electricity cut off, and now we got no lights or hot water or heating or telly-vision.' Mr X stared hard at the window to my right; Mrs X suddenly found all manner of interest about the cuffs of her sweater, her hands, her fingers, her wedding band... her fingernails....

'But I've got nothing to do with your electricity, or your lights or your hot water or any of those things,' I protested. 'That's a matter for Eastern Electricity†. And the account with them is in your name.

---

* A gunnery term; in effect, the load of a shotgun shell up-scaled to and fired from a cannon.

† Then the regional electric-power utility, the company's distribution rights are now owned by Centrica, a multi-fuel holding company... with the result that our electricity bills are headed 'British Gas' (*sic*).

How could I possibly cut your electricity off?'

'I dunno, but you did, Mister. *You did.*'

A pattern… a pattern of evasion, dare I write, seemed to me to be emerging. 'Well, I'm sure we can quickly sort this out,' I said, reaching for my telephone. 'I'll just have a word with Eastern Electricity Customer Accounts.'

As Chang and Eng – the 19th-century, 'original', conjoined, 'Siamese' twins – might have done, Mr and Mrs X snapped upright on the sofa and then awkwardly rose as one from their seats. 'You can call 'oever you wants to, Mister,' Mr X snarled, 'cause it won't make no difference. Our contract's with Sir Roald, not you. And *you*' – Mr X scanned his eyes wildly around the room, looking everywhere except at me – 'cut off our electricity, lights, hot water, heating and telly-vision!' Then, like the not-Duracell-powered toy rabbit running down, Mr X started to stop. 'Now: my Missus and I, we've spent long enough 'ere, talkin'. *We're goin'!*'

Those last words, at least, I found easy to accept. And after seeing Mr and Mrs X to the door – or rather, given their precipitous flight, trailing behind and shutting the door after them – I made my call to Eastern Electricity. One of our tenants, I told the woman who picked up, a Mr X, has had his electricity cut off. Could you tell me why? 'And you are…?' D'Arcy Henry, I replied, Mr X's landlord. There was a moment's pause while the woman brought up the file, then: 'Is that Mr X, of Bottom Cottage, The Heartsease Hall Estate, Norfolk?' Yes, I replied. 'The account hasn't been paid,' the woman said. 'The electricity's been cut off because the Bottom Cottage account hasn't been paid.'

I thanked the woman, hung up, turned to my PC and keyed in: 'Dear Mr and Mrs X; As we discussed, a serious arrears in your rent has occurred. Unless this arrears is cleared and your payments brought up to date by the close of business on Friday, 9 December 1994, I will consider your Tenancy Agreement in respect of Bottom Cottage to be null and void, and your lawful tenancy there to have ceased. You will then have until Friday, 20 January 1995 – five calendar weeks – to vacate Bottom Cottage. Failure to vacate by that date will result immediately in the start of proceedings to evict you.'

· · · · · · · · · · · · · · · · · · ·

Such a tough guy… such a truly 'Ugly American'!

I was only looking out for N's, the boys' and my interests.

Miscreant… un-deserving, even… the X's may have been. But

they were your Brothers: part of the great Family of Man whom you're morally bound to keep.

(Deleted) them!

This petty, misanthropic 'start' to your new life as an English country squire: was it really, I asked you, 'as you intend(ed) to go on'?

(Deleted)!

· ·

Late one evening a few days later, N arrived back from London with the discouraging news that Lord Gowrie, the arts-funding Minister, thought it 'highly unlikely' we'd get monies from English Heritage or any other UK public-sector entity to support T2S2 of the Masterplan and its manifold 'I's', that's to say restore the Hall. His Lordship cited three reasons, N reported: the cost of restoring the Hall was assumed already to have been discounted in the price we paid for it; even if it weren't, as there appeared to be little immediate danger of the Hall's being 'lost to the nation', more-urgent restoration projects would have precedence; and, so far as he could see, restoring the Hall wouldn't significantly further 'the general good' – an indirect reference, I took it, to our intention not to keep the Hall open to the public at large. If, however, we were to change our minds on this last issue, Lord Gowrie hinted, some public funding might be found.

· ·

All that seemed eminently fair and reasonable....

Indeed... if you and I weren't then regularly hearing about all those other schemes having no apparent relationship to 'the general good' which did get public funding.

I recall one such scheme in particular: to have 'Christo' (Christo Javacheff, the Bulgarian-born environmental sculptor) wrap St Stephen's Tower*, in London's Westminster, from top to bottom in skin-colored plastic sheeting.

The wags suggested the tower shouldn't then be known as 'Big Ben'; instead it should be called 'Big Ben's'.

· ·

Our only real hope, Lord Gowrie concluded, would be some private individual or institution with a particular interest in Georgian-Gothic

---

* St Stephen's Tower is the erection at the north end of the Houses of Parliament from the head of which booms out 'Big Ben' – originally, the nickname given to the Tower's principal bell (in honor of Sir Benjamin Hall, London's Chief Commissioner of Works in 1856, when the bell was cast) but now often applied to the clock, or the tower as a whole.

architecture or William Wilkins, Junior or Senior. He doubted, however, that many such benefactors existed.

By this time, Piggy and her piglets – all ten of them, at least 6–7 of which must have been born in transit from Brambledown – were very much out and about, by day rooting in the estate's woods and fields (and the immaculate lawns surrounding the Hall) and generally making a nuisance of themselves, returning to their horsebox 'nest' only at night. Their relegation to the walled garden was, therefore, well overdue.

About mid-morning on 12 November, I finally achieved that relegation and, in the event, other than taking care Piggy and her family's entrance into the walled garden didn't occasion Applesauce and/or Mustard's exit from it, no especial tricks were needed. I got a bucket of nice, fragrant swill and, as Piggy stood on the track trying to decide where to take the kids for brunch, I waved it under her snout. The felicitous import of my initiative registered immediately. I then walked through the gate and into the walled garden; Piggy – her piglets lapping around her like wave-froth on a sea shore – followed as if drawn by some invisible lead. I slopped the swill into the trough; Piggy tucked in for a moment or two then, *pro tem* sufficiently sated, gave her 'Soup's on!' call and lay over on her side. As iron filings to a magnet, ten hungry little suckers suckled down. I exited the walled garden; closed, locked and barred its gate... and departed. 'The End', at last, of the Piggy *et al* removal from Brambledown saga.

The following afternoon, a Sunday, N and I took what was over the years to become our customary Sabbath stroll (and latterly, occasional horseback ride) around the lower lake. This time, however, our usual, in-depth reflections on 'higher things' – rising UK household, regional and national debt, falling standards of public health, education and welfare support... metastasising organized and opportunistic crime... and the seeming failure of the then Conservative Government under Prime Minister John Major effectively to address these important issues – were brought rudely back to earth by the sight of five dogs tearing out of Neate Wood, and running around and barking as if they were mad. Then, from deep within the wood itself, came great shouts of laughter. Hmmmm, as I thought Sir Roald would say. Shortly, four people – three women and a man, all younger-middle-aged and clad in hi-vis (high-visibility) tangerine-orange and cobalt-blue nylon shell suits – also appeared.

I made my all-amiability way over to them with a view to establishing who they were and what they thought they were doing. I learned that two of the women lived in our village, and that the man and the third woman, his wife, were the luncheon guests of one of them. How interesting, I said, trying to sound interested. 'And do you' – I nodded gravely… esquirely… toward the two neighbour-ladies – 'and your dogs walk here regularly?'

'Oh yes, nearly every Sunday afternoon and, in the summer, sometimes weekdays in the evening as well,' one of them replied. Lowering her voice, as if speaking in confidence, she concluded: 'Sir Roald likes us to.'

Hmmm, I said again. Sir Roald might, as a courtesy, have given these women permission to walk here – there being no public right of way, he certainly wasn't required to – but 'liking' them to? I doubted it. His sense of community responsibility aside, Sir Roald had struck me as no less territorial than any other Englishman at home in 'his castle', as various Anglologists have put it. Offering a non-committal 'Isn't that nice!', I bid N's and my *adieux* and continued on; almost immediately, the laughter and general merriment recommenced. I hmmm-ed a third time. And 'liking' in the present rather than the past tense. The sale of the Heartsease Hall Estate had been pretty big local news; didn't these people know – or couldn't they guess – who N and I were?

. . . .

In the autumn of 1994, you'll remember, d'Arcy, 'Right to Roam' – more correctly called 'Right of Public Access': legislation the then in-opposition Labour Party under its leader Tony Blair (Prime Minister 1997-2007) had conceived – was a hot topic of discussion.

I certainly do remember, Alter-natis, and I'm reminded almost daily still.

This proposed new legislation had very little to do with formalizing the relationship between UK taxpayers and estate owners who accepted taxpayers' money to restore their house or its grounds, that's to say the quid pro quo *you referenced earlier in this chapter. It was aimed at landowners generally, and them primarily for three reasons: they owned large swathes of a valuable national asset; they constituted only a tiny proportion of the electorate, so their views could safely be ignored; and some of 'the people' – a much larger and, hence, much more critical demographic – wanted to reduce them via the exercise of some collective right of eminent domain.*

No real benefit was ever intended to accrue to the landowner from Right to Roam; it was, purely and simply, a form of legalised trespass.

'Legalised trespass' is an oxymoron, Alter-natis; 'trespass' means *il*legal... or wrongful entry, for example, upon another's land.

Nonetheless, in 2000 – with the Labour Party now in power – Right to Roam was enshrined in UK law as the Countryside and Rights of Way Act or, as many of those on whom it was inflicted delighted in calling it, the CRoW Act: 'That's with a "C", as in "co-prophagous" ([deleted]-eating).' Implementation of the Act began a few years later.

How did this jurisdiction come about?

The same way the so-called British 'Constitution' came about: the accretion over time of precedents relating to the on-going conflict between the UK's 'haves' and its 'have-nots' – as regards the CRoW Act, those who have land, and those who haven't – and trying to re-solve that conflict non-violently.

I'm still not quite sure what 'Right to Roam' in this context im-plies.

Right to Roam is and remains – partly by design, probably – to some extent a legal 'grey area', that's to say an example of the good, old, face-saving 'British Compromise', d'Arcy. But like waterways and woodlands, the other two pillars of the UK primary economy, land – for mining and quarrying, minerals extraction, etc... and, in your case, farming – is largely nationalized; persons who intend or commit no damage or impairment to UK land may, therefore, 'right-fully' access it. The landowner – you, in other words – can only ask them to leave.

That's very, very, *very* different from the legal position in The Motherland, where trespass is usually treated as a criminal offence rather than just a civil one....

From there, it's only a short step to obliging the landowner – again, you – to allow just about anyone onto his or her land at just about any time.

But what about that first principle of free-enterprise democracy: an individual's right to own property? N and I'd purchased the Heartsease Hall Estate; title to it had been clearly established and properly transferred....

From Sir Roald Festing populusque Angelorum – that's 'and the people of England' – to you and your wife populusque Angelorum.

How about my right to privacy, then?

Certain areas – the 'curtilage' (residential areas) and areas ordi-narily in commercial use, like farming, and recognized Conservation Areas, usually – are all excluded from any generalized right to roam. Other areas may be excluded at certain times – during the wildlife breeding season, or the hunting season, for example... or, briefly, under 'Special Circumstances', that's to say when the landowner reasonably desires it.

And the time and effort I expend managing my land so that uninvited others may, more or less at their pleasure, walk around and enjoy it?

It's possible your hard work may in due course be compensated in some small, indirect way – in the afterlife, say... if there is one.

Were obligations also imposed on those who roam my land... what you're calling the 'legalized trespassers'?

A certain reciprocity applies. People who come onto your land aren't allowed to deport themselves as if they're taking part in a public celebration of some sort – a Fourth of July-type parade, say, or a fun fair – unless it's been done there traditionally, or you invite them to. Loud behavior is prohibited – there's no mention of 'loud', hi-vis clothing, however – and children and pets have to be under control at all times.

In particular, the natural environment must be respected. That means people mustn't ride bicycles or horses, or drive certain types of vehicles (except, of course, on designated footpaths, or bridleways), take part in organized games or commercial activities, bathe in lakes or non-tidal rivers, or use boats, hunt, fish or collect anything from the area – rocks or plants, for example – or camp or light fires.

In theory, I've no quarrel with that...

No, and you couldn't have. Because this sort of public access is closely related to your notion that we're all just tenants of this fraught, fragile earth... a condition which you referenced in your 12 October 1994 letter to Sir Roald and proposed in the Foreword to this book!

... but in practice, just as being a good, responsible landowner is hard work, so also is being a good, responsible tenant. Do you think the Right to Roam legislation will eventually result in the UK's land – and, by extension, *our* land, *our* natural environment... *our* earth – being better protected and maintained?

That remains to be seen. But I don't have to tell you the public sector's record in respect of enterprise management is very mixed.
· · · · · · · · · · · · · · · · · · · ·

A few days later, I wrote to our principal agricultural tenants and/or contractors introducing myself. That end was easily enough achieved; the problem was at the beginning: deciding what, in view of the UK's ever-insidious class system, should be my distinguishing form of address or 'style'. I didn't want to sound too traditional and remote as in 'landowner' or 'squire', or too brash and B-School easy as in 'chief honcho' or 'CEO', or too happy-clappy-matey as in 'fellow Earth-sharer'. In the end, I opted for… 'the new co-owner of the Heartsease Hall Estate'.

The following Tuesday brought a formal offer to purchase Bramble-down – the first such offer we'd received – from Mr and Mrs Military. High indeed were N's and my 'Hosannas!'… for a while….

· · · · · · · · · · · · · · · · · · · ·

Just remind me of The Militarys' offer, d'Arcy. Was it pretty much what you and your wife were hoping for?

Not exactly. The Militarys offered us a cash payment equal to about one-third of our asking price together with their house a few miles away, in Bourton-on-the-Water.

Well, an offer's an offer…. Tell me again: how big was The Militarys' house in Bourton? Was it detached (free-standing) with 3–4 bedrooms? And how much was it worth?

It was a 2–3 bedroom terrace (row) house which, in a white-hot property market, might have fetched a quarter or perhaps a third of what Brambledown was worth.

So The Militarys' offer, all told, equated to perhaps two-thirds of your 'reduced, reduced' asking price for Brambledown?

Yes. And, of course, the offer wasn't what you'd call 'clean'. We'd clear some funds, but we'd still have a house to sell.

· · · · · · · · · · · · · · · · · · · ·

The next day, N telephoned the EA to discuss how best to reply to The Militarys. Like N and me, he was puzzled by the modest worth and complex structure of their offer. Had they had some sort of financial setback, he wondered, and instead of owning up to it were ducking and dodging? (Several months later, we learned that was indeed the case.) Or as N angrily put it, were they 'trifling' with us? (Imagine: a very senior British military officer and/or a performance-tested concert pianist 'trifling' with us… us upstart-American d'Arcy Henrys. The very suggestion beggared belief [!].) Shortly afterward, N and I held a private council of war during which we reconfirmed our preparedness to consider almost anything, provided the bid on the table was close to our ask, and so long as the purchaser's problems didn't become our problems. For as we later faxed the EA: 'We feel we have enough of these last on our plate already.'

In a word, we told The Militarys 'no'.

About mid-day on 18 November, Sir Roald telephoned to say he and Lady Maureen would shortly be in the area and would like, if it'd be convenient, to call in to say 'Hello'. He paused to clear his throat; I thought: Isn't this fine! Our aristocratic, new friends – the 13th Baronet and his wife – dropping by on the spur of the moment to see N and me; what a splendid acknowledgement of our arrival on the north Norfolk social scene....

Throat clear, Sir Roald continued: 'Hello to the donkeys... and to you and your wife, of course.' I replied 'certainly', then rushed out to the doncs' paddock to confirm everything was as it should be, to find... no doncs – just a perimeter of post-and-rail fencing and a partly-open gate jibing gently in the breeze. I whistled up N and Big Fee; the three of us then circled the Hall and its outbuildings looking behind the hedges, under the trees, across the fields down to the lakes and beyond... once, and once again.... Then I split the team up, sending N and Big Fee around one way while I went around the other in case, in our group circumnavigations, we'd just been driving the wretched doncs ahead of us.... Still no doncs.

What to say to Sir Roald and, especially, Lady Maureen whose arrival must now be imminent, I wondered frantically? That yes, your beloved donkeys had asked if they might go for a walk and we – thinking this must be *de rigeur* – had said all right? ('But don't be gone too long girls and, above all, don't go near the road.') That no, we didn't know exactly where the doncs were just now, but we were sure they were OK and that they'd be home soon? Thinking to widen the search area, I raced into the Hall to get the keys to the Land Rover, then raced back out toward its garage glancing, as I did so, into the stables; I beheld two dun-colored rumps, each with a dark-brown, dorsal stripe running down to a swishing tail. I slowed, corrected my course... and jogged over for a closer look. Jubie was in Maggie's stall and *vice versa* but, otherwise, both doncs were present and accounted for, munching hay as content as could be.

At that moment, Sir Roald and Lady Maureen drove into the stableyard. As Lady Maureen got out of their car, she observed brightly: 'Oh, good! You've brought Maggie and Jubie *in*. That's just what I was hoping you'd have done. If they stay out in the paddock too long this time of year and eat too much rich, late-autumn grass, they'll get laminitis* for sure!' I nodded gravely... veterinary-knowledgeably... then I went over and, as covertly as I could, shut the doncs in their stalls and slid the doors' locking bolts home.

---

* An inflammation of the laminate of tissue which, in ungulates, suspends the pedal bone or bones within the hoof.

I spent the last week of November in South Asia on FHA business. While in Lahore, in north-east Pakistan, I'd a few spare hours, so I took the opportunity to review some of the magnificent architecture – ancient and modern, Indian, Mughal (Muslim-Indian) and British-Imperial – on display there. It was a veritable banquet for the eye… which started me thinking about architectural heritage – 'built heritage', in architectural-historian speak – and its classification in the UK, that's to say its listing.

. . . .

Just imagine the time and effort which goes into that process, Alternatis: first establishing a suitable definition of 'built heritage', then developing general eligibility criteria for listing… then specific eligibility criteria for different grades of listing…

Qualitative judgments, all of which must admit of as much quantification as possible….

… and then applying those criteria, that's to say deciding which of the tens of thousands of candidate-structures: habitations – castles as well as caves – fortifications, places of worship, schools and colleges, theatres and other arts facilities, sports facilities, factories, offices, department stores and shopping malls… infrastructure facilities… to include….

Why not, d'Arcy? It gives people who like that sort of thing something arguably worthwhile to do and quite a nice stipend from the taxpayer to do it on….

What I've never understood is why the British authorities haven't introduced some sort of 'National Heritage Site' category – analogous to the United Nations' 'World Heritage Site' category which, as you know, at time of writing now registers more than two dozen UK locations – for structures of truly exceptional importance.

Yes; Heartsease Hall is, of course, a very special building. But compared with some of its fairly-near neighbors – Blickling Hall, Felbrigg Hall, Holkham Hall, Houghton Hall, Raynham Hall, Sandringham House… to name just a few – it's a relatively modest pile, yet they're all lumped together as 'Listed Grade I'. I agree: elements of the UK's present built-heritage classification system could be improved.
. . . .

A couple of days later, I took an away-day from the pandemonium of New Delhi and drove south along the NH2* to Agra, in Uttar Pradesh (state), and the ineffably tranquil beauty – presented once in

---

* The 'National Highway – 2', a rebuilt section of the 1,600-mile, British-Raj-era 'Grand Trunk Road' running from Chittagong in today's Bangladesh to Kabul in Afghanistan.

stone and mortar and again, reflected, in the still waters of the Lotus Pool – of the Taj Mahal, the Mughal emperor Shah Jahan's memorial to his beloved wife Mumtaz, who'd died birthing his child. Rising above the Yamuna river flood plain, its rose-sandstone and white-marble domes and minarets lancing into the crystal-clear cerulean of the northwestern Indian sky, to my mind it's one of the most exquisite architectural achievements on the planet (and, indeed, a UNESCO 'World Heritage Site'). And *it* started me thinking about... how we should re-empark the fields around the Hall.

• • • • • • • • • • • • • • • • • • • •

Back then, I remarked, it didn't take much to trigger your obsession with your new property... and it still doesn't. Anyway, I said, let's have it: T1S2I1 – Title One, Schedule Two, Item One – of The Masterplan.

As you're aware, Alter-natis, in the late 19th century the Heartsease Hall Estate totalled some 6,000 acres. During the early years of the 20th century, however, a good deal of that land – and nearly all of its contained villages – had to be sold off to pay down debt....

My, my: 'de-leveraging' Edwardian-style. Tell me, d'Arcy: were interest rates generally very low back in those days? And did they then have over-leveraged hedge fund managers, and commodities and derivatives traders? I know they had plenty of aggressive 'investment' bankers....

Of the remaining land – including the prime, 'core' land N and I'd bought – roughly a third had originally been parkland, that's to say grassland with scattered trees.

We couldn't re-empark the whole of that area, of course; there'd have been too much sacrifice of farming income. On the other hand, we didn't much like the way the fields were then disposed, with cropping running more or less right up to the Hall's front and back doors. But how much land should we re-empark? Fifteen acres... fifty acres... a hundred and fifty acres?

You needed to establish the estate's phi... its 'golden mean', as Fibonacci might have put it: in this application, the perfect ratio of built-up, constructed area to parkland, lakes, woodlands, pastures and arable fields.

Fibonacci?

A 13th-century Italian mathematician whose real name was Leonardo da Pisa. Like his 15th/16th-century fellow-countryman, Leonardo da Vinci, he was much exercised about the aesthetics of proportion.

Ummm. Well... I *thought* the answer was to swing a nice big semi-elipse, whose perigee was a point about 200 yards due north of the Hall, from Neate Wood in the southeast to Home Farm wood in the northwest. That would re-empark perhaps 50–60 acres which we'd put down to grass for the sheep and later, maybe, cattle and/or some horses.

Together with the contiguous woodlands at either end of that semi-ellipse, and the upper and lower lakes and their associated pastures which comprised its southern extent, a total of perhaps 120 acres – with no public roads, no bridle ways, no footpaths; only sections of the front drive and the east track – would then be parkland.

You could establish your own, mini, nature reserve, I enthused!

And *I* said: could I do that? I mean… if land in the UK is so substantially nationalized, wouldn't all sorts of bureaucratic hurdles be put in my way? For example: would I have to get Planning Permission? And/or the consent of the MAFF (the Ministry of Agriculture, Forestry and Fishing, now called the Department for Environment, Food and Rural Affairs [DEFRA])? And/or the Countryside Commission (now called Natural England)? And/or the Forestry Commission (now called the Forestry Authority)?

And then, having established the reserve, would there be things I might want to do to it sometime in the future – for example, reconfigure the reserve slightly, or take down a few old trees and plant up a few young ones – but, owing to red tape, I couldn't or wouldn't be allowed to do?

I concluded you'd better have a word with honourable land agent before you 'start(ed) as you intend(ed) to go on' with your nature-reserve project.

Instead, I cranked up my rugged individualism and, over a period of years, established a *de facto* mini nature reserve pretty much as I'd wanted to…

… all the while keeping your fingers crossed that no one except you and your family and friends – and the grateful flora *and* fauna, *of course – would notice.*

· · · · · · · · · · · · · · · · · · · ·

On returning to the UK, I learned from Lady Maureen that Sir Roald had been in hospital again, this time with a leg problem. I telephoned him to commiserate but couldn't get through, so I left a message on his voice mail. Then I had a meeting with Joscelyn Steele. The original purpose of this long-scheduled conference was to explore ways in which the estate's farming might be up-rated but, given Sir Roald's indisposition, I decided as well to get Joscelyn's views on a couple of local-interface issues, in particular the pre-emptive 'right to roam' some people – the above-referenced Sunday-afternoon walkers, for example – were exercising through our north and east gates.

The possibilities for improving our farming were quickly laid out

– Joscelyn proved even more knowledgeable of this subject than I'd thought – and so we moved on to right-to-roam. I told him I didn't want to come across as 'over-paid, over-sexed and over here'* but, equally, I didn't want people feeling free just to come in and walk around anytime, anywhere. 'It disturbs the wildlife, invades our privacy, and may have security implications,' I noted. How should I proceed, then? Install no-entry barriers and put up 'Private – Keep Out' signs, or let the isolationist preferences of the new regime become known by word-of-mouth gradually, over time....

The gradualist approach was much the better course, my mentor immediately replied. He continued: 'Then, when you're sure the word is about, you can install a few gates and put up a few signs as a reminder of your preferences rather than a statement of them.'

. . . .

In Howard Newton's words: 'Tact is the art of making a point without making an enemy.'

. . . .

Finally, we turned to nature conservation and preservation of the rural environment – fundamental interests of Joscelyn's in furtherance of which he sat on most of the relevant regional and UK-national committees. We talked about the problems of getting permission for nature reserves, and of managing them once they were established... then, almost as an afterthought, Joscelyn vouchedsafe matter-of-factly: 'As you're probably aware, d'Arcy, planning permission exists right now for some 75,000 new dwellings in north Norfolk – retirement cottages or second homes for city people wanting to get away from it all... you know, that sort of thing.' The news hit me like a bomb blast!

. . . .

Seventy-five thousand new dwellings, Alter-natis! That represented 150,000–200,000 or so more people... 100,000 or so more cars.... A Cotswolds-like population explosion was going to be detonated, substantially right here – within the purview of our 'glorious, Edenic biosphere' – and the fuse on the charge had already been lit! What could I say? What could I do?

Your questions relate to that age-old problem: the use, or abuse, of 'commons', that's to say 'common-pool resources' or 'CPR'. The archetypal 'commons' was almost certainly grazing land, we're told;

---

* A popular British characterization of American soldiers stationed in the UK during the Second World War.

increasingly today, of course, it's the whole of our earth and its forests and seas – and, in a non-material or incorporate sense, knowledge and intellectual property – that are adverted to.

In 1968, the American biologist Garrett Hardin published his famously gloomy paper 'The Tragedy of the Commons'; some years later, the American political scientist – and 2009 Nobel Prize winner – Elinor Ostrom showed conclusively that well-specified 'grassroots' initiatives, leveraged and supported by government, could regularly deliver much brighter CPR outcomes.

'The Tragedy or Otherwise of the north Norfolk Commons' as a microcosm of life on earth; I'd certainly like to know which school of thinking is correct!

In respect of preserving the developed world's countryside, a number of those who've looked closely at the problem (Stewart Brand and Edward Glaeser are good examples.) believe that from an environmental standpoint the best longer-term solution lies in encouraging marginal country dwellers to move into cities and towns – to where in the developing world, as you know, such people have for a long time been moving anyway. ('Increasingly, we're a city planet,' Brand has repeatedly observed.)

In the shorter term, however, there don't seem to be any easy answers, d'Arcy.

My first reaction was to regard this prospective influx of outsiders as a pandemic... a modern-day, socio-economic and environmental equivalent of the Black Plague!

That was a nice, convivial, earth-brotherly-tenantly reaction....

Given that planning permission for the new dwellings already existed, however, it was too late to inoculate, so to speak... to immunize against the contagion; the only option was to try to limit its spread. '*At all costs,*' I ranted, '*this most (un)popular plague must be contained!*'

Like the unfortunate Canute – the Anglicized Viking who ruled England from 1016 to 1035 – you might as well try to hold back the rising, tidal sea, I said.

Surely, Alter-natis, all those people 'wanting to get away from it all' at the same time... going to the same place.... Surely: the 'all' simply trans-locates, with the result that no one – not those who make their living in the country, not those who weekend or vacation in the country... not those who retire to the country – is entirely content.

Right on, Brother-Tenant.

And surely everyone values nature and the rural environment, and wants to preserve it; surely, they can all agree on that....

In theory, yes. In very broadly-categorical practice, however, the issues become: 'value' it how? As lebensraum *(living space) for phys-*

ical bodies, or as an ambience – a sanatorium with a view – where world-wounded souls can relax and recuperate?

I've no quarrel with either of the above! So let's get started....

And 'preserve' it as what? As a theme park with horses and vintage farm machinery, and small parcels of relatively inefficiently-used land... or larger parcels owned by self-impressed landowners – 'squires', maybe – relying on over-worked, underpaid labour... that's to say, representing aspects of rural life as it was 75–100 or so years ago?

No: that couldn't be right....

Or as the dynamic, living, working... contemporary... 'mixed' socio-economic system the UK countryside largely is today?

That's better, it seems to me....

And finally, to close the rhetorical circle: preserve it for whom? The many? The few? An assortment of both, self-selected, chosen by ballot or as a result of drawn straws?

Ummmm. I'm beginning to see just how vexed an issue 'The Tragedy or Otherwise of the Commons' really is....

Meanwhile, of course, life day-to-day in the countryside must go on.

. . . .

Given Joscelyn's dispiriting news, it was perhaps only fitting that the 'Met(eorological) Office', as the UK's official weather service is commonly known, should shortly pronounce November 1994 to have been the warmest since reliable national records began, and note that the month's mean night-time temperatures – an indicator of stored heat, that's to say the green-house effect – were 'exceptionally high'...

. . . .

Global warming as revealed in north Norfolk: Arctic and northern-European ice and snow melting and coursing into the Earth's other waters... undergoing thermal expansion... raising the level of the oceans and, thereby, the level of the North Sea – throughout all of which the East Anglian landmass continues its gradual sinking....

But we're on high ground, Alter-natis; that's why the valuation carried out by the chartered surveyor in September 1994 included the sentence: 'Flooding is not thought likely to threaten the Heartsease Hall Estate's lands or properties.'

Very reassuring. If honorable chartered surveyor's got it wrong, however, your heirs may find the change from mainland to island living takes some getting used to.

. . . .

... 'exceptionally high', and that we'd get a fax from the EA confirming The Militarys weren't prepared to improve their curiously-inadequate offer for Brambledown.

Chapter 9

Eye to Hounds

By almost any measure – social and economic diversity, cultural excellence, 'buzz'... ambient noise generally, some would say – New York is one of the world's truly great cities. Usually, I love it. But in early-December 1994, wound up and distempered by a succession of tense, all-day and into-the-night FHA business meetings there, the place seemed to me to have outgrown any real-world purpose and to exist primarily to replicate and cater for its own like some raucous, smelly, hive-bound queen bee. As I flew back to the UK to confront the pell-mell commercialism that is Christmastide in much of today's developed world, all I yearned for was a little gentle down-time... a little soft repose....

• •

Those high-flyers you'd been advising: they didn't seem to need down-time or repose – certainly not as much as you did... and do still, d'Arcy.

What? Nonsense! I don't need much down-time! I'll take it, of course, if it's on offer but I don't really *need* it.... And besides: there're people who need more down-time and people who need less. Everybody, however, needs some.

Do you think, in general, people get enough down-time?

No, probably not. So many people's lives are such a continuous, mad scramble of business – or what passes for business – and pleasure – or what passes for pleasure – they hardly ever kick back, put their lives into perspective and take the long view. As William Wordsworth wrote in 1807: 'The world is too much with us; late and soon, Getting and spending, we lay waste our powers; Little we see in Nature that is ours.'

Well so what? Why should this... this Down-Time Deficit Syndrome – DTDS as it might be called – concern anyone except those who suffer from it?

People with DTDS are, I would argue, *ipso facto* over-stressed. And stress-related personal illness, stress-related familial and wider social dysfunction, stress-related political, economic and commercial dysfunction – that's to say misappreciation, misjudgment and mismanagement – all imply significant costs to society as a whole.

*So should everyone, including the entirety of your vast Reader-
ship, have their Heartsease Hall? Some nice, quiet place to retreat to
and repose in?*

Not necessarily a Listed Grade I Hall surrounded by hundreds of
acres – something that big and demanding. But a nice, quiet retreat,
certainly; they might then be disposed to read more and buy more
books!

*Even if that nice, quiet retreat is in the countryside? In north Nor-
folk, say? Such that north Norfolk becomes over-run with DTDS-
ers kicking back and elongating their view? Shopping for luxuries
they don't need in chic little shops, eating over-elaborate meals they
shouldn't have in bijou little restaurants... trekking – like hi-vis lem-
mings in their orange and blue nylon shell suits – through conservation areas and wildlife reserves in pursuit of 'nature'? And withal,
driving to and fro', their cars' exhaust fumes fouling the air, and the
cars themselves clogging the roads?*

Stress and fatigue seems to bring out the uncharitable in you too,
Alter-natis.

. . . .

And mostly, soft repose was what I got. Awaiting me upon my arrival
home were only: letters from two of our farming tenants – the body-
copy of one letter written in a rounded, feminine hand (the wife as
amanuensis, presumably) but signed with a jagged, male-paw scrawl
– saying they hoped we'd find the estate, etc, to our liking...

... and my first exposure to deep, north-Norfolk winter cold: daytime temperatures hovering around 10–15° Fahrenheit, accompanied
by winds almost literally straight from the North Pole which chill
to the very marrow of your bones. ('Express winds' some locals call
them because they don't seem to stop at or swirl around you; instead,
they blow straight through.) For Readers accustomed to well weather-
proofed homes with modern central heating systems supplying great
gouts of BTUs (British Thermal Units, a measure of heat) more or less
on demand to every room – and, in some cases, the garage, and the
sub-soil beneath its forecourt and the driveway – the full implications
of such weather for the residents of Heartsease Hall may be difficult
to appreciate.

To begin to do so you must first recall to your mind's eye a substantial dwelling with relatively large windows (many of whose sashes
didn't fit well and still don't) sitting atop a 'hill' which, notwithstanding a narrow shelter-belt of mainly-deciduous trees, is more or less
fully exposed to the Arctic blasts. Upon entering the house, through
relatively large portals (most of whose doors didn't fit well and ditto),

you must re-visualize an array of pretty good-sized rooms, some of which have central heating (*a* radiator or, in the case of the dining room, *two* [see below]), but a few of which – most notably, Yr Correspondent's estate office/library, his and his Uxor's bedroom, and her and her PA's office – have just a single fireplace. The ceilings of the envisioned rooms are very high. (Warm air rises, of course, in such rooms to well above sitting or standing height... before dissipating.)

Finally, you must review (see Ch. 4) the attics: great voids roofed over by weather-boarding and cold, hard, silver-grey-green Westmorland slate, 'floored' by lath and plaster with only a thin overlay of fiberglass insulation and, at the eaves where roof and 'floor' join, deliberately ventilated to allow condensation to escape. By this most expedient of architectural means, nearly all of whatever heat may be available to build up in the habitation below is conveyed relentlessly up, up, up and away.

Experienced denizens of big, old, draughty, English country houses take severe winter weather pretty much in their stride – or try generally to act as if they do. They stoke their insides with rich foods and swathe their outsides with thick layers of underwear, socks, shirts and skirts and/or trousers, sweaters and – in very extreme conditions – overcoats, scarves, hats and gloves, even. Then they close off their mansions' grand rooms – the formal dining room, and the reception and sitting rooms and their associated halls (taking with them as-yet-unfinished jig-saw puzzles or reading materials and photographs of loved ones) – as well as any inessential domestic offices and retreat, initially to their kitchen with its 'range'*, ultimately to their bedroom where a fire may be kept burning continuously... and in between, perhaps, to their 'snug', by definition a smallish room, typically with an over-sized, often 'inglenook' fireplace† where, penguin-like, they huddle together trying to keep warm but, you suspect, never quite succeeding.

N, the boys and I and, bravely, Big Fee – who, after all, could easily have found employment in some more agreeable clime, decorating a catwalk or a beach-volleyball court, perhaps – implemented as far as possible this established, best-UK-country-house, wintertime-survival-indoors practice. We shovelled in the calories, put on lots of sweaters, etc, gathered regularly in the kitchen with its great, four-

---

* A large stove, originally wood or coal-fired but now most likely fuelled by oil or natural gas.

† One within a recess or an enclosure sufficient to take a stool or a chair or two.

oven Aga, and retired early to our electric-under-blanketed, multiple-duvet-covered beds. We had only one serious want: a snug. So for much of the rest of a cold winter's day, like Samuel Taylor Coleridge's 1798 Ancient Mariner – accursed because he'd killed an albatross (venerated by sailors as bringers of good luck) – we roamed the Hall 'alone... all, all alone' and, at least metaphorically, with 'ice... all around' in search of heat.

(Our later Festing predecessors, we were told, had used the dining room – with its south-facing, green-house-like windows, its five-foot-high by six-foot-wide fireplace and its two radiators – as their snug, in the winter importing bookshelves, reading lamps, a sofa and some comfortable chairs, a radio and a television; a grand piano was already *in situ*.... N and I eventually settled on the estate office/library. Although it was northwest-facing and, as noted above, without any sort of *central* heating it had a modern, wood-burning Franklin-type stove extending from the hearth part-way into the room. Supplemented by a portable LNG [liquefied natural gas or, as the British call it, 'bottled-gas'] space heater, it made the library entirely livable... or so Yr Correspondent thought. N was occasionally heard to proclaim a different view.)

It was, therefore, probably inevitable that at about this time we should officially host our first Heartsease Hall guests.

Nell (she who *ab initio* had foreseen where our piano and *bateau lit* sofa should go in the Hall, and how its surrounding display gardens should be reconfigured) and her husband Chris were hardened country-dwellers. And as we knew from skiing with them in the Alps, when the cold winds whistled they just pulled down their hats, turned their collars up, tightened their scarves and enjoyed themselves all the more.

Upon their arrival, therefore, we inflicted on them the full Heartsease Hall Estate Grand Tour, taking in the farthest fields and woods ('The air *is very bracing*, isn't it,' Chris chortled happily. 'It feels much, *much* colder here than in Saffron Walden,' Nell echoed.), the lakes, the inby farm and service buildings, the domestic root and wine cellars... then we supped and drunk them in a dining room meanly furnished as per our inaugural meal seven weeks earlier... after which we withdrew them for coffee to cushions on the drawing room floor and, finally, bedded them down in a guest room 'decorated' more or less in the style of an airplane hangar and 'heated' like a meat cold-store. All of this they bore with their characteristic enthusiasm and good grace.

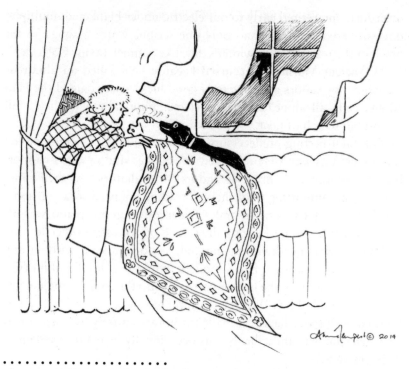

. . . .

I hadn't really thought of it or formulated it until then, Alter-natis. But good fortune provides an easy way to distinguish real friends: they're the ones who share not only your sorrow but more importantly your joy, overcoming avarice, envy, jealousy, and the like, to empathize with it as if it were their own.

. . . .

A few days later Joan M, a former White House work-mate of N's, and her daughter Georgia, both of whom 'just happened to be passing through' from Hong Kong *en route* to New York, came to lunch; 'We simply *had* to stop by and see your new home!' Joan gushed as she and Georgia swept through our front door.

As usual, Joan was clad as if for a 1960s *Vogue Magazine* photoshoot: calf-length mink overcoat (which she never removed!) and matching pill-box hat, orange-on-blue patterned skirt-suit in what looked like Harris tweed, brown alligator-skin handbag and ditto shoes with gold-washed fittings.... And, again as usual, she proved more than willing to apprise us of her recent news: the assumption of 'important' new oversight responsibilities at Harvard, a 'successful' meeting with [a very-senior member of the Indian government], a 'promising' personal relationship with [a well-known, Geneva-based investment banker], the devastation by *phylloxera* and subsequent re-planting of her 'beautiful and historic' vineyards in California.... Whenever Joan paused for breath, daughter Georgia – clearly a chipette off the old blockette – took over, telling us how she'd been funding '(her) real love... (her) painting and sculpting', by night-desk sub-editing at the *Far East Economic Review*. Wow!

Throughout these various promotions, however, Joan repeatedly and enthusiastically congratulated us on our acquisition of the Heartsease Hall Estate, effusing over first this feature of the landscape and then that one (as best she could discern the farther ones without having to venture outside)...

. . . .

The 'real friends' thing again.

. . . .

... and then, of the Hall, remarking on the one hand how 'grand and imposing' it appeared and, on the other – 'speaking as one who knows' – how 'blissfully easy' it must be to manage. (The Hall's icy inclemency seemed to be not quite so blissfully-easily manageable, however. For although we tried several times to persuade Joan and Georgia to stay the night with us – in our hangar-like, meat-cold-store guest bedroom – our invitation was emphatically declined. 'Claridge's [one of London's most exclusive hotels] are expecting us,' Joan opined firmly, 'and we mustn't let them down.')

In short, our all-too-brief... refrigerated... rendezvous proved to be great fun. For as N and I later fondly reflected: some people, fortunately, never change. And after all, we concluded, what's a little self-congratulation – a little self-glorification, even – among friends? If more people had even attempted what Joan had actually achieved – or Georgia aspired to achieve – and done so with as much panache, the world would certainly be a more interesting place and, quite possibly, a better one.

The morning of 5 December – driven by Eddie, one of our farm men – I had my first ride in our largest and most-expensive piece of farming kit: a sugar beet* harvester.

---

* Before the advent of modern, 'artificial' sweeteners, consumers' suchlike cravings were mostly satisfied either by honey – a fructose sugar – or sucrose sugars made from sugar cane or sugar beet. The first-named comes from the tropics, of course; the last is widely grown in temperate zones, e.g. northern Europe.

· · · · · · · · · · · · · · · · · · · ·

Not another glorification of farming, d'Arcy!

Read what follows as a note on farm mechanization, Alter-natis. Way back when you and I were born, harvesting sugar beet was done largely by hand; pulling up, topping and 'heaping' (gathering into piles) just one acre of beet required some 50 man-hours of work, or about one man-week. Today, harvesting an acre of beet requires, all in, maybe 30 man-*minutes*. In short, productivity has increased roughly a hundredfold.

Anyway: this next section's primarily for men who may have never entirely grown up; women Readers – if there are any – can skip it.

· · · · · · · · · · · · · · · · · · · ·

I'd long suspected that the job description 'farm worker' or 'agricultural worker', designations which are is still widely used in north Norfolk, tended to understate the engineering and other technical skills – not to mention the plain old physical strength and stamina – required for employment in modern, industrial-scale agribusiness; today even the humblest tractor driver, I'd noted, ploughing the proverbial 'straight furrow' had, at the very least, to be able to use safely and well what in 1994 was perhaps £175,000–250,000 (then $250,000–350,000) worth of very big, very powerful and, potentially, very dangerous equipment and, in addition, substantially to maintain and, occasionally, to carry out running repairs to it.

My ride with Eddie more than confirmed my suspicions. His job required using safely and well, etc, some £325,000–400,000 ($500,000–600,000) worth of equipment – the sugar beet harvester – a machine about the size of two, side-by-side, double-decker London buses which, when fully loaded, can weigh nearly 50 tons. Powering this monster is a 450 horsepower diesel engine; in addition to providing drive and steering to all six wheels, it enables: 'topping and scalping' (defoliating the beet, and removing a thin sliver of its cost-*in*efficient-to-process crown), 'popping' (squeezing the topped, etc, beet out of the ground, as if it were a splinter), 'lifting' (collecting up and joggle-cleaning the beet), 'tanking' (conveying the beet via 'ring trains' to the harvester's holding tank) and, finally, 'elevating' (offloading the 25 or so tons of tanked beet into an attending tractor-trailer) – a task which is accomplished, without stopping harvesting, in 30–40 seconds!

And this big, powerful… complex… piece of machinery is operated by a 'mere' farm or agricultural worker? Well, he (and, occasionally, she) does have a range of computers on board to help 'fly' the harvester, that's to say manage its travel over the ground (at a top speed of 15–17 mph), to adjust and synchronize its various harvesting and harvest-support systems, to plot the position and time-to-arrival of the tractor-trailers for off-loading into, to calculate the field area and beet tonnage already harvested and estimated still-to-be harvested, and thus the current yield per acre (or hectare), and relay all of this data back to the farm head office. Finally, CCTV cameras to the front, rear and both sides of the harvester, and ditto ranks of megawatt halogen lights, allow the 'pilot' continually to monitor his work from inside a cab which, to protect him from stones thrown back by the toppers and scalpers, has windows fitted with bullet-proof glass.

. . . .

Whew!

. . . .

In the afternoon, I telephoned a local north-Norfolk livestock hauler about transporting our main SHB sheep flock from Brambledown to Heartsease Hall; in passing, I told him I proposed initially to accommodate the animals in a field (Pavilion Paddock) which would be electric-fenced. A move the following Sunday was agreed. What seemed to me a curious exchange then ensued. The hauler asked if our sheep were 'used to electric', that's to say electric fencing. I told him no, and to myself confided warily: 'and neither is their Head Shepherd....' The hauler continued: 'So you'll want the flock with you as early as possible... before noon, for sure.' I'd no idea what the man intended by this seeming parenthesis but, not wanting to reveal to the locals yet more basic farming ignorance, I quickly replied 'Of course!' and thanked him for his consideration.

That conversation concluded, I speed-dialled my long-time, Cotswolds farming friend and mentor David T. Why's this hauler-fellow so concerned about our sheep's acquaintance of electric fencing and that we have the flock here before noon, I asked? Roaring with laughter, David advised that a before-noon delivery would give the sheep some daylight hours to accustom themselves to the unfamiliar field and the apparently-inadequate fencing around it... and, he added mischievously, 'you some daylight hours to round them up and pen them back in again if – "when", more likely – they successfully challenge the fencing and get out.'

(In the event, no problems arose. Sheen put the fencing up for me – thereby ensuring the job was done properly – and wired in a battery and battery-powered 'energizer' [a type of (? transformer) which pulses an electric current through the fence] and the hauler delivered the flock in good time at about 1130. Throughout the afternoon I kept an anxious watch in case the ewes should show an inclination to go exploring. But, it became clear, compared with their cosy Cotswolds' enfolds, north Norfolk's wide-open spaces struck them as egregiously unsafe. After a quick gallop around the periphery of Pavilion Paddock, they flocked up tight in the middle of the field – their heads up and their ears pricked – where they remained until the need for forage drove them to deploy. Another stage in the d'Arcy Henrys' remove to Heartsease Hall was complete.)

Our first evening abroad in north Norfolk 'Society' – drinks and supper (or more correctly 'dinner'; everyone was in 'lounge' [business] suits or long dresses) with honourable land agent and his wife – followed shortly. Before setting off, I'd a quick squint at my Ordnance Survey map (to reiterate: commercial GPS was then in its infancy) and concluded that, as the crow flies, the venue couldn't be more than 10–15 minutes away; our departure from Heartsease Hall was timed accordingly.

But as the Reader may recall (see Ch. 2): in north Norfolk – especially in north Norfolk – you very often can't drive as the crow flies. And in my hasty map-reading, I'd neglected to register the two or three 'dykes' ('watercourses' in this, East Anglian, usage) and 'fens' (low-lying, marshy areas), the couple of infrequently-bridged tributaries of the River Bure... and so the 10–15 minutes became the better part of three-quarters of an hour of intensive orienteering – I hunched over the steering wheel; N ditto over the OS map – along narrow lanes, around hairpin curves, over humped-back bridges and, at regular intervals, into 'Passing Places', fussing and fuming while other presumably-lost souls inched by. More or less as drinks were finishing, we arrived at our destination...

... to find we were the guests of honour. Our host introduced us around: to a farrier*, to a doctor and his schoolteacher wife, to a lady barrister (a lawyer qualified to plead in the higher, English courts), to the chairman of a FTSE 100 (S&P 500 near-equivalent) company and, finally, to the holder of one of England's oldest titles... all of whom lived within ten or so miles of us.†

---

* In Britain, a person who looks after horses' hooves and may, as required, shoe them; today's 'blacksmith' typically crafts or repairs smaller metal wares.

† Some years later, our host characterized his 'broad-church' (inclusive) guest list as intended 'to help (us) appreciate the breadth and depth of (our) new community' – which it certainly did. It also all-but ensured we'd meet some local souls with whom we were *sympathique*.

'Parish-pump' (local-community) matters of which N and I were then largely ignorant exercised the mouths of most of the guests most of the time. But there were also wider-world conversations into which we could enter and, at intervals, expressions of apparently-genuine interest in how we liked north Norfolk and what our plans were for the Heartsease Hall Estate. It was, in short, an evening quietly remarkable for the warmth of its hospitality, the congeniality of its company and, unlike the exclusion we'd frequently known in our Cotswolds days, the fact that we were invited at all.

. . . .

Back in Gloucestershire you and your wife sometimes, privately – and, it must be emphasized, largely in jest – complained of being 'treated almost like Blacks, or Jews'.

That's a huge exaggeration, of course, Alter-natis; the prejudice and discrimination we suffered there was as the morning dew compared with....

But there was some prejudice...?

And we had – and have still – a number of very dear Cotswolds friends....

Even so...?

Well... there were some people who seemed generally to look down on us and disparage our 'dumb', upstart-American ways.

Why on earth did they do that, do you suppose?

First of all, because N and I *aren't* British. The foreigner... the outsider – '*L'Etranger*' in Albert Camus' eponymous novel – is always, everywhere, the object of some insider suspicion and prejudice. And it may be that in land-locked communities, that's to say communities like the Cotswolds which are closed off from the cultural 'cross-roads' of the open sea, the predisposition towards prejudice is somewhat greater.

And secondly, I suppose, because you and your wife are American.

America's energy, its power and reach, its determination – however mis-guided or self-serving those attributes may sometimes appear, and sometimes *are* – to make the world 'a better place' makes Americans very high-profile and thus very tempting targets. For a certain type of Briton, that temptation is....

Would you care to write what type of Brit?

No, of course not, Alter-natis! I wouldn't stoop so low as to....

Are you sure? You're sitting here all by yourself, effectively, writing anonymously; there seems to be an opening in the narrative.... It's an opportunity for redress – for retribution, even – which won't come your way very often....

Well yes; OK, then. In the main those British who generally disparage Americans – as opposed to criticize them selectively/

constructively – are people who lack confidence... who're morbidly – pathologically, almost – unsure they can hack it themselves. But defensiveness like that is a characteristic of prejudiced human beings the world over, not just British ones.

It was Churchill's lovely characterization, wasn't it, of Americans as people who in the end 'could be counted on to do the right thing, but only after (they had) exhausted every other alternative'. Anyway: are there some further reasons why you feel you're sometimes looked down on and discriminated against in the UK?

In exhausting every other alternative – and then, we hope, in doing the 'right' thing – Americans often project an arrogant ignorance of the hard lessons of history which many British – not to mention nationals of other defunct civilizations and colonial powers – have painfully learned.

It may be that N and I aren't entirely without sin in this regard....

How very forthright... how very noble: a public acknowledgement, of sorts, of the possible, occasional, small, inadvertent, delinquency of your ways – in short, the possibility that you and your wife may indeed sometimes behave like 'upstarts'. But let's move on. What have you learned from your passing experience of prejudice and discrimination?

That prejudice and discrimination almost always says more about those who perpetrate it than about those who suffer it, and that suffering it can deepen your self-knowledge, strengthen your character and stiffen your will.

Anything else?

If you're up to it, the so-called 'Golden Rule': 'Do unto others as you would have them do unto you' – some codification of which, I'm told, underpins virtually every major religion – is, on balance a far, far more constructive way to proceed.

· ·

Although I hadn't seen old Groome for many weeks, Sir Roald had kept me informed of his doings, and I knew that shortly after our purchase of the Heartsease Hall Estate had been agreed he'd applied for a council flat (public housing). And I further knew that he wasn't planning to live there... because he'd decided to move in with his long-term ladyfriend – a distant relation of Sir Roald's, whose father had been chairman of a major international publishing house – who'd recently bought a very up-market property on the UK's 'South Coast' overlooking the English Channel. 'But there you are: a relationship which is as sincere and fulfilling as it is improbable,' Sir Roald had confided to me with a twinkle.

So when just after lunch on 7 December Groome dropped by to

say – somewhat self-consciously, it seemed to me – that he'd been allocated a council flat sooner than expected and would shortly be quitting the estate, I nodded... and smiled knowingly. Groome cocked his head slightly to one side and, for a moment, regarded me as a miscreant schoolboy might a teacher who'd found him out. Then he broke into a big grin and laughed heartily.

An un-reconstructed, old-style countryman – a 'man of the road' or hobo, almost – Groome might be I reflected but, withal, he was charming and genuine; I could easily see how Sir Roald's kinswoman – any 'real' woman – would take to him. He thanked me for letting him stay on at Heartsease Hall 'until (his) council flat came through'; I thanked him for looking after the estate while Sir Roald and Lady Maureen moved out and N and I *et al* moved in; we clapped each other heartily on the back, wished each other good luck, shook hands... and that was that. (Bar disposal of the wretched mobile home on which Groome magnanimously gave me first refusal – probably because he knew it would prove very difficult to prize out of its investing rubble-heap and tow away.)

Later that day, Warrener stopped by to say squally weather was *en route* which would drive shore-dwelling ducks and geese away from the rough waters of the North Sea and inland towards shelter, for example on our lakes. He and (Com) 'Mander Steele had concurred that a fine evening's wildfowling was in prospect. '*We could*,' Warrener proposed leadingly – which I took as a request at least for my blessing on the venture and, perhaps, my participation in it – set out at 1600 by which time, he declared, the light would be 'just about right'. (Yr Correspondent estimated there'd hardly be any light at all at that time.) And so came to pass my first Heartsease Hall duck hunt.

It was an interesting couple of hours. As context, I must make clear I wasn't entirely sure I wanted to shoot these birds – it was so lovely just having them about, 'sharing' our lakes with them – and I'm still not entirely sure. But I knew wild duck to be very tasty and, as my father used regularly to enjoin: 'A man should try (almost) anything once.' So there we were, settling into our blinds, Warrener and I on the north side of the lower lake, Joscelyn across from us on the south side... the wintry wind whipping, the sleet and rain slashing, the faint, late-afternoon sunlight rapidly fading... when suddenly, out of the lowering gloom, a pair of dark duck-shapes whistle* overhead like

---

* Literally, as on their wings' down-strokes air is forced through the birds' flight-feathers.

mini-Cruise missiles.

'There's a couple, sir,' Warrener fairly spits into my ear. 'Teal (*Anas crecca*, a relative of the mallard, but smaller)... a drake and a hen. Git em.'

I off the safety and mount my shotgun, my outstretched index finger supporting its fore-end, my cheek and nose aligned tight along its stock, as I'd been instructed, sight the first bird, start somewhat belatedly to swing through it.... A 'crack... crack!' comes from the other side of the lake. One dark shape crumples immediately into the water; the second flies on briefly then falls too.

'You gotta be quick, Mista 'Enry,' Warrener consoles, 'The 'Mander, he'll give you first go... but if you don't go, that's it.'

Well, I resolve, I'll be quicker. It's not right that the New Squire, on his own estate, be outdone by some Established Squire – no matter how kind and solicitous of the New Squire the Established Squire's been.

But first, it occurs to me, I've actually got to see the blessed birds. By now, it's almost totally dark or so it seems to me; I wouldn't, I reflect, want to walk around without a flashlight or good illumination of some kind. And, I muse, if I were a duck, I certainly wouldn't want to fly... or, if there was nothing for it and I *had* to fly, I certainly wouldn't want to land. I'd try to find a thermal so I could circle around and around all night...

. . . .

Ducks – flying birds – may use thermals to speed them on their way, d'Arcy. But they don't 'circle around and around' on them like soaring birds – albatross, for example, or condors and vultures... and some birds of prey – do. They can't; relative to their body weight, their wings aren't large enough.

. . . .

... circle around and around all night – do something... anything... to keep me aloft until the next morning, when I can see the runway better.

And it further occurs to me: even if I do manage to sight a bird early enough, how do I identify and range it in this light? That speeding shape up there could be a little, bitty duck 80–100 yards out or, perhaps, a great big goose two hundred or so yards away. If I can't correctly identify the bird, of course, I shouldn't take a shot at it. And if I haven't got some markers – a conspicuous tree, say – to allow me to calculate how far away the bird is, giving my shot the correct lead is going to be very, very difficult....

Wait a minute! Isn't that a pair of duck coming in, I whisper to Warrener? Over there to our left just behind the 'stag-headed' oak, as they're sometimes called*. 'No,' sighs the long-suffering gamekeeper heavily, 'them birds is pigeons, Mista 'Enry. The way they use their wings... the way they move in the air.... Ducks is different from pigeons. Besides, they's lookin' to roost up in a wood somewhere; they won't be comin' over us here.' He paused, then: 'An' that ole tree's not a oak; it's a sweet chestnut – *Castanea sativa*, also called Italian or Spanish chestnut. But look, jist over there, sir.... You see? Flyin' right outta the moon....' Warrener's voice rises in volume, pitch and intensity. 'Them's four... five mallard....'

'Where, Thomas?'

'There, Mista 'Enry. Don'tcha see? *There!* Jist passin' in front of them tall willas (willows),' he fairly screams.

'Crack... crack!' And suddenly – too late again – I see them: a couple of dark shapes tumbling through the air, unflighted... crashing-splashing down, and three still airborne vectoring up on full thrust... curling... curling... and accelerating away.

'Never mind, Mista 'Enry. They'll be some more come over. You'll git th' 'ang of it. But with the 'Mander, you gotta be quick. You got... ta... be... quick....'

After an engagement (? *dis*engagement) of such epic stress and strain, not to mention humiliation, Yr Correspondent was very much in need of someone or some ones on whom to vent his frustration. A pair of suitable nominees soon came to mind. The deadline for payment of their rent-arrears having passed without my having received any monies, about 1900 hours I faxed Euan instructing him immediately to begin eviction proceedings against Mr and Mrs X.

. . . .

Christmas is coming, I reminded you. And I pointed out that your initiative wasn't altogether in keeping with 'the Christmas spirit'.

What was I supposed to do, Alter-natis: send them down a fruit cake and a bottle of sherry? Turn the other cheek?

. . . .

By now, I was starting to get more into a routine with the doncs, but.... Thank goodness for Big Fee; I'd never thought taking care of

---

* An oak, usually elderly, which has lost its top; the remaining upper branches, when their leaves have dropped, may resemble a stag's antlers.

the brutes could be so demanding! (Indeed, based on detailed observations of donc care-taking made during extended periods spent in the Middle East, I wasn't entirely sure it needed to be.) According to Lady Maureen's prescriptions, however: doncs must have plenty of fresh water, and hay *ad lib* – either to supplement their fresh grass intake or to forestall their taking in too much fresh grass – and morning and evening a little snack such as rolled oats or 'concentrate' (pelletized food, usually vitamin-enriched) with chopped carrots or apples mixed in….

Then they like a good grooming, giving particular attention to their hocks and hooves ('donkeys are very prone to mud-fever*, you know') and along their backs, especially their withers and croup ('donkeys can't reach to groom themselves there, obviously'). All of which might seem less mind-numbingly, gratuitously onerous if just one donc, for only the briefest flicker of time, showed even the slightest acknowledgement of – let alone gratitude for – their carer's lavished attentions.

The most vexed issue, however, remained whether the doncs should be outside in their paddock, or inside in their stalls. Lady Maureen's standing orders were simple: the doncs were generally to be out. But then came the conditionals: unless there was too much grass… or it was too hot or too cold, or too wet or too dry, or too windy or too still. To Yr Correspondent, it seemed the data-processing capabilities of a super-computer and the devotion of a Mother Theresa were required to get it all just right.

The afternoon of 17 December, Sir Roald and Lady Maureen – and Phoebe, of course – began a few days' stay in Dovecote Cottage. That evening, Sir Roald and I exchanged brief pleasantries before going our separate, frantic, pre-Christmas ways….

The next morning, Sir Roald came into the library about 0830 to ask in his attuned, foreign-correspondent way if 'anything (was) going on' – by which, I knew, he meant was there interesting news, preferably breaking, of a local or domestic nature – and to discuss significant developments in the wider world. (He and Lady Maureen, he'd earlier revealed, always awoke to the 0600 BBC World Service News [sadly, now a much-reduced service] and, shortly thereafter, the last-named went out to fetch a selection of newspapers [*The Times*,

---

* *Dermatophilosis*, referred to in the US as 'scratches', a bacterial infection primarily of the skin of the legs and feet which flourishes in warm, wet conditions.

of course, the *Daily Telegraph* and the *EDP*] all of which within an hour or so had been read.)

I wanted desperately to generate 'a story' for Sir Roald or construct 'an analysis' or provide 'a commentary', but I wasn't aware much had happened in the Parish or to the d'Arcy Henry family during the 14–15 hours since Sir Roald and I'd last spoken, and the latest *International Herald Tribune*, which we got by mail, hadn't arrived yet. So I defaulted into some waffle about current prospects for the Anglo-American 'special relationship' which, it seemed, the Old Boy found rather ho-hum as, smiling indulgently, he almost immediately excused himself saying he had to do some laundry.

· · · · · · · · · · · · · · · · · ·

Laundry? The 13th Baronet Festing... doing laundry?

· · · · · · · · · · · · · · · · · ·

An hour or so later Sir Roald came in again, this time with a couple of still-damp mens' shirts and what looked like a woman's blouse draped over one arm. He reported that the iron in Dovecote Cottage was broken and asked if he could borrow ours. I replied certainly; he turned to leave... then, turned back.... 'Mr Henry, what parallels do you see between America's global role today, with the Cold War concluded, and Britain's, say, after the 1815 Treaty of Vienna*?'

Indeed, I thought; what a good question! After a bit of umm-ing and ahh-ing – this time eliciting from Sir Roald an expression of near-despair... before his exit – I made a mental note to find out whether the International Institute of Strategic Studies or the Royal Institute of International Affairs (aka Chatham House) – organizations with which I was then affiliated – had available any recent research on this most interesting subject.

And that evening, Sir Roald and Lady Maureen came over for their first-ever supper as our guests in the Hall: through what used to be their back door, into their former kitchen, onto their chairs, around their table, eating food cooked on their Aga stove... just as they'd done in the good old days. (Phoebe came too and – a little like Mr and Mrs X, perhaps – she seemed less than fully-accepting of the change in ownership of the Hall which had taken place. At intervals

---

* Following the final defeat of Napoleon, the then five Great Powers (Austria, France, Great Britain, Prussia and Russia), held a Congress in Vienna at which Britain, via its Foreign Minister, Viscount Castlereagh, played a pivotal role. The resulting Treaty established a new European 'order' – and thus a new global one – which remained more or less intact until the outbreak of World War I.

uncurling from underneath the shelving next to the Aga – where we'd put an old blanket as a bed for her – she quartered the kitchen floor proprietarily in search of errant scraps of food.)

N, predictably, was her usual, easy, 'go-with-the-flow' California self. Yr Correspondent, however, was plagued by thoughts of how awkward this revisitation must be for Sir Roald and Lady Maureen and, therefore, how careful he must be to avoid topics of conversation, direct and indirect references... innuendoes even... that's to say anything which might give rise to painful memories and/or cause *angst*....

I shouldn't, of course, have worried. Far from finding the subject of their removal from the ancestral abode too distressing, Sir Roald and Lady Maureen told anecdote after anecdote about it: how the local newspapers and then the BBC had picked up the story; how Anglia Television (a regional operating unit of the UK's Independent Television, ITV) and ultimately CNN, even, had sent crews in; and how prospective purchaser after prospective purchaser, to a total of nearly three dozen, had come – several by helicopter – and traipsed up and down and around and through... and found the Heartsease Hall Estate either too big or too small, or too remote or too near, or too daunting or too negligible – that's to say 'just... you know, for us... not quite right'.

· · · · · · · · · · · · · · · · · · · ·

Shades of trying to sell Brambledown, Alter-natis. Indeed: *didn't* we just know!

· · · · · · · · · · · · · · · · · · · ·

And, intriguingly, although several of those who viewed went on to offer for the property, how to Sir Roald none had 'seemed suitable, really'. (Lady Maureen again and again exclaimed her 'delight' at Heartsease Hall having been purchased by N and me 'instead of some awful "yuppies"... or whatever they call them'.)

From start to finish, therefore, the evening proceeded almost like a family celebration: a baptism or a wedding or better, in a sense, an Irish wake. It was as though not just title to a house and some land – a physical property – had been transferred to us but also a spiritual property... a sort-of trust. In certain respects, the Henrys had become the Festing's heirs, N and I felt, and in those respects our heretofore entirely-separate families and very-different individual lives were now conjoined.

. . . .

Just one big, happy symbiosis.

Yes, and very agreeable it was too! We didn't know then how frequently Sir Roald and Lady Maureen – and the inevitable Phoebe – would visit or how long they would stay or, of course, over the longer-term how their visiting and staying might work out interpersonally.

But there was something very comforting about having the Old Folks here, 'in dower'*, gradually winding down their association with the estate as we wound ours up... evolutionary rather than revolutionary change.

Aahhhh: that's a very difficult call, d'Arcy.

What call, Alter-natis?

Your implied preference for evolutionary as against revolutionary change.

I'm a clay-footed, evolutionary sort of guy... mostly. Revolution, upheaval, cataclysm... frightens me like, I guess, it does most people.

'This (United States), with its institutions, belongs to the people who inhabit it. Whenever they shall grow weary of the existing government, they can exercise their constitutional right of amending it, or their revolutionary right to dismember or overthrow it.'

'Revolutionary right... to dismember or overthrow... the existing government' of the United States? Who on earth wrote that?

Abraham Lincoln in 1861, shortly after he was elected President.

I didn't realize Lincoln was such an insurrectionist firebrand!

He wasn't really, according to most scholars; he just believed very deeply in man's inherent right to be self-determining.

Ummmm. But, surely: life on earth, the earth itself, the solar system, the universe... our personal physical and mental selves... not to mention our civilization's great institutions – its arts and sciences, and its politics and socio-economics – represent the triumph of evolution over revolution...?

I won't trouble to pick you up on your choice of the noun 'triumph' in this context; I'll just note that almost without exception the various evolutions to which you refer began with, were and are periodically punctuated by and, very probably, will end in some sort of revolution – a catastrophic one, pretty much by definition – during which much and perhaps all of what was is totally destroyed.

Good Heavens, Alter-natis! Do you think we're going to be caught up in a revolution?

Another very difficult call, obviously. But the mass of conflicts pent up within our increasingly physically constrained and socio-economically inter-dependent global community does sometimes seem to be going critical. Self-obsessed, self-serving governments and

---

* Technically a widow's contractual life interest in her late husband's effects but, by extension, any person's life interest in property which formerly belonged to them or their spouse.

NGOs (non-governmental organisations), and the political classes who wait on them are partly to blame, of course. But ultimately, 'We the People' must be our Brothers' and Sisters' keepers.

Adjudicating and peacefully resolving today's manifold conflicts is everyone's responsibility.

. . . .

... our very-different individual lives were now conjoined.

As if in confirmation of this conjunction, the next morning Sir Roald was in bright and early – as even the most casual Reader will by now be aware was his wont – to ask whether he and Lady Maureen might rent Dovecote Cottage until they found a new, country property. 'We don't want to be a burden or get in your way, of course, but we all do seem to get on well; my wife and I certainly feel we do.... And it would be very convenient for us.' Of course; what a sure honour and what likely great fun! Without bothering to consult N, I quickly agreed terms with Sir Roald.

Well then there was, Sir Roald said, one collateral matter: charge of the Purdy shotgun his father had given him as a 21st birthday present. Would I keep it for him? Put it together with my armaments in the gun room safe? And perhaps, if I didn't mind, might he from time to time take it out after rabbits, squirrels, pigeons, crows and other vermin? I said 'of course' again and made a mental note immediately to get the required documentation off to the police*. For Yr Correspondent – if not, apparently, for Sir Roald – it was another highly symbolic and poignant moment.

. . . .

In nearly all societies – families, tribes, states... nations – permission to bear arms to defend yourself and your property, or for hunting, or even just for target practice, comes ultimately from 'The Chief', doesn't it?

Yes, except in The Motherland, where bearing arms – in some states even semi-automatic versions of assault weapons like the AK-47 and M16 rifle, and the FN Five-Seven pistol – remains enshrined in the Second Amendment as a US citizen's 'Constitutional right'.

And there was Sir Roald, the 'Old Chief', metaphorically surrendering his arms and the means of his and his dependents' survival to you, the 'New Chief'.

. . . .

---

* UK law requires not only that the name and contact details of a firearm's owner be recorded, but also the name, etc, of its current keeper.

Twenty-one December – the eve of the winter solstice when, in England, Helios officially sets out in his chariot about 0800 GMT and garages it again only a scant eight or so hours later – dawned in 1994 brilliant-bright and clear, with a thick hoar frost off which the sun dazzled. Duck and geese paddled the lakes; partridge and pheasant stepped the fields; the sheep cudded contentedly within their electric-fenced paddocks... along Neate Wood's near edge, a hind-herd of red deer grazed. And so before starting work at my desk, I decided the beauty of it all warranted a quick trundle around the south lawn.

Practically as I was taking my first step, however, a sharp 'bang, crackle, crackle, crackle... ka-thump' rent the crisp, hibernal air. Good Lord, I thought, what *was* that *awful* noise? It sounded like a stone falling onto a slate roof and then rolling down... down... down... and finally dropping to the ground. And indeed, that's just what it was! It was one of our dragon-fish scales – our lovely, knapped-flint dragon-fish scales – which, 'delaminating' from its mortar-bed in the Hall's southeast gable-end wall, had fallen onto, and then down from, the roof of our annex. I walked over, picked the flint up, took it inside and put it reverently on the mantelpiece in the library.

• • • • • • • • • • • • • • • • • • • •

You were probably the first person in over 200 years to handle that stone, d'Arcy.
A precious moment in architectural history it may have been, Alter-natis. But uppermost in my mind then was: how many more of our flints are going to come down?

• • • • • • • • • • • • • • • • • • • •

Shifting from such dour speculations into Merry-Christmas mode required some reprogramming. The first stage in this process was accomplished mid-morning on 22 December, when I swept the drawing room chimney preparatory to present-opening in front of a proposed 'Christmas Day Fire'. I put up sixteen 'rods', as they're called in the UK* and brought down a large quantity of soot, twigs, birdlime... even a couple of bird skeletons. That chimney hasn't been swept for many, many years, I noted sourly. But soon I'd a trial fire blazing away, throwing out good heat – and not too much smoke.

And by the afternoon of 23 December, my conversion to full Yuletide glow was more or less complete. While N and Piglet food-shopped in our local village, Bapu and I set off in the Land Rover to

---

* Connectable lengths of stiff plastic tube (formerly bamboo cane) to the front of the first of which a disc-shaped brush is attached; each rod is about a yard long.

cut some holly and ivy branches for decoration, and a conifer suitable for use as our Christmas tree. In Home Farm Wood, we quickly found an abundance of everything we sought and a big ball of mistletoe as well. (Coming back, Bapu asked me anxiously if Santa Claus would know we'd moved house. I was able easily to reassure him on this point but then came his supplementary: 'How does Santa know we've moved, Daddy?' I considered telling him Santa had been granted special access the US military's GPS – 'enabling him, with his on-sleigh computer, to determine the whereabouts of every good little boy and girl to within a foot or so' – but I was afraid Bapu might then ask how GPS worked. So I replied authoritatively-preemptively that Santa was a bit like God or Whomever [or daddies...] and 'just knows things'.)

Christmas Eve was a day of pandemonic preparations: buying and wrapping last-minute presents; garlanding the cut holly and ivy over the fireplace mantles and hanging the mistletoe from the chandelier in the entrance hall; decorating the tree and setting under it the 'Maryland Christmas' model my Father had made over half a century earlier (It comprises a painted, mica-snow-sprinkled representation of 'Whitehaven', the main house on my Harryman grandparent's estate [now tract housing] in Garrison Forest, Maryland, where my mother was born and raised [my father was born and raised near Dorsey, Maryland], and its adjacent St Thomas's Church where she and my father were married.); displaying, somewhat late in the count-down, N's Aunt Betty's Advent calendar (designed, jig-sawn from plywood, and painted by her own hand, and from which one icon should already have been removed on each, prescribed, pre-Natal day); making the stuffing for the turkey (oyster and chestnut, the latter ingredient sourced from our own trees) and the rum-butter sauce for the plum pudding.... Indeed, it was as N observed: 'For our first Christmas at Heartsease Hall, everything's got to be just right!'

And that evening, the Henry family attended Carol Evensong in St Lawrence's Church. Within a simple, unheated, place of worship lit only by tallow candles... in the deep-dark winter still without, great clumpy snowflakes – 'feathers from the angels' wings', Bapu called them – floating down... we and perhaps 60–70 other adults and children harked to messages of wondrous joy and hope, and gladly rejoined in similar vein; by our very presence, I reflected, we were at once constituting and continuing an oblation which in one form or another had been made right here – by people not so very different from ourselves – every Christmas (or *Cristes maesse* [Christ's Mass])

Ann Tempest© 2014

Eve, probably, for roughly the last one thousand years. What an awesome experience, literally!

Then back to the Hall we all went for a light supper, the ceremonial hanging of the stockings and a reading of Clement Moore's famous 1823 rhyme *A Visit from St Nicholas* with its archly betokening opening words: 'Twas the night before Christmas....' Bapu and, next, Piglet shuffled off to bed; the presents were laid out; N shuffled off to bed; the cookies-and-milk 'treat' for Santa was taken – as well as a wee dram (I could all-but hear Bapu asking: 'How did Santa know where you keep the single-malt whiskey, Daddy?') – and, finally, an opportunity presented itself for quiet reflection:

. . . .

'Merry Christmas, Mr Henry! Merry, merry, *merry* Christmas!'

Sir Jacob; what a pleasant surprise!

'I was passing by so I thought I'd call in and conjure up for you a real, old-time 'Ghost of Christmas Past' scene – as might have been before the imposture of nasty old Scrooge, deserving young Bob Cratchet... English-Romantic melodrama... that sort of thing; Charles Dickens's 1843 *A Christmas Carol* initiated a whole new stage in the secularization of what previously had been ostensibly a religious festival, you know.'

I'm very glad you've come; it's been a long while....

'What did you think of this evening's carol service, Mr Henry? The vicar's sermon excepted, perhaps, did you find it moving?'

Yes, of course. You'd have to be anencephalic not to be moved by such an observance.

'I used to love that service. A hundred or so people usually attended – estate workers and their families mostly. We had candles everywhere! It was still pretty dark and dingy, though.... There used to be a little fireplace set into the wall just in front of our pew near where the lectern is today which kept me and my family, and the vicar, nice and warm. But it didn't do much for the rest of the congregation and the choir, I'm afraid.

'We all sang and prayed and hoped and feared together.... Nothing much has changed really except the church's furniture: it's late-18th/early-19th century, of course; one of my successors – an 'Isaac', I think; in those days, there always seemed to be an Isaac Festing about – had it put in. And the ceiling – you know, the one modeled on William Wilkins, Senior's, ceiling here in your entrance hall.... In my day that coved, lath and plaster confection with its running rib moldings didn't exist; above us were just bare roof trusses and the under-boarding of the exterior, pantiled roof.

'Anyway: why was it, do you think, you found the Carol Service moving?'

Do you mean 'why' in the sense of sensory stimuli, that's to say what were the electro-chemical genitors of 'moving-ness' in my brain's parietal, temporal and/or frontal lobes? Semi-darkness and stillness, I suppose, punctuated by words and music age-old yet new... and a sense of communion: of sharing with others of like mind gathered together in a consecrated place....

Is that the sort of answer you were looking for, Sir Jacob? Or had you in mind something deeper?

'I was sort of hoping for something deeper... and more revealing, Mr Henry.'

I find a service such as tonight's moving because it obliges me to confront my mortality.

'What do you mean by "confront (your) mortality"?'

I mean recognizing that my existence... my 'individuality' – my 'singularity' to borrow a word from mathematics, or physics – is part of a great continuum stretching back to the basic, primordial elements of which I once was and forward to the basic primordial elements of which I will be. In the words of that ancient interment prayer: 'Earth to earth, ashes to ashes, dust to dust....'

'Does this recognition make you apprehensive, Mr Henry?'

Not at all, Sir Jacob. In fact, rather the opposite: this recognition is a relief.

'Why is that?'

Because it delimits me, that's to say puts me and my life and my endeavors into a perspective which I think I can know and understand to some extent. It's ignorance and uncertainty, after all, which evokes fear, not knowledge.

'Are you then, my son, finally beginning to see The Light?'

'A Light', perhaps... a dim, far-off 'A Light'; I still don't know what is the 'The Light' or even if there is a 'The Light'. Maybe there's only an 'A Light'. Or maybe the 'A Light' and the 'The Light' are one and the same....

'Well, that's progress of a sort, I guess. But never mind; I'll call in again, if I may, and see how you're getting on.... In the meantime, keep up the good, enlightening work!'

· · · · · · · · · · · · · · · · · ·

Our first Christmas Day at Heartsease Hall was – would you believe it! – a white one. Yee-ah! Four or five inches of... 'angel-wing feathers'... fell, sufficient to work its magic on the landscape but not enough seriously to complicate the logistics of existence. I took some hay to the sheep – more as an excuse to get out and about than because they needed it – and shot a roll of 'wonder-of-it-all' pictures; then I came back (out of film, predictably) to the sight of Piglet and Bapu building a snowman on the lawn south of the orangery and, from the Hall's kitchen, the smell of coffee, frying bacon and eggs, and N's fresh, home-baked bread. In sum: I ran out of superlatives!

That night, looking back – and other than as 'The Henry's First Christmas at Heartsease Hall'; the Reader may be tiring of so many inaugurals – how did we remember this most memorable day? I'll list out a few of the recollections which come to mind:

- the pleasure of giving presents

- the pain of observing the rituals of present opening ('Be careful not to tear the wrapping paper, Dar; I may be able to use it again next year.' 'Oh, N! Just what I was longing for: a pair of sky-blue, nylon ankle socks with a pink-pig motif on!')

- the pleasure of eating good, wholesome food, lovingly prepared

- the pain of over-indulging ('I think it must have been the plum pudding, N. It doesn't usually affect me this way. But I seem to remember that Christmas we spent in Great Budworth [a town south-east of Manchester in the UK's north Midlands] with Robin and Jane....')

- the pleasure of snuggling down in front of the fire in the library to watch television

- the pain of discovering there's nothing on worth watching ('Dad, if we just had "Sky" or "Digital"... one of the cable or satellite TV systems; they don't cost *that* much!')

- the pleasure of at last tucking into bed

- the pain of having another Christmas end ('Well, N, that's it for Noel 94. N? *N*...?' 'Zzzzzzz'.)

Shortly after Christmas, Sir Roald and Lady Maureen, returned from visiting Sir Roald's sister and her family in Vienna, were once again in residence next door. And on 29 December, the first-named – already bored, apparently – telephoned about 0830 wanting to know if there was anything we needed to talk about. As usual I couldn't, at first, think of anything. But then I remembered N's and my forthcoming FHA presentation to [a major US multi-national] which touched on Moscow's current relations with East Europe. Vienna was and is still, of course, a hot-spot for intelligence of this sort, and Sir Roald was egregiously well-connected there. Had his just-ended sojourn turned up any new news, I asked? Five minutes or so later, the Old Boy strode briskly in. Once a foreign correspondent, always a foreign correspondent....

About mid-day arrived on the back porch a box – literally in this case, but in north Norfolk any Yuletide gift may be called a 'box', I learned* – from Warrener and Rosalie. In it were two bottles of home-made damson gin† and the dressed carcass of the biggest, fattest capon I'd ever seen.

The last day of 1994 we achieved (? survived) yet another first: a 'family', as they're called (for family and friends only, as distinct from 'commercial'), 'hoot' (laid-back, upper-class-English *patois* for 'shoot') over part of the estate.... Or, as we plain-speaking, upstart Americans would say: we went pheasant hunting. In overall charge of the event was our neighbour Joscelyn Steele.

A hugely to-be-prized *mise-en-scène* it was, some would argue...

---

* Apparently from 'Boxing Day', traditionally the first workday after Christmas (now observed as a public holiday), when the gentry handed out gratuities, often boxed, to their servants and trades-people.

† Gin in which sugared damsons (*Prunus institia*, a relative of the plum) have been steeped.

among them Piglet. He was up at first light and into a hearty break-fast, then he put on his beaters' outfit (including thorn-proof chaps hand-made especially for him by Rosalie Warrener) and went out to the yard to practise thrashing the underbrush with his stick and shouting 'Whissst... whissst!' (a noise intended to startle the birds into flight, hopefully over the 'Guns', that's to say the hunters). Moreo-ver, what he didn't know was: in addition to having an exciting day out, he was going to be paid the standard 'baby-beaters' wage of ten pounds (then about $15). What bliss!

But for Yr Correspondent, who had again to reveal his indifferent shooting skills as well, possibly, as one or two other seeming imper-fections....

About 0900, I collected Sir Roald from in front of Dovecote Cot-tage and drove in our Land Rover to the meeting-place for the first drive. Joscelyn greeted us and introduced me – Sir Roald, it was im-mediately clear, already knew everyone – to the other Guns, among whom were: a retired Equerry to Her Majesty the Queen, a ditto Vice-Admiral of the Fleet and his wife, two sitting Members of the House of Lords, a former Lord Mayor of London, and the present High Sheriff of Norfolk.

My first thoughts were largely *en passant, viz*: such an *interest-ing* collection of Old-English Establishmentarians Joscelyn's put to-gether.... What on earth am I doing here? My second ones were more situation-oriented and concrete. These fine fellows are, almost certainly, very knowledgeable and experienced Guns. How, there-fore, can a novice Gun like me – and mere apprentice country Squire – take and maintain some semblance of The Initiative? I decided my only practicable strategy was a tactical retreat into deferential American mode...

• • • • • • • • • • • • • • • • • • • •

'Deferential American mode': now that's what I call a real *oxymo-ron!*

• • • • • • • • • • • • • • • • • • • •

... and so for the duration of the event, I 'yes, sir-ed' and 'no, sir-ed' all and sundry like a cadet on parade.

But... I should hardly have worried. With Sir Roald as my social guide and mentor – patron, effectively – the question of my stand-ing... my 'entitlement' to participate... never arose – at least within my hearing. And with Joscelyn as my shooting guide and mentor....

. . . .

What's the problem, I asked you? The beaters put the birds up; you knock 'em – the birds, that is – down. Could it be any simpler?

As you've implied, Alter-natis, safety when shooting is indeed the over-riding concern. And to shoot safely you've got to handle your gun properly: not be loaded up unless you're on your 'peg' (where the Gun stands, often indicated by a stick or suchlike stuck into the ground), shoot only within the prescribed zone in front of and behind you, and never, ever swing 'through the line', that's to say across the Guns pegged to your left and/or right.

It's all common sense, of course.

That may be another reason why you found the experience so challenging.

It's also important to understand how, in the prevailing wind and weather conditions, the birds will fly. On this variable will largely depend the placement of the Guns, the line the beaters will walk and the positioning of the 'pickers-up' (shoot attendants who retrieve downed birds).

A proper British day's shooting is sort of like a military campaign, you know.

You've never been very militaristic....

That's why the Shoot Captain is so crucial. Advised by his Head Keeper, he'll determine the Shoot Plan and give you your shooting orders which, in spite of the turmoil within and all around you, you've got to remember to follow.

Good Lord! You've actually to follow the Shoot Captain's orders, have you?

In fact, however, a good Shoot Captain hardly ever *orders* a Gun to do something....

He calls him on his cell phone... or emails or texts him, does he?

Instead, he advises him in code, saying something like: 'There's a little hollow in the ground over there, just about in range from where you're standing. Sometimes a dog or one of the beaters can pop up quite unexpectedly.' The Gun has to translate: 'Be careful, please, not to shoot a dog or a beater!'

Very clever....

But there's much more to this business than the ritualized slaughter of hand-reared birds, you know.

You could have fooled me!

Oh yes: shooting's substantially – primarily, some would say – a social occasion where old acquaintances are renewed and new ones made; family, local and regional ties are strengthened; and national and international allegiances are re-enforced.

I see: shooting as bonding; no wonder an introvert like you shies away!

. . . .

All told, it was a better-than-expected day out. A splendid, mid-day meal was laid on; the distinguished, invitee 'natives' were without exception friendly and appeared to take a sincere interest in me, and N's and my small doings at Heartsease Hall; and on the 'hooting' front, after a few *pro forma* misses... I popped one pheasant nice and cleanly and then, after a seemly interval, one or two more. So I reckoned I just about managed an honourable passage through my north Norfolk, pheasant-hunting tutorial.

· · · · · · · · · · · · · · · · · · · ·

Temperature well below zero, sleet mixed with snow raking in from the Arctic... and some of England's finest lords, ladies and gentlemen – persons of wealth, status and discernment – are standing, most of the time stock still, out in it. And you're standing out there with them. Why?

It didn't seem to bother them that I was an untitled, upstart American, Alter-natis; they saw the natural aristocrat in me.

I'm not asking why you were in these peoples' company, Dimwit – although I'll just note that 'natural' as in 'natural aristocrat' could be construed as 'out of wedlock' or 'illegitimate'. I'm asking why on earth you – a man fairly full of years and presumed to be of sound mind – were abroad in those conditions. Wouldn't it have been more sensible to be inside, in front of a roaring fire, sipping a good whisky and reading a good book?

It would have, sort of... I guess. But....

But what, d'Arcy?

It's fun, in a way, exposing yourself to the elemental forces of nature, pitting your skills against the swift, soaring birds with crackshot Guns either side of you some of whom are bent on poaching (shooting game, etc, in your zone), accepting the jeers of the beaters and the pickers-up when you miss and their congratulations if you hit.... It grabs you, draws you in... pulls you along... almost in spite of yourself. Besides....

Such a masochist! But: 'besides' what?

Besides, in north Norfolk shooting's what squires do; it's one of their definiens. Cooks cook, writers write... squires shoot; it's as simple as that. 'So if you aspire To be a squire...

'... learn to love to shoot' (with pre-emptive apologies to the 19th-century English dramatist and librettist W. S. Gilbert, who must have penned something like this).

· · · · · · · · · · · · · · · · · · · ·

To my opening list of reservations, however, I'd add in conclusion: hanging around not doing very much. Unlike ice hockey or freestyle wrestling, or tennis or squash, or horse riding or sail boating... or deer stalking – all sports I've much enjoyed – hunting driven pheasant is a relatively leisurely pursuit. On a typical day, a standing Gun (as opposed to a 'walking' one, who patrols alongside the beaters) may spend 5–5.5 hours (7–8 drives x 40–45 minutes per drive) actually in the field; for only forty or so *minutes*, however – one-eighth of his total field-time – will he likely be on 'red alert' or actually shooting.

· · · · · · · · · · · · · · · · · · · ·

Sort of like a first date, you might say, d'Arcy.

Not any more, Alter-natis. In the hot heat of today's so-called hook-up culture, young peoples' 'rules of engagement' appear to have substantially changed.

· · · · · · · · · · · · · · · · · · · ·

But all that time spent on 'amber alert' doing pretty much nothing was... *absolutely exhausting*! So after supper with N and the boys, a quick glass of bubbly with N, and a private review *magna cum gratia* of our manifold blessings, I made an early end to my most-eventful 1994 and hit the sack.

The next morning provided a fine, bright start to our New Year. Snow was forecast, however, so anticipating a directive from Lady Maureen, I brought the doncs in. We did, eventually, get a light dusting of white. By mid-day, however, a southwest wind indicated any really severe weather had passed us by. So I put the doncs out again....

· · · · · · · · · · · · · · · · · · · ·

Ho, hummm. As you're so fond of saying: there's never a dull moment in the country.

As earlier proposed, Alter-natis, everyone needs a bit of downtime.

· · · · · · · · · · · · · · · · · · · ·

January 3 was my [...] birthday: yet another 'at Heartsease Hall' first. We celebrated it with a bottle of bubbly before moving on to a supper of whole roast woodcock* with home-made quince jam, thick-cut, 'game' potato chips, roast parsnips, stir-fried red cabbage and apples, all washed down with a nice claret and followed by chocolate cake with a topping of real-vanilla ice cream. Afterwards, we drank a cou-

---

* *Scolopax rusticola*: an insect-eater, primarily, whose cooked intestines, known as 'trail' (short-form for 'entrails'), are often served on buttered toast as a 'savoury' (salty or spicy desert course); N and I decided we'd save these last for some even-more-especial occasion....

ple of glasses of vintage Armagnac, and I had a Montecristo cigar... with the result that I tossed and turned for much of the night. What a delight – mostly – if birthdays could ever really be so described....

• • • • • • • • • • • • • • • • • •

There are two types of people in this world, d'Arcy...

I've heard that argued, Alter-natis. But surely such a rigorously binate distribution is simplistic. Karl Friedrich Gauss, the 19th-century German mathematician whose work, we're told, led eventually to specification of the 'bell curve'....

... those who reach out to and embrace their birthdays – and, usually, personal anniversaries of any sort – as an opportunity for celebration....

N's like that; she loves birthdays... even her own.

They're the so-called Venusians: sunny, extrovert, fun-loving people with a real zest for life and living.

That's N, all right!

And then there're the so-called Martians, that's to say those who....

Yeah; I know.

• • • • • • • • • • • • • • • • • •

A few evenings later Lady Maureen came to supper – on her own, Sir Roald being in London, she said, 'attending some literary function'. (In fact, he was back in hospital.)

Initially, Lady Maureen seemed concerned to construct and maintain a certain psychosocial distance, which I put down to defensiveness coupled, perhaps, with a slight case of Derivative Spouse Syndrome. After a glass or two of wine, however, her fundamental accessibility reasserted itself ('*In vino veritas*', indeed!) and she regaled us once again with tales of Heartsease Hall in the good old days of yore: of Sir Torvald, Sir Roald's father, the 12th Baronet Festing – in his 90s and severely cataracted, so wearing a homburg (hat) to shade his eyes – sitting at the dining-room piano playing classical music from memory for hours on end; of Lady Elena, Sir Roald's mother, and her sister Tatiana standing at the top of the main staircase arguing, as they regularly did – initially in French* and then, as the argument grew

---

* Throughout the 19th century and well into the 20th, French was the *lingua franca* (literally, 'the language of the Franks', a medieval West German tribe, from which modern French in part derives) of the continental European intelligentsia; in the aftermath of the First World War, however, as The Motherland's reach extended and fresh, 'new-order' practicalities succeeded exhausted, 'old-order' prescriptions, French began to be replaced by American-English.

more heated, in their native, Austro-Hungarian inflected German – and hurling articles of clothing, towels, toiletries... almost anything that came to hand... at each other, all the while seemingly oblivious to the CLA, HHA, English Heritage and other, just-ordinary, every-day, tour-group members tip-toeing warily about below....

. . . .

As I've regularly exhorted, d'Arcy, you and yours must raise your level of eccentricity very considerably if you intend playing in this league.

We've tried, Alter-natis... and we're still trying. But there's a real knack to it. Maybe if they continue to reside in the UK and at Heartsease Hall, the boys will eventually succeed. For Yr (Well-toilet-trained) Correspondent, however – if not, perhaps, for his wife – achieving such exquisite caprice may just be a persona too far.

. . . .

And so our splendid first Christmas at Heartsease Hall – in retrospect, our splendid, Heartsease Hall Christmas holiday-honeymoon – came to a close. It was succeeded by four weeks of near-total absorption in the business of becoming an English country squire which began with a represented 'war' about shooting rights and ended with an almost-real war – or, at least, an almost-real direct, physical confrontation – about....

Well, Dear Reader, you'll just have to read on.

Chapter 10

Blooded

Flash! as news-agency and paper correspondents in the field used to front urgent files, thereby alerting their editors back at 'The Desk' to important, breaking news: 'Shooting War in North Norfolk.' *Flashhead*: 'Heartsease Hall Squire's Sweetwater Skirmish'. *Flash*: 'At approximately 1600 hours local time on Monday, 9 January 1995, Thomas Warrener, Head (game) Keeper to Commander Sir Joscelyn Steele, discovered three men armed with shotguns in Sweetwater Wood, land over which he believed W. d'Arcy Henry – the new, American, Apprentice-Squire of the Heartsease Hall Estate – had given his employer exclusive rights to shoot.' *More....*

'Mr Warrener told the trio in no uncertain terms to clear off and, in due course, the men did but under protest, saying their presence on the land was sanctioned by their employer, The Hon* James Jermyn, who had recently acquired Sweetwater Wood from Sir Roald Festing. The British Prime Minister, John Major, after an emergency audience with Her Majesty the Queen, has issued the following statement....' *More. More....*

Finally, there was some real local news, brought to me direct by fax from Joscelyn. The gist of his message was essentially as dramatized above but with the addition that he'd since received a telephone call from The Hon James – a Festing kinsman nicknamed 'Chaser', apparently – requesting 'clarification'. Shooting rights were sometimes retained even when the land itself was sold off, Joscelyn explained, and in this case he – Joscelyn – thought they had been. In sum, it was accepted that The Hon James did indeed *own* Sweetwater Wood. But the shooting rights: weren't they ours still?

Joscelyn's fax concluded enigmatically: 'Given your supper arrangements for Wednesday evening... I very much regret that this matter has arisen at this time.' Well, N and I had indeed accepted an invitation to supper on Wednesday from some friends of long stand-

---

* The abbreviation of 'Honourable', a courtesy title for the children of viscounts and barons and the younger sons of earls.

ing – Nigel and Trish, who lived 12–15 miles away on the North Sea coast – but how had this invitation and our acceptance of it become so widely known?

Given I neither knew the answer to Joscelyn's question nor was inclined to retrieve from our safe and read through the manifold sub-sub-clauses of our very long contract of sale to find out, I decided to let my fingers do the researching, that's to say I telephoned Sir Roald. He, predictably, was absolutely delighted something local-newsworthy was happening: 'So Chaser got on to Joscelyn right away, did he? That's rich! That's very rich! And then, you say, Joscelyn…?' But, also predictably, he was no more sure of the legal position in respect of the Sweetwater Wood shooting rights than I was.

So I telephoned Euan, intending to ask him to check out the contract, but was advised he was 'away from his desk for the week'…

• • • • • • • • • • • • • • • • • • • •

How things change! In my time – yours as well, probably, d'Arcy – the 'away-from-your-desk' gambit was generally reserved for unavailabilities of relatively brief duration.

• • • • • • • • • • • • • • • • • • • •

… so I got back to Sir Roald, who telephoned *his* lawyers… who said they thought they should be able to have an answer for him 'in 3–4 working days'.

• • • • • • • • • • • • • • • • • • • •

Good Lord! Didn't these people know how serious this matter was, Alter-natis? Didn't they understand that while they dallied away from their desks or thumbed unhurriedly through their secure archives, mothers and sisters and wives and children might lose their sons, brothers, husbands and/or fathers?

• • • • • • • • • • • • • • • • • • • •

Foot-dragging being the order of the day, apparently, I faxed Joscelyn that my reply to his question was in preparation but still some way off, and apologized for the delay.

And, it transpired, my reflex, go-with-the-flow procrastination was very fortuitous. For only moments after my fax went out, a swarm of BT (British Telecommunications) engineers descended on the Hall to install a new telephone system. (The old one having accreted over the last half-century or so, the engineers had great sport trying to establish which wiring was operational and which wasn't – and then which operational wiring was part of the telephone system and which part of the security system. [N did, fortunately, forewarn the local police.] The din was terrific, with telephone bells and intruder-alarm bells ringing almost continuously and, but for N's cell phone, the interruption of our communications with the outside world nearly complete.)

As BT's men assured and reassured us, however, their '24-hour retrofit' would be exactly that; 'this time tomorrow...' they vowed, they'd be gone.

But all of this – or, indeed, any of this! – in the midst of the great Sweetwater Wood Shooting-Rights War? Finding the mental strain of it all too great I took my usual solace in hard, physical work, this time pulling out derelict hedging from around the southern perimeter of the south lawn. To help me – and to forestall her distracting BT's men and, thereby, perhaps causing our private, upstart-American telephone conversations to be mis-routed through to the UK's GCHQ* – I seconded Big Fee. She'd said many times how much she loved being outdoors and doing outdoor work, so I found her a pair of thick leather gloves and work boots, and set her to fastening and unfastening the pulling chain while I drove the Land Rover. She scrambled through the brambles, and around and over the standing and up-rooted cypress trees and other rubble, handling the heavy chain with consummate ease.

· · · · · · · · · · · · · · · · · · · ·

Women remain a very under-utilized resource, Alter-natis, especially in parts of the developing world; indeed, the under-utilization of women there – through the denial of equal opportunity to them... through the outright exploitation of them – is, many sociologists think, a major reason why, politically and economically, so many of those regions lag so far behind.

For 'under-utilization' read 'gross subjugation', d'Arcy. Take, for example, the practice of female geni.... Arrragh: it's so abhorrent, I can't bring myself even to write it!

Why do some men still subjugate women, Alter-natis?

Because being stronger physically they're generally able to, and because what they're told are their societies' long-established traditions – however outdated and hence counter-productive those 'traditions' may be – sometimes encourage them to.

Subjugating women seems such a self-defeating thing for men to do. If women weren't free to flaunt and flirt, for example, and then to run not-too-fast away – and, once caught, to generate all those

---

* Government Communications Headquarters; it's American counterpart is the NSA (National Security Agency).

so-called 'man's jobs' around the house… or hut – what would we do in our spare time? How, mentally and physically, would we stay in shape?

But, at base, most men who subjugate women do so, I suspect, because women – liberated women, especially – evoke in them what's effectively a fear of generative death, aka castration. In other words, men subjugate women in order to protect and project themselves. The Indian-born English poet Rudyard Kipling elaborated lightly on this dark theme in his proto-feminist poem The Female of the Species *which runs in part:*

'Man, a bear in most relations, worm and savage otherwise, Man propounds negotiations, Man accepts the compromise. Very rarely will he squarely push the logic of a fact To its ultimate conclusion in unmitigated act.

'But the woman that God gave him, every fibre of her frame Proves her launched for one sole issue, armed and engined for the same, And to serve that single issue, lest the generations fail…The female of the species must be deadlier than the male.'

Amen!

Closer to home, d'Arcy, the French historian Alexis de Tocqueville writing in 1840 attributed emerging America's prosperity and growing strength largely to 'the superiority of (its) women'. Isn't it wonderful that The Motherland's blessed with such superior women and that, today, they're all so liberated!

What: to work 'Nine to Five' or longer, just like men do, and to head up, 24/7, hugely-demanding private and/or public-sector enterprises, and bear arms and fight wars just like men do and achieve senior officer rank… and, even so, often to have their career hopes of ultimate preferment dashed against the so-called 'glass' or some other sort of ceiling?

Men's hopes are also sometimes dashed, d'Arcy…. Anyway, I'm not talking about all that secondary liberation stuff, like citizenship, or the right to vote, or workplace equality – I'm talking about primary liberation: the freedom to choose when or whether, even, to conceive and bear children. The widespread availability of safe, reliable contraception has wrought perhaps the most fundamental change heterosexual humankind – and thus humankind generally – has ever known, you know; even our earth's runaway population growth is, we understand, now being brought under a measure of control.

Lots of younger people locked in the throws of friendship 'with benefits' have, I suspect, for some time been appreciating reliable contraception….

That's 'throes' of friendship, etc, d'Arcy, unless those younger people are engaging in what some Brits call 'a bit of rough'. Even by this measure, however, most Third World women – many American women, even – still aren't entirely liberated.

They aren't?

No, fortunately. And that they should ever achieve such total emancipation is an eventuality altogether too dire to contemplate. Why, Man, we men could all be over-run!

Liberty means different things to different people, you know. As the poet John Milton observed of arrogant, over-reaching English-Civil-War parliamentarians in 1673: '"Licence" – "immoderation" or "irresponsibility", in other words – they mean when they cry "liberty"; for who loves (liberty) must first be wise and good.' Most women are by-definition good, of course, but – in theory – Milton might just as well have been writing about them.

But tell me, Alter-natis: down deep... fundamentally... just how 'liberated' are most men? Like us, the majority of them have themselves and their families to help support and their taxes to pay... and their own and their bosses' and their society's – not to mention their God's or their Whomever's – higher and wider expectations of them to meet.. Personally, I sometimes think not all that much has changed since the French philosopher Jean-Jacques Rousseau complained in his *Social Contract* of 1762: 'Man was born free, and everywhere he is in chains.'

Only in fantasy-land, perhaps, may anyone ever be totally free.

. . . .

Two days later – 'Wednesday' – N and I set off for our above-referenced supper with Nigel and Trish. As usual, I missed a turning somewhere – not, the Reader will recall, something Yr Correspondent found difficult in north Norfolk – thereby making a 20–30 minute drive into a nearly one-hour one. But also as usual, we were welcomed warmly.

The guests were mostly horsey folk and included: the MFH (Master of Fox Hounds) of the North Norfolk Harriers (or more correctly: 'MH', since their quarry weren't foxes but hares) and his wife, both very robust and jolly; a tall, severely-groomed and diamond-hard-edged dressage woman in training for the British Olympic Equestrian Team; and – all credit to the local grapevine or, perhaps, those tintinnabulating church bells – The Hon James 'Chaser' Jermyn and his wife Diana. She, I learned, competed regularly in dressage, cross-country and show-jumping, that's to say was 'an eventer', and as such had achieved considerable distinction; he also evented but, like several of his forebears, was better known for his exploits in the hunting field and point-to-point racing (also called 'steeple-chasing', of course

– hence the nickname).

As in my experience may many seriously-horsey people, Chaser gave the impression of being ever so slightly – and utterly engagingly – cracked. (Too much time spent in the company of horses, or too many headlong leave-takings of them at speed, or both, perhaps.) His default persona, however, was clearly what the 17th-century English writer Izaak Walton might have called 'The Compleat Countrieman': intuitive, savvy, down-to-earth... deeply committed to his family, his estate, his huntin', shootin' 'n' fishin'... and a certain complementary idiosyncrasy. In short, Chaser struck me as a fully-fledged, genuine English country squire, and I took to him immediately.

(Chaser was also a bit of a philosopher. N quoted him as saying that north Norfolk had 'just the right amount [*sic*] of people in it: not too many... not too few', an observation which, on mulling it over [see below], struck me as very apposite.)

Initially, however, it seemed to me a little something was 'in the air'. For although Chaser was very affable, he was also very concerned to remind me of his family's links with the Festings and Heartsease Hall. And when Yr Correspondent jokingly referred to the Sweetwater Wood shooting-rights controversy and said his lawyer was looking into it, Chaser replied shortly that while a lawyer's views would certainly be very interesting, 'there couldn't, really, be any doubt about who's right': he, Chaser, was. (And... he was.)

The more N and I got out and about in north Norfolk, the more it became clear to us that, at a certain level, everyone knew everyone and *about* everyone, and that these various parties regularly squabbled and – usually – made up. Indeed, we concluded, unless you were known and known about, and squabbled and made up, you didn't really count. The great Sweetwater Wood Shooting-Rights War had already drawn me into the squabbling; the making-up would, I assumed, follow in due course. But was it obligatory that the new, apprentice Squire of Heartsease Hall become known and known about, I wondered? Being an 'outsider' and existing at or beyond the fringes of the common communal pale, as I'd done for most of my life, seemed to me to have its advantages.

. . . .

In a world which so exalts individualism and the cult of the individual, I've never felt I fully understood the relevance of 'community', Alter-natis: what it is... what it entails....

'*Community*' – *you being* '*Your Brother's Keeper*' *and he, or she, being yours* – *is a reciprocated, longer-term predisposition toward social responsibility and caring. At its most exclusive, it's a sort-of partnership, like marriage, between two people; at its most inclusive* – *as in* '*The Community of Nations*' *or* '*The World Community*' – *it's statute-based and co-extensive with The Brotherhood of Man.*

As the exploration of outer space proceeds, we may eventually find it's co-extensive with '*The Brotherhood of the Universe*'!

'Just ET and me, and baby makes three, we're happy in My Blue Heaven,' as the US songwriter George Whiting might have enthused.

At the local level – *and excepting, for the moment, salvation through God or Whomever* – *your community is the platform upon which you build your wider political, socio-economic and cultural relations, and your ultimate refuge in time of need. In short, your community is of fundamental material and spiritual importance to you.*

I can see the importance of community in deep-country areas, where life is often very hard. But is community important in cities where, some might argue, the living is easier?

At times and in its own way, '*deep*' *(inner) city life can be at least as hard as* – *even harder than, some would argue* – *life in the deep country. But certainly: community in cities is very important. And as you know, most cities are rich in community. It may be, however, that community is generally more difficult to establish and sustain in cities.*

Why so?

Community requires that people be physically and mentally avail- able to co-mingle and interact, to define common interests, to agree common goals... in a phrase: to bond with one another. And that physical availability must be relatively continuous and on-going since, self-evidently, you're unlikely to bond properly if you aren't there.

Cities, however, are often characterized by high levels of transi- ence – *of discontinuity of physical availability* – *as people change jobs, climb up or down the property ladder, move in... move out.... In short, it's often difficult for city dwellers to be sufficiently avail- able physically to bond.*

And mental availability?

Even if people spend sufficient time together, they may be so over- stressed – '*the hectic pace of modern life*' *thing* – *and/or so wholly consumed by the need to make a* '*good*' *living, or simply to survive* – '*the competitiveness of modern life*' *thing....*

'I'd really like to, Alter-natis, but I'm too busy and/or too tired right now....'

Exactly! Add to these real or perceived cultural-survival stresses

*the 'standard' urban-environmental ones: air, noise and light pollu-
tion, travel congestion... overcrowding generally.... Again in short,
it's often difficult for city dwellers to be sufficiently available mentally to bond.*

I didn't realize community required so much time and effort!

Finally, there's the quorum *factor which Chaser, with his observation about north Norfolk having 'just the right amount of people',
implicitly referenced.*

Shouldn't he have said 'number'? 'Just the right *number* of people'?

From pre-historic times, it seems, Homo sapiens *has been programmed to regard a community as having a certain size or 'critical
mass'; according to the British anthropologist Robin Dunbar, that
size is 100–230 souls... or roughly 'village-sized'. In sparsely-pop-
ulated deep-country areas, this critical mass may never be achieved
because too few people are about; in teeming inner-city areas, it
may be many times over-achieved and result in a hyper-community
which, as its coefficients of inter-personal bonding are exceeded, becomes unstable and breaks down.*

A loving family, a fine house surrounded by lakes, woodlands and
good farmland, and a community I might join... all right here in
north Norfolk. Indeed, Alter-natis, I'm very fortunate! (But even so,
do I really want to become known and known about?)
· · · · · · · · · · · · · · · · · · · ·

The next day, I'd a meeting scheduled with the land agent for 1730.
So about an hour beforehand – thinking I'd ample time – I made
a bonfire of the south lawn perimeter hedging Big Fee and I'd removed... almost immediately upon my ignition of which honorable
land agent – and, happily, his comely assistant! – arrived, catching
me almost literally *in flagrante* (from the Latin *flagrare*, 'to blaze or
burn') so to speak. (It being a fine late-afternoon, the land agent said
he couldn't bear spending it 'trying to look busy' in the office; shades
of the chartered surveyor back in September, I thought.) The three of
us gazed spellbound... enraptured... into the fire for awhile...

· · · · · · · · · · · · · · · · · · · ·
Fire: *the* essential force for creation, the Greek philosopher Heracli-
tus held. Is it this recognition which makes watching fires and fireworks so compelling, Alter-natis?

*'From Brig o' Dread when thou may'st pass, Every nighte and
alle (or at other times), To Purgatory fire thou com'st at last; And
Christe receive thy saule (soul)'.*

*That description of crossing over the 'Dreadful (awful... ter-
rifying) Bridge' from Earthly Life to The Hereafter's holding pen*

238

is from a medieval Scottish ballad, d'Arcy. Following Divine Judgment, you'd be released from it either to Heaven... or to Hell.

Well indeed, Alter-natis, in religious history fire does traditionally have that association with redemptive purification, but.... Ooooh! I don't really think I'd....

You may prefer this more down-to-earth – earthy, even, you might say – quotation from T. S. Eliot's Four Quartets: 'All manner of thing shall be well When the Tongues of flame are in-folded Into the crowned knot of fire And the fire and the rose are one.'

. . . .

... gazed into the fire for awhile, then I took my guests to the estate office/library and offered early drinks. The main items on my agenda – the coming years' cropping plans, and farming income and expenditure projections – were disposed of quickly and easily. So bearing in mind that often cardinal but rarely observed rule of meeting management about never addressing more than two 'major' issues in any one session, I moved on...

... to what I assumed was a 'minor' one: an invoice which was overdue for payment by a local merchant we'd sold some grain to. I introduced the matter and, as a coda to my introduction, added: 'If, in the future, the merchant made his payment directly to me rather than indirectly, via Sir Roald and/or your firm, my farming cash flow would be improved.' So, I proposed executive-executive briskly: 'Let's action that one, shall we.'

Honourable land agent leaned back in his chair and stretched out his long legs. 'Actioning your suggestion would be very tricky,' he averred, brows knitting, head nodding... sipping a good sip from his glass. 'Very, very tricky.' But why, I asked? All I'm proposing is cutting out middlemen. More brow-knitting and nodding, and a protracted silence ensued. Then brightening and re-engaging with me, honorable land agent vouchsafed his 'solution': 'The important thing, d'Arcy, is owning the Heartsease Hall Estate. Now that the estate's yours, all these other matters will take care of themselves.'

Smiling affably... I weighed the possibility of a further round of mental sparring – even and notwithstanding the splendid, debutant dinner he and his wife had given for N and me, an initial round of *physical* sparring – against the improbability of ever persuading the land agent actually to agree my request. But then I reflected: why make waves? Take this petty *démarche* as another stage in your rite of passage... your initiation... into the squabbling and making up that's the forge-fettle of north Norfolk society. So instead, I contented myself with trying to skewer honourable land agent with my best, apprentice-esquirely glare.

(Later, over supper in our kitchen, I reprised these early-evening exchanges with my ever-supportive Uxor. 'N,' I began, 'I think that rascally land-agent's....'

('Who? Robyn? Surely you don't mean dear, sweet Robyn, with his lovely, soft, greeny-blue eyes and waves of gorgeous dark-brown hair? He wouldn't....'

(I proposed again my suspicions and, this time, was heard out. N reflected for a moment... then delivered her verdict: 'It seems to me, Dar, Robyn's trying to do three things: get as good a deal as he can for the local merchant – who's probably a friend of his – and his former client, Sir Roald; generate a bit more in fees for his firm and, thereby, commissions for himself; and make the best of an opportunity – which he strongly suspects may be time-limited – to stick it to the upstart-American Squire.' N rose, stacked our empty plates, walked over to the dishwasher, stopped, turned back to me and opined loftily: 'I get the impression he's succeeding on all counts.'

(Yr Correspondent let this reading settle for a moment... then he pounced: 'N, have you got a crush on this younger man?')

The last pheasant 'hoot' of the season (a vermin 'hoot' was still to come, Joscelyn informed me) provided some light relief from my heavy concerns. In attendance were the by-now-usual assortment of Joscelyn's friends: a retired Royal Air Force Chief Marshal, the Managing Partner of a major City (of London) investment bank... a High Court Judge – 'They's almost as many toffs about as pheasants,' Warrener observed dryly – and an amazing fellow named Asquith Amoury.

He was an 'older chap' as they say in north Norfolk – in his early 80s – about my height and build but more wiry, and gnarled like some ancient, wind-distressed bristlecone pine. Beneath a glistening, bald pate fringed with tufts of curly white hair, merry eyes twinkled – so far, the portrayal could be of a slim, trim Santa Claus – but then told the side-swept, flattened nose of the ring-battered boxer and the set-square jaw that looked as if it'd been cut from carbon steel. Shaking hands with him was like committing your fingers to the jaws of some bone-and-sinew vice.

Moreover, it transpired, Old Amoury had a shooting eye like William Tell. Yr Correspondent had the misfortune (or the good fortune, if excuse were needed for not dropping more birds himself) of being pegged next to him on several of the morning's drives; anything that came within his range – jays, magpies, crows... and, of course, pigeon, partridge, pheasant, woodcock, snipe... hares, rabbits, squirrels... a rat (!) – whether in my prescribed 'exclusive' fire-zone or that of the Gun to his other side, was taken early and definitively. Come the end of the drive, the carcass-littered ground around old Amoury looked like an 'after' scene from *Apocalypse Now*.

Chatting idly at the end of one of the drives – trying to make conversation while the pickers-up finished picking up – I asked the old fellow about his gun slip: a soft, scabbard-like case made of some sort of gray-brown hide with a few scraggles of yellow-brown fur still on, bound around its edges with leather thongs... almost certainly, I surmised, home-made. What's its history, Mr Amoury, I asked?

'Laoun,' came the mono- or elided duo-syllabic reply. Lone? Lawn? Lie-on? I attempted a translation from upper-class, Edwardian to modern, middle-American orthophony, but had to give up. So I offered an enquiring glance instead.

'Laoun,' old Amoury repeated, amiably. 'Came after me one day in the Sudaun when I was out shootin' for the pot. Big ole male… probably just been turfed out of 'is pride by some enterprisin' young 'un. 'E was fairly spoiling for a fight so I let 'im 'ave it. Then I 'ad the boys skin 'im out, thinkin' the pelt 'ould make a nice rug for m' floor. But the dogs got there first. They et a good bit and chewed holes in most of the rest.' He patted his superannuated gun slip fondly. 'There 'uz only enough left of old laoun's skin to make this.'

· · · · · · · · · · · · · · · · · · · ·

'The laoun in Sudaun preys occasion'ly on you, maun,' as George Bernard Shaw might have scripted for some Dark-Continent Pygmalion.
    Alter-natis, 'I think I've got it! By George, I think I've got it!'
· · · · · · · · · · · · · · · · · · · ·

'What were you doing in Sudan, Mr Amoury? Were you there on safari… to hunt tigers and lions?'
    'Nope. I'd just arrived from Abyssinia (now Ethiopia).'
    'Abyssinia?'
    'I 'uz about twenty-three at the time. Been trackin' ivory… then I got into a part of the country where the British weren't very popular. One of the local tribes – I forget which one – took me prisoner; they said they were goin' to cut me up and feed me to the crocodiles. (Roars of laughter!) Luckily, an old friend – the Headman of the Danakil* – got wind of it. 'E came along with some of his men and sprung me out.'

· · · · · · · · · · · · · · · · · · · ·

Now let's see, d'Arcy: what were you *doing at age twenty-three?*
    Trying to get a secure, well-paying job, behind a desk… in a nice, comfortable office.
· · · · · · · · · · · · · · · · · · · ·

The next day, a Sunday, we'd been invited for after-Church sherry with Sir Desmond and Lady Clementine Platt at 'The Embassy' as, in recognition of the first-named's distinguished Foreign Office career, and he and his wife's *über*-stylish mode of entertaining, their relatively-modest, retirement bungalow was jokingly known. Then well into their 80s, the Platts were an extraordinary couple:
    Sir Desmond – the son of an Anglican missionary in China, where he was born and raised – was a Cambridge University graduate with a string of important Ambassadorships to his credit; in the course of

---

* A northern Ethiopian/southern Eritrean tribe noted for its prowess in fighting.

them he'd been, as he modestly put it, 'generally at the beck and call of the great and good... but also of some others'. His area of especial interest was post-WWII European reconstruction; indeed, if implementation of the 1947 Marshall Plan and establishment of the 1952 European Coal and Steel Community*was your fancy, Sir Desmond was your man.

Lady Clementine came from a medical family. Prior to and during the earlier stages of her tour of duty as a diplomat's wife, she'd successfully raised three children; before that, she'd taught economics at Oxford University. Unlike her husband, however, she'd little time for the EC; indeed, I was told she kept a copy of the 1957 Treaty of Rome (which formally established the European Economic Community [the EEC]) beside her bed, with inclusions she found particularly objectionable lined through in red ink. And I was warned at all costs not to get her started on Britain's then-proposed membership of the Euro – the now-infamous Eurozone single currency – a policy she denounced to all who'd listen as 'criminally ill-advised'. ('Clemmie's not what you'd call shy or retiring,' one guest confided to me. It was a notice which, six or so weeks later, I'd vividly recall.)

That afternoon, Sir Roald stopped by to ask if he and Lady Maureen could continue their stay in Dovecote Cottage through the end of March 1995; I said yes, of course. (The 'rent' we agreed was a pair of Festing curtains in the Hall which N coveted; 'I suppose we should inform Inland Revenue [the UK's Internal Revenue Service equivalent, now called Her Majesty's Revenue & Customs] of our arrangement,' Sir Roald sighed.) I brought him up to date on various estate matters – in particular the results of my meetings with Mr and Mrs X, and the land agent – and offered anecdotal tidbits from the most recent shoot, and Sunday sherry at the Platts; we then moved on to the days' headline national and international news, in respect of nearly every item of which Sir Roald wanted to hear in detail and critically discuss Yr Correspondent's views.

Whew, I respired! In the space of just over one week I'd had to contend with: 'Chaser' and the Sweetwater Wood Shooting-Rights War; the wily, 'greeny-blue-eyed... dark-brown-haired' Robyn (N's 'crush'); old 'laun' Amoury and yet another cohort of Joscelyn's egregiously-Establishment chums; the hugely-experienced and knowledgeable Europhile Sir Desmond, and his at least as formidable, Eurosceptic

---

* The ECSC, the precursor of today's European Community (the EC); I'd taken a post-graduate degree in which the ECSC figured prominently.

(? Europhobe) wife; and, to round off, the relentlessly-attuned, analytic… interrogative Sir Roald.

Aloud to N and carefully-selected others, I rejoiced in the astonishing number of very interesting people we'd met in just our first few months in north Norfolk. Alone, with only the company of my own face in the shaving mirror, however, I wondered if in fact I was up to it. Well, I reflected grimly, if I was going to become a real, card-carrying English country squire and '*Veni, vidi, vici!*', or whatever, I *had* to be up to it. For there could only be more – much, much more, probably – to come.

And there was…. And it started coming soon – the very next day, in fact, shortly after our arrival at Piglet's boarding school in Oxford to which we'd delivered him for the start of his Lent (Spring) Term.

N's and my intention had been to drop Piglet off, continue on to Brambledown for the night and, early the next morning, drive up to Birmingham for an 0900 presentation to a potential FHA client. But when we arrived at the school – a distance door-to-door from Heartsease Hall of some 163 cross-country miles – we saw on a notice board just inside Piglet's dormitory the instruction: 'All Boys – Please Give Your Passport to Matron' (as the woman in charge of the dorm's domestic arrangements was styled).

'Passport?' we thought. We've not brought Piglet's passport with us…. And even if we had, give it to Matron? Good Heavens; what does she need it for? Suppose she mislays it or it gets stolen? While I helped our senior son carry his bags to his room, N went to investigate….

Yes, Dear Reader, it was as we'd by then begun to fear and some of you may have already guessed: the next day Piglet's class was to begin a five-day 'Europe Awareness' trip to France. (Preoccupied as ever with his studies [he went on to become a King's Scholar], our son had neglected to mention the outing, and although it was clearly entered in the school's Calendar of Events – tucked between advisories about the importance of regular head-lice inspections [*sic*] and the forthcoming visit of a travelling magician's show – N and I'd failed to register it.) Indeed, he and his mates were due to depart the school at just about the time we were scheduled to pad the podium in Birmingham.

Animated exchanges with the Master in charge of the outing and then with the Deputy Head Master – known as 'The DHM' – ensued. Mightn't Piglet travel on some alternative documentation and so manage without his passport, we asked? If he was a British national yes, came the reply; alternative documentation could indeed be used. But an American national? Shaking his head, the DHM intoned firmly: 'There is no way.' Cautiously, I raised the possibility that Piglet might therefore have to forego this visit to France in favour of a subsequent one. A look of shock and horror came over the DHM's face. 'Your son... forego this visit to France?' he muttered seemingly incredulously once... and then again. 'There is *utterly* no way,' he eventually pronounced.

I told the DHM that N and I'd consider our options while driving to Brambledown and get back to him. And indeed, during that drive we did much considering. Piglet's passport was at Heartsease Hall, of course, locked in the safe... to which only one person knew – and *should* know, I strongly felt – the combination: Yr Correspondent. (Even knowing the combination, I found the safe very tricky to open.) So instructing Big Fee to dig out the document and deputing a third-party to courier it to Oxford wasn't a possibility. Indeed, once the situs of the passport had been fully appreciated, it was clear there were no possibilities really except one: a return by Yr Correspondent and, presumably, his dutiful Uxor to Heartsease Hall.

Probably needless to write, that was not our preferred option. The Birmingham presentation, for which N and I'd long been prepping, was almost certainly our last chance to sign up a mega-multinational prospect we'd been stalking literally for years; Piglet, on the other hand, could reasonably be expected to have many other opportunities to confront the tormentors of his Huguenot, d'Arcy Henry forbears. So, self-evidently, our decision: N and I would have our planned, pre-presentation sleep at Brambledown then, refreshed and ready, we'd drive up to Birmingham and strut our stuff; our senior son – the DHM's proscription notwithstanding – would have to *faire connaissance de la France et les étroitesses* (narrow-minded), *intolérants, vraiment insupportable* (truly insufferable) *Français et Françaises...* umm... errr... ahhh... *d'autre jour* (another day).

But at 2200 hours – literally within minutes of our arrival at Brambledown – the telephone rang; the School's *HM* – The *Head* Master, a formidable man whom I very much liked but, even more, greatly respected – was on the line. He told me in no uncertain terms that Piglet absolutely had to do the France trip, so he absolutely had to have his passport... so I absolutely had to get off my fat backside (well... he didn't use quite those words) and retrieve it. If it would ease our logistics, he volunteered, he'd dispatch a courier to Bedford (in the UK's industrial midlands) to meet us half-way.

Drawing myself up to my full height, I advised HM of the locked safe, the long drive N and I'd already made, the importance of our 0900 presentation the next day and our desire to be reasonably fresh for it, and rested my case. A protracted silence ensued during which I could almost see HM lifting his jacket and shirt cuffs as he consulted his wrist watch: 2200 hours now, give or take a few minutes... the Henrys due on-stage tomorrow at.... The silence ended. 'Good Lord, d'Arcy,' HM thundered, 'you say your presentation isn't until 0900? Well then; you've got eleven hours! It shouldn't take more than 6–7 hours to do the round trip to and from Heartsease Hall, and an hour or so to drive to Birmingham.... I don't see what the problem is. You can get your son's passport to us and make it to your presentation with at least a couple of hours to spare!'

Indeed, and so N and I did. We went the extra 326 or so cross-country-road miles, in the process achieving a new, personal-best driving time for the circuit (it was a clear, dry night with little traffic to slow us down) and rejoicing... wryly... in the spirit which made Britain – and still makes elements of Britain – 'Great'. (And we got our contract.)

The last few days of January and into February were almost exclusively taken up with my English country squire apprenticeship, that's to say with learning about running the Heartsease Hall Estate. For although it was still effectively the dead of winter, a time...

. . . .

'...the very worst time of the year(:) the ways (are) deep (with mud and snow), the weather sharp, the days short, the sun farthest off....' That's from Bishop Lancelot Andrews' Sermon 15, d'Arcy; he published it in 1622, toward the end of the so-called 'Little Ice Age' which drove global temperatures lower than they'd been for a thousand or so years.

And, in the nearly four centuries since then, have temperatures been mean-reverting higher, we ask? Certain recent meteorological data notwithstanding, N doesn't really think so.

. . . .

... a time in north Norfolk when plants, animals and, especially, humans typically just lie low and wait for the abysmal weather to improve, much, in fact, was going on. In no particular order of chronology or consequence:

1. I embarked on my first, serious act of Hall renovation and discovered for myself the fundamental truth I'd earlier, often, been told: that repairs to old buildings are, almost invariably, more extensive – and thus more expensive – than expected.

. . . .

This 'fundamental truth' you reference: I thought a man of your wisdom and experience would have appreciated it much earlier. Your wife and The Suits certainly did.

I was *un*willing to suspend my disbelief, as the poet Samuel Taylor Coleridge might have written. Or to put it more in the modern idiom: 'Nothing's real till it's local.'

. . . .

The 'renovation' in question was a couple of cracked panes of glass in the front porch sunroof. I'd thought these damaged elements could just be removed and replaced; the builder told me the sunroof was infested throughout with wet-rot* and that virtually the whole of it – ridge beam, rafters, glazing bars, wall plates... as well, of course, as the cracked panes – would have to be replaced.

2. I contacted the Countryside Commission (now Natural England), a government-funded nature-conservation body, and initiated an application process for grant-aid to restore and improve various aspects of the estate's fields, lakes and woodlands which, after months of intermittent hard work on my part, would result in... absolutely nothing.

The immediate object of the exercise was T1S2I1 of The Masterplan: replanting with grass and trees – that's to say 're-emparking' – some of the fields nearest to the Hall which were then being cropped. A very authorized-sounding young man picked up on my telephone call – he was a 'Senior Casework Officer', he informed me grandly – and, after I'd told him generally what I had in mind, he intimated that for 'the right kind of property (and) the right kind of re-emparkation', substantial funding could be available. But, he added, seemingly as an afterthought: 'Some sort of provision would probably have to be made for public access, however, otherwise we could reject you (*sic*) out of hand.'

Notwithstanding the access issue – on which, as indicated above (Ch. 8), N and I were prepared to consider compromise – it seemed to

---

* *Coniophora puteana*, a type of fungal decay; there are also several types of 'dry-rot' fungi (!).

me that restoring parts of the great Nathaniel Richmond's parkland, around the great William Wilkins, Senior's, Hall must, surely, qualify as 'right' on both counts, right? 'This Bud's for me!' I said to myself confidently.

· · · · · · · · · · · · · · · · · · · ·

Riiight....

· · · · · · · · · · · · · · · · · · · ·

So I gave the SCO a more-detailed description of my plans, and ticked off the estate's 'most-notable features' including, of course, its 'Listed Grade I' Hall. The SCO heard me out, and then made what I took to be 'encouraging noises'. And more: he said that if I decided to apply for a grant to let him know and he'd come out and make a preliminary determination of our chances of success. 'The application process is very long and complex... and competitive,' my interlocutor advised me earnestly; 'You don't want to put yourself through it unless you're going to get some cash.' I pondered the matter and, a few days later, wrote to the SCO saying I had indeed decided to apply for a grant and would therefore very much appreciate his preliminary determination.

3. I met with Sheen and settled a couple of lower-order estate issues: the likely impact on farm income of my proposed re-emparkation, and how to deal with what I jokily referred to as our 'covert uninvited guests', or CUGs (as distinct from our OUGs: 'overt' guests who were 'uninvited', like the earlier-referenced Sunday-afternoon walkers).

Happily, less financial downside attached to re-emparkation than I'd supposed. As most of the area to be grassed down and treed up was poorer land – higher and thus more damaged by wind, etc, erosion, Sheen pointed out – not much more income from crops would be lost than could be recouped by increasing our sheep numbers. The only real concern, Sheen felt, was the curvilinear field boundaries Yr (Landscape) Correspondent desired, large-scale farm machinery – particularly big tractors pulling big, 'gang' (multi-shared) ploughs and disc harrows – being designed to work more-or-less in straight lines.

So onto the CUGs... who were of two sorts: 'fly-tippers', as the British call them, that's to say people who illegally dump trash, for example along road verges or in fields or woodlands; and the assorted (in many senses) couples (very often literally, as in 'coupled') – mostly nocturnal but sometimes crepuscular and, occasionally, even full-on diurnal – who frequented our several 'Lovers' Lanes'.

In respect of the fly-tippers, we concluded the only option was to

up-rate our vigilance and try to catch those involved – fines for littering, Sheen told me, could be up to £20,000 (then about $30,000)
– and quickly to clear up anything that was dumped so the site didn't
look derelict; less-hardened fly-tippers, Sheen said, sometimes shied
away from desecrating well-kept land.

(My mind flipped back to New York where, many years earlier, I'd
pointed out to the driver of the taxi I'd just flagged down the empty
Coca-Cola can and crumpled Kleenex tissues on the floor of his passenger bay. He immediately leapt from his seat, tore around to the
nearside rear door of the cab, wrenched it open, took a little whisk
broom out of his pocket and, with a display of mighty indignation,
swept the offending items out and into the street. 'Dese [deleted] nowadays,' he fumed, 'dey don' give a [deleted] 'bout nobody or nothin'
'cept demselves.')

. . . .

Why don't people dispose of their trash legally instead of dumping it
illegally, for example on the Heartsease Hall Estate?

*Some litterers – younger people, often – can't be bothered, d'Arcy;
it's not their land so they don't care. Being careless is 'cool', they
think.*

But in a sense, it *is* their land, Alter-natis; indeed looking to the
future, it's really more theirs than ours. Their land, their countryside, their environment... their earth.

*Other litterers are either so desperately hard-pressed simply to
survive or, alternatively, so deeply addicted to conspicuous over-
consumption, they don't care.*

. . . .

What to do about our several 'Lovers' Lanes' was a less straightforward issue. On the one hand, I reminisced, these facilities probably
give a number of younger people – and, manifestly, even some older
ones – a good deal of (? innocent) pleasure; indeed, I confessed to
Sheen, I'd fond memories as a teenager of several such *sancta* in Baltimore. On the other hand, they constituted an open invitation to
Gypsy 'Travellers' and other mobile-homer types in search of free,
temporary accommodation. As Sheen confirmed, these last two sorts,
once *in situ*, could be very troublesome and, under UK law, very difficult to evict. Reluctantly, I decided we had no choice but to close our
Lovers' Lanes down. (Closing them down proved far easier decreed
than done, however.)

4. I met with one of the local seed merchants or 'seedsmen', as
they're called, and learned that properly re-establishing grassland – as

opposed to allowing it to regenerate naturally – could be a complicated business.

My instruction began... pretty much at ground level. I of course understood that grass seed had to come from somewhere and, more specifically, that since many types of grasses existed there must be many types of grass seed. But my goodness! On offer were perhaps a hundred different varieties – Italian ryegrass, Creeping red fescue, Southend crested dogstail, Highland browntop bent... 'Erecta Timothy'... to give a few of the more picturesque names – permuted and combined into some two dozen standard mixtures each containing, say, 8–12 different varieties. Each mixture was intended for a particular purpose such as hay-making, silage (fermented hay) making, early grazing (sheep, cattle and/or horses), late grazing (ditto), 'utility', sports, 'luxury lawn'... just plain, ordinary lawn; or a particular type of soil ('heavy' [having a high proportion of clay and so slow to drain], 'light' [ditto of sand and thus *fast*-draining]... 'loamy' [in between, and including lots of decayed organic matter]); and/or a particular ambient environment (wet lowland/dry upland, sunny/shady... exposed/sheltered). If none of these ready-made mixtures suited, ones bespoke to the customer's specific requirements could be made up.

· · · · · · · · · · · · · · · · · · · ·

Oh boy! Another one of those fascinating farming interludes....

· · · · · · · · · · · · · · · · · · · ·

There was even, I learned, a special 'Countryside Stewardship Parkland Mixture'. Designed primarily with the preferences of wild animals in mind, it was – so far as husbanded animals were concerned – neither particularly productive, that's to say heavy yielding, nor particularly palatable, that's to say tasty. I made a mental note, however, that if my Countryside Commission grant came through, I'd probably have to use it.

5. I evicted some trespassers. On the day in question I was awakened not, as usual, by my alarm clock but by a serenade from some 30–40 Canada geese tittle-tattling over breakfast in Pavilion Paddock. (I won't suffer upon the Reader yet another ode to pastoral beauty, but I will observe once again what a privilege it was – and is still – to access such beauty so easily.)

That evening, however, sounds of a jarringly different sort arose from Pavilion Paddock: those of two cars – one car's engine roaring full-throttle, the other's winding, grinding... trying unsuccessfully to start. Then the noise of the engines ceased and was replaced by that of male voices loudly cursing. What, I thought, humans disturbing – nay, profaning! – *our* fauna and flora, *our* wildlife... in *our* mini nature reserve-to-be?

I drove down in the Land Rover to discover a pair of twenty-something lads who'd been trying to jump-start the dead-engine car by towing it with the live one and, in so doing, had travelled up the East Track, through the field gate and into Pavilion Paddock itself... where, predictably, they'd gotten stuck. And as they made very clear, they weren't happy with their situation. I told the pair to pipe down, turn their backs to me and put their hands on their heads (at the time, it seemed an appropriate instruction!) while I took their vehicles' details; then I summoned them over to the Land Rover – still with their hands on their heads – to give me their names and addresses. (One lad was from a village about five miles away; the other lived in Norwich.) Eventually, I asked them what they thought they were doing here, on private property, at this time of day – that's to say night – and received by way of reply vocalizations which might transcribe as: 'Wha'cha fink (think) we're doin' 'ere, Guv? 'Avin' a (deleted) pinnick (picnic) or summat (something)?'

· · · · · · · · · · · · · · · · · · · ·

That *was* English those two fellows were speaking, wasn't it Alternatis?

A form of English, yes. Similar dialectal tribalisms – dialectal corruptions, purists call them – also present in American, viz 'gangsta rap'. Top of my pops, however, is that pidgin-English adjectival used by the Bislama speakers of Vanuatu – a south Pacific Islands-State and member of the British Commonwealth – to personify Prince Philip, the Duke of Edinburgh: 'Nambawan (Number-one) bigfala emi blong Missis Qwin'.

Anyway, language isn't set in stone, you know, d'Arcy; it's continually evolving. That's part of its utility and its appeal.
· · · · · · · · · · · · · · · · · · · ·

I cautioned the two that as a father, husband, householder and landowner I held very firm views on 'homeland security', and urged them to advise their friends that anyone on the estate after dark without my prior permission should regard themselves as 'at risk'. (For a moment, the two lads looked incredulously at each other, then one of them observed sullenly: 'Dis geezer's [deleted] serious, I fink. I fink dis [deleted] geezer's [deleted] serious.') Finally, I towed the live car back onto the east track and told the young men to get in it and be on their way. (The dead car, I allowed, could be collected the following morning.) Not an incident of much moment, I concluded, but a useful opportunity to make better and more-widely known the resolution with which the upstart American apprentice Squire would engage any unauthorized foray onto his turf.

6. I repossessed Bottom Cottage. For about a week, Bottom Cottage had seemed suspiciously quiet: no smoke was visible from its chimneys during daytime; no lights showed through its windows at night; along the way giving access to it, no cars or pedestrians came or went. It was as if Mr and Mrs X – anticipating their eviction from the premises – had simply packed their bags and stolen... away.

So about mid-morning on 19 January – clad in a hooded, camouflage hunting-suit and trainers – I drove the Land Rover to the far end of Pavilion Paddock (near where the above-referenced young men had gotten stuck), parked, got out, and crept stealthily through Neate Wood – carefully avoiding the open ground along the east track – to the edge of the little clearing in which Bottom Cottage stood. I looked; I listened.... Nothing. I scented the cold, winter air; no smell of human habitation – food, say, or garbage – could I detect. I crawled to the cover of a shrub on the lawn behind the cottage, then sprinted to the side of the cottage and sidled along its wall until I arrived at the sitting room window. Cautiously, I craned my head around and peered in....

The sitting room was empty – and 'empty' in a pretty thorough way. As I'd anticipated, no furniture, or curtains or carpets... or pictures... were to be seen, but neither were curtain rods or light bulbs or light bulb sockets, even, just dangling bare wires. (Ah well, I reflected, with the electricity cut off, removing light bulb sockets – or just about any other electrical fittings – wouldn't have been much of a problem.) While I was considering what to do next, my gaze lowered to the inside of the window and its sill; the fine, original, 18th-century brass window locks and casement stays were also gone.

Persuading myself that such circumstances justified the Landlord's having a closer inspection of his premises – even an unannounced, that's to say a possibly-illegal one – I tried the front door with the spare key I'd brought along.... I tried the back door ditto.... I tried the front door with the back door key and *vice versa*... but to no avail; the locks had all been changed. So removing...

· · · · · · · · · · · · · · · · · · · ·

Was there no depth to which the upstart-American apprentice English country Squire would not sink?

· · · · · · · · · · · · · · · · · · · ·

... so removing my trainers and making a mental note later to wipe carefully with my handkerchief anything I touched, as I knew from the crime soaps on TV was best practice, I opened the lock-less casement window in the kitchen and climbed in.

Caramba! There was no stove in the kitchen... no refrigerator or washing machine.... In the absence of an inventory, I had to assume these white-goods could belong to Mr and/or Mrs X. But then I noticed the hot water/central heating unit had been removed (it was unlikely that they could belong to Mr and/or Mrs X, I felt!) and, moving on, I saw there was no fine, original, 18th-century brass furniture on the doors – just patches of unpainted wood with empty screw and spindle holes marking where the touch plates and knobs had been. And there were no fireplace surrounds. No fine, original, 18th-century Georgian fireplace surrounds – only the bare brickwork of the chimney breasts where the surrounds used to be. And along the west wall of the sitting room was one much larger bare patch, about one and a half yards long by two yards high. Clearly, something had gone missing from there as well but what, I tried hard to remember? And to where?

I made my tidy exit from Bottom Cottage and trundled along to the adjacent outbuilding which old X used as a workshop. It was padlocked. But looking through its window, I saw a hot water, etc, unit and a vaguely-familiar wooden cupboard, Georgian in style, perhaps one and a half by two yards in length-height dimension; curiously, the sides of the cupboard were painted the same, distinctive, brown-green-slime colour as the walls of Bottom Cottage's sitting room....

And sticking out from behind the cupboard were what appeared to be the corners of a pair of Georgian fireplace surrounds. And on the floor next to the cupboard was a large hessian bag, suspiciously free of the wood dust and shavings that covered almost every other low-lying object in the workshop and containing – to judge from the lie of the cloth – a jumble of small, angular objects. Could those 'objects' be 18th-century brass window and door furniture, I asked myself? Hmmmm.

So back to the Hall I went for my camera and a padlock; then down again I went to 'The Workshop at Bottom Cottage'...

• • • • • • • • • • • • • • • • • • •

Dame Agatha Christie or Sir Arthur Conan Doyle might have built a good murder-mystery around a title like that.

• • • • • • • • • • • • • • • • • • •

... Bottom Cottage' to photograph as much as I could from the window and to hook my padlock through the staples alongside old X's, thereby securing for my own purposes the workshop door. Then I returned to my desk and made two telephone calls: the first to Sir Roald, who confirmed he hadn't disposed of any of the items in question to the Xs (even if he had, we should have had some claim on them as 'fixtures and fittings') and the second to the police, who said they'd send someone around immediately to make a report. (They did, and later they told me they'd 'spoken to' [interviewed] – old X who'd insisted he'd removed the Bottom Cottage items to the outbuilding 'for safekeeping'. Would that all defaulting, departing tenants were so considerate, I mused.)

7. I went head-to-head with 'The Mauler'. Martin Dann – all six-foot plus, 220 or so lean-and-mean pounds of him, aka 'The Mauler' – was one of the estate farming tenants/contractors we'd inherited. He was also, I'd been told, a gifted athlete who'd played several sports at 'county' ('semi-professional' equivalent) level; among them was rugby in which, as a ferocious member of 'the scrum' (analogous to American football's offensive/defensive line), he'd earned his nickname.

One bitter-cold evening in January, Martin came over at my invitation for a get-to-know-you drink; with him he brought his father Billy, who'd preceded him in farming on the estate. I took the two men into the drawing room, sat them down, poured them each a stiff Scotch and water (the temperature in the drawing room was probably in the low-mid-50s, but neither of them seemed to take much notice) and began to try to size them up... as, it quickly became clear, they were trying, bemusedly, to do to me. ('So how long have you been "farming", Mr Henry?' 'Ooh... it must be comin' on for 10–12 years now, Mr Dann. Yep; 10–12....' 'What crops do you grow, sir?' 'Sheep, a few pigs – no, hold on a minute: we've about a dozen pigs now; our dear Piggy's recently had piglets – as well as Grow-Bag tomatoes, onions and radishes, Martin... and lots and lots of weeds.)

(The Danns came from a long line of what in the UK may be called 'yeoman' farmers, that's to say farmers who aren't substantial landowners living in big houses or 'halls' but, as distinct from tenant-only farmers, own some – and, sometimes, very considerable – freehold land. [As the UK's great estates have reduced in size and number, and astute, hard-working 'yeomen' like Martin and his family have enlarged their freeholds, the practical distinction between 'landowner' and 'yeoman farmer' has been eroded.] In agriculturalist circles, the yeoman farmer is generally regarded as knowledgeable, skilled and diligent – in short, almost always ahead of the agronomic curve – and able to grow just about anything well. Over the years, Martin has proved himself no exception to this rule.)

I took two main impressions away from our meeting: first, that in terms of lives lived, the American international management consultant turned apprentice English country squire, and these two north Norfolk born-and-bred yeoman farmers didn't have a lot in common. But second – and at a more fundamental, human level – I understood clearly that Martin and Billy were men of integrity who 'knew where they came from', that's to say were confident of their status, and that if I did my best by them they'd do likewise by me. My hour or so with The Mauler and his father therefore passed very agreeably.

8. Over 'elevenses' (mid/late-morning coffee or tea), we finally 'met' the Hufftons. The Hufftons, who lived at Brunstead Hall about two miles to our southwest (when N and I moved into Heartsease Hall, Sir Antony Huffton, the Reader will remember, wrote Yr Correspondent a letter of welcome; see Ch. 7), were one of the triumvirate of 'established', local land-owning families (the other two being the already-introduced Steeles and the Grenfelds, whom we didn't encounter until awhile later); over the previous couple of months, they'd extended several invitations formally to 'meet', that's to say to begin the process of becoming acquainted, but N and I'd always had prior commitments. On 1 February, however, we were at last able to attend. About 1045 N and I got into our car and set off....

Not wanting to repeat the Steele 'tea-taking' experience and arrive via the stables, I turned into the Huffton's driveway with some trepidation... to discover their home standing a half-mile or so directly in front of us like some misplaced neo-classical caravanserai. Antony and his wife Cordelia greeted N and me at the front door, then led us into the drawing room where, amid antique carpets and furniture, bronzes, *objects de vertu*... a couple of dozen or so portraits and pictures hung in the multi-tiered manner reminiscent of Georgian-era galleries...

. . . .

Oh no, d'Arcy; not another *exquisite, museum-home!*

. . . .

... galleries and – as seemed *de rigueur* in these parts – a miscellany of dogs, we sat and chatted.

I was particularly struck by the drawing room itself. High-ceilinged, south-facing, and with tall, elegant, sash windows, it was closed on two sides by double doors of what I took to be Honduran (but, possibly, Cuban or West African) mahogany, their thick frames carrying highly figured, 'flame-grained' panels – manifestly sawn from a single, massive log – which the early 19th-century craftsman 'joiner' who fashioned them (and also the hall's windows, staircases and stairs, probably) had paired and set mirror-image.

. . . .

I don't expect many trees capable of yielding such splendid close-grained timber are still standing today, Alter-natis.

Good Lord no, d'Arcy; except in remotest Austral-Asia, nearly all of the old-growth, luxury hardwood was logged out a century or so ago. That's why today's antique furniture, etc, restorers generally rely on woods cannibalized from other antiques.
. . . .

Antony who, it transpired, had been CFO (chief financial officer) of [a global primary-resources company], wasn't an imposing presence physically; in size and build, he much resembled the late Baron Home of the Hirsel (as Alec Douglas-Home, British Prime Minister 1963-1964). Mentally, however, he was focused, articulate, commanding... and a veritable encyclopedia of landscape gardening. I learned, among many other things, about the various types of guards which may be used to protect young trees from browsing livestock and/or wild deer (no cheap or easy solutions existed, I was told) and about cattle grids which, the Reader may recall (Ch. 8), I was considering having installed at the top and bottom of our front drive (an easy solution, apparently, but not a cheap one).

Finally, we embarked on a tour of the Huffton's 8–9 acres of English Heritage Listed Grade I display gardens. Beneath stands of huge specimen trees, past clumps of magnificent shrubs and immaculate flower beds, over rippling rivulets and around ornamental ponds padded with lilies our way wound... to end at an immaculately-restored, walled kitchen garden, greenhouse and (head) gardener's cottage complex dating from the 1830s.

. . . .

'The kiss of the sun for pardon, The song of the birds for mirth; One is nearer God's heart in a garden Than anywhere else on earth,' as the English poetess Dorothy Frances Gurney – an ancestor of our Brunstead host, we later learned – wrote in 1913.

That may be for Ms Gurney, and possibly dear Aunt Gertie and old Hughes... and, of course, the Hufftons. But after my years at Brambledown, Alter-natis, even the possibility of closer proximity to The Devine won't prompt me to all that hard, hard work.

. . . .

9. I learned more about the Heartsease Hall Estate's golden, olden days. One morning, bright and early as usual, Sir Roald came into the library, this time to lay carefully on my card table-desk a couple of the estate's Game Books dating from the early 1900s; if only on the basis of these records, what a stupendous enterprise the property must then have been. Signed-in guns included the Duke of York (later King George V) and the Duke of Norfolk (England's 'Premier' Duke and hereditary Earl Marshall [president of the Heralds' College and undertaker of important, mostly-royal, ceremonies]), as well as co-horts of lesser Lords and Gentlemen – and even a few Ladies. And the quantities of game taken! Bags of a thousand or so pheasant and partridge, hundreds of waterfowl of all sorts, as well as hares, rabbits, pigeon and 'various' including the occasional fox were not uncom-mon; if it showed itself, these Edwardian-era grandees dropped it.

(Was Sir Roald's show-and-tell informed by some covert agenda, I wondered and, if so, what was it? Surely the man – a sportsman-in-tellectual rather than a huff 'n' puff, 'mass-slaughterer' shooting type – wasn't seeking to impress.... I concluded the Old Boy just wanted to share with me some of the history of his beloved, former demesne.)

10. I gathered winter fuel. As we were nearly out of logs for the home fires, I drove one afternoon to a woodland on the estate called the Hand of Pork* where I knew lay several big, well-seasoned oak limbs. I chain-sawed them into suitable lengths, then took the lengths back to the Hall's woodshed; when split – which shouldn't take long, I reckoned; the wood was straight-grained and largely-knot-free – I'd have a fortnight or so's firewood for just a couple of hours' work. (And as the old saying goes: with the cutting/hauling, the splitting and, finally, the burning, the wood warms you thrice!) 'Oh, The Good Earth,' I recall exulting then; when cutting, etc, wood for the fires now I add: 'May my cardio-vasculars enjoy the rudest of good health, and may carbon-credits accrue to me without surcease.'

11. I repaired some plumbing. For several weeks, the ball-cock

---

* So named because on the estate plan, its outline resembled that of the fore-shoulder roast, or 'hand' as it used to be known, of a butchered pig.

valve in one of the Hall's attic header tanks* had been malfunction-ing, causing the tank to over-flow; repeated attempts to engage a plumber having been unsuccessful, I decided to deal with the problem valve myself.

. . . .

The apprentice Squire of Heartsease Hall... plumbing?
You seem to have forgotten, Alter-natis, that in the mid-1990s relatively few British young people went into the so-called 'higher building trades'; in the main, they got service-sector qualifications of some sort and sat behind desks pushing papers around.

Plumbers were particularly hard to find. Eventually, the high wages on offer brought literally thousands of suitably-skilled arti-sans into the market – from East Europe and points south mostly, but a few were UK-born – and within 5–7 years the plumber supply-demand balance was largely restored.

Designing things, building things... fixing things, even... can be very restorative....
Anyway... Sir Roald irons.

. . . .

Here again new insights abounded for Yr Correspondent. As earlier referenced (see Ch. 4), the central attic had no natural or wired-in electric light, so all illumination had to be imported; ditto it had no flooring – only teetery walk boards laid across the ceiling joists of the rooms immediately below. Simply getting to the header tank involved clambering, with your light-source, your tool bag and the repair ma-terials and spare parts you thought you might need over, under and around a succession of roof trusses and supports, and along those teetery walk boards....

And, oh yes: 'tool bag, etc.' Woe betide the plumber who arrived on-site in the Hall's attic lacking some essential item(s). 'Central stores' wasn't just a quick trip down to the basement or out to the ga-rage. It was a clamber back across the walk boards, over, etc, the roof trusses and supports, down the equivalent of two very long flights of stairs, along perhaps 45–50 yards of corridors and then, the want supplied, all the way back up again.

12. Finally, we said goodbye to BT's engineers. The workmen did, in fact, go the day after they'd arrived – as they'd said they would. But they came back again... and again... and again. Indeed, it wasn't

---

* From which water gravity-feeds to the heating, hot water, kitchen and bath-room, etc, systems below.

until some fourteen working days after the men started their '24-hour retrofit' that our new telephone system was installed and fully operational, and I'd the means of summoning from my card-table desk in the estate office/library almost anyone – N, Piglet when he was home, Bapu... Big Fee...

· · · · · · · · · · · · · · · · · · · ·

Summoning Big Fee.... Yes! Ye-esss! What a good idea!

· · · · · · · · · · · · · · · · · · · ·

... Big Fee – at any time, from almost anywhere: the annex (where N had established her FHA office), the main bedrooms, the kitchen... the orangery – merely by pressing a button.

· · · · · · · · · · · · · · · · · · · ·

But if you press the button and say: 'The Squire requires your immediate attendance,' will anyone in fact come, I asked you? As even the mightiest mortal powers must ultimately accept, means are not ends, and technology alone does not dominion make.

No, it doesn't, Alter-natis, although it may help. Ultimately – in peacetime as well as in time of war – you have to win those 'hearts and minds'.

· · · · · · · · · · · · · · · · · · · ·

The fourth of February 1995 became for N and me 'a date which will live in infamy' – President Franklin D. Roosevelt's outraged reference before a joint session of Congress to 7 December 1941, the day the Japanese attacked Pearl Harbor.

It began innocently enough: with the shoot Joscelyn had promised to reduce the local population of feral rabbits, squirrels, corvids, etc. But although much consideration was given to which Guns should stand where (The best were put in what were expected to be the hot spots; this day's sport wasn't about 'sport', it was about pest control.) and much beating was done, literally about the bush(es), the wretched vermin mostly declined to show; Warrener had done his keepering too well.

But as Joscelyn and I were driving along Heartsease Lane *en route* to shooting out Church Wood (which partly encloses the round-towered, St Lawrence's Church), I noticed in a field adjacent to but not forming part of our property a smallish, white-cardboard placard fixed to a stake. Long experience of life in the Cotswolds told me immediately it could only be one thing: a local-authority Planning Notice, that's to say the first stage in an application for permission to build or construct something. Joscelyn stopped his Land Rover; then he and I climbed down and walked over for a closer look. The placard, we confirmed, was indeed a Planning Notice, on behalf of Anglian Water* for the construction of two 'Sludge Lagoons'.

Sludge lagoons? *Pro forma*, I racked my brain – and the much better-informed Joscelyn racked his – in a vain attempt to work out what the purpose of these puddles-writ-large might be. For Yr Correspondent, however, such 'rackings' were entirely beside the point; whatever 'sludge lagoons' were, I didn't want any in the middle of this pristine pastorality abutting our Wilkins-Richmond, Listed-Grade-I Hall and its 'back yard'!

'Who owns this field, Joscelyn?' I asked. '[...],' Joscelyn replied, adding: 'he's one of your men, I believe.' Indeed; the at-best accessory to – at worst, actual instigator of – this possibly prospective local-environmental outrage was, in status like the above-referenced Martin Dann, one of our farming tenants/contractors. Figuratively only, as must in this quick to mis-take, gratuitously-easily-offended and greedily hyper-litigious age preemptively be made absolutely clear, I was almost mad enough to kill.

Even as only an *apprentice* English country squire, however, I recognized that on the local inter-personal relations and wider political front I'd have to proceed very, very carefully. Everyone has 'rights' – to build or seek to build on their own land, for example – and, in the deep country especially, any perceived 'infringement' of those rights may be long remembered – particularly, I assumed, if the presumptive infringer was an up-start American who happened also to be a major landowner and the putative defendant's somewise employer. But I took the decision then and there to oppose construction of the sludge lagoons however much time and effort it would take, and however much confrontation it would involve. I returned with Joscelyn to his Land Rover and continued on with a heavy heart.

When ten or so days later I found out what 'sludge lagoons' in fact were, my heart grew heavier still.

. . . .

What did you suppose your tenant, etc, fellow was up to, d'Arcy?

I didn't know then and I still don't know, Alter-natis. He'd a wife and 4–5 children.... Farming's not an easy life, and you have to gen-

---

* Then the 'modest' regional water utility; at time of writing, part of a global 'water conglomerate' owned by a consortium of pension funds, a private equity firm and the Canadian government.

erate income pretty much however you can. Anyway, the matter's history; the man and I get along fine now.

He lived the far side of the next village, didn't he, some 2–3 miles away?

Yes, he did.

So close proximity to the sludge lagoons – and he must have known exactly what 'sludge lagoons' were – wasn't much of a concern for him.

No, it wasn't.

I remember telling you that either the man's culpably careless of your interests or, given the timing of his initiative – on the morrow of your moving into the Heartsease Hall Estate – he's deliberately throwing out some sort of challenge to 'The New Boy'.

You and I agreed, however, we'd no alternative but to give him the benefit of the doubt.

. . . .

Chapter 11

Entering Puppy

Dogs – work dogs, play dogs, hunting dogs, showing dogs, lap dogs, great XXXL dogs... what in the UK today are sometimes called 'PaT' (Pets as Therapy) dogs – preferably assorted packs of them, have always been an integral part of English country life. And 'fat and short, or thin and tall' – with dogs no less than with women some would hazard, if they dared – the English country squire's default mode is to 'love them all'.

I'd loved dogs from earliest childhood (women came a little later) but because of Brambledown's proximity to the heavily-travelled Fosse Way, I'd decided against having any there. The Heartsease Hall Estate's far-removed acres were, therefore, just the opportunity Yr (Caninophile) Correspondent had long been waiting for; indeed, by the time we'd moved into the Hall, I'd already selected my dog's breed and colour. I wanted a 'standard' (full-sized) French poodle, in black.* So when in early February 1995, Big Fee reported an advertisement in our local, *EDP* newspaper for standard French-poodle puppies, I was ready at the mark.

I did the easy work first: getting Big Fee to run a preliminary check on the advertisers to make sure they were genuine and to confirm that at least some of the puppies were black. Then, very cautiously, I addressed the ultimate challenge:

'N, Fiona tells me some poodle puppies are advertised in the local paper.'

'Oh? Are they? Ummmm; that's nice. By the way, Dar, what would you like for supper tonight? There're some lamb chops in the deep freeze....'

'Yeah. "Standards"; that's to say good, big ones – or, at least, they should be. The puppies are about three months old, apparently; I've asked Fiona to check 'em out. Her Aunt's one of New Zealand's top

---

* Poodles, France's national dog, are thought to have originated in Germany. And although they're classed by the American Kennel Club as 'non-sporting', they were originally bred as water retrievers.

poodle breeders, you know.'

'Poodle breeder; no, I didn't know that. That's interesting. Anyway: there're lamb chops, or we could just have pasta. I could make that *putanesca* sauce you like – you know, with anchovies and black olives....'

'They're very intelligent, poodles, and good companions and good guard dogs. And they're clean and easy to house-train....'

'Are they indeed; I'm glad. Or alternatively, we could go out to supper – to The Green Man pub, say, and have some of their scrummy, golden-delicious fish 'n' chips.'

'If Fiona thinks these puppies sound OK, I might just go over and have a quick look at 'em, don't you think?'

'Ummmmh.'

One morning a few days later, I drove N to Norwich Airport from where she was flying to Frankfurt to do some FHA business, hopefully. The total elapsed time from Heartsease Hall to the airport departure lounge was, we clocked, of the order of 25 minutes; check-in took roughly another five. And although the airport offered direct flights to only a few destinations, Amsterdam-Schiphol – another 25–30 minutes only away – was one of them; from there, as the Reader may know, the world's your oyster. Fantastic! Just driving from Brambledown to Heathrow and parking the car, we reflected, usually took two to two-and-a-half hours, after which came the protracted ordeal of checking-in.

And that evening I drove to Heathersett, a village on the southern outskirts of Norwich, to view and, in the event, to acquire... well, whatever we'd decide call him. Big Fee and Bapu – the latter believing we were going shopping – came with me. Arriving at the breeder's modest cottage I rang the bell, harked to a chorus of barks in reply and waited and waited.... Eventually the door opened and out surged a veritable tidal wave of poodles – seven in total, all of them surely pushing the top end of the 'standard' range and absolutely coal black – which nearly bowled us over. 'That one,' the lady-breeder proudly proclaimed, pointing at and then subduing for our closer inspection the largest of the septet, 'is the mum, and these' – she swept her arm over the residual of the churning pack – 'are her pups.'

Bapu, of course, had by then cottoned onto the game and, of course, he thought he'd very much like a puppy. But had he misjudged? Was there more to 'puppy' than he'd reckoned? In their welcoming glee, the boisterous bunch were soon all around and barging into him, whacking him with their thick tails, licking him – because his height and theirs was conveniently comparable – in his ears, his eyes, his nose.... For a moment, Bapu looked as if he was going to panic; then the old Frederick-Henry steel reasserted itself. He put his arms around the nearest animal – 'Mum', I think – and gave her a hug. Then he grabbed one puppy's flailing tail and pulled; the dog turned and retaliated with a playful nip to Bapu's tummy... at which point in the melee, Bapu lost his footing and all but disappeared from view.

'Which one strikes your fancy?' the breeder enquired once we were all – poodles and people – safely back inside her cottage. In the all-wriggling, all-jiggling ruck around us, it was hard enough to tell where one animal ended and the next began, let alone make a selection. But there was a dog with huge paws, already nearly as tall as his mother; Bapu and this puppy seemed to lock onto each other almost immediately. 'Could we have this one, Daddy?' Bapu asked again and then again. 'Could he be ours? Please?'

I held a quiet conference with Big Fee. How did the quality of the dogs strike her? 'Splendid: tremendous size, excellent conformation, and overflowing with health and vigour.' As good as your Aunt's? 'Yes; possibly even better.' And the puppy Bapu'd selected... or *vice versa*? 'He's clearly the boss of the litter, and he's got no physical faults that I can see except, perhaps, one patch of fur – there, on his saddle – where the curl doesn't look to be as tight as with the rest of his coat; that could be a problem if you're going to show him. But it's very difficult to tell at his age.'

'They're all Kennel Club registered and their grandmother was Champion in her class at Crufts'* our hostess, seizing her moment, volunteered.

In due course, money and Puppy changed hands. I put on the latter the length of bailing twine I'd brought along as a lead; then, after great beseechings from Bapu, I let him 'walk' the dog to the car. Puppy not being much accustomed to leads and not having been walked for a while, a wild, careering excursion ensued. Eventually, however, all of the passengers were snuggled up together in the back seat: Puppy in the middle, Bapu at his hind end with his arm across Puppy's flank, and Big Fee at his fore end with Puppy's head in her lap. Thus more or less did things continue until we got to the very top of the front drive – about thirty yards from home – when, copiously, Puppy erped.

---

* The premier British dog show, named after its founder, the late-19th-century breeder Charles Cruft.

We took Puppy into the kitchen and let him have a good sniff around; then after giving him some water and a nice bone to gnaw on – and a little cuddle – Bapu showed him to his 'bed': a converted fire-log box with an old blanket for a mattress on the floor next to the Aga. Almost immediately, the exhausted canine climbed into it and went to sleep.

(Puppy's overnight accommodation soon became something of a domestic issue, however. Understandably, he was unhappy in the kitchen with just himself for company and on this account regularly voiced long, loud protests – exclamations which I felt evinced a considerable musicality. So in what I thought was best English-country-squire practice, I persuaded N that Puppy's bed should be moved to our bedroom... where he proved to be not only a very energetic and noisy sleeper but also a very early riser. At N's insistence, Puppy's bed was eventually returned to the kitchen.)

The next day old Groome stopped by to see how N and I were getting on. We chatted; I introduced him to Puppy, whom he declared to be 'a brilliant little chap'; then, as he was leaving, Groome vouchedsafe off-handedly but with seeming sincerity that he'd recently heard from several local people what a fine game-bird shot I was. Clearly, I thought warmly, the folks around here – my community! – are either the very souls of charity or, I considered less warmly, inveterate liars.

. . . .

They could be both; sometimes, you know, a little hyperbole, a little fabrication – 'a little white lie', even – may be in everyone's interest.

You're probably right in respect of trivial pursuits, Alter-natis, like making social small talk, or writing a book about becoming an English country squire. But where vital personal, national and international interests are at stake – managing population growth and climate change, for example, or electing heads of government, formulating and implementing domestic and foreign policy and, above all, administering The Law of the Land – truth or a very, very close approximation to it, is absolutely fundamental.

And as the regularly self-proclaimed leaders of 'The Free World', Americans could be seen as obliged to set the standard in this regard.

I seem to have pushed another of your hot buttons, d'Arcy.

Essentially, this larger sort of truth is about enabling properly-informed choices. All we really needed to know in simpler times was what kept us, our family and our tribe alive – most of which seemed either to be self-evident or the business of the gods. Today, we need to take cognizance of a wide range of very complex issues, in respect of which huge volumes of information are available. The quanta of this information *per se* makes choosing very difficult; if its particulars have been deliberately 'biased' or 'spun' – distorted – such that *un*truth must first be redacted from it, properly-informed choosing becomes almost impossible.

As runs that modern proverb: 'The first casualty of war is truth.'
Even in peacetime, however, it regularly sustains grievous wounds.

And if we're deprived of the means of making properly-informed choices, ultimately, free enterprise democracy will break down.

I thought you – or I – had suggested earlier in this book that it's already breaking down....

Well... It'll break down faster and further.

· · · · · · · · · · · · · · · · · · · ·

Late the following evening, Bapu and Yr Correspondent – the former pledged to secrecy – drove to Norwich Airport to retrieve N. She and I maundered through the usual just-landed exchanges: How was your trip, Dear? Oh, OK, Dar; the hotel was a bit noisy, but I'd a lovely meal – pork hock with sauerkraut and dumplings – at a little *gasthof* in a side-street just off Kaiserstrasse. And the presentation: did it go well? Pretty well; there were one or two slides which, on reflection, I'd have altered slightly.... Has anything been going on here, at home? I could sense Bapu, in the back seat, was about to explode. So *multo staccato e marcato**, I replied: no, Dear, nothing's been going on here... has... it... Bapu? It's all been pretty routine. Yesterday, old Groome stopped by....

We arrive at the Hall. I garage the car and take N's luggage out of the trunk; the three of us walk through the tunnel to the back door and then along the back hallway towards the kitchen; Bapu's leaping and bounding about, and humming and whistling to himself as if possessed. 'Would you like a glass of wine, Dear? Or something stronger?' I ask. 'I know how stressful your marketing trips can be.' I push open the kitchen door; Bapu's absolutely beside himself with glee now....

Woooosssh! Out like Caliban† hurtles Puppy. He ricochets off me, gives Bapu a welcoming buss or two on the snout, then registers there's a third – and unfamiliar – humanoid to greet. He bounds over to N, runs his muzzle part-way up the front of her skirt, retreats a lit-

---

* In music, a performance instruction meaning 'in short bursts and with heavy emphasis'.

† In Shakespeare's *The Tempest*, the aphasic, ostracized son of the sorceress Sycorax whom Prospero befriends and teaches to speak.

tle… and then jumps up, placing his two big, black forepaws on her chest. As N leans down trying unsuccessfully to fend him off, Puppy delivers a succession of slaverous licks to the underside of her chin. Then, greeting accomplished, he backs away.

Over the years, I'd observed that my sweet little Uxor – particularly when in travel-weary, senior-consultant mode – didn't always take well to invasions of her personal space. How would she react now, I wondered? For all our sakes, I very much hoped her introduction to this newest member of the d'Arcy Henry household would go well.

N scowls dyspeptically down at Puppy; Puppy looks delightedly back up at her. 'So who's this, then?' N asks. Like a balloon that's been inflated and released without being tied off, Bapu streams out the story. 'So he's ours, I take it,' my ever-astute, resident MBA concludes. More mis-matched glances pass between N and Puppy; then Puppy squiggles over and sits next to N. N continues to scowl down at him but, eventually, manages a would-be-dismissive little pat. Puppy squiggles up tight against N's legs, all-but sitting across her feet. Softening now, N bends down and gives Puppy something between a stroke and a caress. N and Puppy gaze into each other's eyes. N sighs, straightens up and smiles a tired smile; Puppy yawns, collapses and goes to sleep.

The morning of 10 February, I telephoned the EA to see if anything was happening on the Brambledown front. EA said there wasn't, but that we shouldn't worry because now was 'the darkness before dawn' of the new property-marketing year. 'How poetic,' I rejoined, sensing I had to say something; to myself, however, I added: 'and please, God… Whomever… let EA's words prove prophetic.' In due course, the EA's words did indeed prove prophetic. But as events over the next few days made clear, late winter's crepuscular drear remained – lightly but also, sometimes, heavily – very much with us.

The following Saturday was 'Pop-a-Pigeon Day': the first of usually four such shoots held weekly throughout East Anglia during February in which everyone, regardless of their station, is encouraged to participate because of the very considerable damage pigeons do to crops. As usual, it fell to poor Warrener keep me out of trouble. He set me up in a hide behind the walled garden and then stood at my shoulder while I blasted away….

What transpired was essentially a re-run of the duck-hunting evening but without the proximate competitive challenge of Joscelyn.

The first trick was to spot the high-flying pigeon through the tall, overhanging trees, many of which were evergreens (read: ever in full, target-obscuring 'leaf'), and track them until – be they so inclined – they turned into the wind and came in to roost. Then, as they applied their air brakes, the trick became to pick out a nice, fat one, work out which branch it was making for – or *looked like* it was making for; a roost-bound pigeon can change its mind very quickly – give it some lead... programming in the sundry bare and leaved branches its flight path would require you to swing through... and, finally, at just the right moment pull the trigger. With Warrener's rolling instructions and Groome's retailed praises ringing in my ears, I ultimately managed five birds with about twenty cartridges – a pretty dismal performance*.

Between seeing off one flight of pigeon and preparing to welcome the next, Warrener and I small-talked away. A recurring topic was Puppy, specifically: what N and I were going to make of him...

Warrener, predictably, wasn't sure we could make anything of him. 'Why dincha git a good, English dog, sir, like a Labrador or a Spaniel?' he fumed. 'Them French dogs, ya know, they're like wimin; they gotta mind a their own. Ya can't teach 'em nothin'!'

... and what we were going to name him. I told Warrener we were considering calling Puppy 'Chien Fou' and suffered upon him our arcane reasoning: the name sounds Chinese – N and I were then, and are still, big into chinoiserie – but is actually French, as in French poodle, for 'Crazy Dog' – which Puppy frequently seemed to be. Warrener heard me out then, shaking his head in mock-dismay, pronounced himself firmly in favour of '"Spot", sir' – of which markings, of course, Puppy had none.

The next day, a Sunday, Sir Roald and Lady Maureen – who'd spent the preceding Saturday night in Dovecote Cottage – left about mid-afternoon to drive to London. An hour or so later, the telephone rang; on the line was Sir Roald who told me that while they were stopped at a gas station on the A11 (the main Norwich-London 'inter-state' highway), Phoebe had slipped her lead, run off, been hit by a passing car and killed. Lady Maureen was very distraught, and concerned that poor Phoebe be laid to rest 'somewhere she'd feel at home'. Might that be in the Pet Cemetery at Heartsease Hall, Sir

---

* Good pigeon shots typically achieve a cartridge-to-kill ratio of one-to-one or better, that's to say they rarely miss and, occasionally, drop two or more birds with a single shot.

Roald asked? Certainly, I replied. Sir Roald thanked me and said he and Lady Maureen would therefore return to Dovecote Cottage for the night and 'undertake'* the following morning.

This presumed solemnity became instead a 'happening' – in the 1969, Woodstock-hippy sense of that gerund, almost – which in Yr Correspondent's experience could only have been achieved in the UK and, even there, only with the connivance of one or more very-especial people.

The funeral *cortège* – comprised of just Sir Roald and Yr Correspondent; Lady Maureen was too upset to attend, so N kept her company over coffee in the Hall's kitchen – set out at 0900 in heavy, driving rain which quickly found its way inside the up-turned collar of Yr Correspondent's waxed-cotton raincoat, through the stitching of its yoke-seams and into its sleeves as he reached up to pull down the brim of his sou'wester-style hat.

The main problem was to determine the whereabouts of the 'current' Pet Cemetery – over the centuries, the Festings had established a succession of them, I was told – and that accomplished (it was in some waste ground behind the stables, deep within a big clump of laurel bushes), to discover beneath the overgrowing branches, brambles and weeds, and amongst the myriad dislodged and perished little memorials and markers, an unclaimed site. Eventually, a nice plot was selected and approved....

And so we commenced the undertaking itself: Sir Roald pall-bearing the late Phoebe, neatly shrouded in a woven-plastic carrier bag; Yr Correspondent, armed with a pick and shovel, opening the grave. I stroked mightily with the pick and – Crrrack! – immediately struck something hard and unyielding just beneath the topsoil. Oh, no, I thought; not the coffin of some wretched incumbent! Well, no... not exactly. It was the remains of an old, aluminum kettle. I lifted it out, set it to one side, probed around with the pick a bit more and discovered in succession: the broken-off neck of a port or wine decanter, a battered, tin, serving tray, a couple of cracked scent bottles, an iron skillet – still in reasonable condition – the leather upper of an ankle boot and then its sole....

Sir Roald, struggling to look funereal, said he'd thought his forebears had all been buried in St Lawrence's Church or its yard. But...

---

* From which, of course, comes the word 'undertaker'... someone who accepts to do the necessary; in instances when burial in the ground is proposed, it's a neat, elliptical *double entendre*.

perhaps not, he chortled. Perhaps some Festings had been interred here surrounded by household items they might need in the afterlife. His eyes twinkling – mine had nearly popped out of their sockets! – Sir Roald cautioned me to dig on very, very carefully just in case.... As I did so, the rain drove relentlessly down... and Sir Roald considered whether these discoveries and, maybe, others yet to come, might be of some value – 'treasure trove' so to speak – and, if so, who was their rightful owner: we who'd bought the Heartsease Hall Estate; him to whose family the items had almost certainly originally belonged; or 'The Crown' (The State) who, he observed grimly, 'always try to grab a piece of everything they can'?

Finally, after the excavation of yet more detritus, I achieved a hole of about the right size. Sir Roald lowered poor Phoebe gently into it; I handed him the shovel; he scattered a few symbolic clods of sodden soil over; I took back the shovel and filled the grave in. So, I reckoned: that's Phoebe properly laid down... and no Festings dug up. It must be time to join the ladies in the Hall's warm, dry kitchen for a mug of hot coffee and a discussion of today's international and national news? Well yes, but....

Rain or no rain, Sir Roald (Desperately, I scrutinized his rain gear. Was it different from, that's to say superior to, mine? No, I concluded; it was more or less exactly the same as mine.) had found yet another subject of interest: the implications of confessionalism for canine 'monumental masonry', aka gravestones. So far as he could remember, Sir Roald began, most of the Festing's other, defunct pets – being presumed to have accepted the Christian faith of their masters – had had their graves marked with crosses. But, he continued, nearly all of those animals had died full of wisdom and years. Phoebe, of course, was still just a young puppy and un-Baptized, as it were. Should she be regarded as Christian by default and, therefore, be memorialized with a cross, he asked me, or should her confessional status be regarded as 'TBA' (to-be-advised, or announced) and some more-ecumenical marker like a pair of clasped hands be erected instead?

I couldn't tell whether Sir Roald was being serious so, opting to play it safe, I put up some fluff about 'the apparently ever-widening appeal of ecumenicalism' and, certain fundamentalist sects excepted, confessional differences perhaps not being so important as they once were. I got back a look of resigned disappointment as if, in my failure more deeply to engage with the issue, I'd let The Side down. Belatedly, the advice of one of my high-school teachers from Baltimore flashed through my mind: if you don't have an answer or can't fabricate a reasonable facsimile of one fairly quickly, just say: 'I don't know.'

. . . .

Religious fundamentalism: hateful, destructive, militant almost-by-definition religious fundamentalism – although many sorts of loving, constructive, pacific religious fundamentalism also exist, of course. Monastic orders, typically, are examples....

Religious fundamentalism isn't a new phenomenon, you know d'Arcy; so far as I'm aware, virtually every major religion extant today has at some stage in its history been driven by some sort of fundamentalism. That's one reason why – as The Motherland's Founding Fathers clearly recognized – it's so important to keep 'Church' separate from 'State'.

I'd forgotten that, Alter-natis. Anyway: in your view, what underlies militant religious fundamentalism? What are militant religious fundamentalism's roots?

They're the same as the roots of political and economic fundamentalism – Communism, say, or Fascism – or academic and artistic fundamentalism, viz the 'battles' which are regularly waged between contending 'schools' of thought, or fundamentalism in sport, viz athletes and/or teams – and, almost inevitably, numerous of their fans – who mindlessly incant some ridiculous mantra like 'I Am/We Are The Greatest!'

All of these fundamentalisms – and militant religious fundamentalisms especially, it seems to me – are rooted in that given of the human condition: insecurity...

Surely, there's more to it than that.

... which presents not as humility – as professed ignorance seeking enlightenment – but as dogmatism and intolerance, that's to say as presumed knowledge seeking omnipotence. Grievance about some real or perceived emotional and/or intellectual deprivation is, very often, also a factor, as may be mental and/or physical ill-health. In short, my view is that no one who's of sound mind and generally comfortable with his or her lot in life would ever choose to become a militant religious fundamentalist.

To suppose otherwise would be to accept the existence of 'Evil' or 'Original Sin'.

But many such fundamentalists seem to be warm and well-fed... healthy... and to all outward appearances, relatively content. Maybe they just need wives, or husbands... or lovers.

Inwardly, a great deal of research suggests, they harbour what the sociologist Emile Durkheim referred to as 'anomie': a deep-seated psychosocial alienation arising out of anxiety bordering on despair.

Which a 'faith' of some sort at first co-opts and then ultimately takes over.

Exactly. The prime mover, of course, is often what the ancient Greeks called a 'hierophant'*: a visionary-charismatic who sees – or represents that he (or she) sees – things no one else can. Once their 'revelation' gains worldly traction, interests – presented as some sort of 'cause' – vest in it, manipulate it, exploit it... and push it forward.

Certain Colonial-era Americans were – and certain here-and-now Americans are – what might diplomatically be called 'of a militant religious-fundamentalist persuasion'....

Is there a cure for militant religious fundamentalism?

Higher living standards, better education, more opportunity, greater hope realized in a sense of greater security.... Other than genetic engineering – identifying and modifying 'the fundamentalist gene' if, as some now think, a DNA/RNA package of that specification exists – the only sure cure for militant religious fundamentalism lies in palliating the mind-body wretchedness which begets and sustains it.

I think militant religious fundamentalists should be taken outside on a clear night and invited to reflect on the boundless, universal sky with its planets – its exoplanets especially, some of them almost certainly habitable and, maybe, actually inhabited – and its galaxies of stars stretching away in their particulate billions upon billions...

At time of writing, the latest count – based on data gathered via the Keck telescope in Hawaii – suggests some 300 sextillion stars are out there; that's a three followed by 23 zeros!

... into the incomprehensible vastness of deep space.

You could show them colored photographs of the Carina nebula or some similar ineffability taken by the Hubble space telescope; alternatively, a good picture of a meteor shower or Vincent Van Gogh's Starry Night *painting might do.*

If the militant fundamentalists see there – really, *really* see there – explicit support for their particular faith... then OK, carry on; maybe there's something we can learn from them. If they fail to see that support, they should give their militant fundamentalism up and join hands with the rest of us poor, benighted Searchers-after-Truth!

It sounds as though you're in favour of more inter-faith dialogue – more ecumenicalism even, perhaps – here on earth.

I am, Alter-natis.

That's a laudable objective, d'Arcy. But you've got to understand that for militant religious fundamentalists... militant 'true believers'... merely thinking about 'inter-faith dialogue' – an act of cognition which, of course, implies more than one 'right' way to 'ultimate knowledge' may exist – constitutes heresy. A priori, therefore, engaging in any such dialogue – let alone embracing ecumenicalism – is categorically ruled out.

---

* From '*heiro*', meaning 'holy' or 'divine'; and '*phanein*' meaning 'to reveal'.

I'm afraid hard-core religious fundamentalists almost invariably see only what they want to see. In some cases – those of suicide bombers, for example – the result is a hyper-literal acting out of that old proverb apparently first recorded in medieval France: 'Qui cope son nès, sa face est despechie.' (He who cuts off his nose spites his face.)

. . . .

St Valentine's day – when without fail... usually, I put in a vase on N's desk a single, blood-red rose (that particular 14 February, I'd thought about substituting a little bunch of heartsease... until I learned the earliest they flower is late-April) – found me with a gap in my work schedule. I took the opportunity of it to telephone Anglian Water's Public Relations Department and try to establish exactly what 'sludge lagoons' were. The obliging young man to whom I spoke explained it all to me – happily or sadly, depending on where you were coming from – very, very clearly.

In the beginning there's raw sewage – 'Yes Sir: "sewage". "s", "e", "w"...' – the fellow said, a liquid which in addition to the obvious might include everything from run-off rainwater to – 'accidentally, we assume' – toxic wastes; this liquid undergoes a succession of treatment cycles during which bio-chemicals and oxygen are added, and any solids in suspension settle or are precipitated out. The liquid is then drawn off for further purification – 'resulting, ultimately, in its being rendered entirely potable' – leaving the semi-solids behind as a sort of sludge.

This residue, the young man continued, analogous in some ways to 'night soil'*, is full of useful fibre and micro-nutrients – but also contains some heavy metals, residual herbicides and pesticides, and longer-lived medicaments such as antibiotics... or the contraceptives estrogen and progestin – and may be sprayed directly onto or injected into farmland as fertilizer. Alternatively, the sludge may be transferred to holding ponds... lagoons... where further treatment – '"digestion", it's called' – may take place, and most of the remaining water drains and/or evaporates away. The resulting, desiccated sewage sludge – which makes even better fertilizer or, alternatively, may be compacted and burned as bio-fuel – is called sewage cake.

'Digestion', I pondered, that's a strange thing for a sludge lagoon

---

* A euphemism for human-body and other household wastes which, until cities and towns were supplied with sewerage systems, were typically collected at night from cesspools and privies, etc.

to do…. Then it clicked: the sludge lagoon doesn't do the digesting, the bacteria in it do… which means 'digestion' is just a PC word for 'decomposition', or 'putrefaction', or 'rot'.

'So that's what "sludge lagoons" are, sir,' my informant recapitulated briskly. 'They're ponds, usually man-made, where treated sewage sludge is "digested" and allowed to desiccate until it becomes sewage cake.'

Good grief! I fairly screamed down the telephone line. A midden… a dunghill… a putrescent, public latrine… right here… right next door to our beautiful, unspoiled-pastoral Heartsease Hall Estate! It was a possibility almost too awful to contemplate.

But contemplate it I had to. 'Does it… this sewage-sludge-becoming-sewage-cake… smell?' I asked, hardly wanting to hear the answer.

'Not really, sir,' the young man replied sincerely/helpfully. 'By the time it gets to the lagoon, the sludge's been sterilized and treated.'

'And health hazard. Does this sewage-sludge-becoming, etc, constitute a health hazard?'

'Again, not really, sir. As I said, by the time the sludge gets to….'

'So with sludge lagoons there's no associated smell and no associated health hazard.'

'That's right, sir.'

That answer may be true relatively, I reflected, but in an absolute sense, it's almost certainly bunkum. Still, I concluded, the young man's not to blame; he's only doing his job. Thinking to slack slightly off the rope of perjure from which the wretched fellow was now hanging, I asked him: 'Would you like to have a sewage sludge lagoon next door to your home?'

There was a long pause as, presumably, my interlocutor struggled with his analysis… and/or his obligation to his employer… and/or his conscience. Then, beseechingly – penitently, almost – he replied: 'I can't honestly give you an answer to that, sir. All I can say is we at Anglian Water do our best fully to comply with all of the relevant British and European Community health and safety, and wider environmental legislation.'

. . . .

Well, I noted, you always hankered after authentic, historical experience. In Georgian times, foul smells and pestilence – in particular, the deadly Vibrio cholerae *(cholera) bacterium – attended humankind pretty much everywhere. That's why fragrances and fumigants were so widely used.*

But we weren't – and aren't – living in Georgian times, I protested. And we couldn't – and can't – fragrance and fumigate the entirety of the Heartsease Hall Estate.

And seriously, I concluded: suppose we wanted or felt obliged to keep the estate 'open'? Would members of the public come to view – should they be encouraged or allowed, even, to come to view – a property which has sewage sludge lagoons so near by?

· · · · · · · · · · · · · · · · · · ·

I rang Joscelyn to report. Being only slightly farther distanced from the proposed sludge lagoons than Yr Correspondent, he was very interested in what I'd learned and offered to provide 'all possible support' in opposing them. I tasked him up immediately.

About this time I mentioned to N that I was thinking of turning my Heartsease Hall diary into a book or so. 'You'll want some entries about north Norfolk wine and food, then,' she advised. 'You know: a local baker with his own, traditional, brick ovens, who uses proper, stone-ground, whole-meal flours… or a smallholder who keeps a few cows, or sheep or goats in pastures he doesn't put chemical herbicides or pesticides – or "sewage-cake" fertilizer! – on, and uses the milk to make cheese in the traditional way, without any nasty additives… or someone with a vineyard – perhaps only a couple of acres – who makes his own, English riesling….'

'And then, I suppose, having referenced these staples of the urban and sub-urban, middle-class, alternative-lifestyle diet, I should go on to include a few "old favourite" north Norfolk recipes: "Hen on her nest" (a chicken casseroled whole above a selection of root and other vegetables) or "Churchwarden's tea" (a tea *cake* made with chopped dried fruits, nuts, port wine, brown sugar, eggs, butter and flour)… or "Cromer (a resort town on the north Norfolk coast) crab cakes with samphire sauce", for example,' I amplified.

'Yeah, that's the sort of thing, Dar,' N enthused. 'In fact, "Cromer crab cakes with samphire sauce" would be quite a good one. Does it exist? Does that recipe exist?'

'Not that I'm aware of.'

'Well then we'll make it up. There must be lots of good recipes for crab cakes from Maryland and around the Chesapeake Bay… old "Down Home", as you call it; we can build on them. And "samphire sauce": that would just be a matter of taking your basic *béchamel**

---

* A sauce said to have been created by the Marquis of Béchamel, Steward to King Louis XIV of France.

– you know: milk, butter, flour, shallots... a splash of white wine or vermouth, maybe, and a few drops of Worcestershire Sauce – and adding some lightly-poached samphire (*Crithmum maritimum*, a white-flowered, seaside succulent). Easy peasy. So that's one recipe done. What other dishes might be nice?'

'Couldn't I just develop the book or books around buying and renovating the Heartsease Hall Estate and mentally "transitioning", as they say, to English country squire status and physically settling in? Colour it up with a few local characters: Sir Roald and Lady Maureen, Sir Jacob, Joscelyn and Leonie, Antony and Cordelia, the Platts at "The Embassy"... Chaser, Robyn, Warrener, old Groome... Mr And Mrs X, even? Stir in some quaint British conceits for the Anglophile-American audience, like His Excellency did in *Over Here*, and garnish it with a few "larger observations" such as might befit a man of my age and experience?'

'Well, if not local recipes, how about descriptions of some of the traditional arts and crafts which are carried on in these parts? Production of essential oils from lavender, and roses... and physic gardening (the cultivation of medicinal plants) for example. Those are nice, appealing notions.'

· · · · · · · · · · · · · · · · · · · ·

Maggot farming? Didn't you recently meet a fellow – he lived near Aylsham (about 15 miles north of Heartsease Hall), I seem to recall – who did that; he....

I'm sure maggots – like earthworms – do much good work, Alternatis, and I expect farming them can be very emotionally satisfying and remunerative. But as the subject of an English country squire's literary attentions, I don't think it strikes quite the right note.

· · · · · · · · · · · · · · · · · · · ·

After much careful consideration, I finally marked out the northeast boundary of the big, to-be pasture south of the Hall – 'Preston's Pride', we eventually decided to call it, in memory of a deceased friend – as a nice, gentle arc running uphill from the near corner of Neate Wood to a point about 150 yards due north of the stables. I knew the tractor drivers would complain – as, respectfully, one did – because working close in to the field side of its cambered, curvilinear boundary would be very difficult. But to me, aesthetically, the line 'felt' just about right.

And, in respect of tractor drivers 'working': towards the end of my labours that day I happened on Kenny, our senior tractor driver, who'd come to pick up and take back to the barns a big, seven-share plough and a set of disc-harrows (used to cleave the 'moulds' [turned-over furrows] of ploughed soil into smaller pieces) which had been left off in Summer Field the previous evening. While we chatted, I helped him 'fold up' (reconfigure for travel as opposed to work) the two implements, then I watched in admiration as Kenny backed the very big, very powerful tractor in to hitch up first the plough and then the disc-set – feats which in each case required positioning the great machinery so that a steel towing hook, or a pin, in section almost the diameter of your wrist, could be inserted into a draw-bar 'eye' only fractionally larger.

Amazing, I thought… but better was to come. For in consequence of these maneuverings and with the tractor now trailing two pieces of equipment with a total length of 17–18 yards, Kenny appeared to have cornered himself in a little 'headland' as they're called – a strip of arable land intentionally left uncultivated – all-but surrounded by fencing and a stand of young trees; before he could exit the head-land, he'd have to reverse his lengthy, double-articulated rig through a fairly tight 'S' curve.

'Kenny, how're you going to get yourself out of there?' I asked.

'No problem, Mr Henry. I'll just push back a bit… make a little space, if ya know what I mean.…

'But can you do that with *two* implements hooked on? Good Lord; I'd be hard pressed to back up properly with only one!'

'With the two implements, ya steer just the same as if y'd no imple-ments on at all, Mr Henry; ya turn the front wheels a the tractor in the direction ya want the back ones a the second implement ta go. You'll see; it'll be all right.'

And so it was. To my astonishment Kenny pulled forward a little, to better align his rig, then with no hesitation whatsoever flicked the tractor's automatic transmission into reverse gear, pushed the plough and the disc-set backward through the 'S' curve, flicked into forward gear… and with a nonchalant wave of his hand pulled away to the barns.

. . . .

Another of those diversions for male Readers 'who've never quite grown up', I take it.

. . . .

By now we'd had Puppy for the better part of three weeks and started to get to know him, but we still hadn't decided what to call him;

I therefore put this matter to the family Kitchen Council one *exeat* weekend when Piglet was home. The Council members quickly accepted that such a 'special' puppy…

. . . .

Every puppy's special, isn't it? Or should be….
    Well… this puppy was our first at Heartsease Hall.

. . . .

… 'special' puppy had to have a 'special' name. That would seem to rule out such time-tested favorites as 'Guy' or 'Harry' or – I pondered how best to break the news to Warrener – 'Spot'.

We then moved on to Puppy's distinctive characteristics in so far as, given his youth, they could be determined. Was Puppy by nature a consequential dog, I asked? A dog which millennia of selective breeding had evolved into, say, a fighting dog or a hunting dog or a herding dog? Or building on his innate sporting potential, perhaps – his excellent nose and his propensity to retrieve almost anything – was I… were we… going to turn Puppy into something consequential: a gun dog, for example? Possible, the Council concluded, but not probable….

At which point Puppy begins spinning around in circles – long ears flopping, big paws plopping – trying to catch his tail. Then, exhausted by these unsuccessful exertions, he collapses and rolls onto his back, all four over-long legs flailing the air, and wags his tail… which at the end of each inverted, abbreviated arc thumps loudly on the floor. The whites of his eyes glint maniacally, and 3–4 inches of bright pink tongue loll from the side of his wide-open mouth. Finally, suddenly

tensing, Puppy sneezes. Roars of laughter erupt from the Council; names such as 'Caesar', 'Rex'... 'Majesty'... were deleted from the list.

And so to Puppy's physical attributes: his probable size and strength. These parameters too were hard to predict exactly. But it seemed clear from the measure of his paws that – if he ever grew into them – he was going to be very big. And if the breadth and depth of his puppy chest were anything to go by, and the girth of his puppy neck... he was going to be very powerful as well. 'Bitsy' and 'Morsel', etc, were therefore also out.

Puppy's likely residential environment also had to be taken into account: whether, in short, he would be an indoor, 'carpet', dog or an outdoor, 'field' one. If only by virtue of our extensive acres and our predominately *alfresco* habit, Puppy – like it or not – would have to be a field dog.

I remembered someone – perhaps my Uncle Bill, Aunt Gertie's first husband, who was an avid outdoorsman (and critically-acclaimed naturalist painter) – saying that with big, rangy, field dogs, you needed a percussive name – a name which in effect exploded out of the throat and mouth – so as to carry well over longish distances. I thought back to my singing-lesson days and the taxonomy of human vocalizations I'd then had to learn. Names beginning with vowels were certainly unsuitable; ditto, probably, were those beginning with fricative or sonorant consonants like 'f' or 's'. Names beginning with plosive consonants, or 'stops' – especially voiced, bi-labial stops like 'b' or 'p' – were strong possibilities, however.

· · · · · · · · · · · · · · · · · · · ·

This section about naming your puppy's getting a bit out of hand, isn't it, d'Arcy?

I'm given to understand that careful consideration of what to call your pet is very British, Alter-natis.

You and your wife didn't spend this much time choosing names for your sons.

· · · · · · · · · · · · · · · · · · · ·

Finally, the wider-world in which Puppy would spend his days had to be considered. I saw it as an environment in which, increasingly, personal identities, family and local identities – 'community' identities, essentially – regional identities... national identities, even... were being absorbed into ever-larger and more anomalous wholes. Perhaps, as a protest against this all-encompassing integration – this geo-political 'levelling'* – we should assert that our poodle and, by extension, the d'Arcy Henry family – said to be descended from the Dukes of Arques, who once held great lands in what are today the *régions* of Haute-Normandie, Picardy and Artois – had strong historical associations with France.

A tiny light began to flicker: Puppy's name should recognize his mirth-provoking abilities – his *ris*-ibilities (from the French word *rire*, meaning 'to laugh') – his physical size and strength, the fact that he might have to be summoned back from fairly far away... and the supposed French origins of his breed. Suddenly the flicker became a flash, as of inspiration: 'Bouff' – short for '*bouffon*', French for 'comic' or 'clown', from which comes our English word 'buffoon'....

'Bouff,' N mulled, reflectively. 'Yes, that's good, Dar. I like it.'

'Bouff,' Bapu and Piglet chimed in turn, the first in his little-boy's treble, the second in his pubescent baritone.

Mr Council Chairman gave leave for a brief debate, during which the about-to-be-named attended energetically to an itch, then proposed and seconded his nomination. Mr Chairman called for a voice vote. Three in favour, one abstention: Piglet, who felt Mr Chairman was trying to railroad his preference through. By virtue of the (tenuous!) authority vested in me as head of this household, I now declare Puppy to be named....

'Bouff,' I called gently, looking from across the kitchen deep into the young dog's limpid, dark-brown eyes. Then pointing to the floor next to my feet, I intoned firmly: 'Bouff, come here.'

The newly-denominated, ears pricked, tail wagging *furioso*, regarded the four faces staring intently down at him. Clearly the centre of attention, he was very much enjoying this new game.

'Bouff,' I called again, this time more firmly. 'Bouff, come here.'

He looked at me, and our eyes – the eyes of a man and his dog... better, an apprentice English country squire and his dog – met... met profoundly... for perhaps the first time. It was as though a covenant – not as between a master and his servant, but as between equals or partners-in-life – was being forged for all time. Slowly, and with a dignity and sense of occasion I'd not expected in an animal of such tender years, Bouff got resolutely to his feet and padded over... to Piglet.

---

* From 'Levellers', a group of radical Parliamentarians who in the wake of the English Civil War advocated the abolition of nearly all distinctions of rank and status.

Chapter 12

Recovery?

The afternoon of 18 February found N and me once again at Brambledown, once again showing the property to some prospective buyers. This time it was a barrister and his wife, a Mr and Mrs Barse, who'd driven down from London. She was smallish and slim, neatly dressed, very intense, very focused, speaking only to sum up the pros and cons of some aspect of the buildings or the gardens; he, by contrast, was large and corpulent – a veritable sumo-wrestler of a man, made to appear even larger by a swathe of sweaters and scarves – from whose great chest-bellows blasted out almost continuously a veritable word-wind of observation, comment, analysis and, most expressly, opinion, which threatened to blow over any competitor credo foolish enough to stand in its way.

(Informing these mighty evaporations was, I felt sure, a mind... an intellectuality, indeed... from which I could learn much. 'If only this fellow would take a time out and let me ask him a few questions,' I grumbled. Alas, old Barse – pausing only to reflate his emptied lungs – bawled belligerently on ... and on.)

. . . .

How did you know old Barse was a barrister, d'Arcy? I don't remember him or his wife telling you....
It was his Ciceronian love of and abundant gift for rhetoric, in combination with his best-defence-is-offence eloquence which gave him away, Alter-natis... although the man could just as well have been a politician, I suppose.
In that ringing adjuration from the 1867 Supreme Court case Mississippi v. Johnson: *'No one is above the law.' But some of those who make, interpret and/or administer the law* do occasionally sound *as if they would be exceptions.*

. . . .

Notwithstanding the above, I thought the viewing went well, as did N. And although the Barses' level of interest was difficult to gauge precisely – because Mrs in her succinctness gave nothing away while Mr in his verbosity kept nothing back, making it difficult to distinguish supposition from proposition – we both felt there was some.

Shortly after the Barses had gone, N and I drove down to West Midlands Farmers, Brambledown's local 'country store', preparatory to heading back to Heartsease Hall. (N needed some sun-dried tomatoes for a Mediterranean dish she wanted to make; I said a real man's mart like WMF wouldn't stock such 'townie' stuff but, sadly, it did.) In the store's parking lot we encountered 'Synthia' (correctly spelled 'Cynthia', of course), an acquaintance from my long-ago days as a presuming 'Debutantes' Delight' on The Motherland's East Coast and, latterly, a fellow expatriate to the UK and the Cotswolds, whom N and I'd occasionally had over for supper.

Even in my youth I'd found Synthia's dogged snobbishness challenging, but way back when… she was very, very pretty. In later life, with her lack-lustre, greying-dyed-blond hair, her over-painted and powdered face, her bony hands with their shrink-wrap of translucent, blue-veined skin… her dieting-wasted body which seemed ever on the verge of collapsing under the weight of the gold jewelry she almost always wore – and yet still vaunting that dogged snobbishness – she invariably brought to my mind the dictum attributed to the Duchess of Windsor (*née* Bessie Wallis Warfield, sometime of Baltimore, Maryland, of whom my Aunt Gertie had been briefly a school-mate) that 'you can never be too rich or too thin'. What an utterly fatuous thing to say!

On this occasion.... After describing in loving detail a party she'd recently given at her Cotswolds home – a seated, seven-course dinner for 200 in a 'huge' pink and yellow marquee with two dance bands, one 'flown in especially from Philadelphia' – but to which N and I hadn't been invited, Synthia asked after our news. I said we'd just bought a nice farm in north Norfolk. 'Oh, north Norfolk,' she replied, sniffily. 'I've got tons of friends there; we do "coaching" – you know: horses and carriages stuff, like Prince Phillip, the Duke of Edinburgh, does. I usually stay at Sandringham*,' she added. 'But even so, I always think: "Whew! What a boring place north Norfolk is. And what an awful, long, *boring* drive it is to get there!'

---

* 'Sandringham' is a village within Her Majesty the Queen's 19,500-acre Sandringham Estate offering a range of public accommodations in which almost anyone may stay. 'Sandringham House' is The Queen's Norfolk seat and one of her official residences. In my experience, it's not unknown for people to imply some link with the latter by adverting elliptically to the former as, I sensed, Synthia was doing.

. . . .

One of those sad Americans who never grew out of trying to be more British than the British, Alter-natis, or who never grew up and into their 'better self'. One or the other or, possibly, both....

Why have you included this mean-spirited little rant? It's not integral to your narrative and it doesn't represent your *'better self'.*

Synthia's snobbishness – delivered from her platform of wealth and privilege – gives wealth and privilege a bad name. Wealth and privilege don't deserve that; they're like any other estimable personal peculiarity: high IQ, athletic ability, good looks, 'charm', ambition, a capacity for hard work and perseverance.... What they are depends on how they're used.

All the woman's really saying, d'Arcy, is that she hasn't very much self-esteem.

Perhaps she should explore – if she hasn't already – other ways of making that point.

. . . .

The following day, one of the up-market British newspapers ran an article at which, N and I quickly agreed, you'd either to laugh or to cry. (After some mutual up-bucking, we managed to laugh... sort of.) Under a headline reading: 'Why (UK) house prices will continue to fall', it forecast just about everything the earnestly-aspiring property vendor and/or the at-long-last-achieved property purchaser – we, of course, were in both camps – really *didn't* want to hear: higher mortgage interest rates, lower mortgage tax reliefs, and decelerating national economic growth leading to increased job insecurity and unemployment.

And to round off, the author of the piece proposed that a substantial house-price decline might in fact be 'no bad thing' because in the UK – and, indeed, in the US, he added – the populace was generally 'over-housed', that's to say had a disproportionate amount of their total wealth tied up in their homes.

N and I'd concluded some months ago (shortly after 21 October 1994, to be precise, the day our purchase of the Heartsease Hall Estate was completed) we certainly had a disproportionate amount of our total wealth so tied up, and that if UK house prices really did 'continue to fall' – or, Heaven forefend, actually tank – we were in big trouble. So characterizing a substantial house-price decline as perhaps 'no bad thing'....

. . . .

How could that British journalist – that mere 'scribbler' – have been so prescient, Alter-natis? Nearly fifteen years before the Great Crash of 2007–08, to have foreseen...

... to have foreseen what would happen when the live coals of mans' greed were doused with the gasoline of easy credit. 'Neither a borrower nor a lender be,' Polonius, in Shakespeare's Hamlet, *cautioned his son Laertes, 'For loan oft loses both itself and friend, And borrowing dulls the edge of husbandry...'*

...or as President Franklin Delano Roosevelt summed up in 1937 when the US was finally beginning to recover from the Great Depression: 'We have always known that heedless self-interest was bad morals; now we know (also) that it is bad economics.... In the long run, economic morality pays.'

Well, when you put it like that, sure.... But what did the UK journalist mean by a house-price decline perhaps being 'no bad thing'?

Back in early 1995, he wasn't referring to sub-prime mortgages 'sliced and diced' into grossly over-leveraged, collateralized debt obligations or CDOs – which 'rating agencies' and 'regulators' either didn't properly appraise and/or allowed substantially to run free – and 'insured' by a great, sprawling pyramid of credit default swaps or CDSs, in respect of which there was effectively no pro bono superintendence whatsoever.

He wasn't?

No. The journalist was referencing a much more fundamental phenomenon and one which was and is still in some respects a defining characteristic of many developed world socio-economies: home-ownership as a symbol not just of material security but of having achieved 'The American, British or wherever... Dream'.

There's no necessary relationship between home ownership and 'dream achievement', you know. More than 80 per cent of Mexicans, Nepalese and Russians own their own homes, we're told, but only 30–40 per cent of French, Germans and Mexicans do; Yanks and Brits, at 65–70 per cent home ownership, occupy a middle ground.

So how did outright home ownership come about?

Some socio-anthropologists see it as arising out of mankind's prehistoric transition from a pastoralist, hunter-gatherer existence – which required that humans range over considerable areas of land no one could ever really 'own' – to a more-settled, farming existence which obliged them to maintain an interest in a particular extent of property...

And its prevalence in Anglo-America?

... others – historians... political scientists and the like – attribute it to the establishment there during the 18th and 19th centuries of free-enterprise democracies, which generally gave people the right to own property, and later – as governments became more and more concerned to propitiate increasingly-powerful, lower-and-middle-

class voters – encouraged them specifically to own their own homes.

The truth, I suppose, lies somewhere in between.

That's where the truth almost always lies, d'Arcy; the trick is to establish exactly where 'in between' it lies. The working lifetimes of many, many very bright people have been and will, I hope, continue to be dedicated to trying to do just that.

Scrolling back, however: what's wrong with investing in 'bricks and mortar'?

Nothing. And as you know, in the US and the UK peoples' owned-homes are typically their primary store of value (financial assets like stocks and bonds are the distant second) and, on this account, their primary political, economic and social anchor.

But...

But an owned home is intrinsically different from a gold bar or a basket of hard currencies in that it's not just a store of value. It's also a consumer good which requires inputs like heating, lighting and water, and maintenance – as well, of course, as timely payment of any mortgage, insurance and tax monies due on it. For this reason a home is often referred to as a 'bundled' good rather than a stand-alone, unitary one.

... but when home-ownership's so 'affordable', that's to say so easy....

Economists often make two points: buying your home isn't necessarily the best way to grow your own personal wealth – over time, and with some notable exceptions (the purported purchase of Manhattan Island for a few handfuls of beads, for example) financial assets can offer a better total return – and, ipso facto, *home-owners in aggregate buying their homes isn't necessarily the best way to grow national wealth. Indeed as a 'driver' of the economy, that's to say as a macro-wealth-creator, many economists regard the money people invest in their homes as largely 'dead'.*

Ceteris paribus, *revivifying some of that dead money would, they argue, create jobs, raise output – and, hopefully, productivity – and increase GDP (gross domestic product).*

So people should view a house price crash, assuming they survive it, as an opportunity to down-size or sell up their homes and diversify? To invest in mutual funds, stocks and bonds, options... indices and other derivatives; or gold, hard currencies, fine art, antiques, pork bellies, chicken livers... that sort of thing? In short: to set a few alternative anchors...?

Proper asset allocation is indeed critically important, d'Arcy. But given on the one hand the rapacity of most governments, viz *the money they take away from us through their often-deflationary fiscal policies (taxes), and through their often-inflationary monetary policies (money supply) and, on the other hand...*

All this '*ipso facto*' and '*ceteris paribus*', and 'one hand/other hand' stuff, Alter-natis! You're starting to sound like an economist... or a central banker.

... and, on the other hand, the rapacity of most financial institutions, viz the money they take away from us through their 'investment' operations, that's to say their equity and other capital-market 'intermediations', and through their commercial operations, viz the control they exercise over the availability of credit....

Tell me, then: how're people going to acquire the financial resources – not to mention the appetite for risk – properly to diversify their investments?

From the security provided by all that wealth tied up in their homes, I guess.

• •

Thinking to lift my over-housed spirits, I roused myself from my desk and went for a little walk-about, in the course of which I encountered Bapu, who asked me if I'd take him for a donkey ride. I said yes; he tripped merrily away and in the blink of an eye returned hard-hatted and booted, so hand-in-hand off to the stables we went.

Lady Maureen had warned me Maggie and Jubie had minds of their own, but....

I tacked Maggie up, clipped the lead onto her head collar and – leaving Jubie behind in her stall in the stables – tried to walk her over to the mounting block where Bapu eagerly awaited. Maggie wouldn't go there. I shortened up on Maggie's lead, pulled her head around, circled her a couple of times, straightened her out and again started her towards the mounting block.... She wouldn't go there. Clearly, I reflected, our Maggie is a chip off the old namesake*.

Thinking it unseemly that the apprentice English country squire's writ should be so emphatically repudiated in his own stableyard by a middle-aged jill donkey, I had a sharpish word with the ungulate in question; then, after another unsuccessful attempt to lead her, I applied the palm of my hand heavily to her haunch (the which action if it wasn't painful for her certainly was for me). She gave me a look as if to say: 'Sticks and stones may break my bones, but you will never move me...' at which point N arrived on the scene. She suggested

---

* In 1980, the then British Prime Minister, Margaret Thatcher (aka 'The Iron Lady', later Baroness Thatcher) famously rejected a policy 'U-turn' (reversal), with the words: 'You turn if you want; the lady's not for turning'. (*The Lady's Not for Burning* is the title of the English playwright Christopher Fry's comedy about a woman falsely charged with witchcraft.) Prime Minister Thatcher could just as well – if not so niftily – have said: 'I won't go there.'

Maggie – 'Mum' – was probably just wanting the company of her daughter Jubie. And so it proved; after putting a head-collar and lead on Jubie, N walked her out of her stall and – with Maggie now practically towing me along behind her – over we all went to the mounting block as easy as could be.

. . . .

Wonderful, isn't it Alter-natis, the lessons which can be learned about human behaviour from observing herd – and pack – animals: the way their group-think minds set, for example, and how they just sort of hang together....

'All we like sheep,' as St Paul is said to have written: going astray... then returning to the fold....

If I'd learned those lessons earlier in life, I might have become a rich merchandiser, or advertising and/or PR executive, or psephologist... or a successful politician, even.

. . . .

The following day, the sewage-sludge-lagoon-proposing, farming tenant/contractor – 'Sslapftc' I'll call him; the acronymic has a suitably, err... something semi-solid hitting the ground sound – arrived at the Hall unexpectedly... on his 1000 cc, canary-yellow, Kawasaki motorcycle. (Wow! I thought, what *is* going on here? If I were an accessory to – the instigator of, perhaps – a possibly-pending, major desecration of the natural environment around his property... his *home*... would I just rumble up without any introduction and plug right in to a chat or whatever with him?) Cautiously, I greeted Sslapftc, then led him into the estate office/library and towards a seat on the sofa.

Physically, Sslapftc was very tall and *émincé*, with steady, direct eyes and a fine, strong-featured face under greying hair drawn back in a pony-tail. Mentally, he seemed a cross between the Dalai Lama in contemplative mode and a hunting tiger: one minute relaxing deep into the sofa, stretching out his long legs, smiling seraphically... the next sitting well forward, crouched, frowning... tense, as if about to spring. In addition to which, although Sslapftc was clearly very able and articulate, at intervals he referred to himself as 'a drop out' (from a range of service-sector jobs including teaching and police work, I learned) who'd come to farming – the vocation his family had followed for many generations and at which he was regarded locally as excelling – largely by default.

In short, I couldn't make my unexpected guest out. Had he stopped by in response to my letter of introduction and invitation of some

weeks ago? Or had he come to lobby in favour of – or, perhaps, apologize preemptively for – his proposed sludge lagoons? No, it transpired
after five or so minutes' conversation, he just wanted permission to
'clear up', by which he meant 'have for firewood', a tree which had
come down next to one of the fields he farmed for us. I said OK but
please to leave 'The Squire' a few good branches… on which note,
Sslapftc departed as enigmatically as he'd arrived.

. . . .

So today Class, I'd like to talk about corporate social responsibility
or 'CSR' – 'business ethic', if you prefer – using management of the
Heartsease Hall Estate as a case….

Yes: Che, my old buddy, my old friend…. Your question? Isn't
'business ethic' an oxymoron – an 'oxymoron' being, in case anyone
here doesn't know…. Yes, that's right: the conjunctive use of syllables or words which are contradictory. 'Oxymoron' is itself an oxymoron, of course, being composed of the Greek words *oxus* meaning 'sharp' and *moros* meaning 'blunt' or 'dull'. Anyway:

No, I don't think 'business ethic' is an oxymoron. There are certainly some companies or divisions of companies which sometimes
operate unethically. But that doesn't imply companies in general or
free-market capitalism as a whole is unethical. So, to take it *da capo*
– that's 'from the top' – again: today, I'd like to talk about….

Yes, Che. How am I defining 'ethical'? I was going to put that
question later. But since you've raised it now and for the purposes of
argument – don't take 'argument' *too* literally – let's say 'ethical' is a
means of furthering the great 18th /19th-century utilitarian philosopher Jeremy Bentham's 'greatest happiness of the greatest number',
that's to say the so-called 'General Good'.

'Unethical' is, obviously, the opposite of that: a means which
doesn't further the General Good… indeed; which may actually stall
or degrade that Good in some way.

But to return to our case study: the Heartsease Hall Estate and, of
course – Ha, ha! – its dynamic, visionary, new CEO….

That CEO has over long, hard years as a management consultant
evolved his own business ethic…. All right, Che! Yes: it could be his
own business '*un*ethic'; we could, I suppose, attempt to characterize
Heartsease Hall's new CEO's approach to business in that negative
sort of way….

Whatever; the new CEO arrives and discovers that an established
farming tenant/contractor of his – acting perfectly within his rights,
it must be made clear – is seeking to do something – specifically:
putting practically in the CEO's back yard some sewage… that's
'sewage' as in (deleted)… sludge lagoons – the CEO doesn't want
done. So the CEO sets out to try and stop him doing that something.

Che, again; what is it *this* time! No, he's not a 'capitalist pig';
the new CEO of Heartsease Hall's not a capitalist pig. A man of
strong principles and strong views inclined, sometimes, towards the
authoritarian, perhaps – but, down deep, he's a person who's fundamentally committed to sustainable free-enterprise democracy. I think
calling him a capitalist pig is unfair. Grossly unfair.

So to continue. The question I'd like to put to the Class is this: is
the new Heartsease Hall CEO's opposition to the proposed sewage
sludge lagoons ethical? Does it further the General Good?

GT, our banker: yes.... Who would 'the winners' be, you ask,
that's to say who would benefit from the sludge lagoons, and how?

Well, let's see: the main beneficiary, of course, would be my farming tenant/contractor who'd be paid for the use of his land and,
probably, get easier, lower-cost access to the desiccated sewage
sludge which he'd use as fertilizer to grow bigger and better crops
which he'd sell at higher prices.

The local utility, Anglian Water, and its shareholders and customers would also benefit, since the sewage sludge they generated
– institutionally and perhaps personally, you could say – would be
disposed of in what we must assume would be a profit-maximized
or, at least, a loss-minimized way.

Yes, Ms Gospel. You want to know who would be 'the losers'?
The losers would be my family and me as well as a dozen or so
fairly-near, downwind neighbours, probably, and all of those en-
vironmentalist *'citoyens'* – in the French Revolutionary sense of
'marginalized masses' – who'd like this bit of English countryside to
remain unspoiled.

It therefore goes without saying that as a farmer trying to make
an honest dollar or an honest pound sterling – but, equally, as someone who's concerned to preserve mankind's natural environment – I
believe a very strong case can be made for....

Now what, Che! No.... NO! Look My Friend: I'm not some
'upper-class bully' trying to throw his weight around. And I'm not
a capitalist pig. Really! So get that Trotskyite 'them-versus-us' chip
off your shoulder. The world's moved on; we've all – together, as
partners in common – got much larger and more consequential fish
to fry.

What? 'Power to The People!' you say? Look, (Deleted): has it
ever occurred to you that 'Power to The People' is what democracy,
the system which gives you – even you – freedom of speech, is all
about? There may be respects in which 'The People' should have
more power – although I'm hard pressed to think of many – and
there may be respects in which 'The People' should have less. Be that
as it may: 'The People' *already have power.*

So why, as regards these sludge lagoons, don't I let 'The People' decide, you ask? Well, if you don't mind my saying: that's just about the most worthy question you've asked all morning.

And I reply: that's what the planning process in the UK is all about. When an application for a construction is first made, it's advertised to 'The People'; that was the placard I noticed on 4 February. If there're objections, an independent, local committee hears them; the committee then accepts or rejects the application... but their decision may be appealed and appealed again right up to national-government level. And the national government, you may recall, is elected by and for 'The People'.

So to propose once again what I'd hoped would be this session's topic of discussion: CSR, aka 'business ethic'....
· ·

On 22 February, the EA telephoned to say he'd just taken Mrs Barse through Brambledown a second time, towards the end of which review she'd 'wondered' if we 'might be prepared to accept [...]' for the property. An offer, N and I asked ourselves? Well, if you looked past the circumlocuitry, yes... probably. But an acceptable offer? Reluctantly, we decided no it wasn't, partly because the mooted bid represented an over-large discount from our original ask and partly because – in spite of the down-beat forecast referenced earlier in this chapter – the word on the real-estate-agency street now was that UK country-house prices might be starting to move up.

Throughout all of these necessary diversions, Yr Correspondent's diligent attentions to his new, esquirely responsibilities continued unabated. In the course of just one week – admittedly a bumper week – my estate-related mailbag spewed out copy letters from the land agent purportedly for '(my) review and comment' but, in fact, detailing how he'd already disposed of the various matters arising: with the MAFF (the Ministry of Agriculture, Fisheries and Food now known as DEFRA, the Department for Environment, Food and Rural Affairs) about payment of AAPS and SAPS (the Arable Area Payments Scheme and the Sheep Annual Premium Scheme, that's to say agricultural subsidies, now merged within the SPS or Single Payment Scheme); with the HSI (the Health and Safety Inspectorate) about complying with new legislation concerning the disposal of farm-arising animal and agricultural wastes; with BS (British Sugar, the beet-sugar producer which together with Tate & Lyle – the *cane*-sugar importer/producer – constituted and continues to constitute a natural-sweeteners duopoly in the UK) about our sugar-beet production quota for the 1995–96 farming year; and with one of our agricultural tenants about his 'too-high' rent...

... as well as original communications sent direct to me from the previously-referenced MOD (the Ministry of Defence), EE (Eastern Electricity) and BT (British Telecommunications) concerning their respective way-leaves; from the EA (in this usage, the Environment Agency) about some drainage ditches they needed to dig; and, finally, from the FC (the Forestry Commission, now the Forestry Author-ity) about a couple of hardwood plantations established during Sir Roald's administration which they wanted to confirm on site were being properly looked after.

· · · · · · · · · · · · · · · · · · · ·

All this deskwork and all these acronyms is farming, I moaned?

As you've somewhat lately come to recognize, a great deal of it is, d'Arcy.

· · · · · · · · · · · · · · · · · · · ·

My in-tray also included: a letter from English Heritage saying that in spite of 'the very considerable merits' of our case, they wouldn't be able to offer us funding to restore the Hall, just as Lord Gowrie had foretold...

... and one from Joscelyn enclosing a copy of the engineering plans for the proposed sludge lagoons which he'd acquired via the NNDC (North Norfolk District Council) and his thoughts on how a cam-paign to oppose construction of the lagoons might proceed. These last included, obviously, references to the lagoons' likely immediate adverse impact on our local amenity but also – less obviously, at least to Yr Correspondent – the appreciation that over time the dimension of this adverse impact could be expected to grow 'as additional sludge lagoons, leveraging the precedent established by the first two, are put in place'.

Oh Ye Gods, I shouted to N. We could wind up with an entire sludge-lagoon farm in our estately back yard!

Thus primed, a few days later N and I met with one of the NNDC's Planning Officers. Putting on a show of injured indignation, I told the cheery staffer who attended us that 'some sewage sludge lagoons (were) threatening my wife's and my bodily health, not to mention our health of mind'. Smiling wanly, the young man sat forward and tidied the folder open on his desk. Then he sat back. 'It's not our job to take sides you know, sir,' he enjoined. 'We just try to ensure all par-ties to a planning issue get a fair hearing.' Free-enterprise democracy

– 'people power' – at work, I reflected, not altogether contentedly.

Shortly thereafter, I drafted a blind letter opposing the sludge lagoons to go out over my signature, or perhaps as a 'round robin'*, and faxed it to Joscelyn for his review; he immediately telephoned back to suggest a few changes and to provide names and contact details of some likely interested parties to whom it might be sent. I also ran up a letter – final copy, not draft – to Sslapftc advising him of my opposition to the sludge lagoons but adding *pro forma* that I hoped he wouldn't take it personally.

On 25 February came what was described by Joscelyn as 'absolutely, positively the final shoot of the season' and the benefaction of a new recipe: breast of moorhen (*Gallinula chloropus*) flash-fried in garlic butter and served on a bed of *radicchio* lettuce and finely-sliced leeks supported by wholewheat toast liberally spread with goose or pheasant-liver *paté*. Is this purported *délice* one, literally, for the book, I wondered? Or were those scallywag locals pulling my leg again.

And the following Monday, 27 February, took place my long-scheduled meeting with the 'Senior Casework Officer' from the Countryside Commission: old SCO. It proved a memorable encounter partly because it didn't begin until 1130, that's to say fully one hour later than scheduled (Never mind, I thought, recalling our first viewing of the Heartsease Hall Estate, it's easy to underestimate driving times around here. Then I reflected: our SCO works out of Cambridge, doesn't he? So shouldn't he know East Anglia pretty well?), but primarily because of the bent of my counter-party and the substance of our exchanges.

The SCO was smallish and slightly-built, and the mental default mode his body language suggested on getting out of his car gave every indication of being in keeping: that of the under-powered, over-promoted, middle-managing gofer who spends most of his time behind a desk or in front of a mirror. By the time he'd reached our front porch, however, the persona he'd assumed was relentlessly up-and-at-'em 'country-hearty', and it was manifestly for this latter role – or, perhaps, the role of Sherlock Holmes – that he'd dressed. Viewing top to bottom, the SCO had on or about him: a 'deer-stalker' cap, a full but immaculately-trimmed, ginger-red beard, a gold ear-ring, a gleaming (but clearly unlit) meerschaum pipe, a plaid shirt of the sort favoured

---

* With multiple signatures arranged in a circle to disguise the precedence-order of signing.

by many of Joscelyn's 'hootin' friends, closed at the collar with a forest-green, knitted-wool tie, a cream-yellow suede waistcoat, moleskin shooting breeches, forest-green, wool knee socks, hiking boots... and a brace of 'border collies', as they're called in the UK – medium-sized dogs, typically black and white, used mainly for herding sheep – which he immediately let out of the car to 'water' and then officiously commanded back in again.

Almost as soon as we'd shaken hands, the SCO began galumphing energetically around (albeit, I noted with bemusement, more or less in circles) inhaling and exhaling deeply, pointing at and then remarking authoritatively on this feature of the landscape and then that one.... Thinking this display of keen interest might represent a good entry point into the *raison d être* of our meeting, I offered old SCO a quick tour around the outside of the Hall so that he might better view at least the estate's in-lying fields, lakes and woodlands... but he said he hadn't built time for such a 'diversion' into his 'busy schedule'. I therefore led him directly inside and along to the estate office/library....

Arriving whereat it seemed to me the SCO looked, for want of a better word, 'uneasy'. So, apologizing for not having thought to enquire sooner – he like his dogs having had a drive of perhaps two hours to get here, I supposed, and therefore also needing to 'water' – I asked him if he'd like 'the small room' (a Victorian periphrasis for 'the toilet'). The SCO said no, so I waved him in the direction of the designated guest seat on the sofa and moved to take up my own usual place behind my card-table desk. Old SCO sat not, however. Indeed, rather than settling in he appeared on the verge of walking out. What on earth was going on? I waved him again towards the guest seat....

Old SCO turned to face me, 'Ahem-ed' a couple of times and, eventually, deigned to inform me that 'his people' (or should I write 'His People') were really only interested in aiding 'very special' properties: 'Listed Grade I buildings with landscapes done by "names", for example.' There was, therefore, little point in his (? His) wasting time here; the Heartsease Hall Estate, he opined, was most unlikely ever to get a CC grant.

· · · · · · · · · · · · · · · · · · · ·

After what you'd told old SCO on the telephone only 3–4 weeks earlier: that Hartsease Hall's architect was William Wilkins, Senior, and that its grounds had been landscaped by Nathaniel Richmond... and that the Hall's 'very special' status was recognized in the prop-

erty's English Heritage listing as Grade I, etc, etc? And after what he having been apprised of all of the foregoing had, in return, implied to you?

And if 'things had changed' – if, for example, he and/or his superiors had had second thoughts about grant-aiding your estate – why didn't he just write to or telephone you and say so instead of driving all that long distance?

He probably just wanted an away-day from behind his desk and/or in front of the mirror in his dreary office.

•••••••••••••••••••••

In desperation, I retrieved from my files and laid before old SCO a copy of the selling agent's Heartsease Hall Estate brochure. And after a bit of displacement activity – a stroke of the old beard, a tug at the old earring… a pull on the old pipe (still unlit!) – *mirabile scriptu*, our SCO seemed suddenly to get the gospel. 'Tell me some of the things you want to do,' he commanded warmly. Even old-hand management consultants don't achieve conversions of this magnitude every day, I reflected. But quickly persuading myself that what I'd heard might in some roundabout way betoken what I might get, I started telling. One of my main concerns was to re-empark the fields to the south and west of the Hall, I informed the SCO.

•••••••••••••••••••••

I said: That's T1S2I1 of The Masterplan, isn't it? Put your proposals to him that way. All those 'titles' and 'schedules' and 'items' in priority order…. That sort of format drives you and me bonkers, of course – as it may have already done some Readers. But it's good bureaucratese; if you lay it out that way, maybe old SCO'll feel reassured.

But was the SCO's expression of interest real or contrived, I wondered? And even if it was real, how were we going to deal with the vexed matter of public 'access'?

•••••••••••••••••••••

I then detailed the preparatory work I'd already done. Old SCO began positively to radiate enthusiasm. 'A relatively modest investment… with the prospect of a very substantial return… just the sort of undertaking we at the Commission really like to back,' he murmured appreciatively. 'This project's a winner… a winner for sure.'

So should I go ahead and actually seed the to-be-re-emparked fields, I asked and, thereby, catch as much as possible of this year's growing season? SCO nodded emphatically in affirmation. 'Just confirm with us the varieties of grass you propose to use – we've got our own proprietary blend, you know; it's called "The Countryside Stewardship Parkland Mixture" (I nodded appreciatively.) – and their application rates,' he particularized. Dumbfounded and unwilling to trust to his fallible memory, Yr Correspondent grabbed a pencil and some paper, and began minuting away like a scribe afire.

But what if my application doesn't succeed, I asked, still minuting frantically. Preparing and re-seeding such a large area will be expensive, Mr SCO. And then there's the opportunity cost of foregone crops. If, at the end of the day...? Don't you worry yourself about that, my newest, best-est advocate assured me warmly; 'the possibility of your application *not* succeeding is very, very low... non-existent, in fact, I'd say.'

I took out the estate plan and TSI-ed one or two other things I had in mind: re-building the deteriorated outfall sluices below and tidying up the banks around and above the upper and lower lakes; improving and extending these field hedges and widening these field 'margins' (perimeter grass strips) here, here and here, to encourage wildlife.... 'Excellent! The crown in which is set your magnificent jewel – Your Hall! – will be completely restored' (or words to that very close effect), old SCO gushed, before concluding: 'We take applications from 1 April to 31 July. Be sure to submit your yours in good time so we can go for what's called Early Acceptance.' After a pause for reflection he added: 'The best thing, probably, would be for you to send your application direct to me. I'll read it through.... Then if I think any fine-tuning's required before sending it upstairs, I can let you know.'

My head spinning from what seemed to be the dramatic improvement in my prospects, and my hand cramping from the effort of recording for posterity the purported understandings on which that prospective improvement was based, I did my apprentice-esquirely best to hang in there while the SCO confided, 'countryman to countryman', that he'd now like to discuss...

· · · · · · · · · · · · · · · · · · · ·

Make sure you get yourself a deerstalker, a pipe, an earring and a couple of border collies asap, d'Arcy.

· · · · · · · · · · · · · · · · · · · ·

... to discuss 'current countryside political issues'. I crossed my fingers and recalled that sublime litotic Chaucer in his *Troilus and Criseyde* of c 1385 scripted for Pandarus, the protagonist's erstwhile procurer (pimp): 'It is nought good a slepyng hound to wake.'

'Access is the paramount concern now,' old SCO opined sagely:

'the extent to which,' he expanded, as if I might have forgotten his earlier, telephone-call advisory or couldn't otherwise know, 'and on what basis members of the general public are allowed onto private land.' I nodded and waited resignedly for the 'slepyng hound' – the individual and group incursions... the invasions of my and my family's privacy, and nature's privacy... that would be the *quid pro quo* for my accepting government money – to leap to its feet and start snarling. Imagine my surprise, then, when the SCO concluded: 'We must all work to ensure that public access is as limited as possible, Mr Henry.'

But when you and I spoke on the telephone, Mr SCO, I queried, you told me if a landowner didn't include adequate provision for public access, the Countryside Commission could reject his application out of hand. 'Oh, no, Mr Henry,' old SCO now confided, mellifluously. 'The way we look at it, public access is just a "bolt-on" (something extraneous or *in*essential). In the case of really exceptional properties, like your Heartsease Hall....'

· ·

What did you make of the SCO's sudden, miraculous conversion to your cause – not to mention his disavowal of his earlier prescriptions in respect of public access?

Much more than I should have; indeed, mine was a classic example of one's heart – I wanted to believe I'd get that funding – overruling one's head.

A useful amount of money seemed to be on offer. And surely, I remember telling you, even the most abject underling in even the most over-bearing government office wouldn't lead you on and strongly imply – if not actually make – promises he didn't intend to keep.

It was substantially your intimation which determined me to go through with the CC application, Alter-natis, in spite of the heavy input of time and effort it would require.

Well, it gave you something to do and, in that well-polished phrase, helped 'keep you out of trouble'. In the end, you learned a lot from your mistake.

· ·

Later that day I got a telephone call from the Secretary of the Irish Georgian Society to ask if members of his group, as well as a few fellow-travellers who were into vintage Bentley and Rolls Royce cars, could visit Heartsease Hall the second Bank Holiday in May. There'd be perhaps 40–50 people and their vehicles, and they'd be coming from a similar look-in on the Steeles at Caiston and the Hufftons at Brunstead, Mr Secretary said, matter-of-factly. But they wouldn't require much in the way of hospitality, he assured me: 'just a cup of tea, perhaps, and some biscuits'.

I said yes immediately and, afterwards, reflected: so that's how it happens. The telephone rings, a bit of easy conversation takes place and, without further ado, the upstart Henrys are booked to host their first public open house! I made a note in my diary to get instruction from Sir Roald on what to and not to do then, thinking better of it, I struck that out and jotted: 'ask the 13th Baronet himself to preside'. That way, I felt sure, the Irish Georgians *et al* would get their money's worth.

By end-February, Old Groome's mobile home had finally been prized out of its associated detritus and repositioned slightly, as if about to be taken away; my goodness, I rejoiced, how very nice it will be at last to see the back of that eyesore! On closer inspection, however, I noticed all of its tyres were flat, and that one of its iron, under-frame supports – vital to holding the mobile home together, presumably – had rusted through. Mine old eyes were going to be sore for a while yet, I suspected.

So I displaced my estate-proud frustrations onto some wooden cargo pallets which were littering the south bank of the lower lake. There were at least two dozen of them, I'd counted, put down many years ago by Sir Roald so that day-trip 'coarse' (as opposed to 'game') fishermen, who paid him a fee for their sport, would have something solid to stand on; now, most of the pallets were deeply embedded in the mud. Taking them up proved very tedious work. If the pallet was badly rotted, it came up easily but in little pieces each of which, with their protruding rusty nails, had to be carefully collected. If the pallet was still fairly sound, the pieces were larger but more difficult to extract, such that the harder I pulled up on them the deeper into the mud I sank down.

And as regards sinking into mud: north Norfolk's lower-lying terrain could be very deceptive, I learned. One post-pallet-picking evening, driving back to the Hall in the Land Rover across what appeared to be firm ground in the middle of Pavilion Paddock, I suddenly bogged down front and rear up to the hubcaps; not even four-wheel drive with the differential* locked could get me out.

What to do? I thought of telephoning one of the farm men – Sheen,

---

* The differential (gear) allows a vehicle's wheels to turn at different speeds, for example, when cornering; if it's locked, all four wheels turn at the same speed thereby somewhat improving traction.

perhaps, or Eddie or Kenny – and asking him to come over with a tractor and tow-chain...

• • • • • • • • • • • • • • • • • • • •

What? You considered doing that?

Why not, Alter-natis?

Revealing your incompetence as an esquire to one of the farm men?

I didn't think there was much of my incompetence they weren't already aware of.

• • • • • • • • • • • • • • • • • • • •

... a tractor and tow-chain. Then I remembered the pallets I'd just taken up. Mightn't some of their larger pieces serve as duckboards* for the Land Rover to run on? In a marvellously short space of time Yr (Problem-solving) Correspondent, his self-esteem still pretty much intact – I'd gotten myself stuck but then, after all, I'd gotten myself un-stuck – had a glass in his hand and his feet up in front of his home fire.

The un-farmed grass verges either side of the front drive represented perhaps 3–4 acres of additional grazing for the sheep and, when I'd re-landscaped and widened them, so as to take in strips from the two adjacent fields, substantially more. All that was needed was new perimeter fencing, which I planned to erect myself, and a pair of cattle grids like the Hufftons had: one at the top, Hall, end of the drive and one at the bottom, Front Lodge/main gate end. I telephoned the builder to discuss the job, and as he quickly made clear, installing cattle grids was trickier than I'd reckoned.

The iron grids rest on thick concrete supports, he pointed out, which typically were set across a driveway, right-angled to its line of travel, at the extremities of an excavation perhaps three yards long and 2–2.5 feet deep; from pouring the concrete to when the supports were 'cured' (hardened sufficiently to bear the weight of the grids) would take a minimum of a week... during which time, I understood immediately, the front drive – the only access to the Hall for non-farm vehicular traffic – would have to be closed. An alternative, the builder suggested, would be to make the supports up off-site, transport them to the estate by truck, and then lift them into place using a crane. This option would, obviously, very considerably reduce driveway down-

---

* Boards or some such laid as an overpass across wet or muddy ground.

time but, with transport and crane-hire, etc, expenses, very considerably increase installation costs.

Saying I wanted to give the matter more thought, I said goodbye to the builder and hung up. The grids I proposed to use were very strongly-mounted all around ('able to take the sixty-plus-ton weight of a Chieftain battle-tank' and so used by the MOD, the supplier had assured me); provided their cross-members ultimately wound up where they should be, that's to say 'crossing', I began to wonder.... At that moment the telephone rang; it was the builder calling back to say he saw no reason why the supports shouldn't be set either side of the drive, parallel rather than right-angled to its line of travel. That way the concrete could have as long as was required to cure without interrupting traffic to and from the Hall. Then when everything was ready, the redundant section of driveway between the supports could be excavated and the grids fork-lifted into place. Total driveway downtime, the builder estimated, would probably be of the order of only a few hours. Perfect!

• • • • • • • • • • • • • • • • • • •

Not exactly rocket science. But this anecdote could, I suppose, introduce a case study on the benefits of lateral thinking – literally – for your business school class.

• • • • • • • • • • • • • • • • • • •

'And into every gloomy nook a ray of light shall come,' as surely someone must have writ, I reflected happily/hopefully. For on 2 March, a firm offer on Brambledown only slightly below our reduced 'reduced' original guide-price was received from the Barses. N and I said 'yes' quickly – but not *too* quickly; we didn't want to give (? confirm) the impression we were desperate to sell! – and fridged a bottle of bubbly. Contract exchange was pencilled in for ten days later.

The purchase was, of course, subject to search and survey, and then there were all those other unknowns – 'known' as well as 'unknown' – which could still de-rail it. So although both the EA and Euan thought this offer was for real, N and I discussed between ourselves and then with Euan how the Barses might be discouraged from even thinking about backing out. Euan suggested requiring that their deposit monies be paid directly into our joint, personal bank account rather than, as was usually done, an escrow account. N and I had little problem with Euan's proposal. But, we wondered, would the Barses – Mr (Bawling-barrister) Barse in particular – accept it?

....

There wasn't anything illegal or unethical about such a ploy; it was just unconventional.

Indeed. And talk about 'unconventional': when we were buying Heartsease Hall, you'll recall, the matter of putting down a deposit – never mind what account it was to be paid into – never actually arose!

Sir Roald was a man full of years, experience and wisdom. From very early on – the time of your first viewing, probably – he under-stood that you and your wife were deeply committed to his proper-ty; having received your formal offer to purchase it and then having met with you several times 'man to man' to discuss contingent is-sues, he came to regard you as a gentleman in whom he was content to repose his full trust.

Yes, and what a responsibility....

As an earnest of your intentions, deposit monies were therefore irrelevant.

No, although apparently his lawyers and trustees weren't entirely happy.... Amazing!

In any event: the Barses eventually agreed your proposal.

....

That evening N and I went to supper – or, *much* more correctly, black-tie *dinner* – with Sir Desmond and Lady Platt at their 'Embassy' where, once again, we were the guests of honour. We arrived, relin-quished our overcoats, took on glasses of champagne... and squared up to the inevitable introductions: to Viscount and Viscountess [...] 'your neighbours at [...]'; to Robert, Lord Blake, 'The Conservative Party Historian' (as, indeed, even N and I were aware); to a steely-eyed Scotsman who'd been CEO of a major Middle East oil company, and his Junoesque wife (who we later learned was sometimes privily referred to as 'The Duchess'); to a clean-cut but rather nondescript man represented as lately 'Military Attaché' (a post sometimes used as cover by intelligence-service operatives) at the British Embassy in [...]; to an immense, bejewelled dowager coifed and dressed as if for some Restoration-era ball; to a petite, immaculately-turned-out Quentin Crisp* analog said to move (? mince) in the art world... and two or three others. 'Good Lord!' I undertoned to N, 'what *are* the Henrys doing here?'

....

Hobnobbin' wi' de Gran' Folks... livin' away up high on de hawg!

---

* A New Yorker by adoption Crisp, who died in 1999, referred to himself in his memoirs as the 'stately Homo of England'.

It just shows what a little inheritance and a big house can do for you, Alter-natis.

And all too often does, d'Arcy; and all too often does.

. . . .

Everyone present seemed very welcoming and, given the convivial warmth and freely-flowing drink, after a while I began almost to feel at home. I sipped and chatted and chatted and sipped…. In due course, dinner was announced; taking my arm, Lady Sylvia led me into the dining room – with the by now 'standard' long mahogany table effulgent with crystal and silver – and to my seat at her right.

The first and main courses – gravadlax (dry-cured salmon) with a caper sauce, and breast of roast partridge basted in lemon and thyme with wild rice – were passed very agreeably eating and small-talking; Yr Correspondent began further to relax and enjoy himself. But gradually, as her hostessing responsibilities eased, Lady Sylvia began to morph into her Oxford-don persona, offering analyses of and asking questions about Anglo-American commercial and trade policies and how they complemented, and did not complement, those of the European Union. I lowered my voice and thereby, I hoped, my profile and tried to punch up to my mid-prandial weight. And, I congratulated myself, I was doing so pretty well until, as the table was being cleared for the desert course, there came one of those moments when for no apparent reason all conversation in the dining room suddenly ceased. Into this great quietude my hostess noisily dropped:

'So, d'Arcy, do you think Britain should join the Euro?'

. . . .

Especially in view of all the exposure the Euro and its troubles have recently received, is this section going to interest a non-European audience… specifically, an American one, d'Arcy?

It should, Alter-natis. Taken as a whole, the at-time-of-writing 27-nation European Union – of which 17 are members of the so-called 'Eurozone' – is the world's largest economy, and its geo-political clout can, in some respects, arguably be said to be commensurate in size….

Zzzzzzzzzzzzzzzzzzzzzz.

Building a genuinely sustainable, free-enterprise, democratic international society will require the closest possible high-level and on-going co-operation among all the world's peoples and, fundamental to that entente, will be ditto co-operation between the UK and the United States.

. . . .

In the mid-1990s and periodically for many years thereafter, 'membership of the Euro' was a hotly-debated topic in the UK, equal in moment to – greater even, perhaps, than – the future of the Royal Family or the role of the Established (Anglican) Church. That 2 March 1995 evening, I could almost feel the assembled Lords, Ladies and gentlepersons thinking: now beckons real sport. 'The New Boy' – the apprentice English country squire of the Heartsease Hall Estate – has got to give his opinion on our joining the Euro, right here live on stage at The Embassy... in 'the lioness's den', so to speak. Would he – could he – rise to the challenge? Down the table to my right, Lord-Historian Blake bemusedly elevated an ennobled eyebrow; directly across the table from me, the redoubtable oil-company CEO – who must have pondered this mighty matter often – fixed me with his psyche-piercing gaze.

At which point the Restoration-retro mega-lady – a bit deaf and, perhaps, not yet fully in the loop – turned to the Quentin Crisp analog and asked in a thunderous whisper: 'Who did you say that young man is?' Shielding his mouth with one hand, the diminutive Crispy directed some inaudible reintroduction into the Dowager's elephantine ear.

Elsewhere, the anticipatory silence wore heavily on. I swallowed hard, assembled some thoughts, and plunged in: 'I firmly believe a country must, as John O'Sullivan proposed 150 years ago for the United States, be free to pursue its "manifest destiny" – albeit now in an increasingly globalized context. It follows that I'm very wary of most types of "entangling alliances" – marriage excepted, of course. Ha, ha... ha!' I paused, winked nervously at N, looked around... and understood clearly from the circle of polite but ruthlessly expectant faces that this declaration was OK as far as it went but.... There was no turning back. 'So, Sylvia, I believe the answer is "No"; I don't think Britain should join the Euro. Indeed, for what it may be worth, I think such a course would be an unfortunate anachronism, premature in some ways and, in others, senescent, retrograde... *dépassé* (already overtaken by events).'

. . . .

Wow!

. . . .

Still the general silence prevailed. But it was somewhat relieved now by slow, seemingly-automatous head-noddings as the assembled luminaries considered this Delphic pronouncement from their newly-arrived, recently-loosed and, as a late addition to the playbill, now

friskily free-ranging Yankee-Doodle-dandy. Lord Blake's eyebrow ratcheted up another notch or two; Mr CEO's gaze drilled deeper. And from The Great Dowager came a scatter of supplementary questions to Crispy: 'Are you sure? Americans? At Heartsease Hall… Rolly Festing's old family home?'

. . . .

Had you really any idea…?

Relax, Alter-natis, I hushed. As revealed in Chapter 10, my post-graduate studies had included courses on the development of the European Community and, as a management consultant, I'd researched and/or written at least half-a-dozen reports purporting to weigh up its shorter and longer-term prospects. I was pretty sure I could….

But, I reminded you, a number of your audience had had extend-ed, real-time, hands-on exposure to this issue at the coal face.

. . . .

'Very interesting, d'Arcy,' my hostess mused. 'But how could join-ing the Euro be both premature, that's to say ahead of time, but also *dépassé?*'

'Premature, I think' (I tried to stress the 'I' but, in what's sometimes referred to as 'uptalk'*, the emphasis somehow transferred itself to 'think'), 'because at present the European Union remains just a collection of largely-disparate nation states. Most notably, there's no real EU political union – by which I mean a broad consensus informed and driven by agreed, "popular" EU interests.

'As you know, there's not even a common language. Informally, the EU mostly makes do with Anglo-American English; as regards its formal, "official" proceedings, it's a veritable Tower of Babel! Until true political union is achieved, realization of effective EU "homeland", foreign and defence policies will remain virtually impossible...

'...as also will realisation of effective EU economic policies. In consequence, the Eurozone – assuming it endures – will likely continue to be just a work-in-progress of primarily trade-related codes and legislations within which "core" and "peripheral" member countries – essentially, the Eurozone's "haves" and its "have-nots" or, as some prefer to say, its "prudent" and its "prodigal" – battle to establish and maintain their individual, national interests.

'Again as you know, no over-arching, EU economic authority – no EU Chancellor of the Exchequer equivalent, or Treasury Secretary – with the devolved power generally to levy taxes and issue bonds, exists; there's just a Central Bank whose remit is largely confined to setting interest rates. Until true economic union is achieved – and, within that framework, true fiscal union – the Eurozone simply won't be able to raise the capital necessary to meet member-states' larger-scale investment and/or longer-term economic and financial-support needs.

'In short, the European Union still isn't truly a nation – it's a confederation. And until a quorum of its constituent members summon up the political will to become a nation – in the sense that, say, those of the United Kingdom or the United States have done – the Euro will remain more a currency of intra-Eurozone convenience than of global commercial exchange.'

That's the 'premature' bit done and dusted, I exhaled, rewarding myself with a deep draught from my wine glass and then a second one; now on to the...

'And *dépassé*, I think' (ditto, regrettably, the uptalk irruption), 'for two main reasons: first because the original objective of European unity – the intradiction of further, terrible European wars – seems, mercifully, to have been accomplished...'

---

* A rising, terminal inflection which has the effect of changing a declarative into an interrogative.

Once again, I sought *securitas in vino*... only to discover my glass was empty.

'... and second because, increasingly on this small planet... this earth... individuals, companies, nation-states – nation "unions", even – who really want to get ahead have to think and act globally and, in particular, with a mindful eye to the desiderata of the developing countries of Africa, Latin America, the Middle East and, above all, Austral-Asia. The "Pacific Century", led by China, impends. The Euro – however important it may be to Europe and Europeans – is just an embarkation point for travel along that paramount, worldwide way.'

. . . .

So, Class, how did that seem? Right – Ha, ha! – on the old money, as it were: the Euro as 'just an embarkation point for travel along (the) paramount, worldwide way' towards globalization? BS, chilling out in the back row, what did you think?

I see: you don't know much about globalization... but you've heard it's an American-backed, capitalist-imperialist plot to take over the world. Who'd you get that (deleted) from? Our old buddy Che?

By the way: Che isn't here today. He's not fallen into some bottomless Pit of Eternal Fire and Damnation, has he... maybe? And where's the spangly Ms Goldstar; she's absent too. Yes... third row on the left... you say what? That you saw the two of them a few minutes ago in the cafeteria having breakfast together? Well.... Good for them!

Anyway BS, it *would indeed* be very interesting to discuss 'globalization' and establish what we think we mean by it... perhaps in some future seminar. But right now, here, today? Yes: Ms Gospel....

You thought my reply was tending toward the long-winded and pompous. Well, yes, it could have been... it could have been, I suppose; particularly after a little ingestion – and a little imbibition – I do have a tendency to ramble on. But my question was really an invitation to you to address not so much the style as the substance of my remarks.

Intense-looking young man with glasses and a briefcase overflowing with papers on the floor next to him ... new to the class... could be an aspiring accountant or corporate lawyer, maybe; 'Compliance', we'll nickname you, or 'Comps' for short....

Much time has passed since the evening of 2 March 1995 and the foregoing representation of my purported dinner-table talk, you note and, during that period, many Euro-related socio-economic tendencies which were then inchoate have coalesced and been made clear. What sources did I draw on in developing my above, purported thesis, you ask, and have I properly acknowledged all of them?

Ummm. I drew on a great number of sources, Comps, but I can't recall the names of all of them; that's how it is when you get older. However, the arguments I laid out and the conclusions I reached were based entirely on my own thoughts and analyses... well, almost entirely.

But we're all, of course, deeply indebted to the great minds who've gone before; 'If I have seen further it is by standing on the shoulders of giants,' as Sir Isaac Newton wrote in 1676 to his close friend and rival, Robert Hooke.

. . . .

From around the table came murmurs of what I took to be at least qualified approval; Lord Blake, looking directly at N, actually appeared to mouth: 'Here, here!' And from across the table, the hitherto implacable oil-company CEO seemed now to be nodding agreement slowly. But from The Mother of All Matrons came yet another incredulous interrogative, this time broadcast to the gathering at large: 'Will they be staying at Heartsease Hall long?'

Emboldened, Yr Correspondent continued: 'Then collaterally, there's the Anglo-American "Special Relationship" – an *entente* which in its World War Two and later form, Sir Winston Churchill is generally credited with having forged and named. It reflects Britain's and America's substantial, shared, socio-cultural and political heritage and, today, the ease with which we work together – the *dis-ease* with which we work together, some of you would probably argue – as contrasted with, if I may put it so, the profoundly conflicted relations which frequently obtain between the UK and certain parties in Europe: the French, for example, come readily to mind...

'... and also our two countries' trade links. The preponderance of Britain's goods trade – especially trade in critical SITC (Standard Industrial Trade Classification) 6 and 7 goods: manufactures, and machinery and transport equipment... and, of course, weaponry – is with the United States, making America this country's most important non-EU trading partner by far; in addition, there're our intensive and extensive financial services links, and tourism. Did you know Americans bring some £2–2.5 billion (then about $3–3.75 billion) a year into the UK – roughly one-eighth of the total foreign-visitor spend? Finally, there's our shared pre-eminence in critical industries of the future: biological and/or chemical technology... information technology....'

'And "information" just by itself, assuming stand-alone "gen" (short for 'general, [security-related] information') without its technology platform qualifies as an industry,' the heretofore-silent 'Military Attaché' suddenly interjected; 'plain-old, all-seeing, all-hearing "hum(an-sourced)-int(elligence) gen" is very often our trump card.' I regarded him quizzically. 'You know,' he elaborated enthusiastically: 'collaborations such as the 1946 "ExCMIN Agreement" (for the exchange of classified military information) or, more recently, "The Activity" (established in 1980 following the failed attempt to rescue American hostages in Iran) and increasingly now, "Five Eyes"* stuff: sat(ellite) and sig(nals)-int… that sort of thing. Next after your lot, you know, we're the ones with the best insights,' he concluded. Oh… yes, sir…. Indeed!

Yr Correspondent wound it down: 'The Anglo-American "Special Relationship" is itself, of course, just an embarkation point for travel along the way toward a greater, global unity. But if Britain were to join the Euro, elements of the Special Relationship – and some of the benefits which flow from it to all of us here this evening – would be forfeit. I don't believe such a loss would be in our best personal, national and bi-lateral interests.'

· · · · · · · · · · · · · · · · · · ·

I remember thinking: Whew! You made it… probably.

· · · · · · · · · · · · · · · · · · ·

Even if the audience didn't altogether agree with me, I felt they'd accepted I'd a case and had put it reasonably well. The sweet – a huge steamed pudding laced nearly to extinction with Grand Marnier – arrived; the parliament dissolved once more into a babble of genteel voices. It was left to Her Ladyship The Dowager to sum up: 'Very interesting,' she mused to no one… to everyone… to herself. 'Americans at Heartsease Hall….' She paused, stared balefully at old Crispy, and concluded her catechism: 'Have they *bought* the place, then?'

Later in the week came gale-force winds and, about 0300 one morning, a sense those winds were howling uncommonly close about my empillowed head. I hauled out from under my duvet, grabbed a flashlight, and went to investigate; sure enough, a pane of glass had been sucked out of the deteriorated upper sash in one of our bedroom windows. I closed and barred the window's wooden, interior shutters

---

* The informal name given, we're told, to the intelligence partnership composed of the United States, the United Kingdom, Canada, Australia and New Zealand.

and snuggled back into bed.

It wasn't until a few days later that I got around to replacing the missing glass. And my goodness: what an exercise! As anyone who's washed sash windows knows, so long as both sashes slide fairly freely – the top sash down to the sill; the bottom sash up to the lintel – the outsides of all of the panes can be accessed by reaching out, and up or down, from the inside (except in the case of very tall windows, of course). If either of the sashes doesn't so slide, access to at least some of the panes must be from the outside only.

In the case of our bedroom window, the lower sash slid as if on well-greased rollers. But over the decades (or centuries), the critical, upper sash – from whose top row the pane was gone – had been painted and re-painted shut... nailed shut, effectively. Could it be slid down? By some stronger or more-ingenious Correspondent, perhaps, but not by Yr This One. Reaching through the opening where the pane had been, however – the cold, late-winter wind fairly flaying my face – I was able to clean, prime and bed-putty the glazing bars from the inside... which was all very well and good. But, of course, I couldn't actually insert the new pane of glass from the inside and press it into place, and pin it and weather-seal putty around it; the only way to do that job....

· · · · · · · · · · · · · · · · · · · ·

'How pleasant to sit on the beach, On the beach, on the sand, in the sun,' I rehearsed to myself, grimly.

· · · · · · · · · · · · · · · · · · · ·

So I got our longest ladder and positioned it at maximum extension next to the window; then I climbed up as far as I could... but because the ladder wasn't quite long enough, I still wasn't able easily to reach the work area or, having reached it uneasily, be well balanced. However, grabbing with one hand under the upper sash bar to achieve a degree of stability and groping up and over it with the other, like a basketball player doing a lay-up – but taking care not actually to look up, in case I over-balanced backwards – I managed to insert the new pane, pressing firmly around its edges, trying to bed it in.... Then I climbed back down to get some glazing pins and a tack hammer, climbed back up, established mostly by feel where the pins should go, started them (dropping only a few) then drove them more or less home – all without really being able to see what I was doing – dressed more putty around the pane as the weather-seal and finally – still 'blind' – pressed the putty in and bevelled and smoothed it with my putty knife....

. . . .

'With the ocean galore within reach, And nothing at all to be done!'

. . . .

At last, the repair was finished – provided, of course, there weren't
more high winds before the putty hardened, which might suck the
glass out again. And how did it look? Was it all seemly and neat,
as befitted a window in The Seat of an apprentice English country
squire? I didn't know – the pane itself excepted, hardly any of my
hard-won result was visible from ground-level outside, and not much
more of it was from floor-level inside – and at the time I didn't care.

. . . .

*Those gloriously languorous lines you've inserted are from Ogden
Nash's poem* Pretty Halcyon Days, *in case you couldn't remember,
d'Arcy.*

. . . .

But, of course, life at Heartsease Hall offered manifold compensa-
tions for such trivial trials. The first Sunday in March was one such:
a day with no delivery or work people coming and going, no urgent
'to-do's' requiring my attention – just a few chores like checking on
the sheep – and, because it was a 'closed' Sunday, no service to attend
at the church.

. . . .

'"Remember the Sabbath day, to keep it holy," Mr Henry. "Six days
shalt thou labour, and do all thy work: But the seventh day... thou
shalt not do any work." That's God's Fourth Commandment and
even the workaholic Germans, mindful of the time-out for *seelische
Erhebung* (roughly: 'spiritual uplifting') they've traditionally enjoyed
– now a "right" enshrined in their national Constitution, apparently
– mostly, I'm told, observe it.'
  '... keep the Sabbath holy.' Yes, I like that, Sir Jacob; down deep,
I'm a sort-of closet Sabbatarian. Or at least keep it especial. I find
one completely down-day a week's very refreshing; indeed, I could
probably manage more than one completely down-day if I was
obliged to.
  'But considering more widely and deeply: how do you feel about
big-time, "institutionalized" religion, Mr Henry? You know, all the
bells and whistles... and the ecclesiastical clap-trap? I have to say it's
always bothered me.'
  I like most religious music very much, and I find elements of the

traditional liturgy – even when I don't entirely understand the words – and the occasional sermon very inspiring. And I love the pageantry of church high-day and holiday festivals and services.

From my childhood in Baltimore, I remember a Christmas service at the Church of the Redeemer on North Charles Street when the choir – augmented with soloists from the Peabody Institute (of music); that's part of Johns Hopkins University now – sang sections from Handel's *The Messiah*... and an Easter service there which was introduced by a trio of trumpeters playing Jeremiah Clarke's famous *Voluntary*...

'Clarke was joint Organist at the Chapel Royal in Windsor, and Master of Choristers at St Paul's Cathedral in London you know until, rejected in love, he shot himself in 1707.'

... and I remember being taken by my African-American sometime nanny, Bertha, to a service at the Glory Hallelujah Baptist Church on Pratt Street. It was just an ordinary service, but from the way the congregation behaved you'd have thought it was that 'Great Gettin'-up Mornin' (Resurrection Day). It didn't matter that you couldn't tell exactly what the preacher was preaching about; his delivery, with its driving cadence and resonance, was by itself sufficient to shiver your soul!

And the 'Glory Hallelujah Gospel Choir', as they called themselves: in their surplices – bright blue for the men; bright red for the women – over immaculate, white cassocks above which their radiant faces bobbed and swayed... singing and clapping... and expressing a sense of togetherness... an *ensemble* – a unison-articulation absolute – the source of which, I felt persuaded, must somehow be divine....

'I've not had direct experience of black choirs, Mr Henry; indeed in the whole of my lifetime I only ever saw one black – or "blackamoor" as we called them – and that was in Yarmouth (a major North Sea port about 20 miles east of Norwich) where the poor fellow'd fetched up after a boat trip from the Barbary Coast (the western Mediterranean littoral of North Africa), I seem to recall. But I've been told black people are profoundly musical and have surpassing voices, so I can easily imagine the beauty of their singing.'

From my early 20s, after I'd begun my travels abroad, I've a clear mental image of watching a Holy Week procession of hooded penitents in Sevilla, in Spain, showcasing the awesome majesty and power of Catholicism, and a similar, Advent train winding through the Kremlin citadel in Moscow during which the earthy mysticism of the Eastern Orthodox Church was proclaimed. Sometimes, religious pageantry carries me away...

'But all the posturing and preening you have to put up with? As Thomas Paine wrote in *The Age of Reason*: "The (Christian) church has set up a system of religion very contradictory to the character of the person whose name it bears... (one of) pomp and revenue in pretended imitation of a person whose life was humility and poverty."'

... and I remember visiting the gilded, incensed... but somewhat shabby... and, to me, stifling and claustrophobic Church of the Holy Sepulchre in Jerusalem, which as you probably know is said to have been built on the site of Christ's crucifixion and burial. But to take your question: there are, of course, many religious institutions... religious systems – 'confessions' – other than Christian ones....

'Indeed, but aren't they really, fundamentally, all the same? The philosopher Thomas Hobbes wrote in his *Leviathan* of 1651: "Religion; which by reason of the different fancies, judgments, and passions of several men, hath grown up into ceremonies so different, that those which are used by one man are, for the most part, ridiculous to another." In the end, he decided how one confessed – *whether* one confessed, even – should be entirely a personal matter.'

So it may indeed be as the 17th-century French mathematician and philosopher Blaise Pascal concluded in his *Pensées* No. 184: 'We shall die alone.'

'I've long felt that old proverb – thought to be of Anglo-Saxon origin – about not throwing out the baby with the bath water sums up our dilemma pretty well, Mr Henry: we must continue to seek, as an "end", our private spirituality however much various of the public "means" of so doing may seem to conspire against us.'
. . . .

... no service to attend at the church. N and I spent the morning of it in the oval room reading and listening to a live BBC radio broadcast from Westminster Abbey commemorating the 300th anniversary of the funeral of Queen Mary II and featuring the *Ode*, with its exquisitely-afflicted 'Thou Knowest, Lord' anthem, Henry Purcell wrote especially for it. (As my Aunt Gertie, who towards the end of her life lost her eyesight, was fond of saying: 'If you have to go blind, England's a good country to do it in; there's always something worth listening to on the BBC.' Amen.)

And in the afternoon, we sat in the open-fronted 'gazebo' (a recreational building, usually small, sited to command a view) on the south lawn. Below us – parading across Preston's Pride and Pavilion Paddock, paddling around the lower lake or preening on the lake's reedy banks – was the most wonderfully cosmopolitan (? 'global') mix of wildfowl including: an assortment of UK-native gadwall, mallard, pintail, pochard, shoveler and teal ducks, some shelducks (*Tadorna tadorna*) of Eurasian descent, a gaggle of graylags (ancestors of the 'barnyard' goose) also originally Eurasian, two pairs of Egyptian and a flock of Canadian geese, a trio of so-called 'mute' swan (*Cygnus olor*) which, as juveniles, peep and, as adults, snort and hiss (two of the swan were 'cobs' [males], who battled at intervals to establish and/or hold their nesting turf), a brace of oyster-catchers (*Haematopus ostralegus*), a moorhen or two and a few coots... 10–12 red-legged, French partridges (the native, English partridge has grey legs) and the inevitable pheasants virtually all of which, of course, derive from Southeast Asian stock.

Closer by – *too* close, sometimes – Bapu and Bouff frolicked: throwing and fetching, chasing and catching, exerting and resting.... And throughout, the blessed early-spring sun shone down, penetrating deep into our bodies, our minds... our very innermost souls... and keeping us in ways at once both physical and spiritual, warm and well.

(What a difference a few hours make! Some weeks earlier, N and I'd invited Mr and Mrs Gullet, our tenants in Front Lodge, to come up for a get-better-acquainted drink and, that Sunday evening, up they came. Mr Gullet – Tom – was stocky and open-featured, with ginger hair drawn back into a pigtail, and dressed in a white polo-neck shirt, casual black jacket and trousers, and patent-leather black shoes. He was a professional musician, it transpired, who played both the piano and the organ as well as arranged and composed, and also had his own band; I felt sure he and I'd get on very well. Mrs Gullet – Magda: shortish and stout, with dark, bobbed hair framing a southeastern-European, Romany [Gypsy] sort of face – was, doubtless, also very amiable. But she seemed somewhat tense... the 'grand' surroundings to which she [like the rest of us...] wasn't much accustomed, in combination with the penetrating cold, perhaps. For with the sun long down, the outdoor temperature was at or below freezing and, in the drawing room, where we sat with just one small radiator and the hearth fire to dispel the deep-in-the-walls winter chill, it felt only a few degrees warmer.)

Several days later, the Festings – just back from *langlaufing* (cross-country skiing) in Austria – were back in Dovecote Cottage, so I had the pleasure of my customary, early-morning, 'interrogation' by Sir Roald, who was refreshed and raring to go...

... or, rather, to stay. Indeed, he vouchedsafe he and Lady Maureen were on the verge of offering for a property in Aldeburgh* – 'A house of about the right size, with nice gardens, and far enough away from

---

* A North Sea coastal town 40 or so miles southeast of Norwich which is the venue of a renowned summer music festival.

here... but not too far away; in due course, I expect you'll understand what I mean,' Sir Roald detailed elliptically – but that it required some renovation. So, he asked, *pro tem* might they continue to rent Dovecote Cottage until the building work was done? Of course; what could be better, I replied.

· · · · · · · · · · · · · · · · · · ·

Not what you'd call 'typical' after-sale intercoursings between the vendor of a property and its purchaser, d'Arcy.

No, Alter-natis. The English 13th Baronet and his wife, and the upstart Americans, living and having their individual and communal beings cheek by jowl with each other...

The first two looking on in dismay...

... and, probably, biting their lips to keep from crying out...

... while the latter earnestly 'improved' – that's to say selectively laid waste – parts of what they once held dear.

On the other hand, as Sir Roald regularly remarked, we did all get along very well and have great fun together.

And, of course, Lady Maureen was handy to help look after the donkeys!

· · · · · · · · · · · · · · · · · · ·

On 12 March, Groome's wretched mobile home was finally stabilized structurally, loaded onto a flat-bed truck and transported away. Watching with me as it disappeared down the drive was Sir Roald, who commented once again what a fine man Groome was, how very helpful he'd been during what Sir Roald had taken to calling 'Our Inter-Regnum' – the changeover in the management of the Heartsease Hall Estate from him to me – and how very much he'd like to be a fly on the wall while Groome settled into his new, 'grown-up' home with its property taxes, utility bills, 'mod cons'... and ubiquitous, noisy, nosey, tidy-house-proud neighbours!

The next day (a *Monday* the 13th, not a Friday, I noted thankfully), Brambledown was to be surveyed. N and I couldn't imagine the Barses would find much to complain about – some chipped plaster and peeling paint, maybe – after all, we'd lived there healthily and happily for the better part of twenty years. But little things often weigh big, we reminded ourselves. Our prospective purchasers might ignore the fact that the house was built like a fortress and fairly recently re-roofed, re-plumbed and re-wired, and pick up on the inconsequential. All our digits and even limbs were, therefore, figuratively firmly crossed.

Chapter 13

Dwelling & Boo Hoo

N and I found our first mid-March through early-April in north Norfolk – even present the manifold delights of the Heartsease Hall Estate – a depressing time of year.

We attributed our 'down' in part to the UK macro-climate which, in spite of the moderating effects of the Gulf Stream, approximates in hours of darkness, degrees of dankness and general overhang of winter drear to that of its seaboard latitude-mates at 50–60° North: Labrador or British Columbia, for example*, and in part to what's known locally as the north Norfolk coastal micro-climate, one aspect of which is that relative to parts of the UK like the West Country or the Cotswolds, the seasons tend to arrive late. Warm, dry, summer-like weather may prevail well into calendar autumn; on the other hand – and as we were as above discovering – cold, wet, winter-like weather may last well into calendar spring.

However, in the bold words of Herodotus as freely translated by the architect William Kendall (and inscribed, among other places, on the US Post Office Building in New York City which he designed) and customised by Yr Correspondent: 'Neither snow nor rain nor heat nor gloom of night stays (the apprentice English country squire) from the swift completion of (his) appointed rounds.' Or more acutely: whatever the weather, the squire must continue to generate the funds necessary to restore his estate and/or maintain it in good living and working order, as well as pay a few other bills; see that those restorations, etc, are properly carried out, or try properly to carry them out himself; and from time to time make the fruits of his labours available for the delectation of third parties, that's to say wider-family members, friends, and representatives of the specific-interest or general public.

Our hopes for money to restore the Hall and its outbuildings from

---

* If the UK were an 'inland' rather than an island at that latittude, its macro-climate would be much more severe, approximating to that of Alberta, Saskatchewan or south-central Siberia.

UK sources having come to nothing, N and I decided to explore the possibility of funding from The Motherland. N made a number of telephone calls, set up a few meetings, and considered the advice of various friends that fund-raising in the US – particularly raising the quantity of funds we were after – wasn't so much a matter of representing need as building a bandwagon, that's to say it required promotional materials, a presentation of some sort and, if possible, the endorsement of 'names and celebrities'. Armed with none of the above but with the expectation of spring in her step, on 15 March my intrepid Uxor set out for San Francisco by way of New York, Boston, Chicago, Houston and Los Angeles.

From my card-table desk in the estate office/library, I continued the search for UK monies to restore the estate's grounds, that's to say I progressed my grant-aid application to the Countryside Commission. In near-final draft, this document ran to twenty-seven, 1.5 line-spaced text pages – nearly 10,000 words – plus fifteen appendix pages of detailed diagrams, costings and maps, each and every one of which, I reflected contentedly, was of a quality FHA would be proud to present and its prospective clients honoured (well... maybe) to receive. Assuming old SCO gave it the fine-tuning he'd promised – and, of course, the support he'd promised – I felt confident we could get started TSI-ing the parkland and the lakes more or less right away.

Which was just as well. For concomitant with these happy thoughts – but also heavy sleet-and-snow showers – arrived in the stableyard the seed I'd ordered for the to-be-reinstated Preston's Pride parkland, and the south lawn extension. In all, a dozen bulky hessian bags – eleven Countryside Stewardship Parkland Mixture and one Luxury Lawn, with a total weight coming on for a quarter of a ton – were unloaded into the depths of the carriage house tack room. Good Lord, I thought: remember, back in Baltimore, when father used to bring home lawn-grass seed in a little brown-paper bag?

(I glanced at the invoice and swallowed hard. Grass seed wasn't like other seeds of which I'd had experience, I confirmed: flower and vegetable seeds for the gardens at Brambledown, say. It was very, very expensive. Fortunately, seedsmen in the UK – like most suppliers to the UK landowning and farming trades – typically offer fairly generous payment terms.)

With sufficient restoration funding in prospect – or so I thought – and some of the restoration work itself all-but underway, it remained only for the various third parties to turn up or apply to turn up. And so they did. Almost immediately the seedsman's truck had departed, I took a telephone call from a Brigadier [...] on behalf of the Royal British Legion (an association for British and Commonwealth military ex-servicemen) asking if their local chapter might celebrate the fiftieth anniversary of 'VE' (World War II 'Victory in Europe') Day on 8 May with a bonfire in one of our fallow fields.

Quite a 'do' was planned, the Brigadier told me. Perhaps 700–800 people could be expected to attend, implying maybe 250 or so cars, and there'd be a professionally-catered barbecue and bar, singing, dancing, fireworks... and, of course, The Bonfire: one of thousands to be lit across Europe – apparently even in Germany and Italy, the principal, defeated Axis Powers – and recorded for posterity not just by us and other ground-based archivists but, clear skies permitting, spy-in-the-sky TV. Wow!

· ·

Did you feel the upstart-American W. d'Arcy Henrys were ready for this?

Do you mean personally or as *de facto* representatives of The Motherland?

Both.

The United States, of course, eventually played a critical role in the WWII European theatre and, because of its close proximity to that theater, a number of American servicemen were, in fact, based in and around north Norfolk. Heartsease Hall itself was, you'll recall, the administrative headquarters of the Norfolk Auxiliary Unit, which was part of what became known as 'Churchill's Secret Army'.

But it was the Russians who bore the brunt of the Allied fighting in Eastern Europe and, in Western Europe, it was the Free French and especially the British who did so, in the process expending the lion's share of their materiel and – much more than that – sacrificing the flower of their man and womanhood: the frontline and support troops who in the reworked and reapplied, fine, epitaphic words of the poet John Maxwell Edmonds 'for (our) tomorrow... gave (their) today'.

I see: as an American, you wondered if it was seemly that you host this celebration. How about just as yourself?

I was prepared to do it, if I had to; I felt it could be part of my 'coming-out', so to speak, as an English country squire. But such a prominent role so early in our residence here.... I wasn't sure how N and I should deport ourselves.

You could be high-profile and ambassadorial, I suggested, mingling with those who attended – most of whom, of course, wouldn't know you from Adam, or Eve – and 'graciously welcoming' them to

a function to which you were largely ancillary....
That wasn't what I had in mind, Alter-natis.
Or you could be low-profile – subterranean, almost – and aco-lytic, not even showing yourself until well after dark.
Yes; that seemed more like it.
. . . .

I took a deep breath... and told the Brigadier N and I'd be honoured to host the VE-Day celebration. 'Splendid Chap!' my interlocutor boomed by way, I took it, of concurrence and, without further ado, he advised he'd stop by to carry out a 'recce' (British soldier-speak for 'reconnaissance') of the proposed 'Operations Zone' in a day or two. (When the Brigadier arrived, I showed him to an 8–9 acre field about 200 yards northeast of the Hall which from the standpoint of crowd, bonfire and pyrotechnics control he pronounced 'entirely satisfactory'. But he was concerned about the site's distance from the designated parking area – 'It's a very long walk for the elderly or disabled,' he noted. – and he said our two, small, plumbed-in public toilets would have to be supplemented *pro tem* with a quantity of rented, chemical ones*.)

Meanwhile, I continued gradually to grope my way up and out the apprentice-squire learning curve:
1. I wrote to the SCO confirming I intended to seed the to-be-re-emparked fields in accordance with the Countryside Commission's specifications, using its Countryside Stewardship Parkland Mixture at a rate of about 20 pounds per acre. (I concluded my letter by noting that as spring was presumably 'just around the corner', the favour of a formal go-ahead from the CC for that seeding – not to mention an eventual contribution towards the cost of it – would be greatly ap-preciated.)
2. Having received letters from two men requesting permission to fish in our lakes, I... ducked the issue because I couldn't decide what to do. I felt sure my petitioners would respect the ambient environ-ment – our ambient environment... our Conservation Area – and so it seemed churlish to deny them their sport. But inevitably, their pres-ence – particularly during the breeding season – would disturb the wildlife I so much wanted to have stick around and multiply. And as Warrener – ever solicitous of his game birds' weal – pointed out,

---

* Among the firms then specializing in such services, it transpired, were 'Spot-a-Pot' and 'Portaloo'.

anglers in the UK are a very close-knit fraternity. He felt sure the two fishermen who'd written to me would have fishing friends and, in turn, their fishing friends would have fishing friends... all of whom, in due course, might seek to thrash our waters. Where would I draw the line, Warrener asked anxiously? Indeed. I paper-clipped the two letters together... and filed them in my 'pending' tray.

· · · · · · · · · · · · · · · · · · ·

Sometimes, the right decision is to not take one, Alter-natis.

Yes, d'Arcy. Most times, of course, it's a cover for plain old pro-crastination.

· · · · · · · · · · · · · · · · · · ·

3. I got Bottom Cottage ready for new tenants, re-fixing and re-fitting the various items the Xs had removed and redecorating throughout. In the process I discovered, under a section of old linoleum flooring, un-opened electricity bills to a total of some £350 (then just over $500). It was almost certainly more trouble than it was worth to try to catch up with the Xs and make them pay – these bills, and the cost of repairing the damage they'd done – but, I vowed, if I ever *did* catch up with them....

4. I met with the Chairman of [a prominent, British nature-conservancy group] – we'll call him Mr NCG – who'd heard from Joscelyn about our sewage-sludge lagoons problem. Physically, Mr NCG was an unprepossessing man – medium height, medium build... pleasant, unassuming, medium-manner – but he'd eyes like searchlights and a disconcertingly-intense gaze which seemed almost intrusively to register and study, like some omnibus anatomist, everything that came within his purview.

As well, he was very workman-like and efficient. Before he'd even gotten out of his car, Mr NCG informed me he'd already inspected the site proposed for the sludge lagoons and concluded that putting them there would be 'an absolute disaster for the local environment'; as we were walking up the front porch steps, he asked if I'd assembled any materials arguing against the sludge lagoons which he could have to adapt for his own use. I said yes and, leaving him standing in the entrance hall, retrieved same from my files and handed them to him.... And that was that. Mr NCG having, apparently, no further concerns specific to his self-appointed task, the business of our meeting was accomplished in roughly 3–4 minutes.

So we repaired to the drawing room for coffee and a talk about painting and pictures. Mr NCG, it was revealed, was a semi-professional artist – a 'figurative expressionist', he called himself which, we easily agreed, was a particularly challenging school – who'd exhibited nationally and been critically acclaimed. Eventually, I asked him what he thought of the pictures we'd brought from Brambledown. Mr NCG said he very much liked them... and then added diplomatically that, in his opinion, the general absence of furniture in the drawing room 'clarified' their hanging.

5. Thus inspired – and by way of welcome-home for my little Uxor – I repainted the drawing room. On the basis of the manufacturer's sample card, 'primula' yellow seemed a nice, bright colour but not too chromatic or cloying and one which, I thought, should background our pictures well. I did a test panel, which established that primula was far too lemony and cold, so I tried 'candlelight'... which proved to be practically indistinguishable from the existing, soot-and-grime-darkened, curdled-cream-white of the dado and wall moldings. Clearly, I told myself, there's more to colour selection than meets the lay eye. (I could almost hear N reminding me of her advice that we call in a professional interior designer.) In the end I mixed my own 'perfect' colour which, as even N now agrees, has stood the test of time very well.

6. Warrener having provided a brace of them which I plucked, drew and cut up, and N having put them in the deep freeze as a 'Hubby Meal, ready-to-cook' for me while she was away, I dined on flash-fried breast of moorhen. This delicacy (see Ch. 12 for the recipe) – which, when eventually she was persuaded to try it, N dubbed breast of 'mud hen' – is, I have to admit, probably an acquired taste: somewhere between wood pigeon and barnyard goose... with, indeed, just a hint of good, fermented, lake-bottom mud. But given a hearty appetite, and alongside generous helpings of thick-cut, 'game' potato chips and steamed, farm-fresh vegetables... and washed down with a glass or two of rich claret, it wasn't too bad at all.

. . . .

As the French satirist François Rabelais observed in Book One *of his* 1534 Gargantua: *'Appetite grows by eating.'*

He'd certainly have so observed in this age of endemic, developed-world obesity, Alter-natis, because... for the vast majority of over-weight people that's the main problem, isn't it! If only our poor, benighted fatties would find the self-discipline to take more exercise and, one way or another, compensate-eat less.

Perhaps the purveyors of calorie-dense fast foods could put more breast of moorhen on their menus.

. . . .

7. I rejoiced in Bouff. Lively, intelligent and good-natured, Bouff was proving to be an ideal general-purpose dog and also an ideal playmate for Bapu. Indeed, being in 'dog years' more or less the same age and having many interests in common, the two were nearly inseparable. They took long walks together 'exploring', from which excursions both invariably returned hungry and tired.

Indeed, such were Bouff's charms that even the scholarly, reserved Piglet was drawn in. One day, I found the last-named down on his knees talking nose-to-nose with Bouff, all the while looking deep into the dog's eyes and gently stroking with his fingertips up the dog's brow to the crown of his head. (Our fine, increasingly-self-aware young man seemed slightly embarrassed to be so discovered!) Bouff, ears cocked, sat mindfully to attention and wagged his tail enthusiastically. But how much of Plato's retailed philosophy or Euclid's ditto geometry or Newton's ditto physics – or his adolescent confidant's fervent hopes and fears, maybe – the dog was taking in wasn't clear.

(My main concern about Bouff was his suitability as a guard dog. Sometimes he growled at just about anything that moved [he so terrified two sweet, old, Jehovah's Witness ladies they wouldn't get out of their car] and sometimes he lavished – or attempted to lavish – great, salivary kisses on just about anything that stood still [a suspicious-looking trespasser, for example, who'd 'got (him)self lost' just outside the door to our farm-machinery repair shop wherein were kept all manner of expensive tools]. In short, his 'friend or foe' recognition algorithm needed sharpening up.)

On the first day of calendar spring, with its import of regeneration and re-growth – the weather remained relentlessly wintry, however – N returned from San Francisco and points east with confirmation that neither was charity from The Motherland going to put back Hearts-ease Hall's delaminating flints. I'd thought that by playing the 'Special Relationship' card, and/or the 'Great Migration' card, and/or the 'preserving for future generations an example of the world's "great" architecture' card, even, perhaps we'd have managed to scrounge a little something. (And we probably could have done that: some 'nickels and dimes'.) But old-money American Anglophiles, etc, had already been pretty well dunned, N reported, by the likes of Oxford and Cambridge Universities, Westminster Abbey, St Paul's Cathedral... Windsor Castle, even (in November 1992, it had been badly damaged by fire and needed costly restoration).

· · · · · · · · · · · · · · · · · · ·

No-one would suggest those institutions weren't deserving, Alter-natis. But relatively speaking, they were already pretty flush.

The principle to which you're alluding applies, as well, with individuals, d'Arcy. The very able, diligent and lucky excepted – and the very unscrupulous – it takes money to make money. That's why, as Gus Khan and Raymond Egan wrote in Ain't We Got Fun: *'There's nothing surer, The rich get rich(er) and the poor get... children.'*

So what on earth are the poor supposed to do?

Apply that famous mock-formula for success apparently coined by the oil tycoon and financier J. Paul Getty: 'Rise early, work hard... strike oil.'

No, seriously, Alter-natis....

Another billionaire oil-man, John D. Rockefeller, described his ability to make money as a gift from God and declared that that gift must ultimately be 'developed and used... for the good of mankind'. In short, he argued that those of us who can must help the poor help themselves by providing better health, educational and welfare facilities for them.

And if certain elements of the poor are ultimately revealed as unwilling or unable to help themselves because they don't and/or won't make good use of the support we offer?

In the run up to 'ultimately', however, Rockefeller was a Darwinist. He saw business success as 'survival of the fittest' and success in life generally – or in an aggregate of lives: a community or a nation – as 'evolution by natural selection'.

So tell me: in a free-enterprise democracy like The Motherland's – one teeming with politicians catering to and voters gorging on their particular, special 'entitlements' – how's 'natural selection' going to play out?

Over the longer-term, badly, probably – even if, in the shorter term, some right-minded 'redeemer' may be able to pull us back from the brink. The rot in the US' social fabric, and in that of the First World generally, appears to be too well established.

That's a pretty dire forecast!

In the words often attributed to the 18th/19th-century Scots historian and lawyer Alexander Tytler, aka Lord Woodhouselee (but not, Fred Shapiro op cit *tells us, actually found in his writings): 'A free-enterprise democracy will continue to exist until the electorate discover they can vote themselves generous gifts from the public treasury.*

'From that moment on, the majority will always vote for the candidates who promise (them) the most benefits... with the result that free-enterprise democracy will collapse.'

· · · · · · · · · · · · · · · · · · ·

And *new-money* American 'Anglophiles', etc, hardly existed, apparently. Regularly, N was told that The Motherland's recently-minted mega-rich were mostly of Asian and/or continental European extraction, and looked first to support worthy causes either in their country of origin or their host country, or in the developing world. As one informant summed it up: 'Most high-end potential donors simply don't have the UK programmed in.'

I spent the morning of 27 March tidying up the estate's books in preparation for the end of the 1994–95 UK accounting year*. My general unfamiliarity with farming-accounts procedures, however, in combination with specific issues raised by the handover to me from Sir Roald, made this year's annual chore a particularly onerous one. So as a self-indulgence, I took the afternoon off and 'checked the fences': the landowner's equivalent, I remembered my old Cotswolds farmer-friend David T saying, of playing golf or fly fishing. The weather was lovely and warm and sunny, so before returning to the Hall I stood for a few moments with my back against a big beech tree, looking southwest across the fat of the estate and admiring the view. It was beautiful; absolutely, breathtakingly....

. . . .

Ecce scutarius, *I said. That's:* 'Behold the shield-bearer'; *the Latin for shield-bearer is* 'scutarius' *which in old French became* 'le scuier' *which in old English became....*

And I said: Hello, Sir Jacob! How....

It's not Sir Jacob, I exclaimed! It's me: your beloved Alter-natis.

I apologized for my mistake, but observed that your interjection was just the sort of etymological recitation Sir Jacob might have given – 'He's very erudite,' I noted, 'or certainly wants us to think he is.' – adding that you and he were both lodged together up there in my mind somewhere... I thought.

So by then, you were en route *to becoming an English country* 'le-squire'. *Drop the* 'l'....

Well, I by then had some of the physical appurtenances of an English country squire.

If you mean the rubicund face, the corpulence, the general untidiness about your person – like Squire Weston in Henry Fielding's 1749 Tom Jones... *that sort of thing – you'd had those physical appurtenances for quite some time, d'Arcy.*

Smart-ass! I meant I had the land, the house, the chattels....

'The Seat' as, I see from Chapter 12, you've taken to calling it.

---

* Almost any date may be agreed with the British tax authorities; the default date used by most payers, however, is 5 April.

But being a country squire's about much more than those collateral things.

It is? Good Lord: what else could you possibly have needed?

I needed the squire's particular aptitudes and abilities – his huntin', shootin' 'n' fishin' skills, especially – and his down-to-earth – clay-footed, even – mind set, so I could walk the squire's walk and talk the squire's talk.

I had visions of your old school and college chums, your dear, prematurely-departed friends Robin and Johnny, your late mother and father... Sir Roald and Lady Maureen... holding their sides and falling about positively unhinged with glee: W. d'Arcy Henry – 'little Dar', the buzz-cut, be-spectacled, all-American, Baltimore, Maryland boy... 'The Professor' as he used teasingly to be called – with his wide-eyed, all a-twit-twitter, California wife... a walking, talking, apprentice English country squire!

All right, now, Alter-natis, that's....

But seriously: how did you expect to acquire those esquirely aptitudes and abilities, and behavioral impedimenta?

Partly by precept... desk research... and partly by example, that's to say by seeking out exemplar squires and observing how they acted – disported themselves, very often literally – in the field.

'Exemplar squires'?

Role models like Antony Huffton, or Chaser Jermyn, or Joscelyn Steele or, more cerebrally, Sir Roald; you're spoilt for choice of them in north Norfolk. Then, over time, I'd build up a personalized, Identikit-like master-model of a country squire....

Did you really think you could do that? English country squires are renowned for their idiosyncrasy; given the truly vast range of their particular peculiarities, I'd be surprised if you could find an Identikit with enough pieces. And to derive your personal master-model from it, you'd then have to sort through all the pieces and decide which of the peculiarities best suited you....

I knew that. But 'where there's a will....' So, I reckoned, if the Barses would just hurry up and buy Brambledown, that's to say get out of my way and let me get on with it....

· · · · · · · · · · · · · · · · · · · ·

The very next day, however, it was revealed that the Barses had opted not so much to get out of my way as to get more in it, which they did via a letter – addressed to the estate agent, predictably, and faxed through from him to N and me – beginning 'it is with the very greatest of (*sic*) regret', continuing on to qualify that regret, *viz* 'because Brambledown is so charming and so beautiful... so exactly what we're looking for', and concluding: 'we therefore do *not* intend to proceed with our purchase of the property owing to the very considerable cost of essential repairs'. My first take was that these (deleted) should be frog-marched away for a long walk off a short pier.

· · · · · · · · · · · · · · · · · · · ·

Brambledown needed no 'essential repairs', Alter-natis. Desirable repairs, certainly, but not essential ones...

... and saying they found Brambledown 'so charming and so beautiful... so exactly what (they were) looking for...'

... and – unless they were outright frauds – of sufficient means to offer for the property in the first place, being put off by the cost of a little redecorating?

A better deal: that's what they were looking for, the B-arses. Something more off your 'reduced-reduced' asking price.

Well, (deleted) them! (Deleted) the bloody B-arses!

Gently, gently, My Friend; remember that (adapted) old proverb: 'the (prospective) customer is always right'.

It's a relatively-young proverb, Alter-natis; the first known use of it was apparently by Cesar Ritz – the eponymous Swiss hotelier – in 1908. And Ritz' exact words were said to have been: '*Le client n'a jamais tort,*' which translates as 'the customer is never wrong'. Being 'never wrong' is very different from being 'always right'.

· · · · · · · · · · · · · · · · · · · ·

My second take was: thank goodness for middle-men or women, that's to say agents and, specifically, their timely institution between you and your disobliging counter-party. For if at that moment a B-arse – in particular, an over-dressed, over-stuffed, orotund and bawling barrister B-arse – had come within earshot of my cursing, or sight of my up-thrusting middle finger, or reach of my would-be throttling grasp....

A telephone call from the EA followed almost immediately. As by then N and I'd ourselves concluded, the B-arses' about-face wasn't so definitive as their letter had made it appear, he said; all they were really seeking was 'recognition' of what they'd have to put into Brambledown 'to make it livable'. As civilly as I could, I replied that Brambledown was an exquisite property overall and in first-class general-structural and service order; that I and my family had found it eminently livable for the better part of twenty years, etc; in any event, I concluded, the B-arses' notion of 'livability' was no concern of mine. After authorizing – nay, urging – pretty much a verbatim transmission of that message to the B-arses, I hung up...

... and stormed out to the woodshed. 'Waack!' I struck with the splitting axe into a length of oak limb similar to one of those I'd cut

a couple of months earlier. There's one for you, Mr B-arse, I muttered through clenched teeth. Two nice semi-cylinders fell open on the floor. I set the two semi-cylinders up on end.... 'Waack!' on the first one.... And there's one for you, Mrs B-arse. Two nice quarter-cylinder fire-logs fell open.... 'Waack!' on the second semi-cylinder.... And there's one for all of the prospective purchasers – all of the prospective *counter-parties* anywhere in the world, why not – who've ever told N or me – or, for that matter, anyone else – they were going to do something and then gone back on their word.

· ·

This sustainable, free-enterprise democracy you're so enamoured of... which, you believe, underpins so much of The Motherland's and the world's economic progress, and so much of the improvement in peoples' standards of living...

... ultimately, after all the to-ing and fro-ing, the positioning and re-positioning, the confronting and conciliating... sustainable, free-enterprise democracy is founded on and derives much of its dynamic from trust. I believe serial, major, pre-meditated betrayals of that trust should be prosecuted as a form of treason and sentenced as a capital crime!

· ·

At that moment, N arrived in the woodshed; she said the EA'd just telephoned again, this time because he'd learned 'only a couple of "Ks" (thousand pounds)' now stood between what the B-arses were prepared to give for Brambledown and what we were prepared to take. Surely, N cajoled, in view of all the time and effort expended to reach this point, the logistical considerations, the financial considerations... FHA's research-direction needs, the estate's general-management needs... the myriad other, more-important family and wider life needs.... She paused and jabbed her index finger at me before continuing: '*your own personal-development needs, Dar, if you're really going to progress from apprentice to "journeyman"* (fully-qualified or entitled) *English Country Squire....*' Surely, I should accept just one more little concession?

. . . .

So, Class: 'bargaining' or, somewhat more formally, 'negotiation'. What's the single, over-arching aim of this time-honoured pursuit? Yes, BS. You say you'd like to be excused to make a telephone call? Now, in the middle of our seminar? Why? Ummmm. You'd rather not tell me, but 'it's very important', you say.

Give me some indication of how you're defining 'important'. Is it important as in: 'If I don't contact him now, he may think I don't want the job'? Or is it important as in: 'If I don't contact *her* now, she may think I don't love her'?

More the second than the first, you say. Hummm. Well, that *is* very important. Have you and your girlfriend had a row? Who's the guilty party... who's the one to blame? She did what? My goodness! Why? Oh, I see: because – Don't cry, Big Fella; it's OK. – because you.... So you accept you could be partly to blame, huh. What're you going to tell her, then: 'I'm sorry'? Yep; anything else? That you 'love her very much'. Well, that's pretty up-front... pretty positive.... But Good Lord, Man, after what you say she did – but then, of course, after what you say *you* did – have you, or she, no pride?

All right then; off you go. But make it quick. And tell her how much you're giving up – how much you're *sacrificing* – in taking time out from our very interesting and informative discussion to make your call.

To resume then, ladies and gentlemen: the single, over-arching aim of negotiation? Yes, GT.... Indeed: to achieve your goal... that's to say, to win. Ego may *drive* negotiation but, in the end, negotiation's not about getting even... not about 'saving face'... it's about winning. 'Blessed are the *meek*,' as St Matthew is said to have written. And what did they win? What did 'the meek' win? Yes... Ms Gospel. You're absolutely right: in the end... mostly, we hope... they won 'the earth'.

Give me an example, Class, from your recent experience – something you've been a party to or observed – of a 'winning' negotiation. Yes, Comps, our prospective lawyer/accountant, maybe....

Sure: BS, now out talking to his girlfriend. He negotiated with me to get permission to make his telephone call; it didn't deter him that, to do so, he had to reveal in public some private things – admit the error of his ways, even – and submit himself to the judgment of you and me, his peers. And he won. He got my permission and as well, I sense, the sympathy – the support even, perhaps – of at least some of you. Now almost certainly, he's negotiating again, this time with his girlfriend. How do you think he's going to do? Is she going to forgive him? Take him back?

Well there's no need to speculate: here's Mr Negotiator himself, returned from 'The Table'. We can get it straight from the stallion's mouth, as it were – uhhhh... that's if the 'stallion' weren't, at the moment, looking more like a weanling colt. How'd it go, Boss Man; everything all right? Oh; she hung up on you. That's too bad. But in love as in life, you've got to be persistent. Remember those immortal words of the 19th-century American writer Thomas Palmer: 'If at first you don't succeed, Try, try again.' Ummmm. You say you called her back... and she hung up again.

. . . .

... just one more little concession? I told N I'd think about what she'd said. Then I went back to the woodshed, got another length of oak limb, set it on its end, swung the splitting axe.... 'Waack!' A half-hour or so later – sweated up but cooled down – I agreed N should telephone the EA and say we were prepared – 'err... better make that "delighted", I suppose, N' – to meet the B-arses half way.

About mid-morning the next day – just as I was hitting peak FHA work flow – my Heartsease Hall apprenticeship unexpectedly resumed with a telephone call from Mrs Gullet at Front Lodge who wanted to know if I was 'happy' with her and her husband as tenants. She put the question one way... she put it another... without, in her relentless disquisition, giving me the chance to offer my reply. Then, for good measure, she put it yet another way....

I tried to get a whiff of her breath – not an easy thing to do through a network of routers, switches and transmission lines, etc – but then, as she droned on, her real agenda became clear: had I in mind to increase the rent for Front Lodge and, if so, by how much? The new UK Rent Act, she advised (or ill-advised; I hadn't until then been aware of the statute) gave landlords the right to impose 'phenomenal' increases, she said, which she and her husband 'just wouldn't be able to afford'.

Eventually, I was given leave to reply that periodically, yes, their rent would probably have to be 'reviewed' – the British circumlocution for 'increased' – but that it would never be my intent to impose 'phenomenal' increases and certainly not, I crooned, on 'such good tenants'. These reasonably-comfortable words, however, weren't enough. On and on Mrs Gullet went, seeking an absolute assurance I couldn't give, so on and on *I* went, offering a conditional assurance she wouldn't accept. Phew!

(Some while later, I learned via 'back channels' [one of the farm men] that at the time of our conversation Mrs Gullet and/or her husband was the owner of a holiday cottage on the north Norfolk coast which was rented out, and that income used to cover some or all of the rent paid to me. Knowing in advance how much I intended to charge them made it easier to work out how much they should charge their tenants, that's to say balance their books.)

The following day, Kenny and Brian grass-seeded Preston's Pride and the south lawn extension. For Yr Correspondent, still trying desperately to up-scale from previous incarnations, it was a bemusing sight: two top-of-the-line tractors – each with a nominal power output equivalent to nearly 400 horses, and trailing twelve-foot-wide drills loaded with Countryside Stewardship Parkland Mixture (one in due course to be re-loaded with Luxury Lawn) – industriously quartering the ground like a pair of monstrous, four-wheeled hounds scenting for foxes.

. . . .

Pro forma, it'd be nice to have had confirmation from old SCO that my Countryside Commission grant was going to come through, I reflected.

Relax, I said; there couldn't be a problem. Old SCO's all-but given you his word, and you're using the CC's proprietary seed mix and sowing it at the rate they prescribe. It'll be all right.

. . . .

(As prelude to 'the quartering', I learned, lengthy discussions had taken place between Sheen and the two drivers about how best to sow the seed without leaving unsightly mini-furrows which might take years to disappear. The conclusion they reached was to carry out the usual operations to produce a nice, fine 'tilth' [tilled (cultivated) seed-bed], then sow using a standard agricultural drill from which the 'coulters' [blades which cut a groove in the soil to receive the seed] had been removed, so as just to drop the seed – not, in fact, 'drill' [implant] it – then rake over with a tine harrow a few times, to joggle the seed down into the tilth and cover it over... finishing off with a couple of passes with a 'press' [a ribbed roller or set of rollers] to compact the tilth firmly.)

Again, my mind went back to patching the lawns in Baltimore: roughening the soil with a garden rake, scattering little pinches of seed carefully by hand, then smoothing the seeded soil and, finally, over-laying it with lengths of fine-mesh, galvanized wire netting to discourage marauding birds....

. . . .

You've come a long, long way, d'Arcy.
But as I'm sometimes increasingly aware, Alter-natis, I've not arrived There yet.

. . . .

That evening the Hufftons came over for 'kitchen supper' as it's called in these parts, that's to say an informal meal. (And still with little proper furniture in the dining room, where the 'kitchen' supper in fact took place, so it had to be.) Just prior to their arrival, I happened to look out a front window and saw Antony down on all fours next to our Hall-end new cattle grid, inspecting it closely. Cordelia later told me how 'very impressed' he was, particularly with the positioning of the concrete grid-supports. When they'd installed their cattle grids at Brunstead, she confided, for ten days or so all household deliveries had to be made to the farm office, and all visitors to their hall had either to come via their circuitous and indifferently-paved back drive or park outside their front lodge and transfer to a Land Rover. Score one for the upstart American apprentice squire, I crowed privily!

This small triumph aside, the evening was notable primarily for the agreeable company in which it was spent and the local intelligence which it confirmed, in particular the intelligence that Antony and Cordelia and Sir Roald and Lady Maureen – all four of them each to the others – were, like members of a clan, distantly inter-related.

. . . .

When, those centuries ago, the north Norfolk gentry had their family get-togethers – or should I write 'family-gets together' – they certainly took the 'getting' and the 'togethering' literally, Alter-natis.
It must have been a bit like Iceland which, I seem to recall, is the

most genetically homogeneous nation on earth...

... or like one of those isolated sodalities in The Motherland: the Amish away in western Pennsylvania, for example, or the hillbillies deep in the backwoods of Appalachia or the Ozarks.

When next you shake hands with one of these old-line north Norfolkers, I suggested – or if you ever happen to be out walking barefoot with them... perhaps on the beach – try to establish how many fingers and/or toes they have.

No wonder 'at a certain level... everyone around here knows everyone and about everyone'!

• • • • • • • • • • • • • • • • • • • •

Country people, I like to think – *real* country people – aren't so concerned with how 'good-looking' you are, how 'fashionably' you dress, what sort of title or style precedes your name or how many honourific acronyms – 'OBE'* like – follow it... how much money you have, even, although these ancillaries certainly register; some don't even seem to mind if you're American.... They're concerned with what you are down deep, in the most fundamental of your 'self-ness' they're able to perceive. And 'real' country people are, in my opinion, as cunning as foxes – that's to say they perceive deeply and well. It's why I've always liked them.

So when on 4 April, The Hon Chaser Jermyn stopped by unannounced – parking, as I've since found most north Norfolk country people do, not outside the front door but in the stableyard at the back – and took time out from his busy, esquirely, morning for a cup of coffee with us, N and I regarded it as a great compliment. His purpose, he said, was 'to see how (we were) getting on', and I'd no reason to doubt that interest was genuine. But, I suspected, he also had a covert agenda: to spy out what the upstart Americans might be getting up to with his old family home.

The devil in me determined to keep Chaser guessing, at least for a while. Having been brought up on that old saw about the best defence being a good offence†, I regaled him with a selection of our local-parochial trivia and then launched into a series of lengthy ex-

---

* 'Order of the British Empire': an 'honour', as such recognitions are collectively known; sartorial evidence of them usually includes a 'decoration' of some sort – a ribbon or sash and/or a medal or medallion. (A medal is sometimes dismissively referred to as a 'gong'.)

† An edited and abridged version, apparently, of George Washington's 1799 pronouncement: 'Offensive operations, often times, is (sic) the surest, if not the only... means of defence.'

tracts from my Heartsease Hall restoration 'Masterplan'. Predictably, Chaser soon began to squirm with boredom and, watching his eyes glaze over, I took it his intelligence-gathering mission had been well and truly stalled. But, shortly, Chaser made his counter-move: reca-pitulating the long list-out he'd given me at Nigel and Trish's 11 January supper of which of his ancestors had lived in our property and when… and following that up by another explanation, this one even more detailed, of how his Jermyn limb axiled into Sir Roald's Festing-family tree-trunk.

• •

You've never been much interested in genealogies, d'Arcy.

No and I should be, Alter-natis, if only in deference to that vener-ated adage: 'Blood is thicker than water.' Families and their inter-relationships – their metamorphoses, in other words, into tribes and beyond – are fundamental building blocks of civilization.

Did something turn you off? Or were you just never turned on?

A bit of both. In my youth, I probably *was* overdosed on all that d'Arcy Henry and Harryman 'CC', and 'SAR' and 'DAR'* mem-bership stuff. But by temperament and inclination, I'm not a social historian; I don't have that concern to explore and represent my and other peoples' lineal and collateral descendings. I'm too much taken up with my own present and future, I guess.

Too much taken up with your own 'vanity of vanities', the great Preacher-King in Ecclesiastes *would say.*

• • • • • • • • • • • • • • • • • • • •

After a few more exploratory exchanges – places we'd visited, restau-rants and pubs we'd eaten or drunk at, which children attended what schools… hobbies we pursued – we tacitly agreed to call it quits and just chatted amiably. Chaser, I confirmed, was indeed a very engag-ing fellow and one with whom, in time, I became good friends. Then Chaser announced he had to leave. We got up; I saw him out the back door and through the tunnel into the stableyard, and across to his car…. Whereat Chaser turned to me:

'By the way, d'Arcy,' he began, 'I meant to ask you earlier: what are the ages of those two sons of yours?' Piglet was ten last September, I replied, and Bapu's shortly to turn four. Chaser, his brow furrow-ing, nodded earnestly. 'Your elder son,' he continued: 'I'm very sorry to say we haven't a daughter his age. But your younger son… he'd

---

* As used here, acronyms for: the Society of the Cincinnati, and Sons/Daughters of the American Revolution.

be just about right for our little Jasmine. In a few years, we must make sure the two of them get to know each other.' Chaser chuckled mock-conspiratorially. As we shook hands, I thought to myself there's absolutely no question about it: that man's a real countryman... as cunning as a fox.

· · · · · · · · · · · · · · · · · · · ·

What's your view of arranged marriages, Alter-natis?

It depends what you mean by 'arranged'. If the arrangement is coerced, that's to say made primarily by and for the benefit of the arrangers, it's an execrable constraint on the matrimonial principals – although, almost invariably, it's the woman and her children who suffer most.

If the arrangement is consensual and made as far as possible in the matrimonial principals' best interests, I've no quarrel with it. The balance of probability, research makes clear, is that arranged marriages of this sort work.

After all, most younger-peoples' prescribed congregations today – the sandboxes they play in, the schools and colleges they go to, the parties and dances they attend, the jobs they take up... the leisure activities they pursue – are, overtly or covertly, prescriptions for marriage arrangement. Why not go the whole hog? Think of it as internet dating intermediated by experienced spouse-hunters who know and love you.

And if the consensual, arranged marriage were to bring one family back, wholly or partially, into a substantial property which years earlier had 'got away' from them?

Why not. But remember: should one of your sons ever become the target of such a ploy, you must hold out for a very substantial dowry – at least a couple dozen good, fat sheep or goats and 6–7 prime Arabian horses or camels, say, as well as a fine, hand-knotted carpet or two, some gold, frankincense and myrrh... and, perhaps, a well-tempered saif (sword). Their 'new blood' is of the very highest quality, you know.

· · · · · · · · · · · · · · · · · · · ·

Later that day I got a letter from Sir Roald saying he and Lady Maureen had had their offer on the property in Southwold accepted but that it'd become clear the house required even more doing up than they'd thought – which would take most of the summer to complete – so could they have the let of Dovecote Cottage for awhile longer, please. Again, I made haste to say yes.

And in his final paragraph, Sir Roald asked would I mind if from now on he addressed me as 'd'Arcy' instead of 'Mr Henry'.

. . . .

Imagine, Alter-natis: in this informal, 'matey' day and age…

… when, increasingly, social and other civilian hierarchies based on rank and status are routinely ignored – if not, in fact, deliberately 'disrespected' – and Jack regularly presumes himself to be as good as his master…

… a distinguished 13th Baronet – a Peer 'of the Realm' – *asking* an upstart American if he may call him by his first name?

Many Europeans, of course, observe the so-called 't/v distinction', between 'tu' and 'vous' in French, or 'tu' and 'voi' in Italian ('du' and 'sie' in German), which reserves the second-person singular form of 'you' for family and close friends, and uses the distancing, second-person plural *form when addressing pretty much everyone else.*

The 'd'Arcy/Mr Henry' distinction was Sir Roald's English-language equivalent. In asking if he could call you by your first name, he was signaling his acceptance of you as an intimate.

How gentle, old-world quaint, I thought and – coming from Sir Roald – how agreeable.

. . . .

On 5 April, I met with the land agent's comely assistant ('You may call me Lois,' she cooed; suddenly, it appeared, everyone was moving to first names.) to finalize my 1995–96 submission to IACS, the Integrated Administration and Control System through which was then administered the UK's agricultural subsidies programme*. It comprised: a 12-page 'Base Form' (essentially, a farm census), sixteen pages of detailed field data including what areas of which combinable crops, as well as forage and other crops, were planted where – to the first decimal place if you accounted in acres or to the second if you accounted in hectares (one hectare 'officially' equals 2.471 acres) – and nine maps showing fields registered with IACS as unities but which for the crop-year in question had been subdivided.

Bureaucracy run riot and running rioter, it seemed to me. But our Lois was very much in estrus and in charge, crossing and uncrossing her lovely, long, slim legs and fixing me repeatedly with her schoolmarm/dominatrix look, *viz*: 'This is important, Sir, so you listen to me!' Preparing IACS documentation not being the most riveting of pastimes, Yr Correspondent has to confess his mind wandered occasionally.

And that evening I completed and fair-copied the final draft of my

---

* As earlier noted, essentially the same job is now carried out within the so-called Single Payment Scheme referred to as the SPS.

grant-aid application to the Countryside Commission; the next morning – 6 April: four working days into the CC's four-month application period and thereby 'early', I reckoned, as in 'in good time... for early acceptance', by any reasonable standards – I mailed it off Special Delivery to old SCO for his critical review. (To it I attached a note asking if my earlier communication regarding the grass-seed, etc, had been received – not that by that time it made much difference.)

Then N and I drove to Brambledown to show the flag and retrieve, in the horsebox, our small, 'hobby' flock of Jacob sheep*. A curious letter from the Cotswold District Council awaited us there. Captioned 'Ref CD.2843/C – Application for full Planning Permission for change of use from residential to six-bedroom hotel at Brambledown', it detailed the structural alterations, etc, that change of use would entail, and the procedure for lodging an objection to the change should we so wish.

· ·

Brambledown? That was our house... still!

Change of use from residential to six-bedroom hotel? What a great idea! In fact... wasn't that what your wife proposed when you and she and old Atta-Boy were discussing how Brambledown might be marketed?

Lodge an objection? *I certainly wouldn't, Alter-natis!*

Nor would I! But wait a minute, d'Arcy. Wait just a minute, I cautioned. Who put this application in? You certainly didn't....

N certainly didn't, the EA certainly didn't, and the Barses almost certainly didn't....

As the 18th-century English poet William Cowper observed: 'God moves in a mysterious way His wonders to perform.'

Maybe. But, you'll recall, we were never able definitively to chart this particular 'mysterious way', nor did any appreciable 'wonder' ever result from it. In short, it was all very strange.

· ·

Early the next day, Toby and I carried out an inspection of Brambledown's grounds. The lawns – recently-cut and with the sun glinting off the dewy grass – looked like green velvet which had been silvered or gilt. (No daisy, dandelion or plantain seed-heads anywhere, I noted contentedly.) The paths were smooth-raked; the flowerbeds on the terraces were planted up and straight-edged; the perennials in the herbaceous borders had been pruned well back and from their stumps

---

* Two or four-horned, brown-and-white pied sheep from whose fleece Israel's arch-patriarch's 'coat of many colours' is said to have been made.

new, yellow-green shoots were breaking; the leaf and flower buds on the shrubs and trees were swelling; the hedges were clear of 'litter'....

Surely, I reassured myself, the Barses – someone... anyone with an eye for the Cotswolds countryside and horticultural beauty – must fall madly, irretrievably in love with Brambledown now. After proposing this resolution to the Whomever, again, I loaded up the Jacobs and drove with N back to Heartsease Hall.

And *laus Deo*, within days the sale of Brambledown was back on track! The EA reported the Barses even wanted to buy the two, life-sized marble statues in the garden N and I'd been debating what to do with, although he wasn't sure how much they were prepared to pay for them. (One statue was almost certainly a 19th-century reproduction of the Greek sculptor Praxiteles' famous, c 350 BC *Aphrodite*; the other was so old and eroded it resembled something Barbara Hepworth or Henry Moore might have turned out on a bad day.) Do we crack the champagne now, N and I asked ourselves? My little Uxor, of course, was up for a bit of bubbly anytime, anywhere. But Yr Correspondent – 'Mr Prudentia', concerned, as ever, not to provoke the Whomever, or whomever – ultimately prevailed: we would *carpe* a subsequent *diem*, it was agreed, when contracts had been exchanged and the deposit monies paid into our account – a consummation which, honourable EA assured us, would 'without doubt' be achieved within 2–3 weeks.

In the immediacy and intensity of the interaction with people and animals to which it gave rise and, collaterally, its sheer, pell-mell preposterousness*, 11 April 1995 represented the essence of what, to me, an English country squire's life could and should – very occasionally – be all about.

The day's schedule of events kicked off just before 0900 hours with what older-generation Britons might call 'a jolly romp': fetching the main sheep flock from 'Hobarts', as it was known – an outlying field in which the ewes had over-wintered – back to Pavilion Paddock – which I'd recently joined up with the widened front drive verges to make one large, 'L'-shaped field running all the way from the east track gate through to and including the parking area for the Front Lodge – where they'd 'lamb down' (give birth). As the ewe ambles, it was a distance of only about a mile but, all told, well over an hour

* A word which melds the Latin *'prae'* and *'posterus'* – 'before' and 'after' – in practical terms, manifestly a 'ridiculous' or 'absurd' conjunction.

was required to negotiate it.

(For the sheep, it was *terra incognita*: wide open and, in the main, recently-ploughed – that's to say fodder-less and untracked – so, predictably, they ranged this way and that, then dispersed outward in a fan until they reached the occasional remnant of fence – often with fresh grass the other side – at which point they sub-divided, amoeba-like, into three or four smaller flocks each with its own, individual sense of expedition. I'm always amazed at how quickly heavily-pregnant ewes can move when they need or want to.)

Participants in the 'romp' included N, Big Fee and Yr Correspondent, and a couple of the farm men and their wives – as well as various of their friends and relations – to a total of about fifteen people. (A couple of days earlier, I'd asked Sheen if he'd lay on 'a little shepherding help' for me; few of those he'd approached could resist an opportunity to observe the up-start American apprentice English country squire in action, it would seem.)

Big Fee was absolutely magnificent, cantering clean-limbed and fluid-graceful alongside the leading edge of the flock, pacing it, keeping just the right amount of pressure on it, overpowering potentially-rebellious ewes with her 'strong eye' (a look of incontestable command)... taking just the right line to turn it – or encourage it to turn itself – at critical junctures; in short, she was every shepherd's dream of a shepherdess. (As I huffed and puffed along, it became clear the only problem was the preference of virile, young, male troop for 'supporting' on her side [? flank] of the flock; I and a couple of other old silverbacks were left to manage the non-Big-Fee side pretty much on our own.)

· · · · · · · · · · · · · · · · · · ·

The previous week the lovely-leggy Lois, that day the filly-form Big Fee....

'The everlasting miracle of spring', as the early-20th-century British poet John Drinkwater wrote.

Or as the 17th-century Scottish poet William Drummond wrote: 'Spring... delicious, wanton, amiable, fair.'

· · · · · · · · · · · · · · · · · · ·

Eventually, the shepherding was satisfactorily concluded. I returned to my deskwork and, a couple of hours later, prepared to partake of one of N's delicious, hot lunches....

But as really deep-dyed *rustiques* (country-folk) are fond of observing, there's never a dull moment in the country. I'd just sat down, tucked in my napkin and picked up my knife and fork, when from Pavilion Paddock, with its newly-ensconced flock of ovine mothers-to-be, a great clamor of shouting voices arose. What on earth was going on? Looking out the kitchen window, I beheld 4–5 men in white overalls running around and, from time to time, excitedly waving their arms in the air. Who on earth were they? Escapees from some local lunatic asylum? I didn't know there was one, and I was surprised (although perhaps I shouldn't have been...) that the Heartsease Hall selling agent, or the land agent – or Sir Roald, surely – hadn't at some point told me of it. Whatever: the that which was being perpetrated by the whoever was perpetrating it was precisely the sort of aggravation expectant ewes (expectant anythings, I suppose) shouldn't have. Reluctantly, I quit my delicious, hot lunch, climbed angrily into the Land Rover, and drove down...

... to discover an immense but severely-wasted Shorthorn* bull which, I was given to understand, had escaped from the little slaughterhouse in the village, passed through our east gate, traveled up our east track, gone over, under or around the fencing (but manifestly not through the field gate, which was still closed and locked) and into Pavilion Paddock... where the slaughterhouse owner and his men had finally caught up with it. By then tiring – but still defiant – the big, raw-boned bovine was rummaging back and forth through my ewes like a sheepdog on steroids, scattering them in all directions. How to deal with this great, lumbering intruder, I asked myself?

On getting out of the Land Rover, however, I quickly reset my action algorithm to how to deal with the slaughterhouse owner – a sort of Anglicized Obelix (albeit with a thatch of unkempt brown hair instead of the blond pigtails with which Albert Uderzo adorned his creation) who was very large and powerfully built (he'd been a British Armed Services light-heavyweight boxing champion, apparently) and probably, it occurred to me, pretty handy with a knife... (but whose surname, I later learned, was Goodfellow).

In sum, old Obelix looked to be the sort of man who, should he choose to engage the errant bull in hand-to-hand combat, was more than capable of dispatching it by himself on the spot.

Or by way of warm-up, I reflected, dispatching me on the spot. For Mr Obelix seemed to have no idea who I was or, if he had, he just

---

* In UK parlance, typically chestnut or chestnut-roan in color, with mid-length, downward-curving horns.

didn't care. So assuming my most-portentous demeanor, I introduced myself to him – adding for clarity that I was the new co-owner of the Heartsease Hall Estate – laid out my fears about the hazard to which my precious, pregnant ewes were now being exposed by his rampaging bull and, finally, enquired what exactly he proposed to do retrieve the situation.

For a moment, Obelix eyed me up and down as might a sergeant major some impious new recruit who'd presumed to get in his way. Then his attitude softened. He took a deep, thought-collecting breath, balanced his body, squared his shoulders... and started in. '"Shorty" – tha's 'is name, sir – belongs to a cousin a mine,' he began, disconsolately. 'I've known 'im for years an' years... ever since 'e was a little calf.' Obelix paused... and took another deep breath.... 'In 'is time, 'e was a workin' bull, o' course... but 'e's allus been very good-natured and gentle.... Shorty's just a family pet, really!' At which point, his massive shoulders hunching and heaving, my hulking interlocutor broke off his chronicle and turned away, seemingly to attend to something in the corner of his left eye. For a moment, it seemed to me it might be a tear welling up, but then I thought: no, from a hardened, professional slaughterman like this fellow, that just couldn't be.

'The poor ole boy's got a 'fection (infection) in 'is jaw,' my conversant continued eventually. 'It's a'ready cost 'im most a 'is chewin' teeth (molars).' More massive-shoulder hunching and heaving.... 'M' cousin'd like to keep 'im... let 'im work another year; 'e's such a lovely bull... an' 'e throws ever such good calves....' Obelix paused to steady himself.... 'But I tole 'im that with that 'fection, Shorty's in too much pain... so 'e won't eat proper; 'e'll just go on suff'rin'... an' deteri'atin'.... We've 'ad the vet out,' he added, 'but 'e don't seem able to do nothin'....

'There weren't really anythin' for it, I said, an', after awhile, m' cousin came 'round (agreed).... The best thing now 'ould be to get Shorty back to m' (slaughterhouse) yard' – again old Obelix paused to attend to that something in his eye – 'and put 'im down nice an' quick,' he concluded, miserably.

After offering such condolences as seemed might be appropriate, I asked Obelix how he proposed to achieve old Shorty's relocation. The slaughterhouse-owner thought for a moment, then replied he'd in mind to fetch from a field adjacent to his premises a few of the wretched bull's 'mates', that's to say other bovines awaiting slaughter, 'includin', mebbie, a dry (not in-milk or pregnant, but perhaps ready to be 'served') cow or two' – a group of herd-animals is more likely to go where you want it to than is a singleton on its own, he reminded me – and drive them through the east gate, etc, and into Pavilion Paddock; when old Shorty'd herded up with them – and just possibly, I mused, engaged more intimately with one or two of the cows – he'd drive them all back again to his slaughterhouse and, in due course, into what he called 'the killin' room'.

Ummm…. I went through the motions of carefully considering old Obelix' plan but, immediately I heard it, I knew I wasn't happy with it and, after a suitable interval, I told him so. When cattle (or, in my experience, any herd-animals) are introduced into a strange enclosure, I pointed out, they almost invariably gallop around it – behaviour which, in this case, would not only further discomfit my ewes but, given the parlous state of the fencing, could result in a mass breakout.

And even if we did get old Shorty herded up, and he and his 'mates' headed back towards the slaughterhouse, I continued, animals who've once been introduced to such premises – with its sights and sounds and smells of death – are, I'd always understood, very shy of returning there. Could Shorty *et al* be persuaded to re-enter this end zone? Or would they be so terrified they'd keep travelling straight on through the village and away down to the nearby, fairly-heavily-travelled main road. 'Remember: if one of your animals causes an accident, you'll be liable,' I concluded.

Obelix pondered my objections… then nodded in reluctant assent. 'What we need's a sharp shooter,' he muttered, as if thinking out loud, 'so we could bring Shorty down right 'ere in the field all natural-like, with the grass… an' the trees… an' the fresh air…. 'E wouldn't 'ave ta get hisself all upset then.' He paused, gazing into the middle distance…. 'Yeah: that'd be the kindest… the most 'umane thing ta do.' Obelix again wiped his eye… and looked hard at me. 'But where'd we get a sharp shooter from?' he asked pensively, rubbing the thick, gnarled fingers of his great right paw along the left side of his great, grizzled jaw. 'I only know of one such, an' – asumin' we could get ahold of 'im – 'e lives twenty or so miles away; it'd take 'im the best part of an hour ta get ta us. Shorty mayn't accept to stop (stay) 'ere that long. 'A course, we could allus call in the police. But once you get them buggers nosyin' around….'

I looked hard back at Obelix… and considered my position. 'I'm a reasonably good shot, and I've got a high-powered rifle which I use for stalking red deer,' I volunteered in due course. 'I ought to be able to bring your bull down.' After one last, racking review of the possible options... and their possible outcomes... I went explicit: 'If you're serious about wanting to bring in a sharp shooter – this may be my land, but it's your animal – I'll go and get my gun.'

Looks of disbelief, scepticism and, finally, springing hope – of his release from his loose-bull dilemma, and of Shorty's release from his burden-of-life one, I assumed – in succession transited old Obelix' face. (Meanwhile, the wretched bull resumed his fitful rummage through my ewe-flock. 'E's still got a bit a life in 'im,' my interlocutor observed proudly... sadly... forlornly....) I pressed on with the operational peripherals: 'But everyone'll have to pull back... get well out of the way and stay there. Stalking in and executing a safe shot... possibly having to follow up a wounded animal... will be difficult enough without you and your people in your bright-white overalls running and jumping about.'

More deliberative rubbing of thick, gnarled fingers, etc, ensued. Then with a rumbling, deep-throated grunt of resignation, and a slow nod of his great, shaggy head, Obelix agreed Yr Correspondent's plan. So up to the Hall I went for my rifle and some cartridges – passing *en route* the kitchen, with its fragrance of my delicious, now-rapidly-cooling 'hot' lunch – then back down I came to Pavilion Paddock for some careful calculation.

The best approach was from the southwest, I decided eventually, because it would let me ground my shot into the foot of Preston's Pride hill. Was anyone in or near that line of fire? No; all was clear. And how about the nearby carr* into which old Shorty, even if hard hit, might run? As agreed, not a white-overalled body was anywhere to be seen. (But what were those rustlings... those murmurings... those titterings... I thought I heard coming from behind the big trees just inside Neate Wood?)

From there on, *laus Deo*, all went according to plan. I stalked in to a distance of 60–70 yards...

. . . .

For posterity, don't you want to make that 160–170... 260–270 yards, even? And, perhaps, have the pain-crazed bull trying to charge you down?

Killing animals shouldn't be an opportunity for self-aggrandize-

---

* Boggy lowland; in southeast England, typically studded with alder and other scrub.

ment, Alter-natis; it should be an opportunity – which people who genuinely live close to nature almost invariably take – to give thanks for animals and reflect on how much they and the natural world in general mean to us.

You carry on like that and you'll wind up a vegetarian!

Besides, I don't know of any animals which charge over the longer distances you propose; their perceived 'sphere of vital interest', that's to say their 'turf', doesn't usually extend so far.

. . . .

... 60–70 yards, fronted up to a sturdy fence post I could use as a support, chambered a round, mounted the rifle, peered through its scope.... Shorty – poor old Shorty! His grossly-swollen, edentulous jaw, with its oozing pus, was clearly visible now; I too found the sight very, very distressing – paced for awhile in a little circle and then stood stock still, head carried (held high) and quarter-turned toward me, like the massive stag in Sir Edwin Landseer's famous painting 'Monarch of the Glen'. I off-ed the rifle's safety... peered through its scope some more.... Slowly, Shorty turned his head away, offering me the whole of his upper body in profile. I inhaled, exhaled, and gently squeezed the trigger.... Bang! Struck in the first or second cervical vertebra by 140 grains of high-velocity .275 'Nosler partition' (bullet), old Shorty – like a derelict building dynamited – came crashing down.

I walked over to the prostrate bull and cautiously tapped an eyeball, just to make sure he was dead; then, after thanking the Whomever for his help in bringing this sorry saga to its quick-and-easy – better, perhaps, 'easeful' – end, I unloaded and shouted the all clear. As if by magic, from behind the trees in Neate Wood a whole crowd emerged: old Obelix, of course, and a diminutive woman who I later learned was his wife, the white-overalled slaughtermen, a 'shepherd' or two left over from the day's earlier diversion... plus a few people I'd no idea who they were. I accepted the thanks of Obelix – who now had what was clearly a runnel of tear-water down his left cheek – acknowledged the acclaim of the gathered, miscellaneous band and then, with as much nonchalance as I could muster, sleeved my rifle and excused myself saying I wanted to finish (start!) my lunch. Our security rating, surely – and, perhaps, the wider regard in which the upstart-American apprentice English country squire is held – must rise as a result, I mused.

. . . .

Even with its overtones of euthanasia, is this really the sort of mate-

rial you want to include in your 'light' read? It's a good tale, and you've told it fairly well. But for Readers of delicate sensibility – impressionable, younger Readers, Green Peace-makers... right-to-lifers... pacifists and other conscientious objectors, say – is the killing of a sentient animal....

I appreciate your concerns Alter-natis and, to address them, let me make the following points: in writing up this story, I've focused on its lighter, more anecdotal aspects... and played down its blood and gore; the killing isn't mindless, gratuitous violence... wholly extraneous to the narrative – like so much 'entertainment' violence is nowadays – but an integral part of it; and, above all, the account isn't fabricated or contrived – it's authentic and genuine, that's to say real.

That's my next point. This isn't a story about some third party... some A. N. Other; it's a story about you. So ipso facto, it's not about violence you've observed as a journalist might; it's about violence that's been perpetrated by you.... And it's not the first representation of violence you've included in this book; earlier material describes you killing – or attempting to kill – waterfowl, game birds, vermin....

With its seemingly careless – 'trivializing', it reads to me – leitmotif about your foregone 'delicious hot lunch', as if the killing of old Shorty was 'all in a day's work'.... As a writer, is this how you want to be remembered?

Well... yes and no. It's a commonplace, of course, that violence... aggression... is a basic instinct. And it's in me – and, therefore, you – as, I'd suggest, it's in many people... most people, probably. Violence's over-arching, definitive expression is war, obviously, and capital crime... and, of course, capital punishment; the on-going 'greed is good' driven destruction of much of our anthroposphere – the recent, episodic, ditto of much of our financial-services and wider-world economy, even – is, in a sense, violence.

The 14th-century English prelate and statesman, William of Wykeham, was adamant that 'Manners makyth man'. What you've just been writing about – what you were back then actually engaging in – is hardly 'mannerly'.

Violence also figures prominently in our less-definitive exploits: the way we play or watch sport, that's to say proxy-fight; the way we put forward and strenuously argue our opinions and, sometimes, agree only to disagree; the way we seek dominance or offer submission in courtship, or while making love.... Great cinema, great literature, great graphic art... the greatest, most-sublime music, even... often represent violence.

Just because it's all around you....

And let's be very clear: at some remove, represented violence begets pleasure both in the performer and in the audience. Think of the enjoyment you get (maybe…) from listening to or helping me try to play, however badly, on the *hammerclavier* – that jagged, jarring, German adjectival for the piano, that's to say a keyboard instrument whose sound is produced by striking rather than by plucking as with harpsichords, or by blowing as with wind (? pipe) organs – '*Sturm und Drang*' ('storm and stress') passages from Beethoven's 'Appassionata' Sonata, his Opus 111 Sonata… his initially contemplative and serene but ultimately tempestuous and raging 'Moonlight' Sonata, even….

There's no need to get yourself so worked up….

Inevitably, violence – like death – is an adjunct of life… in some ways an affirmation of life, even. If more people better understood violence's fundamental role in society – instead of trying to deny it or dismiss it as some sort of aberration – they'd probably lead happier, more fulfilled lives. Our world's not entirely a kind, gentle, cooperative one… yet.

Well… maybe we should all be more prepared to accept that nature is indeed 'red in tooth and claw with ravine' (or 'rapine': seizure by force), as Alfred Lord Tennyson proposed in his In Memoriam A. H. H. *of 1850. You certainly seem to be more prepared….*

And finally, Alter-natis….

Yes, d'Arcy?

In my opinion, if you're really desperate for something to witter on about, why don't you criticize my failure more explicitly to condemn unrestrained population growth, un-relieved malnutrition and disease, un-remediated under-education, our current 'Great Extinction' of our earth's *flora* and *fauna*, our desecration of the environment… and, above all, our unspeakable inhumanity to our fellow man…?

Here's why: because as the English religious reformer John Wycliffe, also an inhabitant of the 14th century, wrote: 'Charitie schuld bigyne at hem-self,' that's to say 'at home'. And because you've yet fully to acknowledge – let alone repent of – your own role as an accessory to these dreadful, nihilistic modes…. In other words: you're… still… 'travelling'.

· · · · · · · · · · · · · · · · · · · ·

My pell-mell, preposterous day concluded with a telephone call from the Brigadier, this time to ask if N or I in our capacity as hosts of the VE Day celebrations would care to light the bonfire 'as Her Majesty the Queen will be doing in Hyde Park, in London'. I thought on it… reflected, wistfully, that it would certainly make a nice diary entry….

· · · · · · · · · · · · · · · · · · · ·

… if pretty much foreclose the possibility of your adopting a 'subter-

ranean' profile on the evening in question....
· · · · · · · · · · · · · · · · · · · ·

However, I held to my view that the VE-Day celebration should properly be a paramount British moment. The honour of lighting the bonfire should therefore go to a national of – better still: someone, or a relative of someone, who actually fought for – what the poet and painter William Blake in the preface to his *Milton* of 1804–1810 called 'England's green & pleasant Land', not just bought a little piece of it. After thanking the Brigadier for thinking to ask us, I told him 'no'.

Over the next week or so, spring finally sprung or, alternatively introduced, our first-ever Heartsease Hall lambs began to arrive.

From the standpoint of the UK flock-owner's business accounts, lambing is the most-critical period in the sheep-farming year. If the lambing is good and lots of baby ovines 'drop', his or her profits may be good; if the lambing is bad, little profit – or even losses – may ensue. And assuming the ewe-flock is healthy and the lambs drop easily, lambing is also a very pleasurable time of year. Two bugbears loom large, however: cold, wet weather which when lambing outdoors in the open fields – as we did – can lead to potentially-fatal hypothermia in the newborn lambs (and, it sometimes feels, in the shepherd as well!); and orphan lambs, that's to say lambs who lose to death, get separated from or simply don't properly bond with their natural mothers, and for whom the shepherd has then either to find foster mothers or care himself.

(Most ewes are ferociously attentive to their own lambs, but they tend determinedly to reject the lambs of other ewes. Sometimes a 'carrot and stick' approach works: the shepherd gives the proposed foster mum a bit of especially tasty feed, then puts the lamb on to suck*; if the mum doesn't 'take' the lamb, the shepherd gives the mum a stern talking to and a little more feed, then puts the lamb on again.... This – mutually, presumably – exhausting cycle can be repeated any number of times. In my experience, however, it's usually the shepherd who capitulates and breaks out the formula milk for bottle feeding.)

---

* Getting and holding the disgruntled ewe in the right position while getting and holding the fidgety lamb in the right position... then getting the disgruntled ewe's big, milk-swollen teat into the fidgety lamb's little, tight-closed mouth – using only your two arms and hands, your two legs and feet, and your head, neck and/or torso – requires some practice.

Initially, the weather was kind to us, and Pavilion Paddock quickly began to fill with shoals of little, curly-white-fleeced ovines. Moreover, I'd only a couple of 'fosters' – both of which, happily, were good, strong-sucking fellows, as the adoptive mothers I volunteered for them took some time to fall into line. But then the weather changed....

My recollection of one foul-weather *accouchement* is particularly vivid. I'd noticed the ewe's protruding waters (amnion) during my pre-bedtime field round but, as she was an experienced mum, I'd thought little of it. By about 0200 the next morning, however, when I made my graveyard round, it was clear the ewe was in trouble. For the better part of an hour – in the pitch-dark, with a bitter-cold, north-east wind driving sleety rain almost horizontally – Yr Correspondent tried to wrestle a very large, breech-presented and, he noted uneasily, suspiciously-flaccid lamb into this world. After awhile, the long-laboring ewe – her birth canal by then inflamed and dry – began to grow tired and dispirited; I could sense her *élan vital* was ebbing away. An emergency caesarian – not a good bet for the lay shepherd anytime, but particularly not under the conditions which then obtained – seemed the only solution.

Eventually, however, I managed to get the lamb out. And in so doing I confirmed not only that the lamb was very large, etc. It was also very rotten-dead.

. . . .

President Truman wasn't it, d'Arcy, quoting one of his aides, who advised: 'If you can't stand the heat, get out of the kitchen.'

. . . .

On 12 April my parents-in-law, Jo and Lew Frederick, had arrived from Sacramento for their first look at our new abode. Not surprisingly, they loved it – 'a perfect jewel of a castle', Jo enthused – and also its collateral perquisites: for Jo, a scratch senior-women's player, golfing at the course attached to the hotel where we'd stayed during our several visits to view, etc, Heartsease Hall; and for Lew, an accomplished outdoorsman, the even closer-to-home fishing in the upper and lower lakes.

(As usual, Jo and Lew seemed wondrously immune to jet lag. When I made this point, Lew observed: 'If so, it's got to be just about the only benefit of growing old.')

One subsequent evening, N, her parents and I went for cocktails with Antony and Cordelia Huffton at Brunstead Hall. Some 35–40 people attended, mostly all shouting to each other in the shooting-deafened, 'traditional' local way. The weather was turn-of-the-season beautiful; lovely drinks and *canapés* were offered; and a tremendously convivial buzz was achieved. (As well, Yr Correspondent managed to remember the names of most of the other guests, that's to say his new friends and neighbours.)

I kept waiting for Jo or Lew further to enliven the proceedings with a selection of their famously *risqué* jokes. But no; determined to help N and me make the best possible impression, they stuck dutifully to the straight and narrow: swapping tales of new northern California for those of old north Norfolk, comparing food, wine and travel experiences, small talking… and telling only decorous jokes.

(Just before we quit the party, I told Antony about a cache of old documents Sir Roald had entrusted to my care, some of which referenced Brunstead Hall. He said he'd like to see them and, the next day, he came over to do so. As earlier noted, Antony'd been Chief Financial Officer of [a global primary-resources company], that's to say was highly skilled with numbers and, in his Brunstead capacity, he'd had direct experience of the Countryside Commission, so I took the opportunity to show him the file copy of my recently-dispatched grant-aid application to the CC. Antony skimmed it, asked a few probing, CFO-ly questions about how I'd derived my costings, and then volunteered he thought the application was very good. He warned me, however, that the CC people 'have a pretty high opinion of themselves… and like making applicants jump through hoops'. I ground my teeth. If there's one thing I don't need now, I reflected grimly, it's having to play up to a bunch of self-impressed paper-pushers.)

Then – after what seemed like only the Biblical (I Corinthians) 'twinkling of an eye' – we put Jo and Lew on the Norwich-London train for the first leg of their return home.

. . . .

It's nice having the older folks around mingling with the younger folks… mixing the generations…. It instills a sense of family and social continuity, Alter-natis.

In today's helter-skelter world, long-distance travel – long-distance communication generally – has become so easy and, as a result, so routine….

It's not like it used to be when people had to travel on foot, or by horse or donkey, or by 'oars, sail and steam'… or by early-generation train, car or airplane, even.

Now, visiting with family and friends is, physically, almost as simple as Skyping – if you can tune out the hassle at the airports, of course.

You often forget to remember that one day they – and, indeed, you – won't be there.

Carpe diem.

. . . .

Chapter 14

Accounted For

The evening of 16 April 1995 began as had so many over the swiftly-passed months since N and I'd moved into Heartsease Hall, and Sir Roald and Lady Maureen had moved into Dovecote Cottage, with drinks and supper *à quatre* in the Hall's kitchen. Sir Roald was in high spirits, regaling us with stories of his childhood:

'I grew up in the "Roaring Twenties", as the period became known: the age of jazz and "flapping" – "sleaze", some called it – and other heretical fads... and, in your country, of that so-called "Noble Experiment", prohibition. I've never really understood the prohibitionist mind-set, d'Arcy,' Sir Roald digressed, 'humankind's been enjoying alcohol in one form or another for thousands of years – responsibly, even, for some of that time... depending on what you mean by "responsibly", of course. Anyway,' he resumed, 'there was a song-writer named Jack Yellen who wrote "Happy days are here again! The skies above are clear again! Let us sing a song of cheer again...." His ditty was conceived in the summer of 1929, I think, when the United States seemed to be pulling out of what was thought to be a shallow recession; then, in October, came "The Crash", which was followed by "The Great Depression",' Sir Roald's voice trailed off....

'At that time, we were living in Vilnius where my father was Minister Plenipotentiary, that's to say the presiding British diplomat – Lithuania didn't rate a British Ambassador then; its "Grand Duchy" days, when it rivalled the Holy Roman Empire in extent, were long gone – and, I can tell you, what with the Russians pushing in from the east and the Poles pushing in from the southwest, there was precious little "roaring" or "jazzing" or "flapping" going on there! And drinking was a way of life; anyone even suggesting Prohibition would've been whisked straight off to the nuthouse! Part-way through his posting, my father pretty much gave up on being a diplomat – other than low-level consular, there wasn't any real business to be done, he felt – and devoted himself to his music: composing generally, and writing operettas and ballets... "trying to address the higher needs of the wider World Community", as he put it. To keep me out of harm's way, I was shipped off to Westminster School in London.'

... and stories of present-day 'local notables':

'A retired diplomat friend of ours named Stephen [...] – he and his wife have a cottage in Seething (a village just south of Norwich) now; you may have already met him (I shook my head.) or, if not, you almost certainly soon will – was in his time the youngest-ever candidate to place first in the entrance examinations for the Foreign and Commonwealth Office, that's to say our equivalent of your State Department... as I'm sure you're aware. After a distinguished career representing the UK in embassies around the world – he was an outstanding Arabist who served as Ambassador to several Middle Eastern countries, for which services he's recently received a knighthood – Stephen was invited to submit his *curriculum vitae* for inclusion in *Who's Who*.

'In the section entitled "hobbies" Stephen entered, along with a few of his manifold other interests, "gossip" which, as he'd long recognised, was a particularly efficient means of gathering and disseminating useful intelligence. The editors of *Who's Who* declined to accept this formulation, however, on the grounds that "gossiping" was beneath the dignity of a *Who's Who* man... whereupon Stephen altered his submission to "exchanging with friends and acquaintances information of a private or semi-private nature". When telling this anecdote, Stephen usually concludes: "With more-open minds and closer editing, the publishers of *Who's Who* could save a lot of trees!"'

... offering us literary and linguistic insights:

'I've just been re-reading – or trying to re-read – Aleksander Pushkin's *Yevgeny Onegin* which, as you may know, was written in verse format and published serially between 1823 and 1831; many critics regard it as the first great Russian novel. With its plots and sub-plots and their twists and turns, its imagery, its fantasy, its reality... just following the book's storyline is challenge enough. But given the lamentable state of my Russian vocabulary now....' Sir Roald sighed. 'There're so many basic words I just can't remember; I keep having to stop and look them up.' Again, his voice trailed off.

· · · · · · · · · · · · · · · · · · · ·

... and generally keeping you and your wife on your toes.

· · · · · · · · · · · · · · · · · · · ·

'Anyway, what could be nicer: after a hard day's work, spent mostly indoors in a comfortable chair with the sun streaming though the window, reading Pushkin, I come over here and sit down....' He winked at N, smiled enigmatically at me and then looked innocently but lingeringly at the bottle of red wine breathing gently on the Aga's warming plate. 'Someone puts a quaff of something fragrant and fresh in your hand....' I nearly knock N over in my rush to fill glasses for Lady Maureen and him.... 'Having said that, I'm not sure you can use "quaff" as a noun; in fact, I'm pretty sure you can't – at least not in German, which is where the word comes from. Anyway: a real, *family* supper – relaxed, convivial... just as it used to be when my mother and father were living in the Hall – is laid on....

'So what's this evening's culinary *pièce de résistance?*' Sir Roald cross-tracked briskly. Pork stroganoff over basmati rice, with sautéed courgettes (zucchini) and leeks, N replied. 'Perfect,' Sir Roald crooned, 'just perfect: nourishing, easy on the old teeth and very appropriate to my day's reading. Count Paul Stroganoff, after whom your main dish is named, was a 19th-century Russian diplomat, you know.'

Eventually we moved on to the usual small talk: how Piglet and Bapu were doing at school ('so bright and such perfect young gentlemen,' Lady Festing effused, 'real "hope-of-the-future" boys') and then to how Sir Roald's nieces, Eutopie and Celeste, were getting on in their careers. ('It's hard to know where they'll finish up,' Sir Roald reflected warmly. ['Married, I hope,' Lady Maureen interjected.] 'Eutie's just accepted a position translating at the International Atomic Energy Agency in Vienna – one serious mistake by her and we could all be toast! – and Cele's recently written, directed *and produced* a play at the International Theater there. But sadly,' he continued, 'neither of them has carried on with their music studies.' [The girls' mother, Oriana – Sir Roald's sister – had been a soloist with the renowned Gilbert and Sullivan opera company, The D'Oyly Carte; their father, Eugene, although American-born and educated, had lived most of his adult life in Europe and was a highly-regarded composer of the post-Schönberg persuasion.])

Lady Maureen reminded us that it was a year almost to the day since they'd received our offer to buy the Heartsease Hall Estate. 'My how time flies!' she exclaimed. To Yr Correspondent, this observation seems a good excuse for a toast. I raise my glass and, after confirming I have an audience, make ready to hold forth, at which point....

'By the way d'Arcy,' Sir Roald interrupts, 'Maureen and I've been intending to say for some time now...'

I lower my glass and look deferentially to Sir Roald....

'... that you and Nikki really should start calling us by our first names. After all, as Maureen's just said, we've known each other – been, by most measures, seeing a lot of each other – for quite a good, long while. And most important: we all get along very well... at least it seems to us we do. So, if you're content, we'd like that from now on you call us "Roald" and "Maureen" or better, if you'd feel as comfortable, "Rolly" and "Maureen".'

'Well, certainly, Sir Roald,' I reply without thinking, 'I mean "Rolly... and Maureen"; I'd....' I glance at N, who positively radiates concordance. 'We'd like that very much.'

'Good; that's settled, then. So if *I* may propose' – the 13th Baronet's hooded, raptor eyes glint congenially – 'a toast to the four of us: Nikki, Maureen, you, d'Arcy, and myself... and absent friends, of course. Getting to know you and your sons has given Maureen and me great pleasure, and the appreciation that Heartsease Hall is in your capable hands is a source of great comfort to us. So: *Na Zdorovye!* as Pushkin might have said – almost certainly *did* say; like most Russians, he was a great tippler – *Prost! Santé!* To good health and long, happy lives!'

. . . .

So, Class: concluding the case study of our acquisition of the Heartsease Hall Estate. To date, we've discussed various *tangible* assets like land and buildings – components of 'book value' as, in aggregate, they're called.... What, then, is 'goodwill'? Yes, Ms Gospel. I seem to remember that last session you told us about the meek inheriting the earth; today, then...? What St Luke is said to have said The Multitude of The Heavenly Host said, you say: 'Glory to God and on Earth peace, good will to men.'

Well, young lady, that's certainly an answer very appropriate for our troubled times. But as we're a business school, not a seminary, perhaps you'd....

What's that? Yes, Ma'am; you're quite right, of course. Some recognition of deeper, more philosophical issues – ethics... CSR... call it what you will, as we tried to essay in our February tutorial – should form part of every business school curriculum; otherwise we risk becoming accessories, or worse, to what the late British Prime Minister Sir Edward Heath notably called 'the unpleasant and unacceptable face of capitalism'.

And let me make this absolutely clear: un-checked, that bloated, corrupt face can threaten the very foundations of our free-enterprise, democratic society. That's why I believe.... No, Ma'am, I'm not planning to run for public office. That's why I believe business fraud,

351

accounting fraud, financial-market fraud, etc, should be.... You say what? That I've made this same point many, many times before? Well perhaps I have. How thrilling that you should remember!

Anyway; 'goodwill'.... Yes, GT. Indeed: a class of asset... *intan*-gible and thus difficult to value, which can be defined as an enter-prise's brand and its reputation... in other words the affirmative re-lations which may exist between it and its suppliers and customers, and elements of the wider environment in which it operates and, in a narrower usage sometimes – for example in corporate M & A, that's to say mergers and acquisitions – between the incoming and outgo-ing managements involved. Excellent!

Many would argue that this last category of goodwill – we'll call it intra-management goodwill or, better, 'team spirit' – is often *the* make-or-break factor in determining whether a merger or an acqui-sition succeeds. Why's that? Why's team spirit of such paramount importance? Someone... anyone...?

BS, gazing out the window... thinking about that new girlfriend of yours, perhaps. I know 'In the spring, a young man's fancy lightly turns to thoughts of love,' as Alfred, Lord Tennyson wrote in 1842; I was young once. But now, at the climacteric, so to speak, of this seminar, this case study... perhaps even this whole course-year.... Never mind. BS, now you're back with us: why is team spirit so im-portant?

So you can 'win one for the Old Gipper,' you say. That's certainly a worthy ambition – a very worthy ambition – but not quite the an-swer I had in mind.

I see the immaculately-manicured hand of Ms Goldstar in the air; to what do we owe.... Yes: because the outgoing management know where the skeletons are, you say. They can either reveal that knowl-edge and help the incoming management anticipate likely problems, or let them find out the hard way, by experience. Bravo!

Any more? Any more reasons why team spirit's so important? More forward-looking ones, perhaps? Yes: Che, my old friend, now also returned to our academic fold. Because the outgoing manage-ment's goodwill may facilitate the incoming management's access to The Great and Good. And just who might those last-named wor-thies be? I get it, you're being cynical; by 'The Great and Good' you in fact mean 'the fat cats of the commercial establishment and their running-dog lackeys, that's to say self-serving politicians and other public-sector people'. Yeessss.... In some respects... in some instanc-es... sometimes, perhaps, you could be right... I'm afraid....

Incidentally Che, cynicism and *its* 'running-dog lackey', sarcasm, can become addictive and, let me tell you, in my experience that's not good.

Wrapping all this up, then: our purchase of the Heartsease Hall

Estate: along with the Hall, the outbuildings, some cottages, the land, the standing crops, etc – the tangible assets... the 'book value' – have my wife and I bought any goodwill?

Yes, Ms Gospel. You say what? Goodwill – team spirit in particular – can't be bought? What about all those 'golden hugs' – 'golden kisses' now, probably, in some cases – and 'golden parachutes' like share options and 'consultancy' contracts, which are so much a part of M & A today? No? Well, I agree; in spite of its importance and in spite of the very considerable time and effort often put into *trying* to buy it, goodwill – team spirit, especially – is ultimately an interpersonal and intra-management, corporate-cultural thing. Try as you will to value it, it still largely remains beyond price.

So have we *acquired* any goodwill, then? Yes...? No...? Come on! Last question... absolutely the last. BS...? Good Man! Of course we have; that's what our 16 April supper with Sir Roald and Lady Maureen – 'Rolly' and 'Maureen', now – was all about. And if we behave ourselves, we should enjoy the benefits of that goodwill – be able to write it down... to amortise it, so to speak – over many, many years to come. Particularly in a small, close-knit community like north Norfolk, that's a most splendid gift to have been given, and a very great honor and privilege, I'd take this opportunity to say.

• • • • • • • • • • • • • • • • • • • •

0830 the next morning found 'Rolly' outside the library as usual, ready for our morning editorial conference. Notwithstanding the previous evening's familiarities, he still knocked gently and awaited my acknowledgement before coming in, then stood quietly until I indicated him to 'The Seat'; for my part, I still wasn't able fully to suspend my sense that in this house I was the guest and he the host let alone, in the sober light of day, call him Rolly. However, we eventually settled into our customary places – he on the sofa, I in the chair behind my card-table desk – and began.

'There's not much on the overnight (news) agency wires,' Rolly informed me gloomily: 'a couple of murders here, an earthquake there... yet another probably-doomed Israeli-government plan to improve opportunity for Palestinians in the Occupied Territories....'

Nor, I surmised, was there much going on locally that we hadn't already put to rights the evening before. How, then, to keep ourselves amused, I pondered aloud? Rolly, his eyes twinkling, said he'd 'a suggestion': we could discuss what to do longer-term with the Festing family portraits in the Hall. As though shot with steroids, my pulse-rate soared.

Rolly reiterated that a number of his relations had expressed interest in the paintings – 'strident interest' in some cases, he made clear – and that he'd considered distributing the portraits among them. And no wonder, I thought, hardly daring to breathe; many people would almost give an arm or a leg to be the custodian of such treasures. But, Rolly noted, most of his relations already had more family portraits than they knew what to do with – 'although theirs aren't nearly so good as ours', he added with pride.

Or alternatively, he conjectured, they could be sold, either privately – to some wealthy collector, perhaps, or the National Gallery (effectively, the UK government) in lieu of inheritance taxes – or publicly through one of the auction houses like Christie's or Sotheby's. 'They're not world-class portraits in the sense that the "greats" of the Middle and Late Italian or Dutch Renaissance are, or "our own" greats like Holbein (the Younger; a German) or Van Dyck (Flemish), or Hogarth or Reynolds or Gainsborough... to name just a few,' he confided, 'but they'd certainly fetch good prices.' I bet they would, I nodded grimly. 'But that would almost certainly mean the Festing "family" would have to be broken up and dispersed,' he continued. I nodded again, this time as pro-stirpes supportively as I could – perhaps even, I hoped, conclusively so.

'So it seems to me, d'Arcy, the best thing might be...'

Lady Maure... I mean 'Maureen', full of the joys of life, appears suddenly at the library door. 'Goodness Gracious,' she exclaims, 'are you two boys still talking? Rolly, we've got to be in the centre of Norwich in an hour!'

'I'll be with you directly Maureen,' Rolly replies brightly. Then he turns back to me. 'Where were we d'Arcy?' he asks. I swallow hard and prepare to leap with all my heart and soul into what appears to be my interlocutor's memory-breach. 'Oh yes, the portraits; the best thing, it seems to me,' he pauses, his expression serious almost to the point of caricature but with his eyes starting to smile, 'would be for the portraits to remain here *pro tem* in the old Festing family home they've graced for so long.'

I hardly knew what to say. Other than owning the portraits outright – a resolution which, given Rolly's relations' far more-direct interest in them, seemed to me bordering on the unfair – this result was about as close to perfection as I could've imagined. And I desperately wanted to make sure Rolly understood how very much I appreciated his most generous offer.

Some gesture of reciprocation was clearly called for, I concluded.

But what? My mind raced. If – 'when', I corrected myself – we ever sold Brambledown, we'd have enough paintings reasonably to decorate a couple of the Hall's main rooms – the library and the drawing room, say – but that would still leave bare walls in the rest of the main rooms: the dining room and the entrance hall, and the staircase hall. A bright light suddenly shone: we'd establish on these bare walls a 'Festing Gallery' where the portraits could all hang together and be exhibited as a group. That would at once confirm their especial status within the Henry's newly-acquired ambit but also, within the portraits' long-established ambit, their essential, conjoint 'Festing-ness'.

I put my idea to Rolly. He thought for a moment... then said he rather liked it 'provided it doesn't inconvenience you. I know you've a quantity of family portraits and other pictures which you'll be wanting wall-space for.' As earnestly as I could, I said for him not to worry... that, somehow, N and I'd find a way to accommodate them all.

'I've only one suggestion then,' Rolly concluded: 'rather than calling the exhibition a Festing "Gallery", you call it a Festing "Conclave". A "conclave" – from the Latin *con clavis* meaning "with a key" – implies a room having a door which can be closed and locked, thereby creating secure premises within which people can talk privately. Having such a facility might encourage those assembled here to chat and get to know each other better... to commune across the centuries, so to speak.' Rolly rose hurriedly from his seat on the sofa. 'D'Arcy, you must excuse me. The weekly "Wrinklies Brunch" as we call it is on at The Club today, and I've promised Maureen we'd go.'

As I saw Rolly to the library door, I kept repeating to myself: imagine, all these lovely portraits continuing to reside on these walls! And although I tried very hard to maintain a proper, businesslike demeanor while saying goodbye to him, I suspect I failed utterly.

. . . .

And so the Festing Conclave at Heartsease Hall came into being, Alter-natis.

You referred in the previous Chapter, when your parents-in-law were visiting, to the desirability... the pleasurability, even, of 'mixing the generations'. Establishing the Festing Conclave – all those portraits hanging around 'talking privately' to each other and, maybe as well, to real, live people passing by at floor level – certainly gave that concept a new dimension!

Yes, and it reminds me: we haven't heard from Sir Jacob for awhile.

. . . .

The day had one more surprise in store, however. That evening, the extended Henry family was, as usual, in the kitchen: Bapu and Big Fee were building a model helicopter out of cardboard; Bouff was doggo in his bed; Yr Correspondent, a malt whisky to hand, was bottle-feeding a hypothermic lamb who'd been rejected by its mum; N was cooking supper... when the telephone rang. At the end of a long, hard, acquisitive (!) day, it was a relaxed, easy domestic moment and neither N nor I wanted to let it go. Finally N, with hands more easily freed, grasped the metaphoric nettle:

'Hello? Oh, hello, Euan. How are....'

Egad! I grumble testily. Honorable solicitor, calling at this hour? What on earth does he want? I plop the lamb back into its box next to the Aga, then strain forward in my chair trying to work out from N's occasional words, or her body language, the import of our caller's message. N seems a bit on edge... a bit up tight. 'Oh? They don't?' I strain further forward.... 'Unnnhh. Why's that?' A long, long silence ensues during which N hunches her neck and shoulders, and begins vigorously to massage her left temple and forehead with the fingers of her left hand. Immediately, I diagnose classic UAS, aka Uxorial Angst Syndrome. Oh no!

'I see. So the Barses have "changed their minds" once again, have they,' I hear N say. 'They say they've "no further interest... no further interest whatsoever", not even at a lower price?' That recitation's not really an interrogative, I note, it's just masquerading as one. At base, it's a plain old unvarnished declarative. N's nodding, reluctantly apprehending head recesses still lower into her shoulder girdle. 'So that's it, is it? After all that, it's all over... all done.' In the ensuing, deafening silence, I can practically feel my pulmonary and cardio-vasculars constricting, pumping up my blood pressure, and hear my red-alerted heart pounding away. 'No further interest' from these people – these bloody, (deleted) B-arses, aptly nicknamed after all – who'd described Brambledown as 'so charming and so beautiful... so exactly what we're looking for'? And with whom we'd haggled over this and over that, and to whom we'd made concession after concession after concession... and who only a week ago – 10 April, to be precise – had reconfirmed their intention to buy the property, had now 'changed their minds'... indeed, had '*no further interest whatsoever*'? (Deleted... deleted, deleted, DELETED!)

'Well, thanks for calling, Euan,' N intones disconsolately. 'Yep, you too. Keep well; we'll be in touch... I hope, maybe... soon....'

N replaces the handset and looks at me with empty, lifeless eyes, her face a masque of woe. She compresses her lips, shakes her head and sighs dejectedly/resignedly. I mumble a few more expletives – and, for good measure, a few more still – scowl down at the hapless lamb, and reach for my drink.

. . . .

In view of the 'call me Rolly' moment you'd achieved some 24 hours earlier, I didn't understand why you couldn't have become an English country squire – of the Heartsease Hall Estate, for example – and, at the same time, still have kept Brambledown. As you've often argued, it's hard to beat bricks and mortar as an investment; having the two properties would, therefore, almost certainly have been better than having just the one....

It was a matter of asset allocation and cash flow, Alter-natis, and logistics and, above all, mental strain.

That last sort of thing hadn't ever bothered you before, d'Arcy. You'd spent most of your so-called 'fat' years lean and hungry, going flat out, dancing on the edge... chasing your tail. You must indeed have been starting to get old!

Being an English country squire – a *real* English country squire – requires 'inner space', tranquility... and peace of mind... so that the whole of your body and soul – the whole of your being – can be devoted to...

Devoted to what?

... to being in charge and trying to understand why I'm here, and you're here... in a phrase: what it's all about.

Good Grief!

. . . .

'The Barses don't want the statues,' says N, seemingly on the verge of tears.

'What?' I say.

'They don't want the two marble statues. Not even at a lower price.' A little bit of a sparkle... a little bit of a gleam... comes into her eyes.

'But the house, the cottage, the outbuildings, the gardens, the fields... they want those, don't they? The bloody B-arses still want those, don't they? Surely....'

A little more of the sparkle, etc, rises. Then, suddenly, the rising becomes an eruption. N does a little twirl, like one of those wind-up propeller-disc toys, and begins almost to levitate from the kitchen floor. 'Oh, yes; the Barses still want those. They still want those. Contract exchange, Euan says, is still on track; it's still "Go, go, go!"'

Bapu and Big Fee 'test-fly' their helicopter; Bouff wags his tail and yawns; I take a big slurp from my glass, and another one – emptying it – give the lamb a comforting pat, and slump back into my chair; N resumes her station next to the stove. She and I look at each other, grinning like cartoon-character imbeciles. Then I straighten up and square my shoulders. I say in a deep, authoritative, all-but-journey-man-squire voice: 'Wife, bring me drink. I must have more drink and my supper. Wife: supper, Ho!

'Yes, M'lord. Right away, M'lord,' my little Uxor replies, winking at Bapu and Big Fee. 'And will that be dry, white toast or whole wheat with your glass of skimmed milk?'

In view of the Barses' re-reconfirmation of their intention to purchase Brambledown, a further, cautious exposure to the rights and responsibilities of an English country squire's living seemed in order. The next day, therefore:

1. I wrote again to old SCO at the Countryside Commission, this time asking how he was getting on with fine-tuning my request for grant-aid; reminding him, again, that we were now even further into the specified application period, that's to say that our prospects for 'early acceptance' were, presumably, fast fading; and, finally, again reiterating my concern to have the already-accomplished re-seeding of Preston's Pride officially approved, 'if only *pro forma*'.

2. I wrote to Lois thanking her for completing and sending off the IACS forms, and agreeing the observation she'd made during our 5 April meeting that the subsidy payment I should eventually receive from the MAFF would, indeed, 'come in very handy'. (It did… but for fine-print contractual reasons I'd not sufficiently appreciated, the principal beneficiary for that particular farming year was Joscelyn Steele, not me.)

3. And I received in the mail – Hallelujah! – a nice, fat cheque (less honourable land agent's fees and commissions, of course) representing our first half-yearly agricultural rents. (Well no, Chief Stoneface, sir; it's not, in relative terms, *really* very much income – certainly not when set against our pending estate restoration expenses. But you'll note it compares well with that from 'gilts, or high-grade corporate bonds'. And as I rationalize our operations and bring more of our land 'into hand' [farm it directly rather than through agricultural tenants/contractors] that income should increase.)

The day after that came, at last, some literally into-hand (better, per-

haps, *hand-into*) esquirely business: attending a young ewe in Pavilion Paddock – about mid-way between the front drive and the gate
into the east track – which was having trouble giving birth. It was the
usual problem: the head of the lamb – a ram, I felt pretty sure – was
too big and/or the ewe's birth canal was too small. The lamb's presentation looked good, however; indeed, its muzzle was already part way
out. Nothing was seriously amiss, I concluded; it was just a matter
of discovering the forelegs and bringing them forward then, with the
ewe pushing and me gently pulling....

So I set to work and, after delivering one foreleg, pause to give myself and the mother-to-be a break. I look up at the lovely, clear spring
sky – a sky redolent of new-season's promise, I reflected. I look out
at the trees, their leaf and flower buds – many of the latter really fruit
buds, of course – beginning to open.... I look down at the lower lake,
its surface dotted with wildfowl resplendent in their dress-to-impress,
breeding plumage and its depths home to fat, tasty fishes and sleek,
tasty eels – more new-season's promise, I reflected. I look along the
bank of the lake, its littoral plants and reeds just starting to deck
themselves out in their vernal yellow-greens, and towards the front
drive....

· · · · · · · · · · · · · · · · · · · ·

*You offer these paeans to 'glorious Nature' pretty regularly, you
know, d'Arcy. It's possible – although, I concede, improbable – that
the long-suffering Reader could tire....*
    Just hang on a minute, Alter-natis; keep calm.

· · · · · · · · · · · · · · · · · · · ·

... towards the front drive.... And Hello: what's that? It looks like a
small party of hikers, or 'ramblers' as they're called in the UK. There's
no public right of way here; this is private property and a Conservation Area to boot, I say to myself. I'll have to ask them to be very
quiet and, when they've had a little *shufti* (Arabic for 'peek' or 'look-
around'), to take their leave. Well, I console myself, at least I won't
have to chase after them to deliver that message; although they're
milling around and, at intervals, consulting what appear to be maps,
as if lost, the ramblers seem to be trending this way. In just a couple
of minutes....

Ohmygosh: in just a couple of minutes, they'll be right here! Right
here, right in the delivery room, with me with my hand.... Help! And
don't a couple of the ramblers – well, just about all of them, for that
matter – don't they have long or long-ish hair? Yes; good Lord! They

all have long or long-ish hair, and chesty chests and hippy hips. It's a party of female ramblers.... A party of ramblettes!

And they see me now. And now they've started walking towards me quickly, probably because they're worried about being late back to wherever they've come from and need directions urgently so they don't miss their bus or whatever. And, yes, I can see quite clearly: it's a party of six ramblettes, perhaps 13 or 14 years old, just out for the day, maybe, from their middle or high school. What *am* I going to do? Continue the obstetrics while I talk to them but put my jacket over the ewe's croup (rump), covering it and the lamb's protruding muzzle and leg? Or carry on just as I am as if it's a Sunday afternoon and I'm washing the car, but ask them to avert their gaze?

The figure prostrate below me gives a long, anguished groan as another contraction comes on. Clearly she's wanting this lamb out now – not after some superannuated old geezer's deferences to (? mis-) perceived conventional modesty, or advisories about private property and Conservation Areas, and why the front drive and the east track aren't Public Rights of Way, and what the ramblettes' quickest exit route from here may be but please, Mr Shepherd: out... right... now.

'Good afternoon, ladies,' I say genially, pressing the right side of my head tight down on the ewe's wooly loin, pinning her to the ground, as my left hand gropes deep inside her for foreleg number two.... Ah, here it is: folded back, hard up against the pubic symphysis. So I've got to push the lamb partway back in, to create a little space, and then rotate it 45° or so before I can straighten the limb and pull it out.... 'You all having a ramble? It's a *lovely* day for a ramble....'

Silence. Absolute, profound, pin-drop silence from the ramblettes, all of whom have now stopped about 3–4 yards to my left. I look up at the young girls, thinking perhaps to introduce myself and welcome them... possibly, even, to try to explain what I'm doing and why. I see six heads angled slightly forward and down like reading lamps, with gaping mouths and wide-open eyes almost literally out on stalks, and twelve arms – three with Ordnance Survey maps attached – hanging limply.

'I'm d'Arcy Henry; welcome to the Heartsease Hall Estate. I'm just now in the middle of....' With exquisite timing, the young ewe gives another long, anguished groan. 'Well, no, let's update that: I'm just now *on the point of* delivering this lamb which's got stuck. Its muzzle's already out and one foreleg, as you can see; I'm just trying to get the other foreleg....' A little more pushing back... a little more rotating.... There; that's got everything lined up just about right. 'The normal birthing position for a lamb – for all ungulates, I'm pretty sure; I expect you know this already from your school biology lessons – is muzzle-between-forelegs as if it's diving into a swimming pool....'

Now for the her-pushing, me-pulling part. I grasp the lamb's two forelegs with my left hand and, with my right, take hold of its neck just behind its ears, set my feet – heels into the ground, one at the top of the ewe's croup, the other at the crook of her hamstrings, just above her hocks – and tension up....

'Sir, should you be doing that? Should you *really* be doing that... to *her*?'

'Yes, sir. Shouldn't you really just stop and let her do it? After all, she's the mother; she's the one who knows....'

'Nature's way's the best way, sir. You mustn't....'

Sensing a contraction coming, I put a little more pull on the lamb; the ewe gives a little more push and, *in extremis parturio* now, voices her ovine equivalent of the crucified Christ's '*Eli, Eli, lama sabachthani?*' ('My God, My God, why hast thou forsaken me?' according to St Mark).

'No. No, sir! *Stop*. You're *hurting* her. STOP!'

The lamb's shoulders start to emerge. I maintain my gentle pull; the ewe gives another push; the lamb's chest comes out, then the fetal process of its umbilicus becomes visible; the pelvis comes out....

Wooooosh! The entirety of the lamb – a ram, indeed – and the rest of the umbilicus and the amnion still partly filled with fluid plash onto the grass. I reposition myself and clear the mucus from the neonate's mouth and nose; the exhausted ewe gives a little sigh of release.... I glance up at the girls; they're like a *tableaux vivant* of mannequins, freeze-framed in real time.

Then like some badly-programmed robot, the lamb jerks himself into a semi-upright position, shakes his head tentatively and gives a little bleat. Mum, prostrate, gives a weary answering nicker. I pick the lamb up and lay him next to mum's head so she can reach easily to clean him off. The lamb gives another little bleat; mum gives another answering nicker, raises her head and sets to work.

The profound silence above me and to my left continues. To see the angle-poise heads, the slack mouths, the staring eyes, the dangling arms with their attached maps... this time, I don't even have to look around.

'Wow: is that it, sir? Is the birth all over? Is that it?'

'Yep, it should be,' I reply authoritatively. 'Unless she's got twins which, judging from the large size of this lamb and the fact that she's a *prima gravida*... aaahhh, that's to say this is her first pregnancy, I rather doubt.'

The lamb struggles to its feet and, after several attempts, accomplishes a full-body shake. Mum, too, decides it's time to assay the next stage and, with an assist from me, gets up. A few sniffs and an exchange of calls... and mother and son start slowly to saunter off.

'Golly. Isn't he cute?'

'He's just *adorable*. That little, speckledy face....'

'And those big knobbledy knees... and his *tail*; look at his little, squiggledy *tail*.... Sooo coool!'

'His mummy keeps licking him all over. Why's she doing that, sir?'

'That's what she's supposed to do,' one of the ramblettes replies, 'that's her job. When Petal – she's our dog, sir – had puppies....'

'Ooooh. When I have a baby I'm not sure I'll want....'

· ·

So ended another inspiriting lesson in the endlessly entertaining school of English country esquiredom and estate life.

As with your earlier, shooting-Shorty story and its laid-back – casual, almost – account of bovine euthanasia, d'Arcy, so also this entry about birthing lambs: treating parturition and the beginning of a new ovine life not as some great, affirmative experience but as just another seasonal farming chore. What sort of message do you think

*that sends to young women intending motherhood and feminists
seeking empowerment, not to mention the yahoo, ultra-conservative
political right wing?*
  Alter-natis, you sound like you need a good, long vacation.
. . . .

April 28, 1995, kicked off and continued for most of its duration as
just another of N's 'thirty-ninth' birthdays, in recognition of which I
offered the customary congratulations and condolences. It ended as a
turning point in our lives.
  A 'glittering' black-tie dinner hosted by Angus and Anthea Doug-
las-Montague, the oil-company CEO and his wife ('The Duchess')
we'd met at the Platts' dinner on 2 March, provided a suitable, if
occasionally challenging, prelude to our momentous moment. As by
now we'd come almost to expect ('Practice may make less imperfec-
tion,' John Adams might better have written in his 1761 *Diary*.), N
and I were the guests of honour and the usual lords, ladies and gentlepersons were in attendance; I remember rejoicing yet again in how
prepared these well-bred and accomplished people seemed to be to
welcome us, to take us up and get to know us... to partake of whatever it might be we had to offer.
  The table talk ranged onto and off of a variety of interesting sub-
jects: an Odilon Redon Exhibition then at the Royal Academy of Arts
which N and I shortly went to view; a purebred Arabian (horse) stud
near Long Stratton, about ten miles south of Norwich, which an An-
glo-Argentine lady (who gloried in the style/name Baroness Marinella
de Poppescu; she was married to a Rumanian aristocrat, apparently)
was dispersing, some of whose breeding stock N and I eventually
acquired; and then, inevitably, back to Britain's proposed membership of the Euro. My goodness, I reflected, what a nest of Europhobes
was (and is still) this little corner of the UK!* The ringing declaration
attributed to the American Revolutionary-era patriot James Otis –
'Taxation without representation is tyranny!' – leapt into my brain.
And I was on the verge of interjecting same into the discussion but,
still traumatized by my near-intellectual-death experience at 'The Embassy', I decided instead to keep my head well down...

---

* 'It's not that we're against the Europeans *as a race*,' I recall one male guest con-
fiding, seemingly in ignorance of his own genetic inheritance, 'it's that we don't
like surrendering fundamental national rights to the Europeans or, more particularly, to a bunch of arrogant, un-elected, un-accountable, over-paid, under-
performing... *boondoggling*... Brussels-based bureaucrats.'

... until the conversation, led by Angus, our host, and a Sir some-one-or-other to whom I'd earlier been introduced but who's name I hadn't registered, turned to the Middle East. Surely, I thought, on this topic I could – should even, as a *quondam* 'specialist' in the area – attempt a profundity or two and, at an appropriate moment, I plucked up my courage and did: on the receptiveness of the various regional Arab sub-cultures – North African, Nilotic (of or relating to the Nile), Arabian Peninsular, Gulf, Levantine (of or relating to the Eastern Mediterranean, from the French word *levée*, or 'rising', as in 'of the sun'), Trans-Caucasian, Mesopotamian, South Asian, etc – to westernization.

• • • • • • • • • • • • • • • • • • • •

You really were *asking for it!*

• • • • • • • • • • • • • • • • • • • •

The pretty, later-middle-aged woman seated to my right listened atten-tively and then in a clipped, no-nonsense voice suggestive of old-style, British-blue-stocking academe asked if by 'westernization' I actually meant 'Americanization', and what effect on Arab receptiveness to Americanization I thought Arabs' colonial-era experiences, that's to say their 18th–20th-century experiences of the European powers, had had. Just as at the Platts', I felt the hairs on the back of my neck start to rise.

• • • • • • • • • • • • • • • • • • • •

Let the record show: I warned you!

• • • • • • • • • • • • • • • • • • • •

'You seem very well informed about the Middle East,' Yr Correspond-ent countered, playing desperately for time.

'Oh, my husband and I' – the lady nodded in the direction of the 'Sir' whose name I hadn't registered – 'spent a good while in that part of the world: in Iraq, Jordan... the UAE. We've only just returned from three years in [...].'

'How interesting. How very interesting. Was your husband, like our host, involved in the oil industry?'

'Well, almost everyone in [...] is involved, one way or another, in the oil industry. But no, not actively... not directly, anyway. My hus-band was....'

Suddenly it hit me. 'You and your husband – He's "Sir Stephen", isn't he? – have a cottage in Seething don't you,' I blurted out. 'He's... he's that celebrated Foreign Office "gossip".'

'My husband was Her Majesty's Ambassador there.'

Ah yes. Well… it was a lovely evening nonetheless. N and I drove home; I kissed the Birthday Girl off to her bed, put Bouff out for his walk and poured myself a nightcap to celebrate yet another narrow escape from the garroting of my self-esteem. Then I had a little wander around. I looked out a front window toward St Lawrence's Church, with its 1000-year-old round tower outlined against the clear night sky; I looked out a back window across the re-configured and re-seeded south lawn, and the re-emparked Preston's Pride, and along the northern flank of Neate Wood toward St Michael's Church – the 600-year-old, 'junior' church – and experienced once more a *frisson* of delight at being able to live at Heartsease Hall… and then, once more, a sharp wrench of apprehension. If only… *if only* progress toward contract exchange would go smoothly; if only Brambledown were finally sold.

For some reason or, perhaps, just out of habit, my wanderings eventually brought me to the fax machine in the Hall's annex 'office'. While we were being entertained by Angus and the Duchess – and Ambassador […] and his formidable wife – a communication had, in fact, come in. From whom? Almost literally with trembling fingers, I snatched the paper from the tray, glanced at its letterhead and started. It was from Euan. I took a draught from my nightcap, exhaled deeply… and read: 'Contracts exchanged today with the Barses and their deposit monies transferred to your account.'

. . . .

So that was that. Endgame; done. At long last you were free to devote the whole of your being to becoming an English country squire and being in charge, etc, etc – or whatever was that drivel you wrote the other day.

Nothing's certain in this world, of course. But as you know, Alternatis, the sale of Brambledown – to the Barses – was in due course completed.

And your long search was all but over.

My long search? What long search?

Your long search for material and spiritual security, as we'd discussed just over a year earlier, on 26 March 1994, to be exact.

There's been so much going on I'd forgotten about our discussion.…

Never mind. Do you now feel secure? Ensconced here, surrounded by your extensive acres… your 'Good Earth'… a holding which in Pearl Buck's China – in China today, if the country had a western system of freehold land registry – would certainly confirm you as a man of very considerable means.

I still have to keep The Suits happy, of course, and make sure they've an ample supply of Impressionist pictures or whatever.

You're heavily invested in food production, and people have always got to eat.

That's true.

What's more, your corporate balance sheet looks pretty much as forecast: that's to say good.

Yes; it's very solid.

By the way, that 'current ratio' of 2.71828 which, back in Chapter 2 of this epic narration, your wife derived from projected, rolling-average cash flow 'just from the estate's farming operations', and in which ever since you've reposed so much mammonite faith? I've suddenly remembered what's so especial about that number.

What is it, then?

It's what some mathematicians regard as 'a nonsense number': a number which ontologically – as regards understanding The Nature of Being... or, in your words, 'what it's all about' – is illogical or absurd... that's to say, irrelevant.

Oh, no; no, *no*, NO! You're telling me that a prime financial metric, proposed in good faith and accepted as attesting to my wife's and my solvency going forward – and hence to our material security in later life – is, when all's said and done, a nonsense number... irrelevant to what it's all about?

Yes; it's pretty much the same with all metrics of material security, I suspect. But there's always that spiritual security you keep going on about....

Ummmm. Achieving spiritual security seems even trickier to me now. It requires that little bit more effort and takes that little bit more time, *viz* St Matthew's fine observation: 'It is easier for a camel to pass through the eye of a needle, than for a rich man to enter into the kingdom of God.'

An increasing number of Bible scholars believe 'camel' is a mistranslation, and that the correct noun-of-passage should be 'hawser' or 'thick rope'.

What a pity; 'camel' is so gloriously surreal. It really scintillates in your mind's eye.

Anyway, what you appear to be saying is: you haven't yet achieved spiritual security.

No, Alter-natis, I haven't. But I'm still working at it, and I feel I'm making progress.

Are you going to continue to chronicle your quest for spiritual security – your 'great travail', we might say – and inflict on the poor Reader an ECS (English Country Squire) Something Vol. II?

As runs that old proverb: 'There is many a slip 'twixt the cup and the lip'...

Or alternatively: 'Many things may come between mouth and morsel'. That's how the 2nd-century BC Roman critic and statesman Marcus Porcius, aka Cato the Elder, put it in his Noctes Atticae... *which you may know as his* Athenian Nights.

... but yes: writing an *ECS Something Vol. II* – and, if there's time, a ditto *Vol. III* – is my intent. And God or Whomever willing, in it I hope to be able to record further progress towards my achievement of spiritual security.

So as the New York Yankees' great Number 8, the catcher Yogi Berra, might have signed off: it's au revoir *until we see you again.*

. . . .

'And until *we* see you again, Mr Henry. Now you're able to devote yourself full-time to the Heartsease Hall Estate, there's so much more about its architecture and history, and the Festing family's history, I'd like to tell you. And we can converse about philosophy and religion, and politics and socio-economics, and Love and Life... and Art.'

Sir Jacob: welcome back!

'You must call me "Jacob" now. And, if you're agreed, I'll call you "d'Arcy".'

I hadn't appreciated you'd be coming along too....